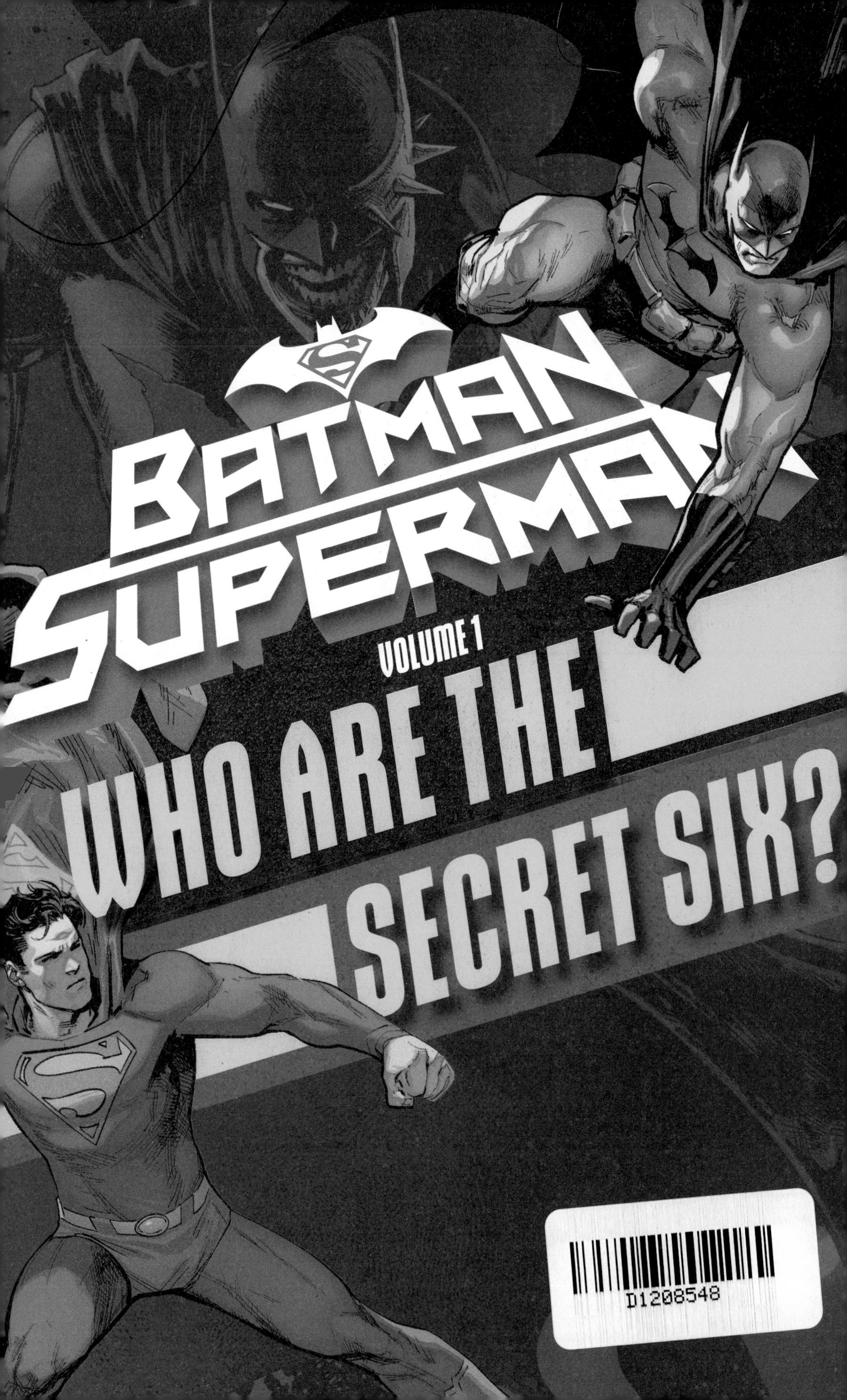
BATMAN SUPERMAN
VOLUME 1
WHO ARE THE SECRET SIX?

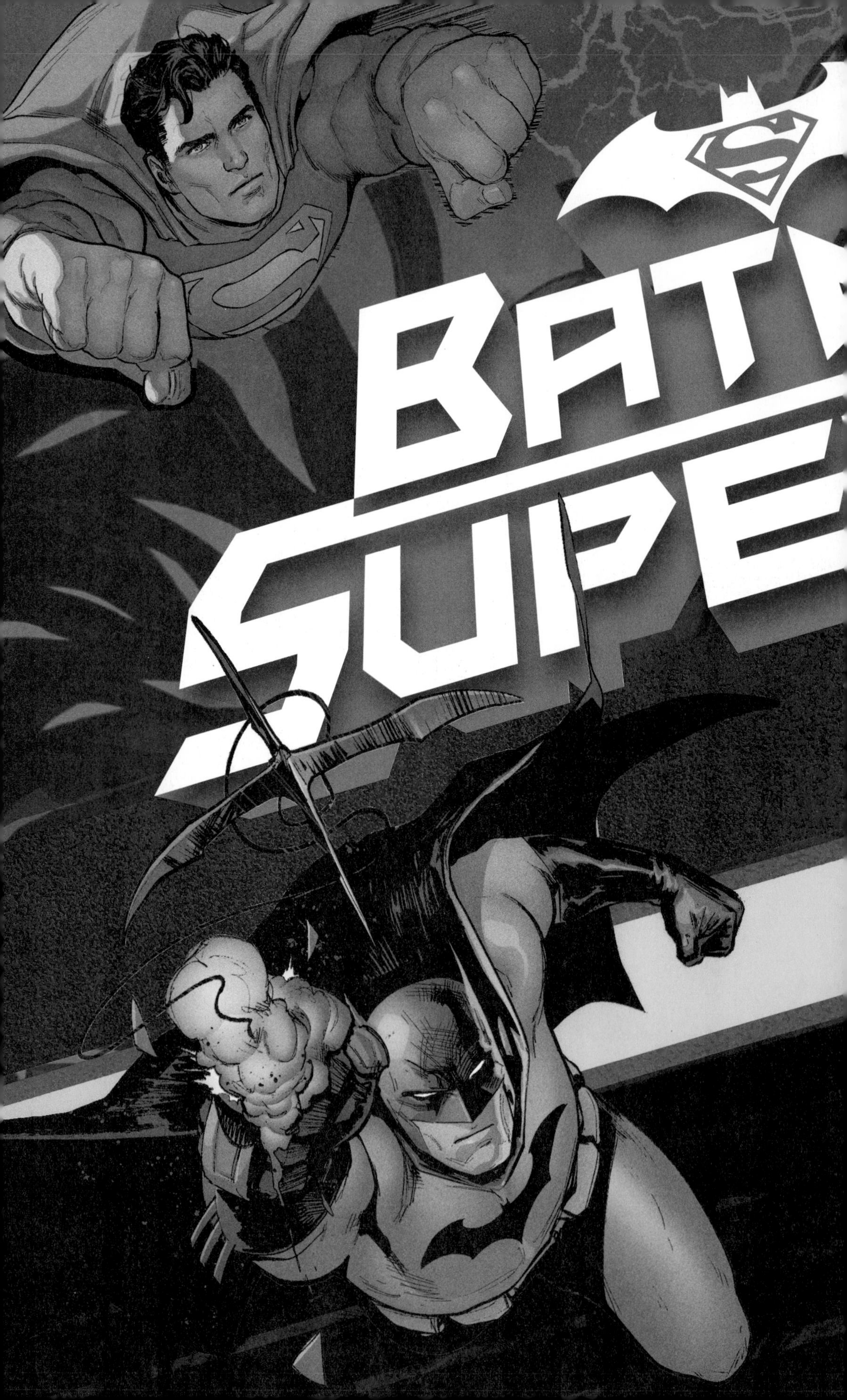

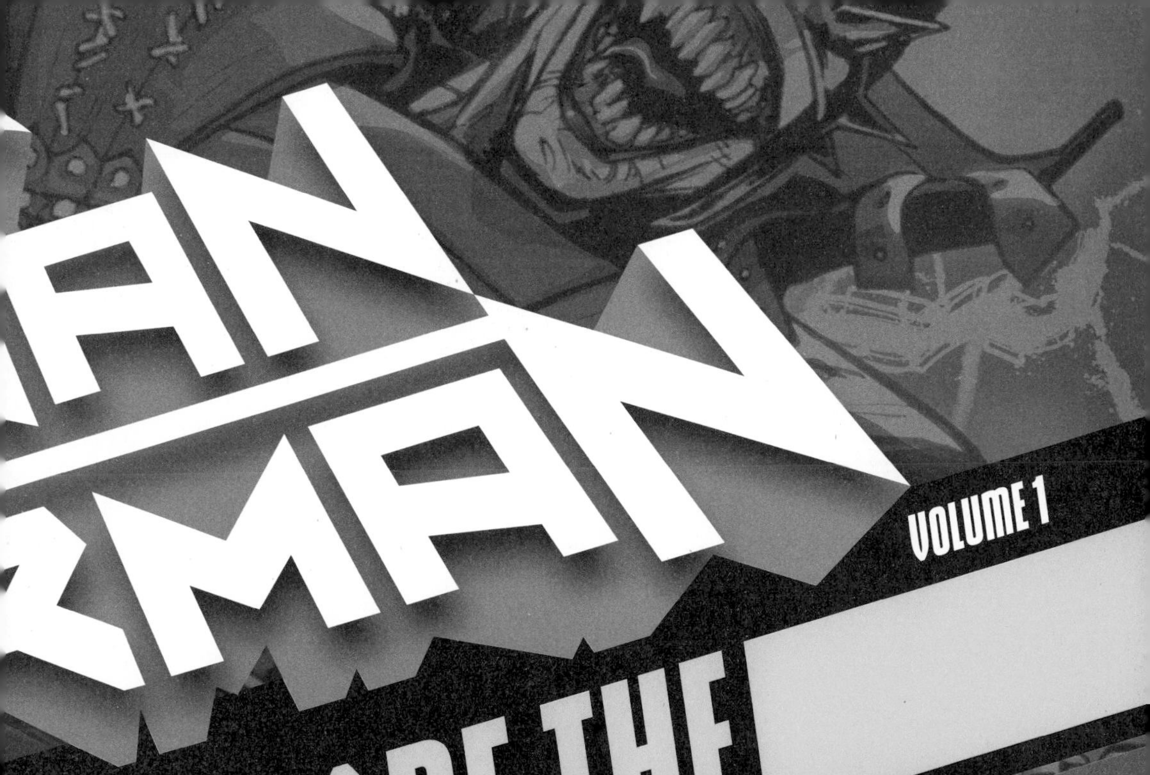

AN
RMAN

VOLUME 1

WHO ARE THE SECRET SIX?

JOSHUA WILLIAMSON
WRITER

DAVID MARQUEZ
ARTIST

ALEJANDRO SANCHEZ
COLORIST

JOHN J. HILL
LETTERER

DAVID MARQUEZ AND ALEJANDRO SANCHEZ
COLLECTION COVER ARTISTS

BATMAN CREATED BY BOB KANE WITH BILL FINGER

SUPERMAN CREATED BY JERRY SIEGEL AND JOE SHUSTER

BY SPECIAL ARRANGEMENT WITH THE JERRY SIEGEL FAMILY

PAUL KAMINSKI Editor – Original Series
ROB LEVIN Associate Editor – Original Series
BEN MEARES Assistant Editor – Original Series
JEB WOODARD Group Editor – Collected Editions
ERIKA ROTHBERG Editor – Collected Edition
STEVE COOK Design Director – Books
DAMIAN RYLAND Publication Design
ERIN VANOVER Publication Production

BOB HARRAS Senior VP – Editor-in-Chief, DC Comics

JIM LEE Publisher & Chief Creative Officer
BOBBIE CHASE VP – Global Publishing Initiatives & Digital Strategy
DON FALLETTI VP – Manufacturing Operations & Workflow Management
LAWRENCE GANEM VP – Talent Services
ALISON GILL Senior VP – Manufacturing & Operations
HANK KANALZ Senior VP – Publishing Strategy & Support Services
DAN MIRON VP – Publishing Operations
NICK J. NAPOLITANO VP – Manufacturing Administration & Design
NANCY SPEARS VP – Sales
JONAH WEILAND VP – Marketing & Creative Services
MICHELE R. WELLS VP & Executive Editor, Young Reader

BATMAN/SUPERMAN VOL. 1: WHO ARE THE SECRET SIX?

DC Comics, 2900 West Alameda Ave., Burbank, CA 91505
Printed by LSC Communications, Owensville, MO, USA. 9/25/20. First Printing.
ISBN: 978-1-77950-567-5

Library of Congress Cataloging-in-Publication Data is available.

PEFC Certified
This product is from sustainably managed forests and controlled sources
PEFC/29-31-337
www.pefc.org

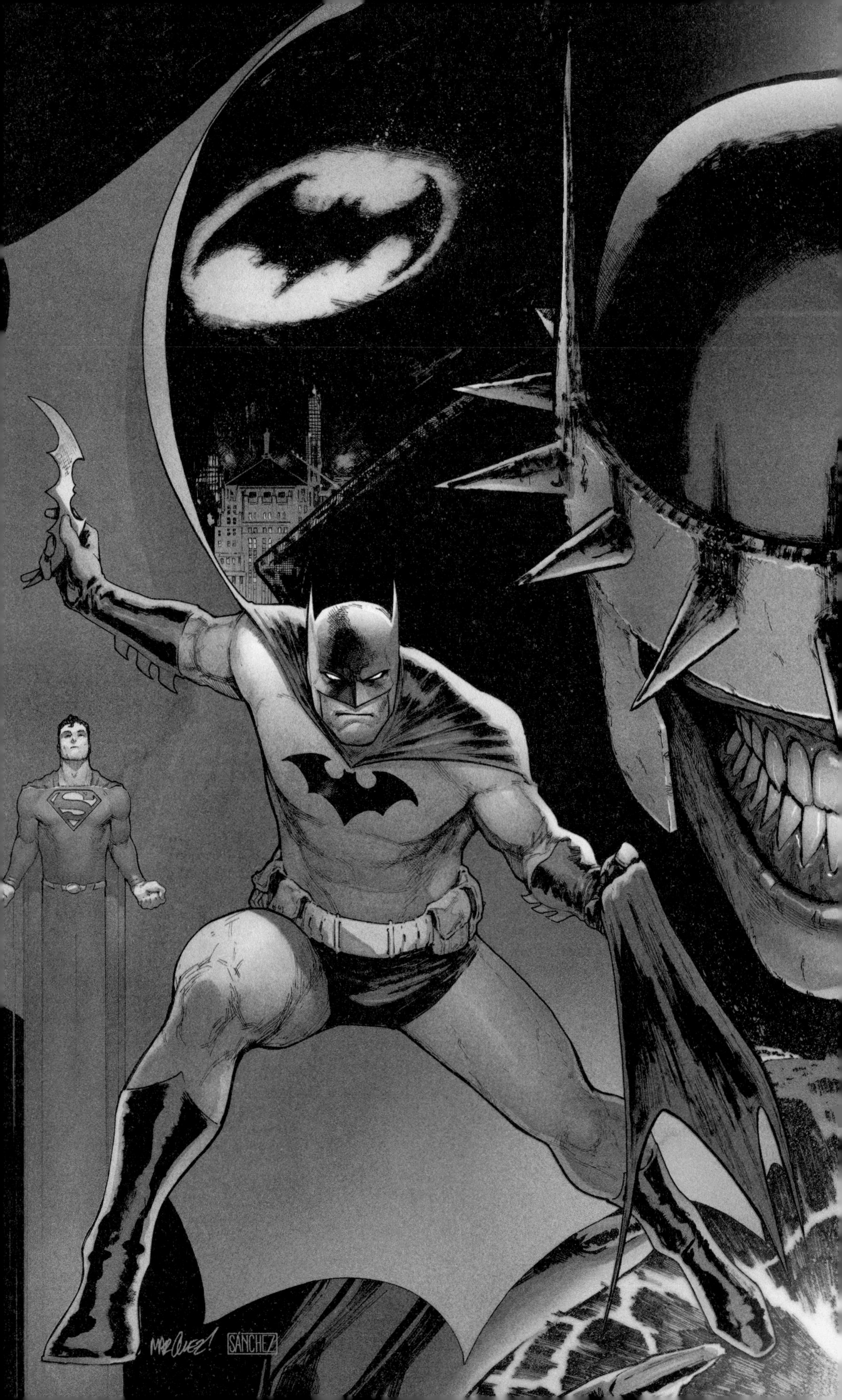
SÁNCHEZ

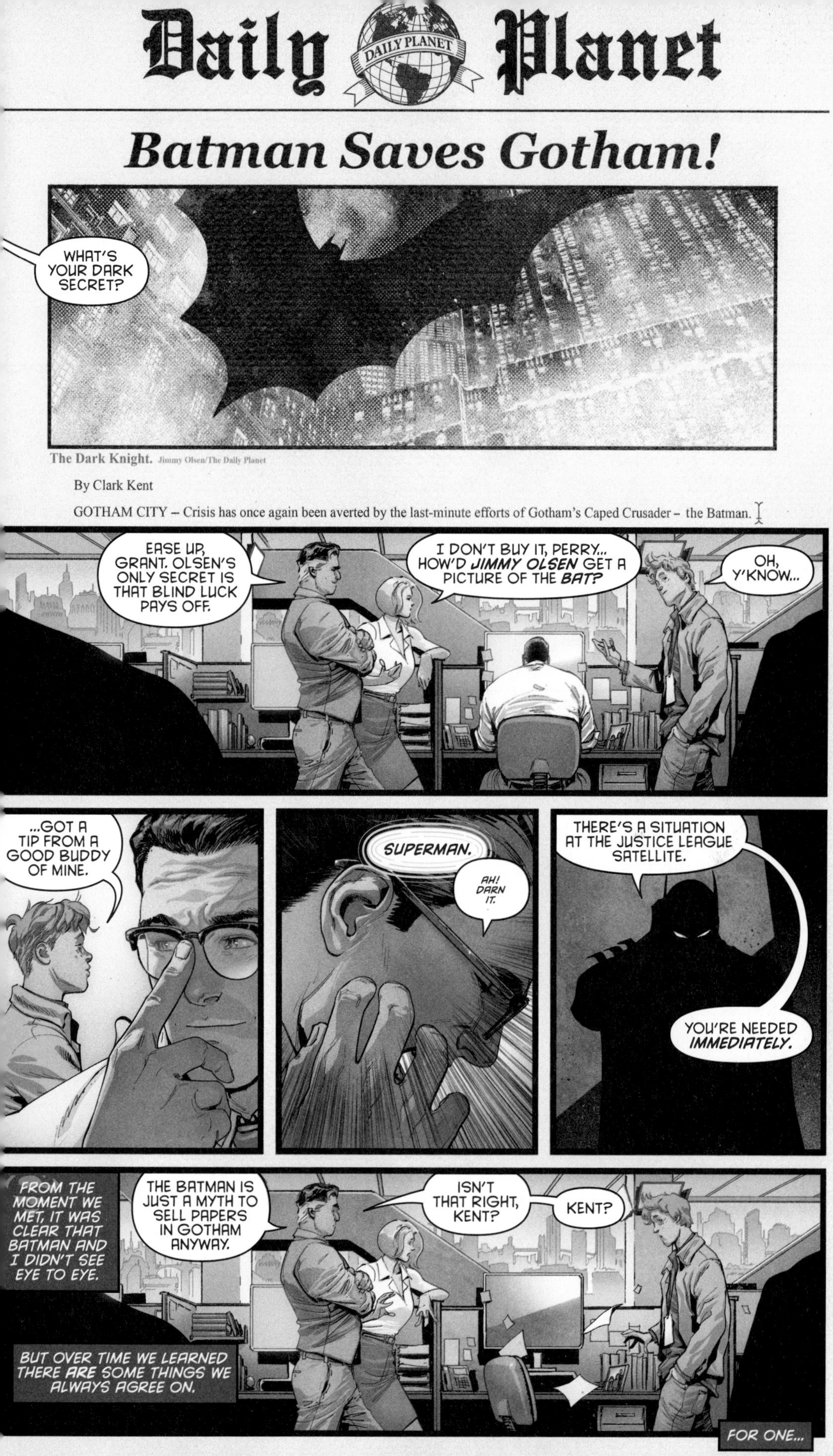

Daily Planet
DAILY PLANET
Batman Saves Gotham!
WHAT'S YOUR DARK SECRET?
The Dark Knight. Jimmy Olsen/The Daily Planet
By Clark Kent
GOTHAM CITY – Crisis has once again been averted by the last-minute efforts of Gotham's Caped Crusader – the Batman.
EASE UP, GRANT. OLSEN'S ONLY SECRET IS THAT BLIND LUCK PAYS OFF.
I DON'T BUY IT, PERRY... HOW'D JIMMY OLSEN GET A PICTURE OF THE BAT?
OH, Y'KNOW...
...GOT A TIP FROM A GOOD BUDDY OF MINE.
SUPERMAN.
AH! DARN IT.
THERE'S A SITUATION AT THE JUSTICE LEAGUE SATELLITE.
YOU'RE NEEDED IMMEDIATELY.
FROM THE MOMENT WE MET, IT WAS CLEAR THAT BATMAN AND I DIDN'T SEE EYE TO EYE.
THE BATMAN IS JUST A MYTH TO SELL PAPERS IN GOTHAM ANYWAY.
ISN'T THAT RIGHT, KENT?
KENT?
BUT OVER TIME WE LEARNED THERE ARE SOME THINGS WE ALWAYS AGREE ON.
FOR ONE...

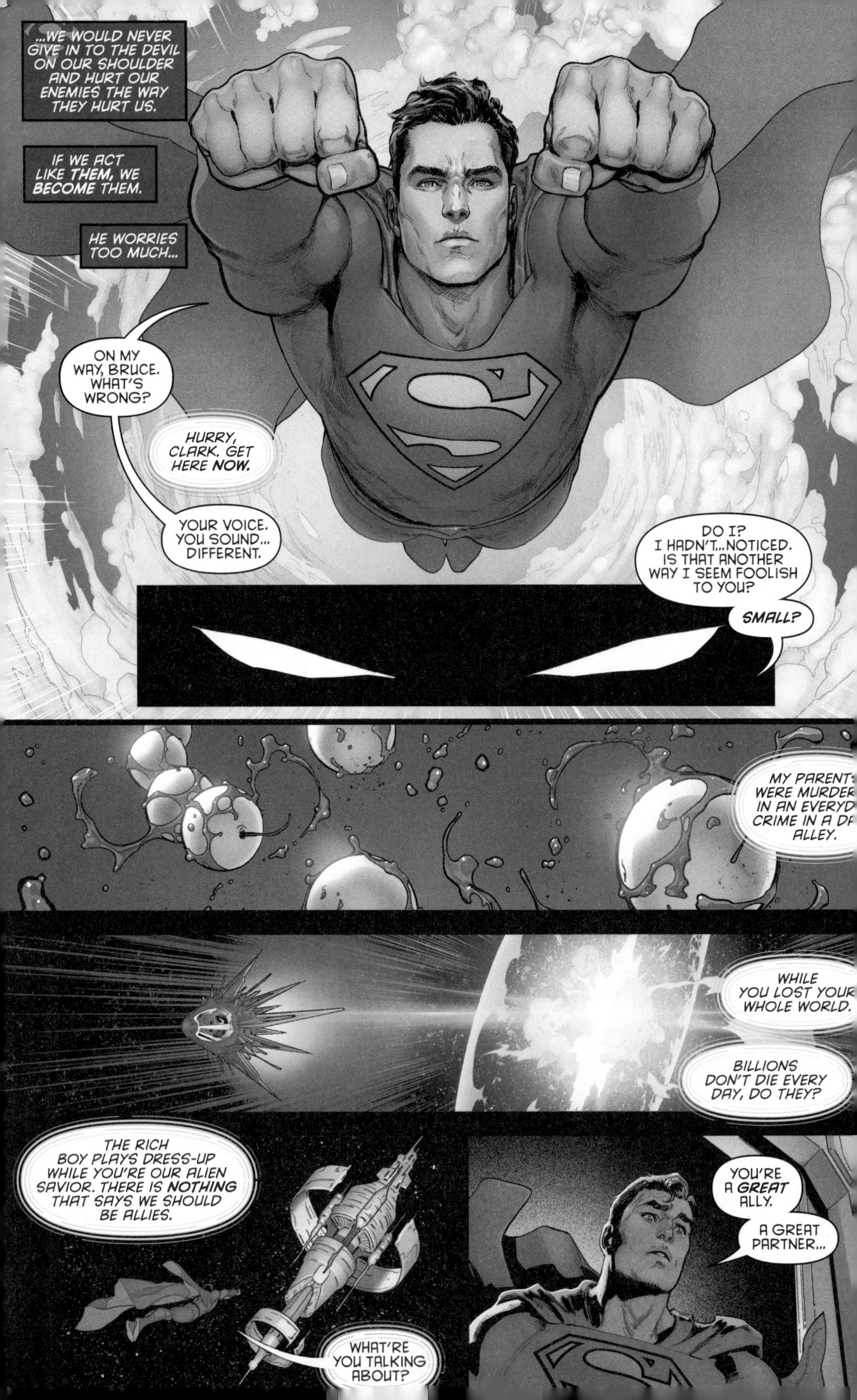
...WE WOULD NEVER GIVE IN TO THE DEVIL ON OUR SHOULDER AND HURT OUR ENEMIES THE WAY THEY HURT US.
IF WE ACT LIKE THEM, WE BECOME THEM.
HE WORRIES TOO MUCH...
ON MY WAY, BRUCE. WHAT'S WRONG?
HURRY, CLARK. GET HERE NOW.
YOUR VOICE. YOU SOUND... DIFFERENT.
DO I? I HADN'T...NOTICED. IS THAT ANOTHER WAY I SEEM FOOLISH TO YOU?
SMALL?
MY PARENTS WERE MURDER IN AN EVERYD CRIME IN A DA ALLEY.
WHILE YOU LOST YOUR WHOLE WORLD.
BILLIONS DON'T DIE EVERY DAY, DO THEY?
THE RICH BOY PLAYS DRESS-UP WHILE YOU'RE OUR ALIEN SAVIOR. THERE IS NOTHING THAT SAYS WE SHOULD BE ALLIES.
WHAT'RE YOU TALKING ABOUT?
YOU'RE A GREAT ALLY.
A GREAT PARTNER...

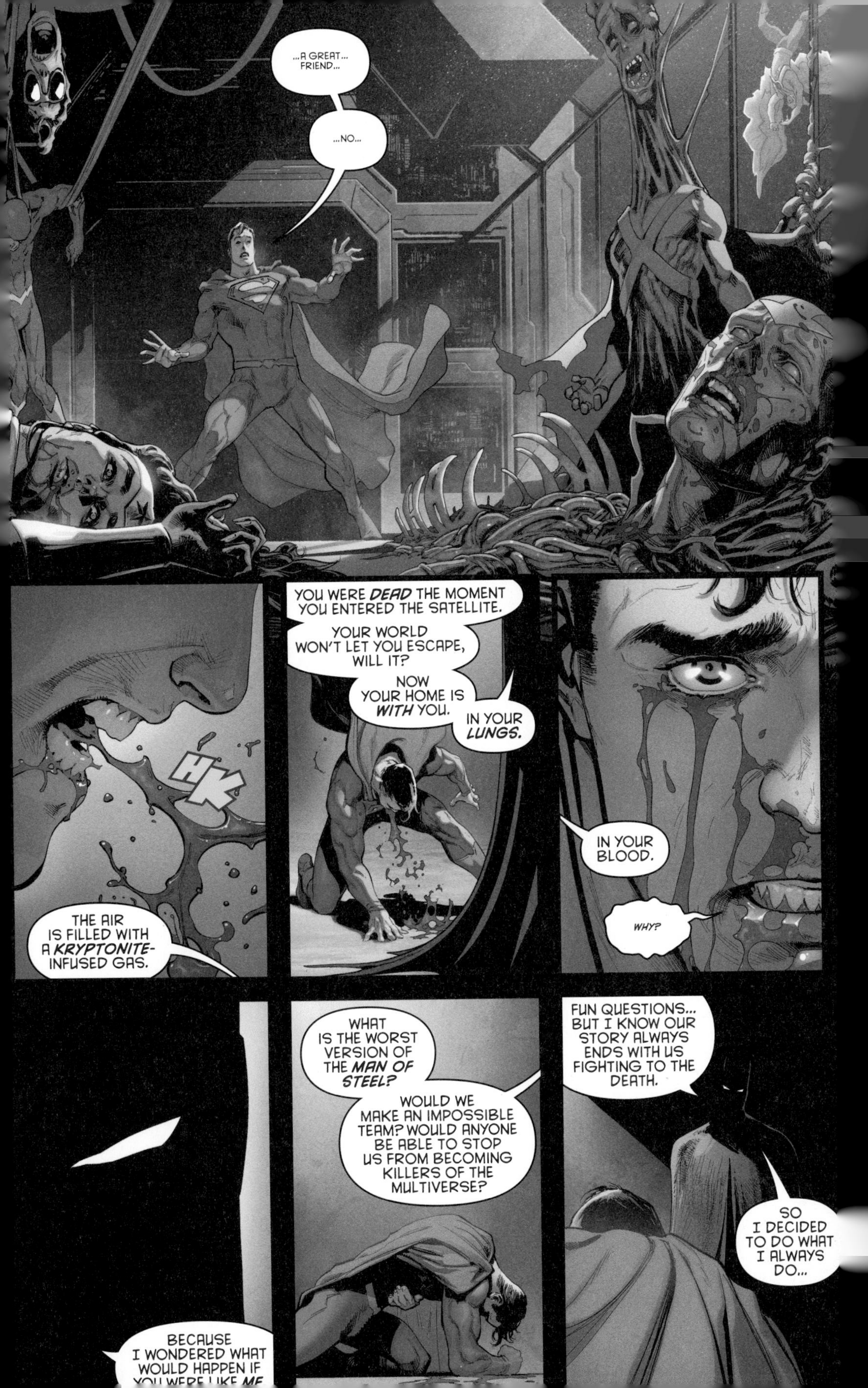
...A GREAT... FRIEND...
...NO...
YOU WERE DEAD THE MOMENT YOU ENTERED THE SATELLITE.
YOUR WORLD WON'T LET YOU ESCAPE, WILL IT?
NOW YOUR HOME IS WITH YOU.
IN YOUR LUNGS.
HK
THE AIR IS FILLED WITH A KRYPTONITE-INFUSED GAS.
IN YOUR BLOOD.
WHY?
BECAUSE I WONDERED WHAT WOULD HAPPEN IF
WHAT IS THE WORST VERSION OF THE MAN OF STEEL?
WOULD WE MAKE AN IMPOSSIBLE TEAM? WOULD ANYONE BE ABLE TO STOP US FROM BECOMING KILLERS OF THE MULTIVERSE?
FUN QUESTIONS... BUT I KNOW OUR STORY ALWAYS ENDS WITH US FIGHTING TO THE DEATH.
SO I DECIDED TO DO WHAT I ALWAYS DO...

PLAN AHEAD.
HAHAHAHAHAHAHAHA!
"HE'S THE BATMAN WHO LAUGHS.
"A BATMAN FROM A WORLD IN THE DARK MULTIVERSE SO SIMILAR TO OURS IT'S FRIGHTENING.
"AFTER HE KILLED HIS JOKER, HIS MIND WAS POISONED BY A TOXIN HIDDEN WITHIN THE JOKER'S HEART.
"ON HIS WORLD HE WAS AN APEX PREDATOR WHO SLAUGHTERED EVERY HERO. EVERY VILLAIN."
HAHAHAHAHAHAHAHAHA!
BOOOM
"AND LAUGHED AS HIS

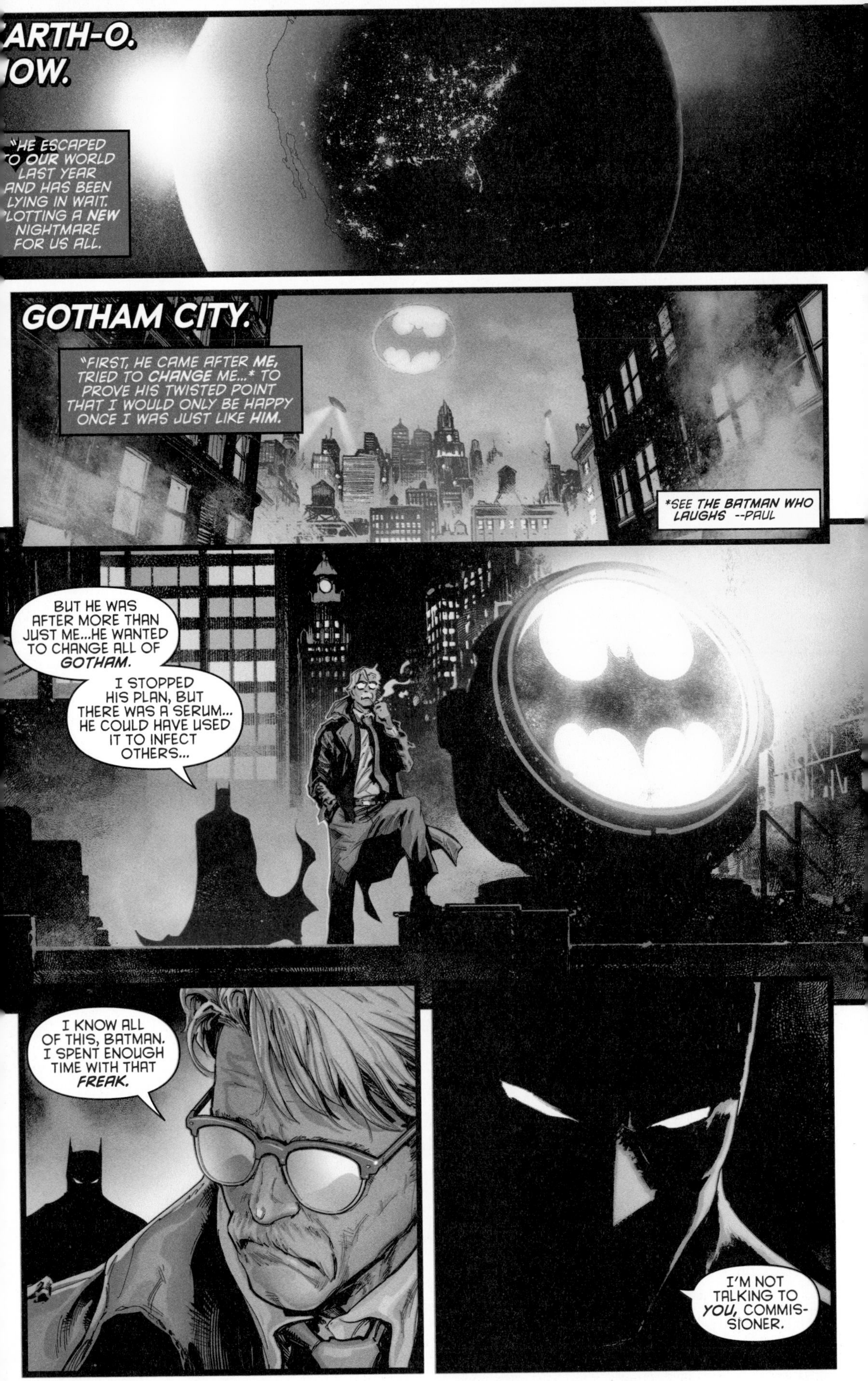
ARTH-O.
OW.
"HE ESCAPED O OUR WORLD LAST YEAR AND HAS BEEN LYING IN WAIT. LOTTING A NEW NIGHTMARE FOR US ALL.
GOTHAM CITY.
"FIRST, HE CAME AFTER ME, TRIED TO CHANGE ME...* TO PROVE HIS TWISTED POINT THAT I WOULD ONLY BE HAPPY ONCE I WAS JUST LIKE HIM.
*SEE THE BATMAN WHO LAUGHS --PAUL
BUT HE WAS AFTER MORE THAN JUST ME...HE WANTED TO CHANGE ALL OF GOTHAM.
I STOPPED HIS PLAN, BUT THERE WAS A SERUM... HE COULD HAVE USED IT TO INFECT OTHERS...
I KNOW ALL OF THIS, BATMAN. I SPENT ENOUGH TIME WITH THAT FREAK.
I'M NOT TALKING TO YOU, COMMIS-SIONER.

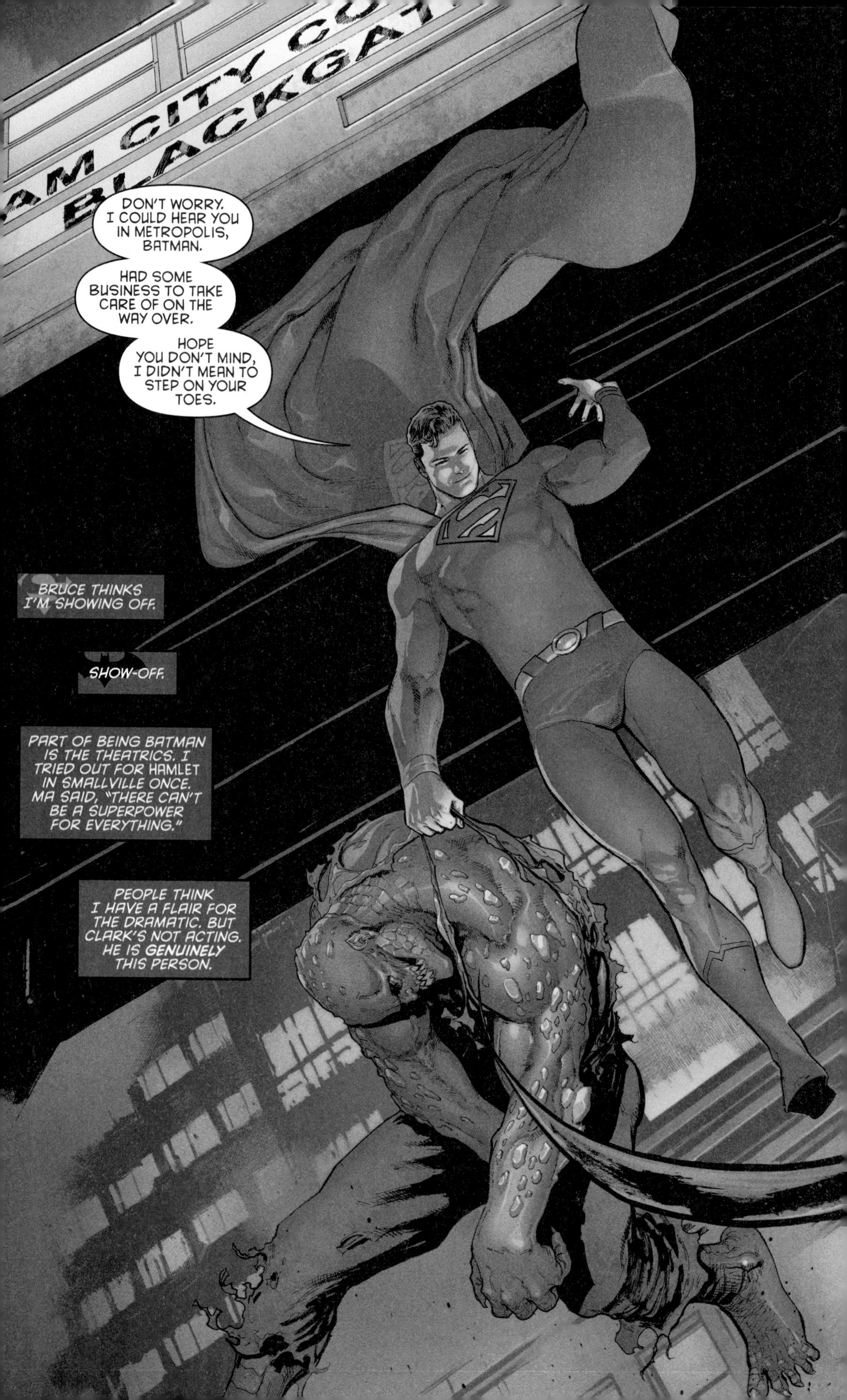
AM CITY CU
BLACKGAT
DON'T WORRY. I COULD HEAR YOU IN METROPOLIS, BATMAN.
HAD SOME BUSINESS TO TAKE CARE OF ON THE WAY OVER.
HOPE YOU DON'T MIND, I DIDN'T MEAN TO STEP ON YOUR TOES.
BRUCE THINKS I'M SHOWING OFF.
SHOW-OFF.
PART OF BEING BATMAN IS THE THEATRICS. I TRIED OUT FOR HAMLET IN SMALLVILLE ONCE. MA SAID, "THERE CAN'T BE A SUPERPOWER FOR EVERYTHING."
PEOPLE THINK I HAVE A FLAIR FOR THE DRAMATIC. BUT CLARK'S NOT ACTING. HE IS GENUINELY THIS PERSON.

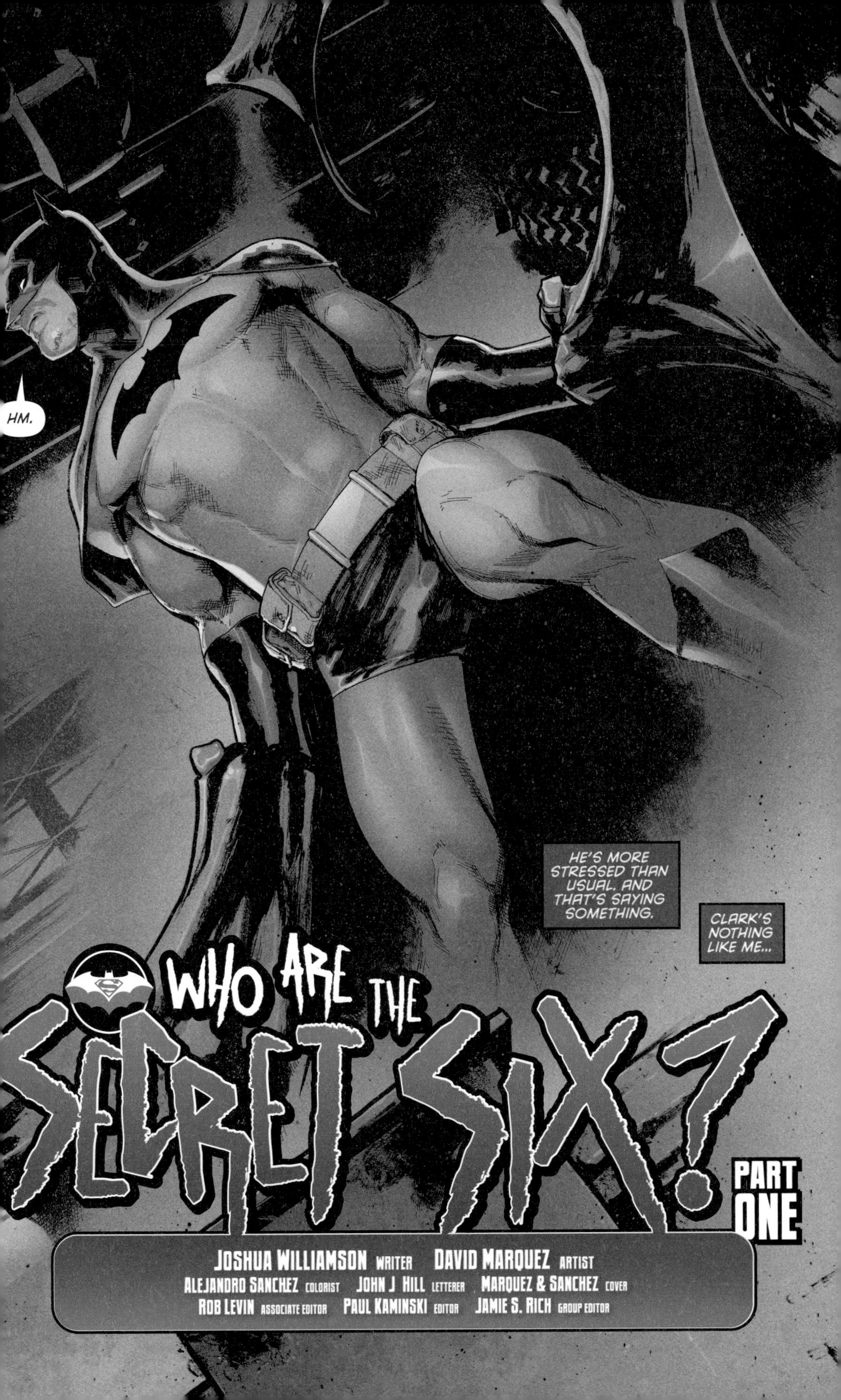
HM.
HE'S MORE STRESSED THAN USUAL. AND THAT'S SAYING SOMETHING.
CLARK'S NOTHING LIKE ME...
WHO ARE THE SECRET SIX?
PART ONE
JOSHUA WILLIAMSON WRITER DAVID MARQUEZ ARTIST
ALEJANDRO SANCHEZ COLORIST JOHN J. HILL LETTERER MARQUEZ & SANCHEZ COVER
ROB LEVIN ASSOCIATE EDITOR PAUL KAMINSKI EDITOR JAMIE S. RICH GROUP EDITOR

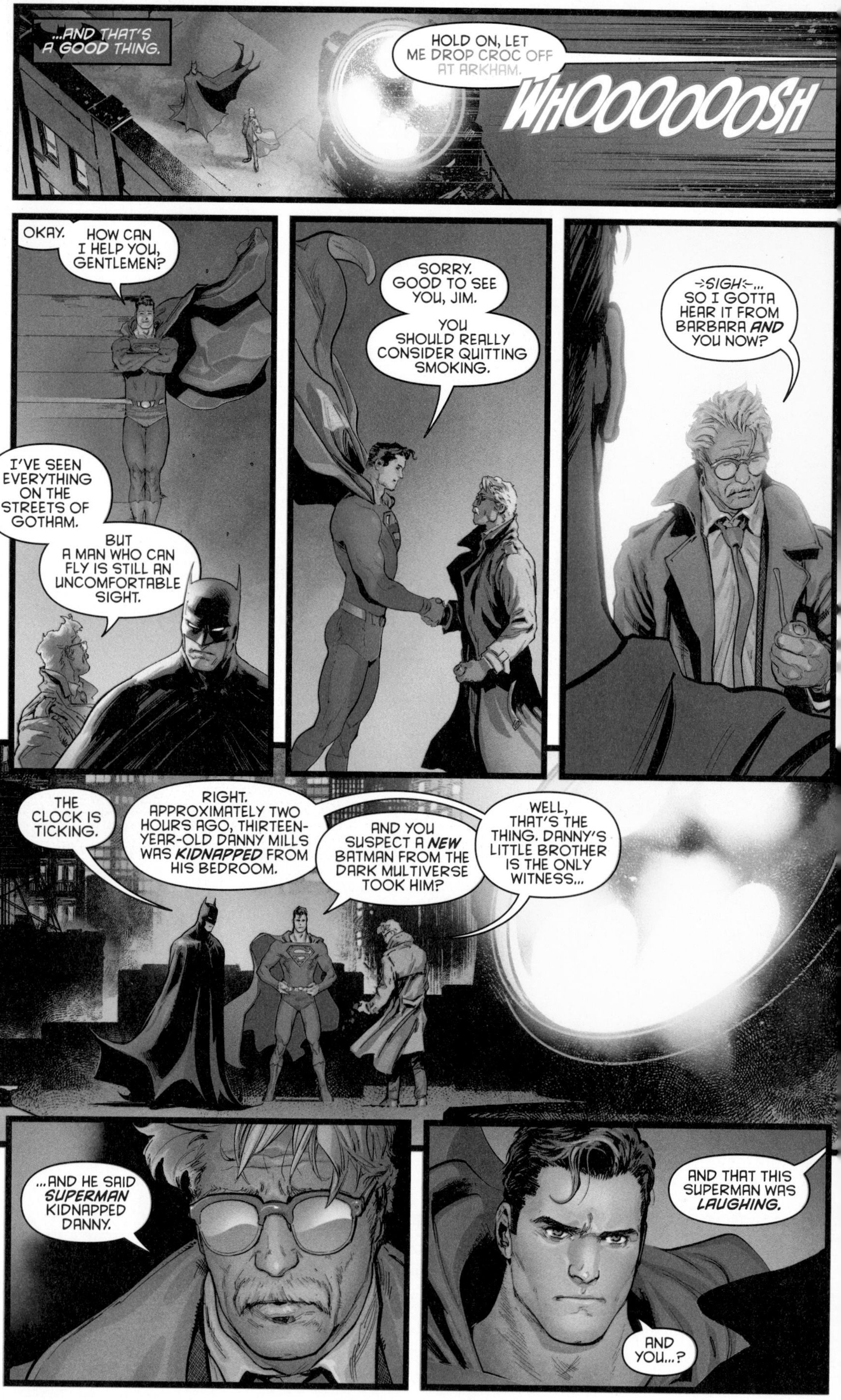
...AND THAT'S A GOOD THING.
HOLD ON, LET ME DROP CROC OFF AT ARKHAM.
WHOOOOOOOSH
OKAY.
HOW CAN I HELP YOU, GENTLEMEN?
I'VE SEEN EVERYTHING ON THE STREETS OF GOTHAM.
BUT A MAN WHO CAN FLY IS STILL AN UNCOMFORTABLE SIGHT.
SORRY. GOOD TO SEE YOU, JIM.
YOU SHOULD REALLY CONSIDER QUITTING SMOKING.
SIGH... SO I GOTTA HEAR IT FROM BARBARA AND YOU NOW?
THE CLOCK IS TICKING.
RIGHT. APPROXIMATELY TWO HOURS AGO, THIRTEEN-YEAR-OLD DANNY MILLS WAS KIDNAPPED FROM HIS BEDROOM.
AND YOU SUSPECT A NEW BATMAN FROM THE DARK MULTIVERSE TOOK HIM?
WELL, THAT'S THE THING. DANNY'S LITTLE BROTHER IS THE ONLY WITNESS...
...AND HE SAID SUPERMAN KIDNAPPED DANNY.
AND THAT THIS SUPERMAN WAS LAUGHING.
AND YOU...?

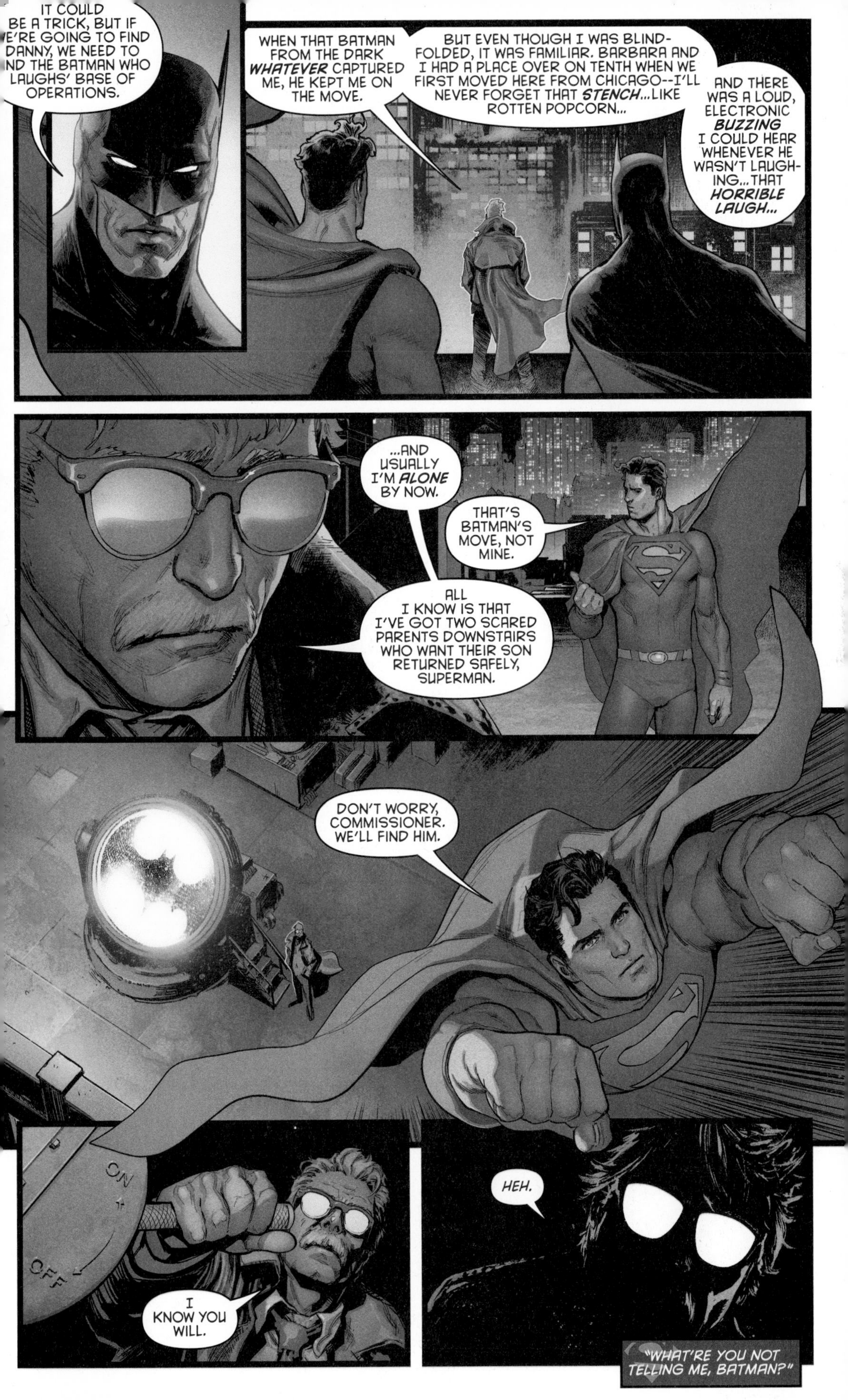
IT COULD BE A TRICK, BUT IF WE'RE GOING TO FIND DANNY, WE NEED TO FIND THE BATMAN WHO LAUGHS' BASE OF OPERATIONS.
WHEN THAT BATMAN FROM THE DARK WHATEVER CAPTURED ME, HE KEPT ME ON THE MOVE.
BUT EVEN THOUGH I WAS BLINDFOLDED, IT WAS FAMILIAR. BARBARA AND I HAD A PLACE OVER ON TENTH WHEN WE FIRST MOVED HERE FROM CHICAGO--I'LL NEVER FORGET THAT STENCH...LIKE ROTTEN POPCORN...
AND THERE WAS A LOUD, ELECTRONIC BUZZING I COULD HEAR WHENEVER HE WASN'T LAUGHING...THAT HORRIBLE LAUGH...
...AND USUALLY I'M ALONE BY NOW.
THAT'S BATMAN'S MOVE, NOT MINE.
ALL I KNOW IS THAT I'VE GOT TWO SCARED PARENTS DOWNSTAIRS WHO WANT THEIR SON RETURNED SAFELY, SUPERMAN.
DON'T WORRY, COMMISSIONER. WE'LL FIND HIM.
ON
OFF
I KNOW YOU WILL.
HEH.
"WHAT'RE YOU NOT TELLING ME, BATMAN?"

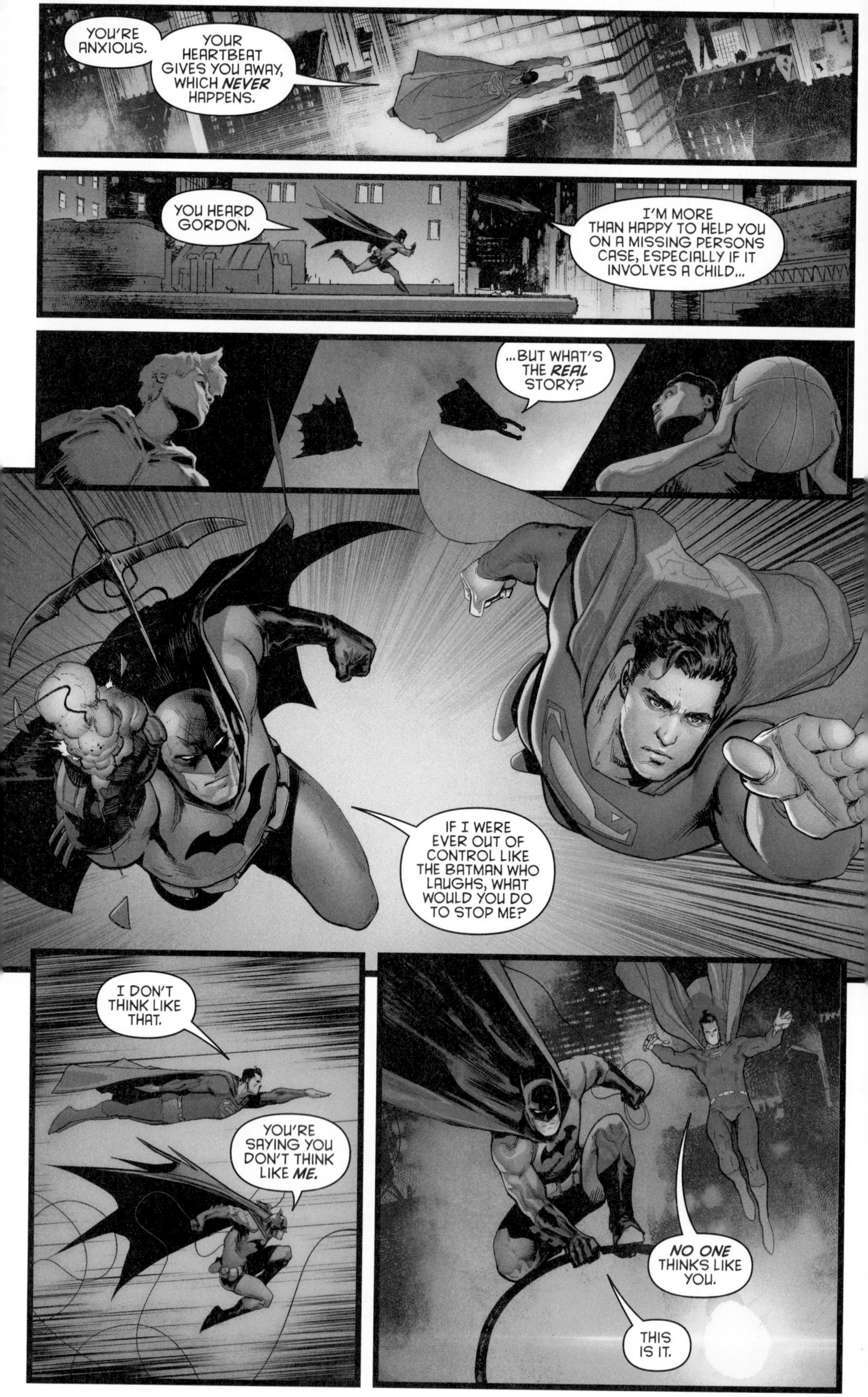

YOU'RE ANXIOUS.
YOUR HEARTBEAT GIVES YOU AWAY, WHICH *NEVER* HAPPENS.
YOU HEARD GORDON.
I'M MORE THAN HAPPY TO HELP YOU ON A MISSING PERSONS CASE, ESPECIALLY IF IT INVOLVES A CHILD...
...BUT WHAT'S THE *REAL* STORY?
IF I WERE EVER OUT OF CONTROL LIKE THE BATMAN WHO LAUGHS, WHAT WOULD YOU DO TO STOP ME?
I DON'T THINK LIKE THAT.
YOU'RE SAYING YOU DON'T THINK LIKE *ME.*
NO ONE THINKS LIKE YOU.
THIS IS IT.

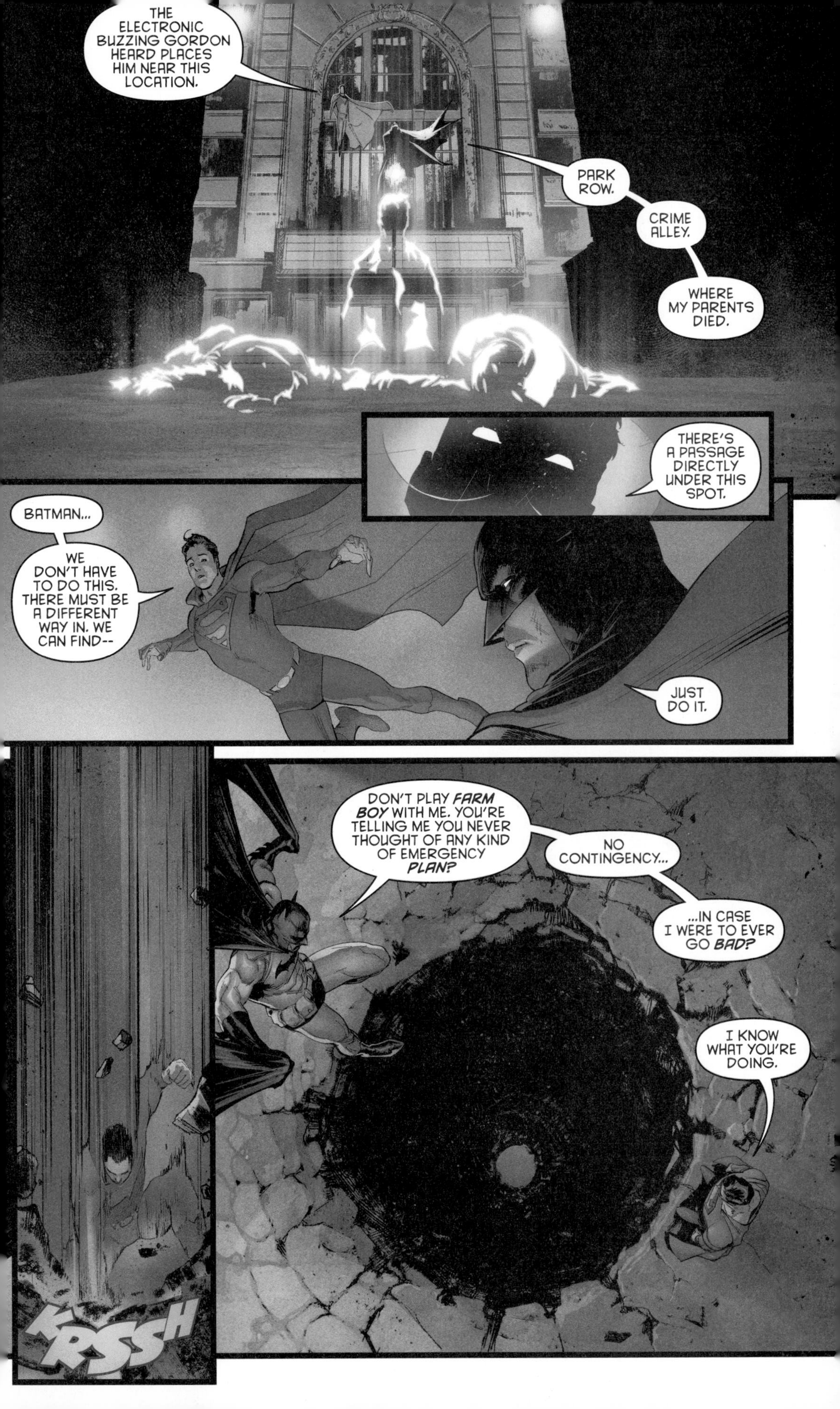

THE ELECTRONIC BUZZING GORDON HEARD PLACES HIM NEAR THIS LOCATION.
PARK ROW.
CRIME ALLEY.
WHERE MY PARENTS DIED.
THERE'S A PASSAGE DIRECTLY UNDER THIS SPOT.
BATMAN...
WE DON'T HAVE TO DO THIS. THERE MUST BE A DIFFERENT WAY IN. WE CAN FIND--
JUST DO IT.
KRSSH
DON'T PLAY *FARM BOY* WITH ME. YOU'RE TELLING ME YOU NEVER THOUGHT OF ANY KIND OF EMERGENCY *PLAN?*
NO CONTINGENCY...
...IN CASE I WERE TO EVER GO *BAD?*
I KNOW WHAT YOU'RE DOING.

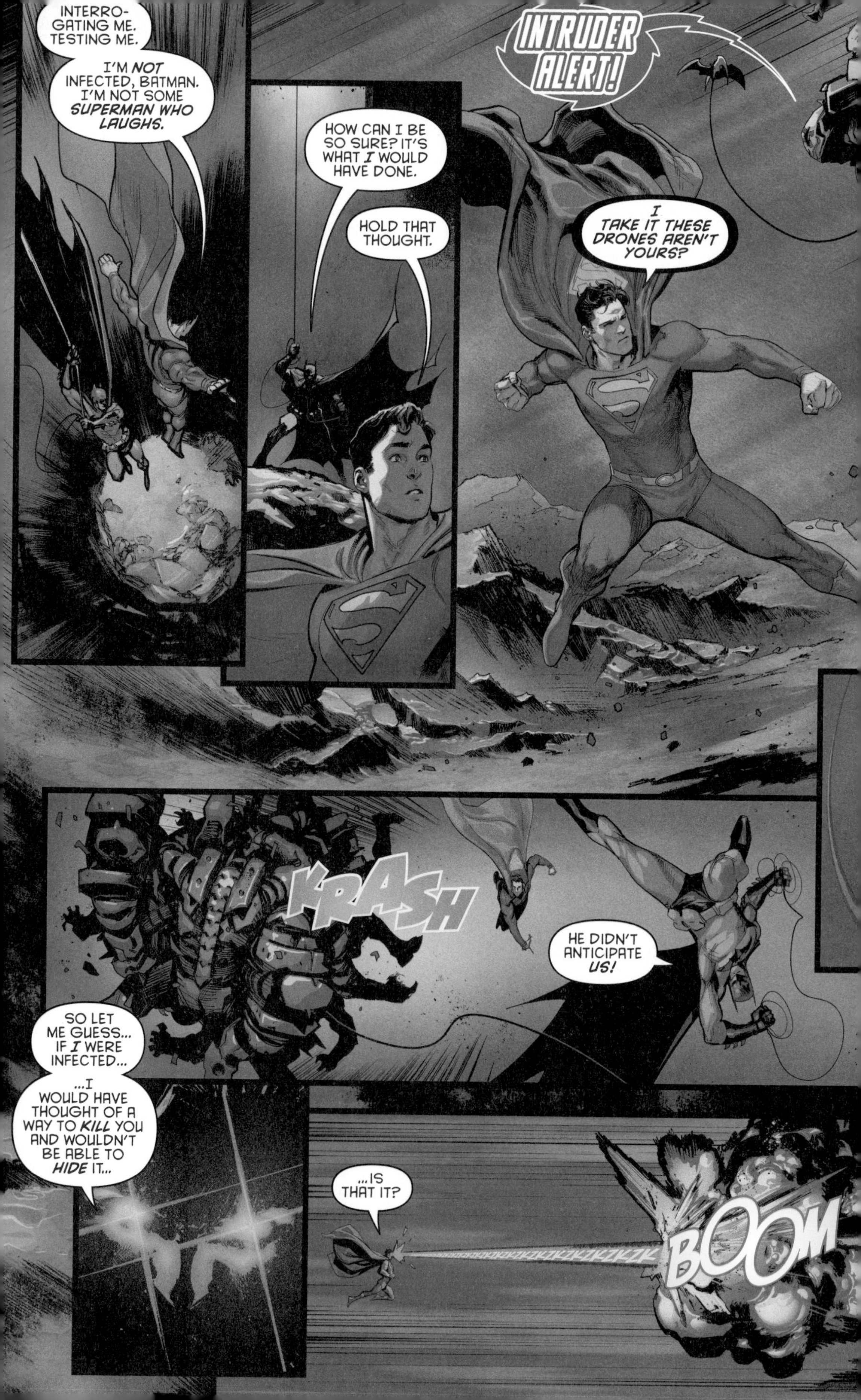
INTERRO-GATING ME. TESTING ME.
I'M NOT INFECTED, BATMAN. I'M NOT SOME SUPERMAN WHO LAUGHS.
HOW CAN I BE SO SURE? IT'S WHAT I WOULD HAVE DONE.
HOLD THAT THOUGHT.
INTRUDER ALERT!
I TAKE IT THESE DRONES AREN'T YOURS?
KRASH
HE DIDN'T ANTICIPATE US!
SO LET ME GUESS... IF I WERE INFECTED...
...I WOULD HAVE THOUGHT OF A WAY TO KILL YOU AND WOULDN'T BE ABLE TO HIDE IT...
...IS THAT IT?
BOOM

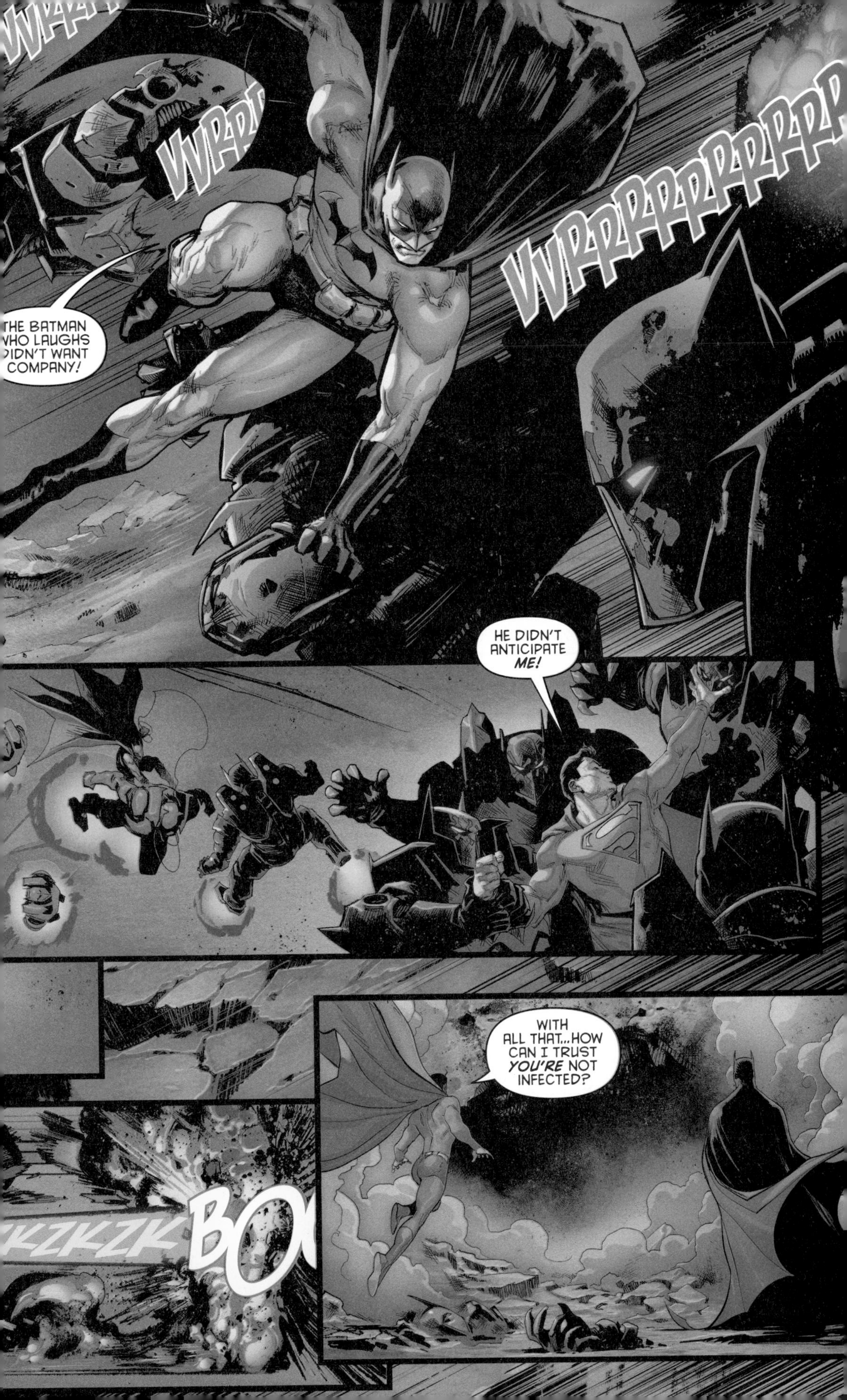

VVRRR
THE BATMAN WHO LAUGHS DIDN'T WANT COMPANY!
VVRRRRRRRRRR
HE DIDN'T ANTICIPATE *ME!*
KZKZK
BO
WITH ALL THAT...HOW CAN I TRUST *YOU'RE* NOT INFECTED?

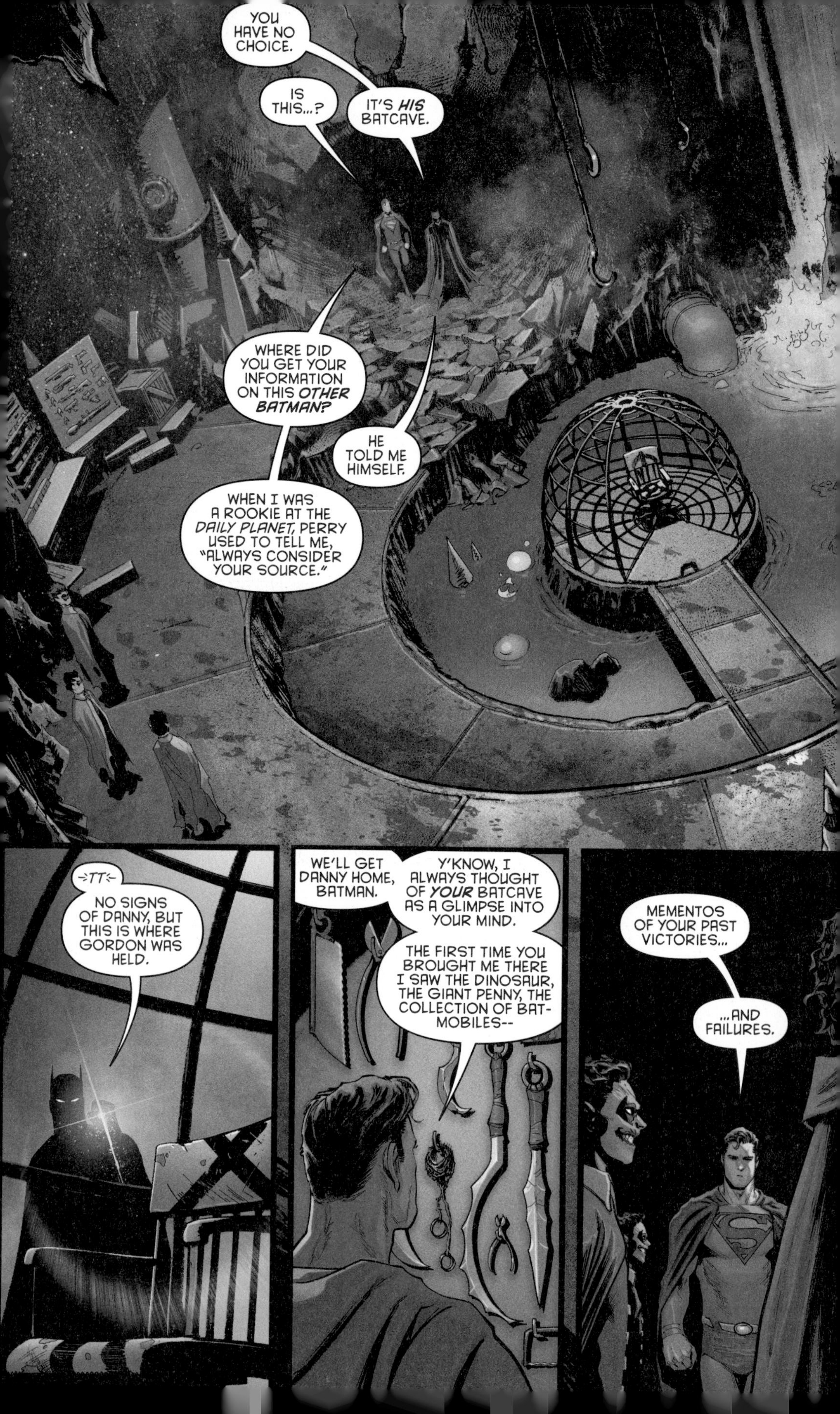
YOU HAVE NO CHOICE.
IS THIS...?
IT'S *HIS* BATCAVE.
WHERE DID YOU GET YOUR INFORMATION ON THIS *OTHER BATMAN?*
HE TOLD ME HIMSELF.
WHEN I WAS A ROOKIE AT THE *DAILY PLANET*, PERRY USED TO TELL ME, "ALWAYS CONSIDER YOUR SOURCE."
-TT-
NO SIGNS OF DANNY, BUT THIS IS WHERE GORDON WAS HELD.
WE'LL GET DANNY HOME, BATMAN.
Y'KNOW, I ALWAYS THOUGHT OF *YOUR* BATCAVE AS A GLIMPSE INTO YOUR MIND.
THE FIRST TIME YOU BROUGHT ME THERE I SAW THE DINOSAUR, THE GIANT PENNY, THE COLLECTION OF BAT-MOBILES--
MEMENTOS OF YOUR PAST VICTORIES...
...AND FAILURES.

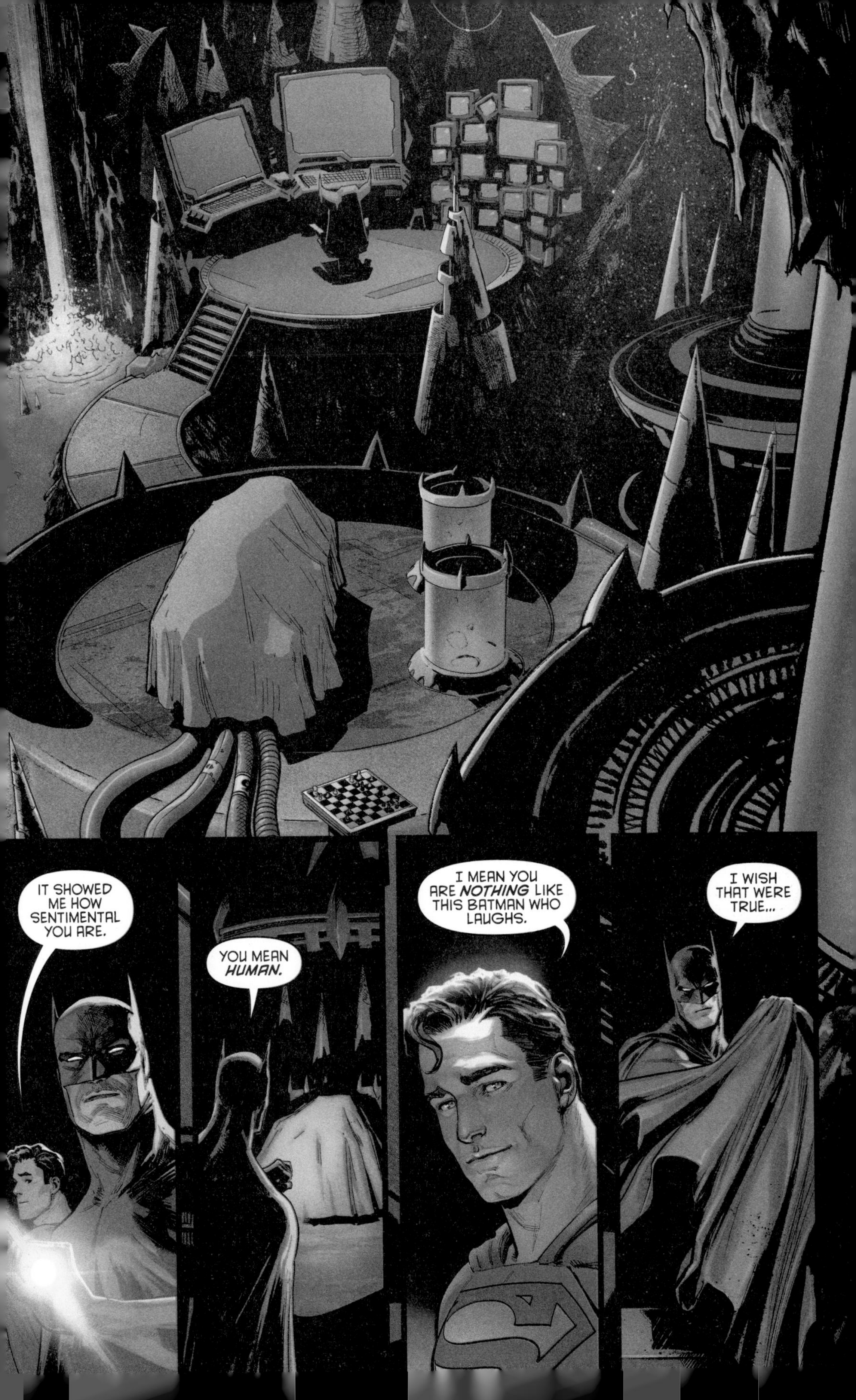
IT SHOWED ME HOW SENTIMENTAL YOU ARE.
YOU MEAN *HUMAN.*
I MEAN YOU ARE *NOTHING* LIKE THIS BATMAN WHO LAUGHS.
I WISH THAT WERE TRUE...

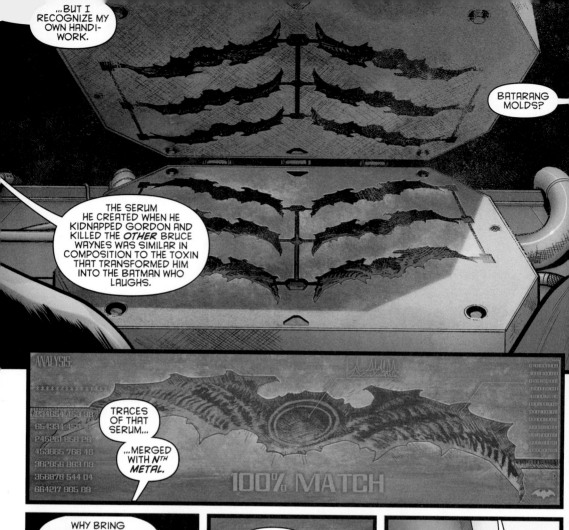

...BUT I RECOGNIZE MY OWN HANDI-WORK.

BATARANG MOLDS?

THE SERUM HE CREATED WHEN HE KIDNAPPED GORDON AND KILLED THE *OTHER* BRUCE WAYNES WAS SIMILAR IN COMPOSITION TO THE TOXIN THAT TRANSFORMED HIM INTO THE BATMAN WHO LAUGHS.

ANALYSIS:

****

1234654 453 38
854334 450 18
245261 856 26
453665 766 48
382856 863 09
356878 544 04
664217 985 89

TRACES OF THAT SERUM...

...MERGED WITH N^{TH} METAL.

100% MATCH

WHY BRING GORDON HERE? SEND SOMEONE TO KIDNAP DANNY MILLS?

HE HAD TO KNOW YOU'D FIND HIS BATCAVE. MAYBE THAT WAS THE POINT.

IF YOU'RE CORRECT AND HE'S JUST LIKE YOU, THAT MEANS HE HIDES THINGS IN PLAIN SIGHT, RIGHT?

THIS IS A MESSAGE.

BOTH SIDES ARE AT A DRAW.

ANY MOVE FROM EITHER PLAYER WOULD RESULT IN A LOSS.

PA AND I USED TO PLAY EVERY SUNDAY AFTER FOOTBALL.

WHAT HAPPENS WHEN WE STOP PLAYING THE BATMAN WHO LAUGHS' GAMES?

BEEP

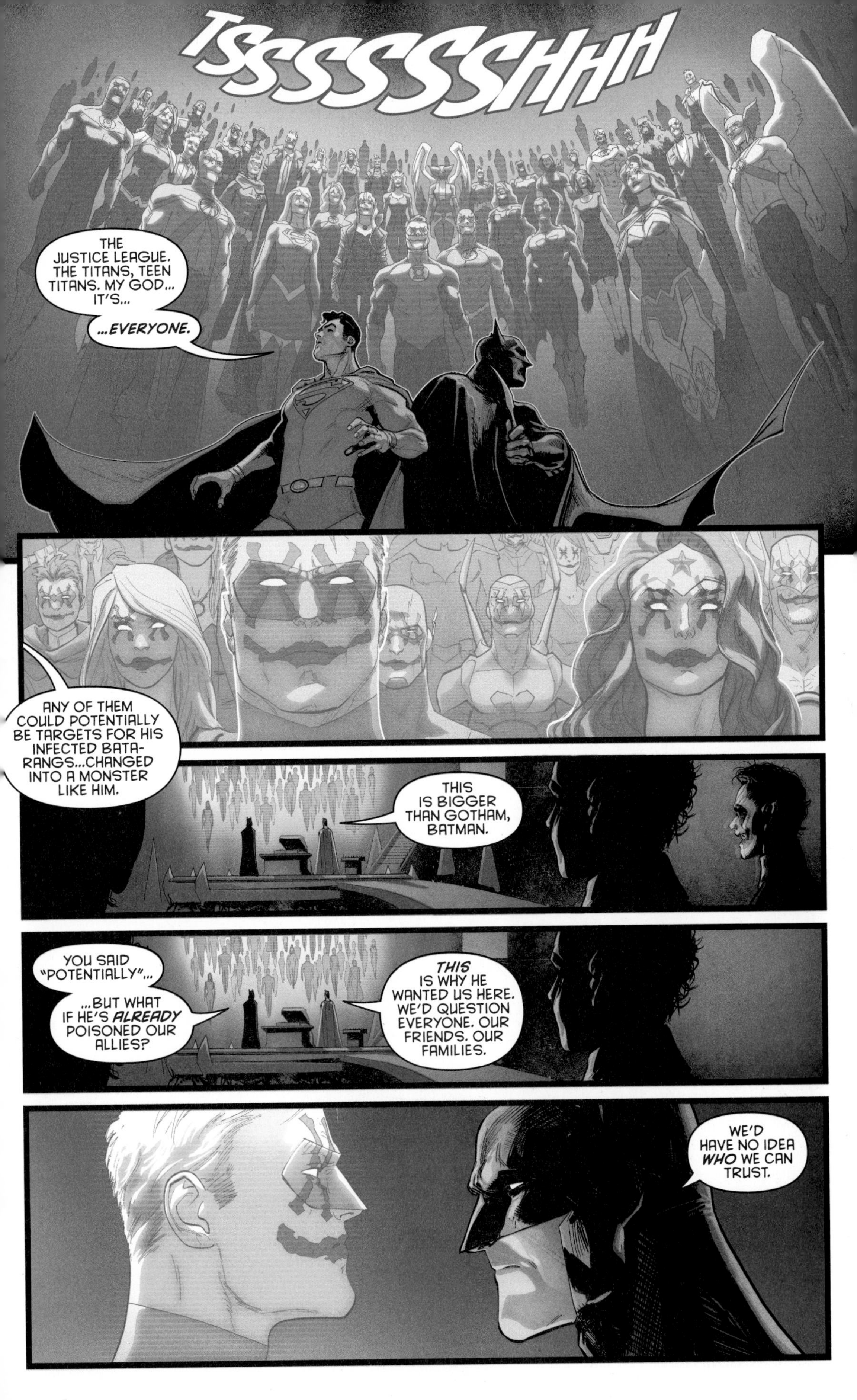
TSSSSSSHHH
THE JUSTICE LEAGUE. THE TITANS, TEEN TITANS. MY GOD... IT'S...
...EVERYONE.
ANY OF THEM COULD POTENTIALLY BE TARGETS FOR HIS INFECTED BATA-RANGS...CHANGED INTO A MONSTER LIKE HIM.
THIS IS BIGGER THAN GOTHAM, BATMAN.
YOU SAID "POTENTIALLY"...
...BUT WHAT IF HE'S ALREADY POISONED OUR ALLIES?
THIS IS WHY HE WANTED US HERE. WE'D QUESTION EVERYONE. OUR FRIENDS. OUR FAMILIES.
WE'D HAVE NO IDEA WHO WE CAN TRUST.

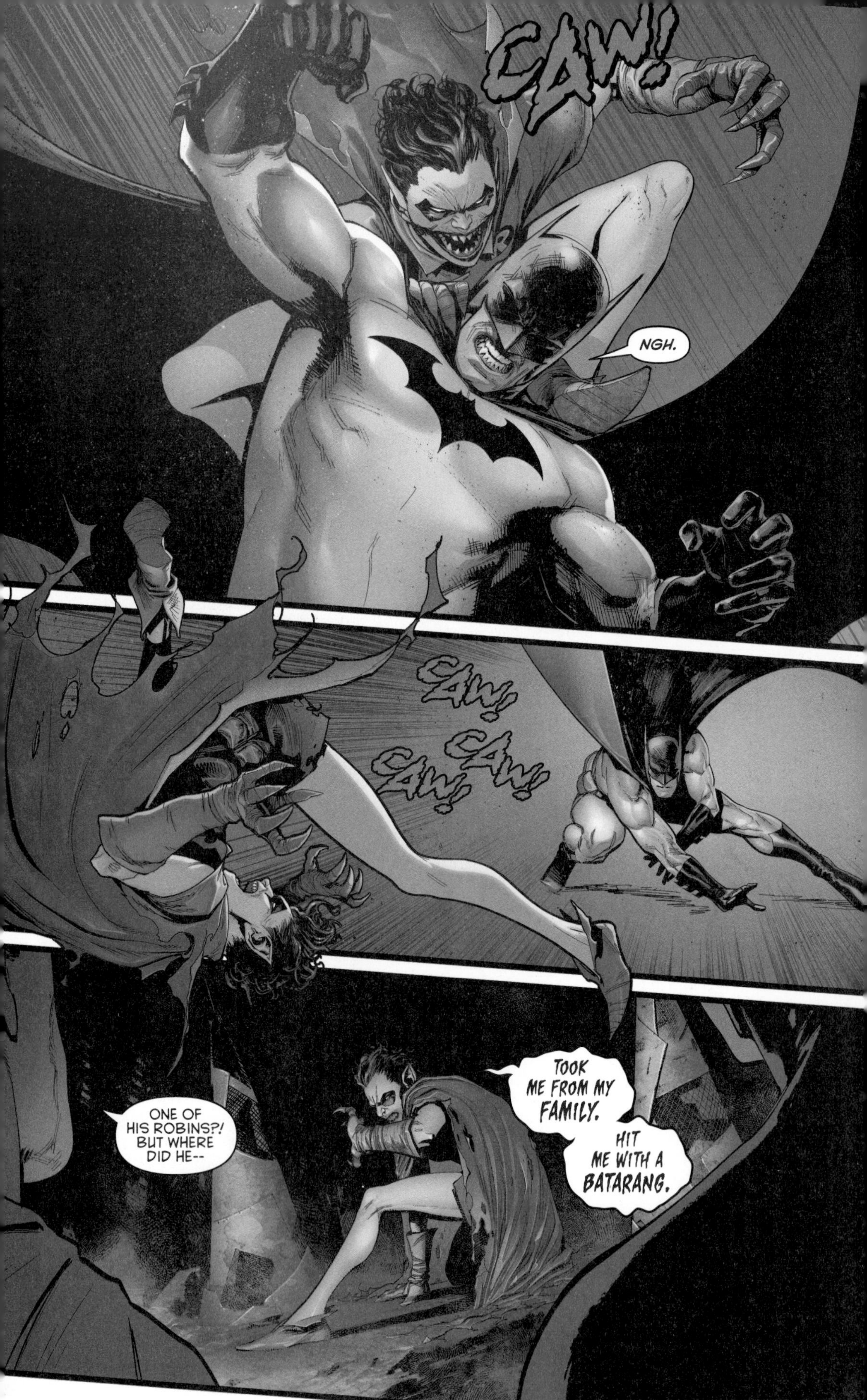
CAW!
NGH.
CAW!
CAW!
CAW!
ONE OF HIS ROBINS?! BUT WHERE DID HE--
TOOK ME FROM MY FAMILY.
HIT ME WITH A BATARANG.

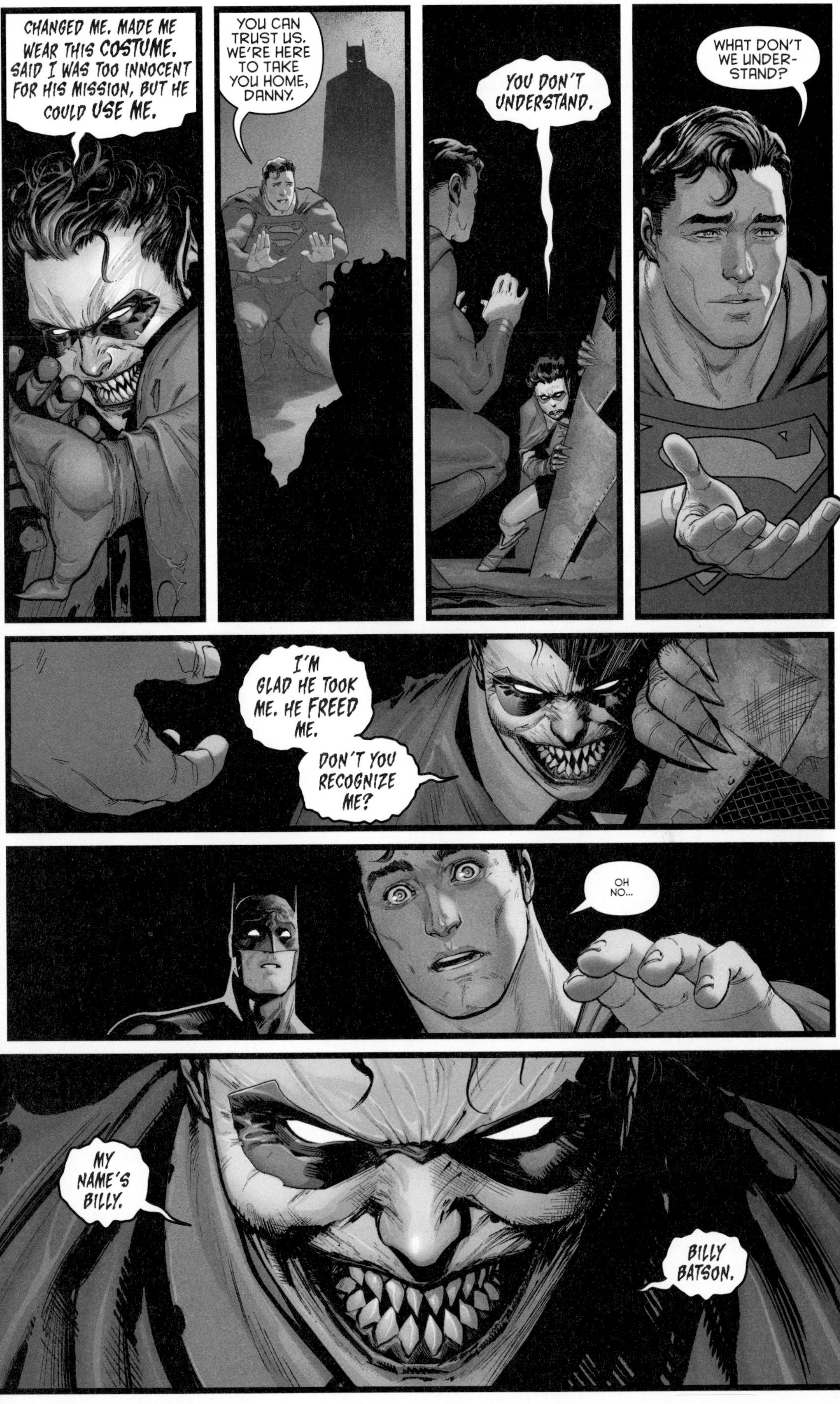

CHANGED ME. MADE ME WEAR THIS COSTUME. SAID I WAS TOO INNOCENT FOR HIS MISSION, BUT HE COULD USE ME.
YOU CAN TRUST US. WE'RE HERE TO TAKE YOU HOME, DANNY.
YOU DON'T UNDERSTAND.
WHAT DON'T WE UNDER-STAND?
I'M GLAD HE TOOK ME. HE FREED ME.
DON'T YOU RECOGNIZE ME?
OH NO...
MY NAME'S BILLY.
BILLY BATSON.

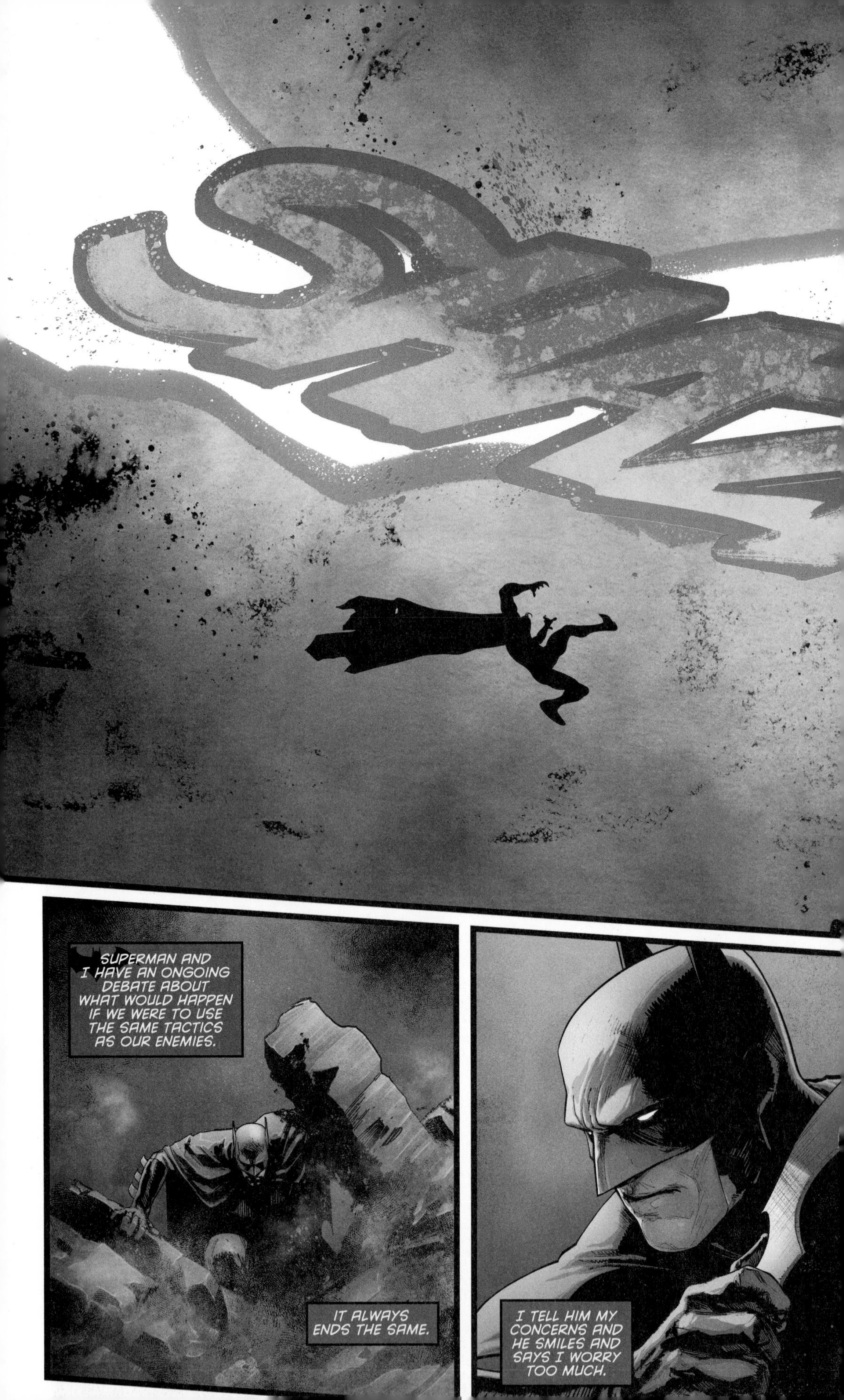
SUPERMAN AND I HAVE AN ONGOING DEBATE ABOUT WHAT WOULD HAPPEN IF WE WERE TO USE THE SAME TACTICS AS OUR ENEMIES.
IT ALWAYS ENDS THE SAME.
I TELL HIM MY CONCERNS AND HE SMILES AND SAYS I WORRY TOO MUCH.

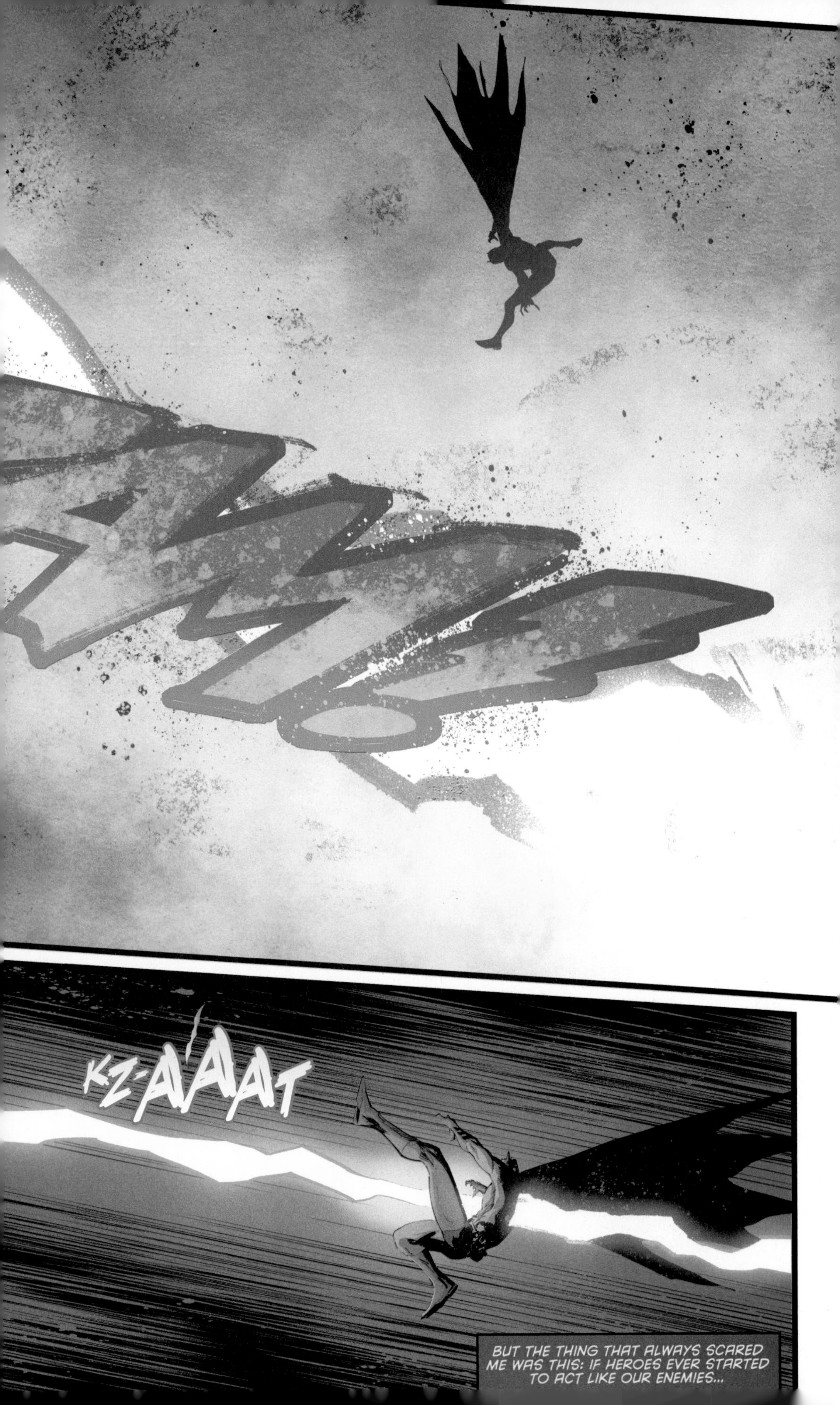
KZ-AAAT
BUT THE THING THAT ALWAYS SCARED ME WAS THIS: IF HEROES EVER STARTED TO ACT LIKE OUR ENEMIES...

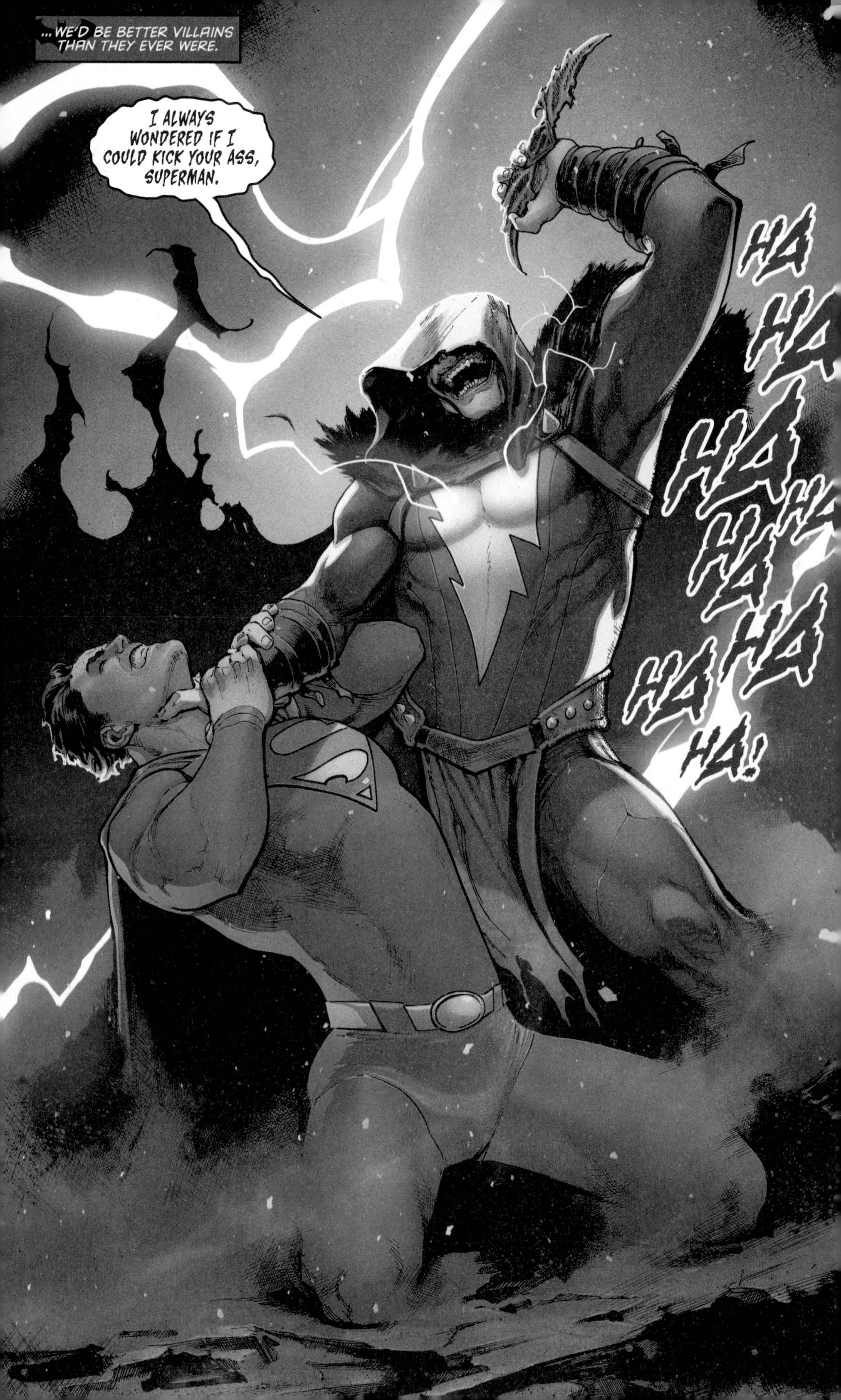
...WE'D BE BETTER VILLAINS THAN THEY EVER WERE.
I ALWAYS WONDERED IF I COULD KICK YOUR ASS, SUPERMAN.
HA HA HA HA HA HA HA HA HA!

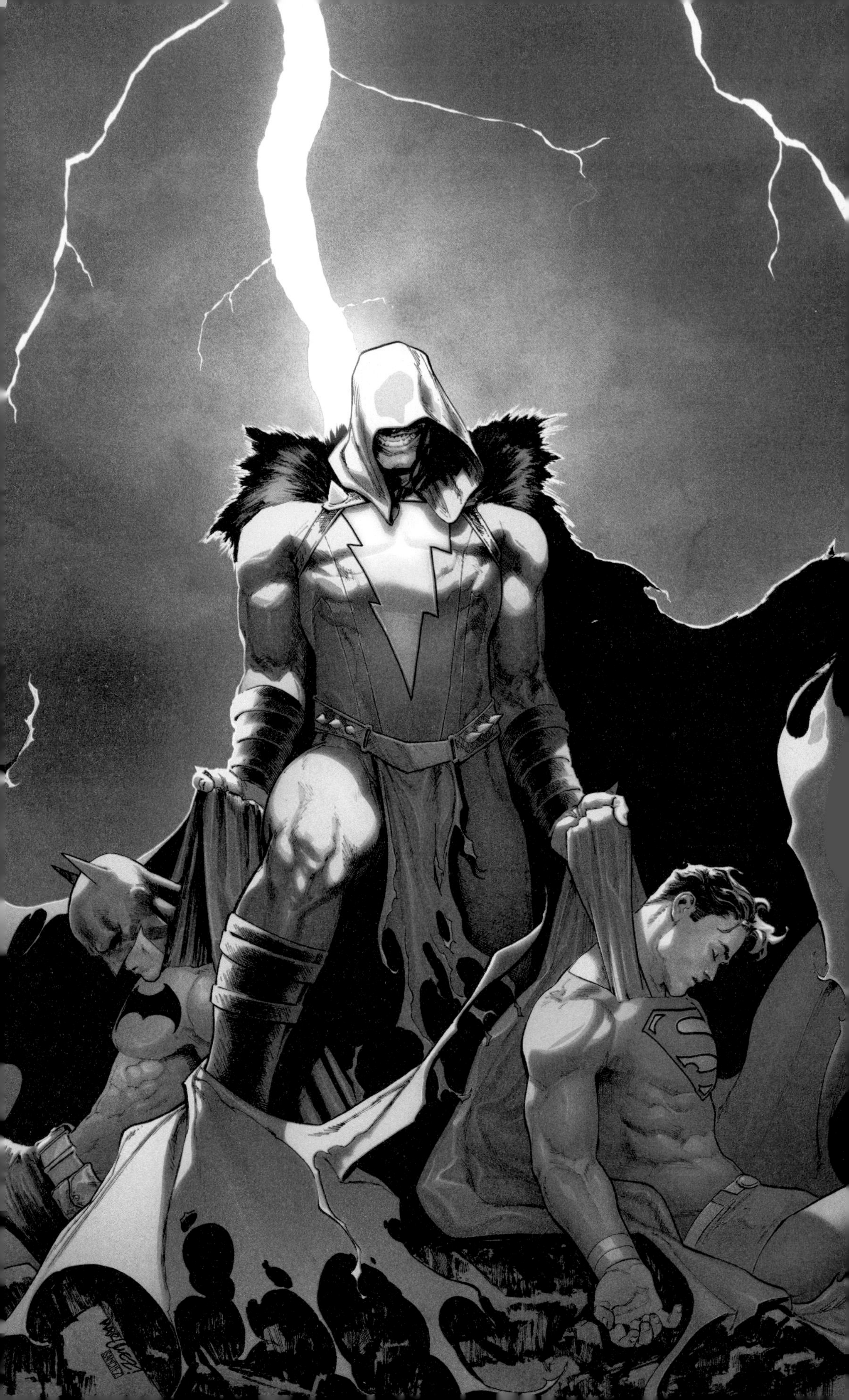

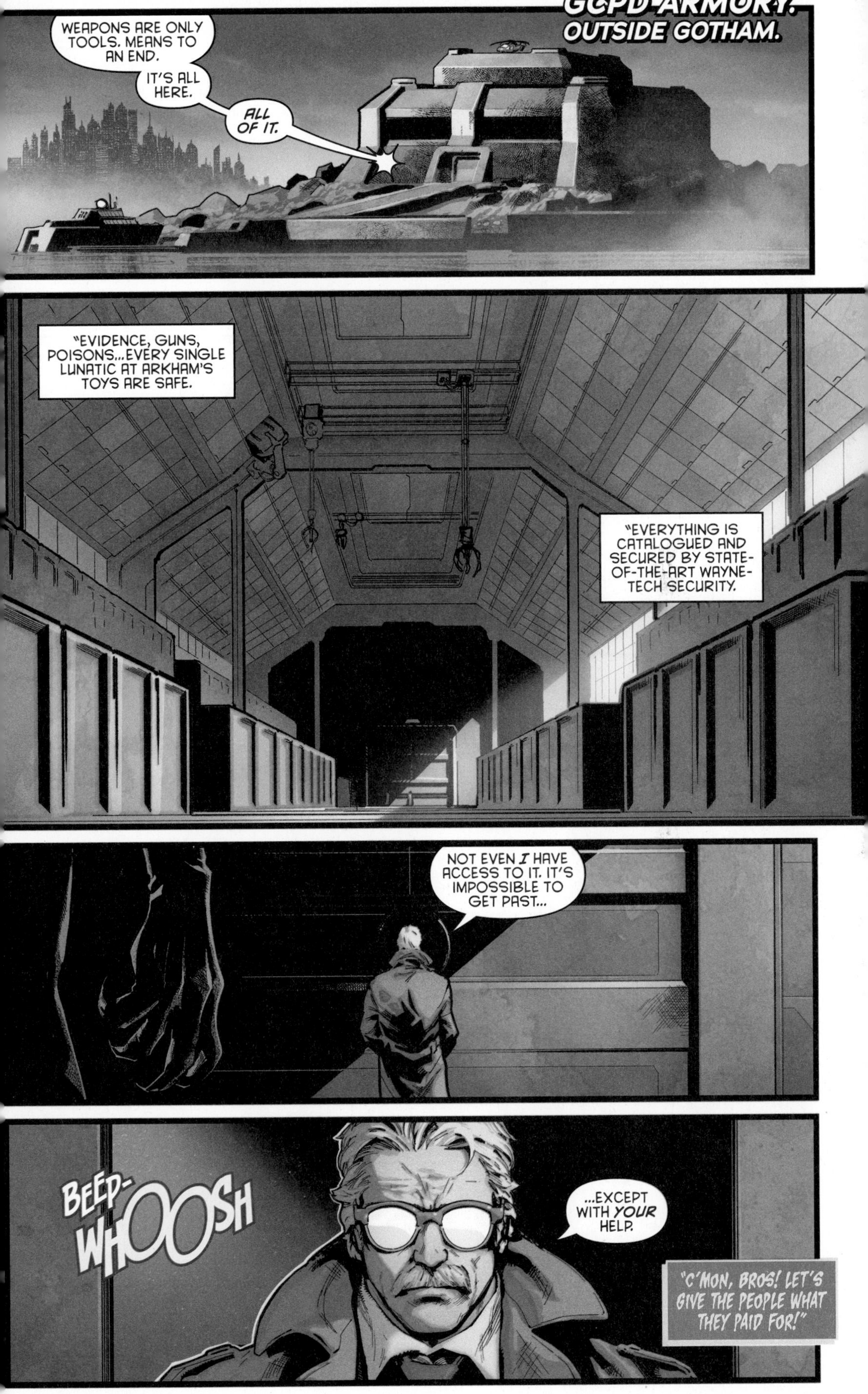
GCPD ARMORY. OUTSIDE GOTHAM.
WEAPONS ARE ONLY TOOLS. MEANS TO AN END.
IT'S ALL HERE.
ALL OF IT.
"EVIDENCE, GUNS, POISONS...EVERY SINGLE LUNATIC AT ARKHAM'S TOYS ARE SAFE.
"EVERYTHING IS CATALOGUED AND SECURED BY STATE-OF-THE-ART WAYNE-TECH SECURITY.
NOT EVEN I HAVE ACCESS TO IT. IT'S IMPOSSIBLE TO GET PAST...
BEEP-WHOOSH
...EXCEPT WITH YOUR HELP.
"C'MON, BROS! LET'S GIVE THE PEOPLE WHAT THEY PAID FOR!"

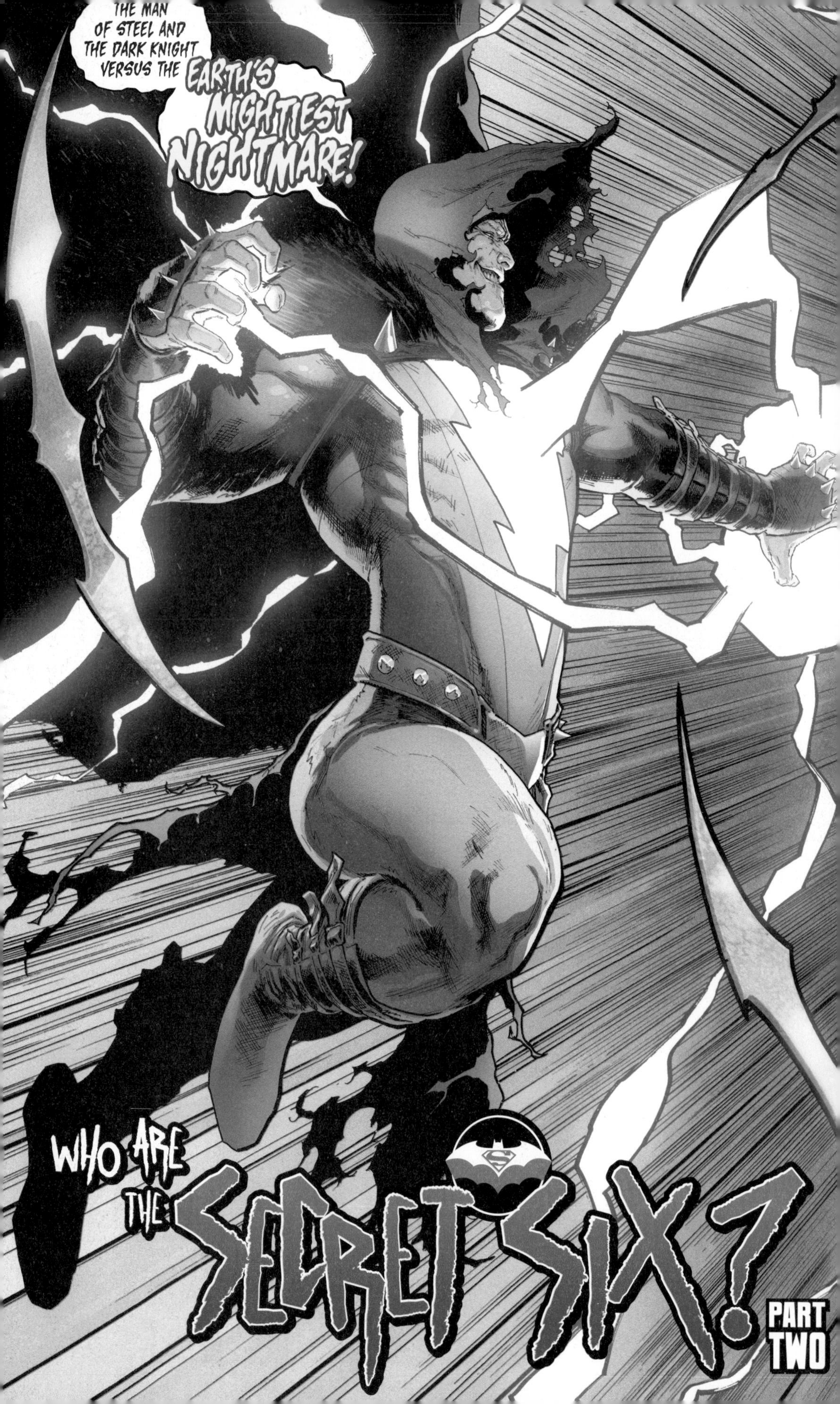
THE MAN OF STEEL AND THE DARK KNIGHT VERSUS THE EARTH'S MIGHTIEST NIGHTMARE!
WHO ARE THE SECRET SIX?
PART TWO

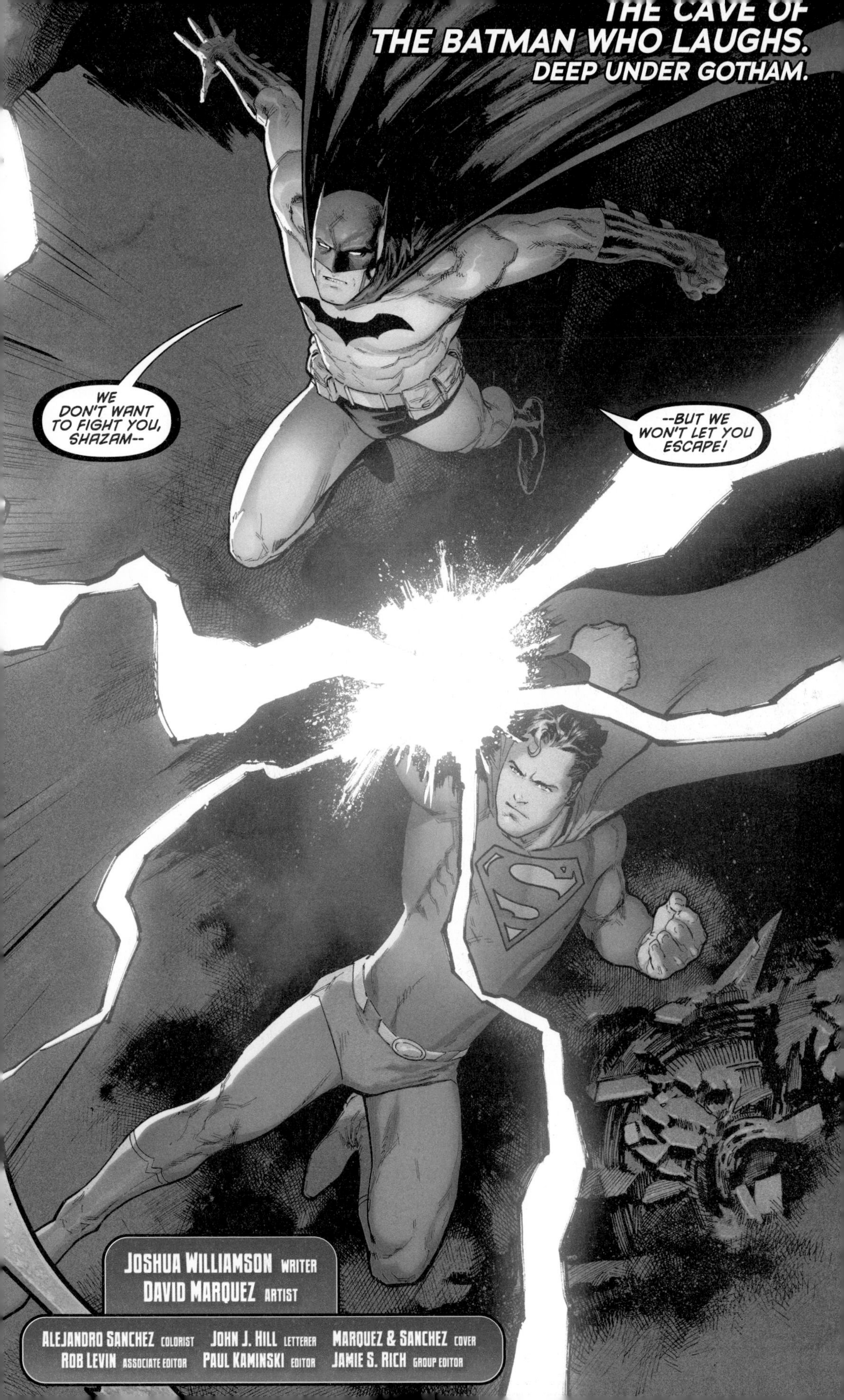
THE CAVE OF
THE BATMAN WHO LAUGHS.
DEEP UNDER GOTHAM.
WE DON'T WANT TO FIGHT YOU, SHAZAM--
--BUT WE WON'T LET YOU ESCAPE!
JOSHUA WILLIAMSON WRITER
DAVID MARQUEZ ARTIST
ALEJANDRO SANCHEZ COLORIST JOHN J. HILL LETTERER MARQUEZ & SANCHEZ COVER
ROB LEVIN ASSOCIATE EDITOR PAUL KAMINSKI EDITOR JAMIE S. RICH GROUP EDITOR

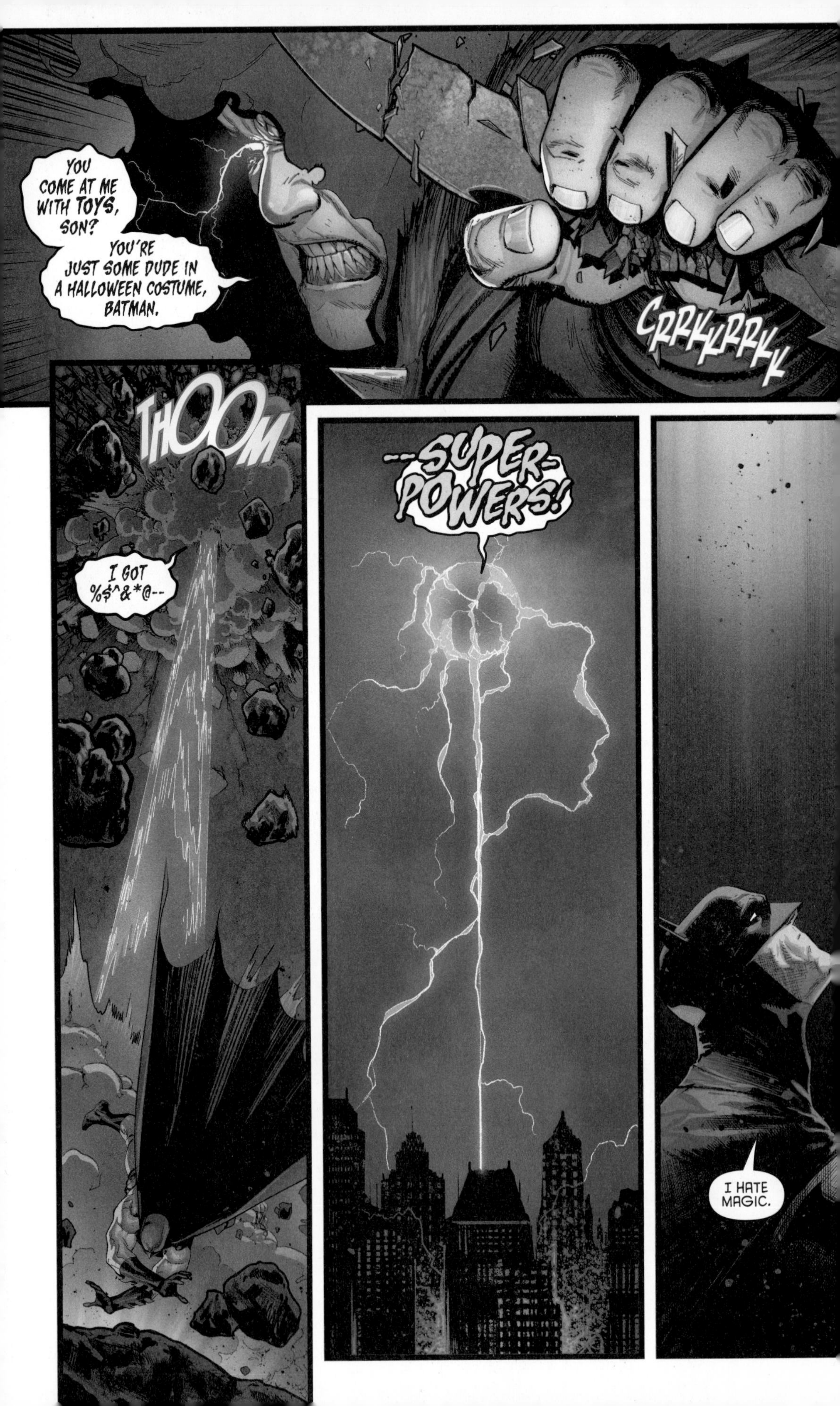
YOU COME AT ME WITH TOYS, SON?
YOU'RE JUST SOME DUDE IN A HALLOWEEN COSTUME, BATMAN.
CRRKKRRKK
THOOM
I GOT %$^&*@--
--SUPER-POWERS!
I HATE MAGIC.

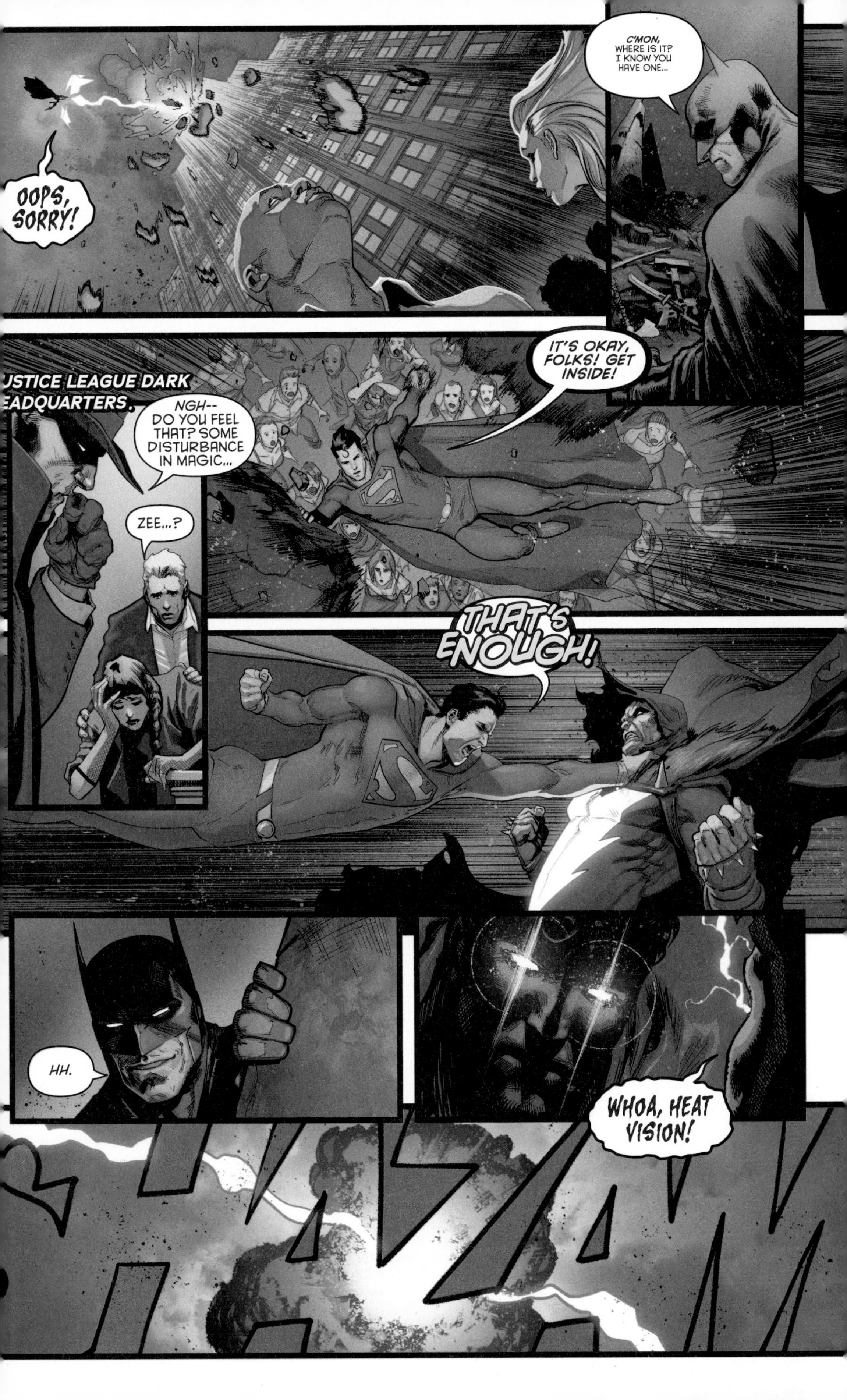
OOPS, SORRY!
C'MON, WHERE IS IT? I KNOW YOU HAVE ONE...
JUSTICE LEAGUE DARK HEADQUARTERS.
NGH-- DO YOU FEEL THAT? SOME DISTURBANCE IN MAGIC...
ZEE...?
IT'S OKAY, FOLKS! GET INSIDE!
THAT'S ENOUGH!
HH.
WHOA, HEAT VISION!

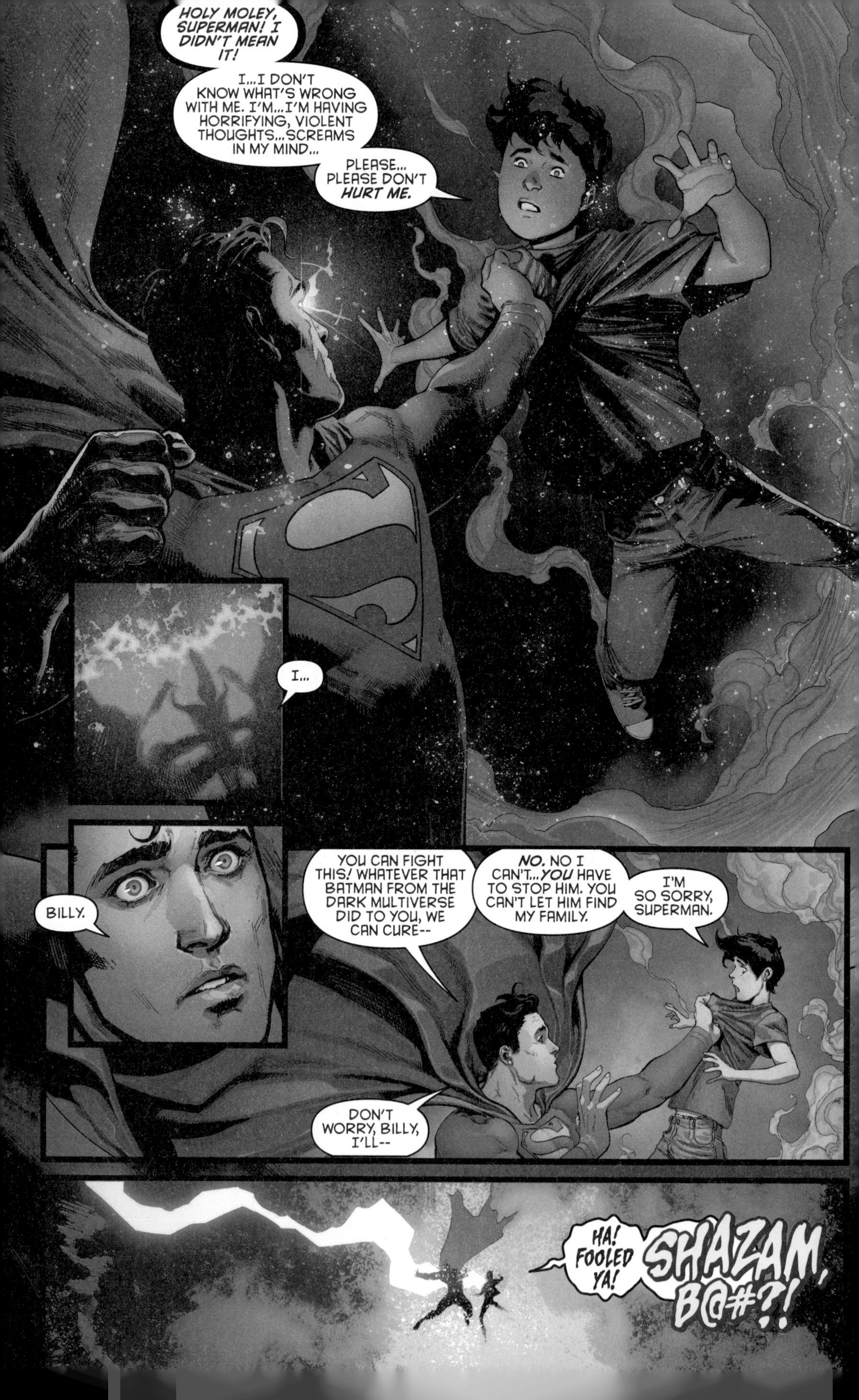
HOLY MOLEY, SUPERMAN! I DIDN'T MEAN IT!
I...I DON'T KNOW WHAT'S WRONG WITH ME. I'M...I'M HAVING HORRIFYING, VIOLENT THOUGHTS...SCREAMS IN MY MIND...
PLEASE... PLEASE DON'T HURT ME.
I...
BILLY.
YOU CAN FIGHT THIS! WHATEVER THAT BATMAN FROM THE DARK MULTIVERSE DID TO YOU, WE CAN CURE--
NO. NO I CAN'T...YOU HAVE TO STOP HIM. YOU CAN'T LET HIM FIND MY FAMILY.
I'M SO SORRY, SUPERMAN.
DON'T WORRY, BILLY, I'LL--
HA! FOOLED YA!
SHAZAM, B@#?!

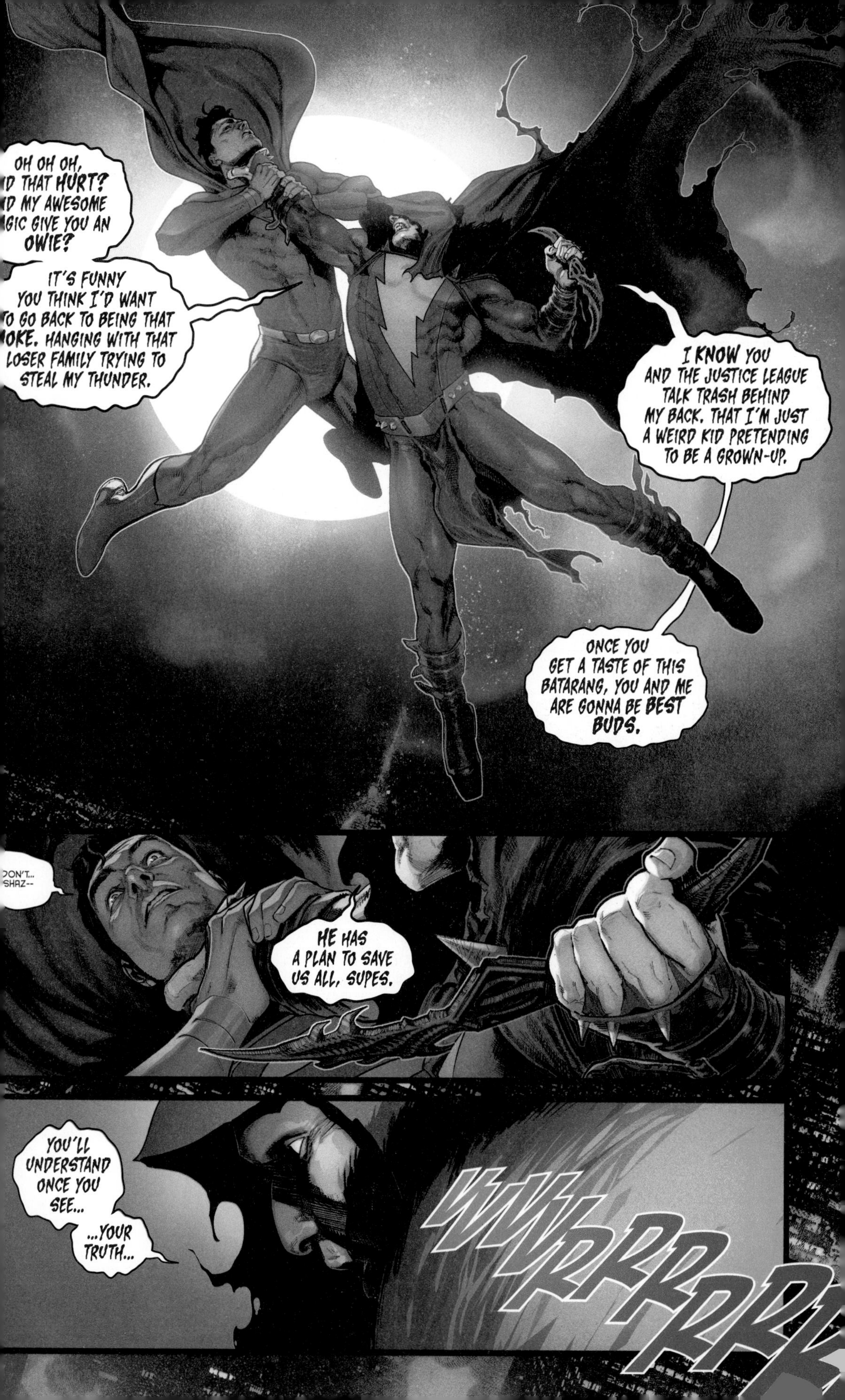

OH OH OH, ID THAT HURT? ID MY AWESOME GIC GIVE YOU AN OWIE?
IT'S FUNNY YOU THINK I'D WANT TO GO BACK TO BEING THAT OKE. HANGING WITH THAT LOSER FAMILY TRYING TO STEAL MY THUNDER.
I KNOW YOU AND THE JUSTICE LEAGUE TALK TRASH BEHIND MY BACK. THAT I'M JUST A WEIRD KID PRETENDING TO BE A GROWN-UP.
ONCE YOU GET A TASTE OF THIS BATARANG, YOU AND ME ARE GONNA BE BEST BUDS.
DON'T... SHAZ--
HE HAS A PLAN TO SAVE US ALL, SUPES.
YOU'LL UNDERSTAND ONCE YOU SEE...
...YOUR TRUTH...
VVVRRRRRK

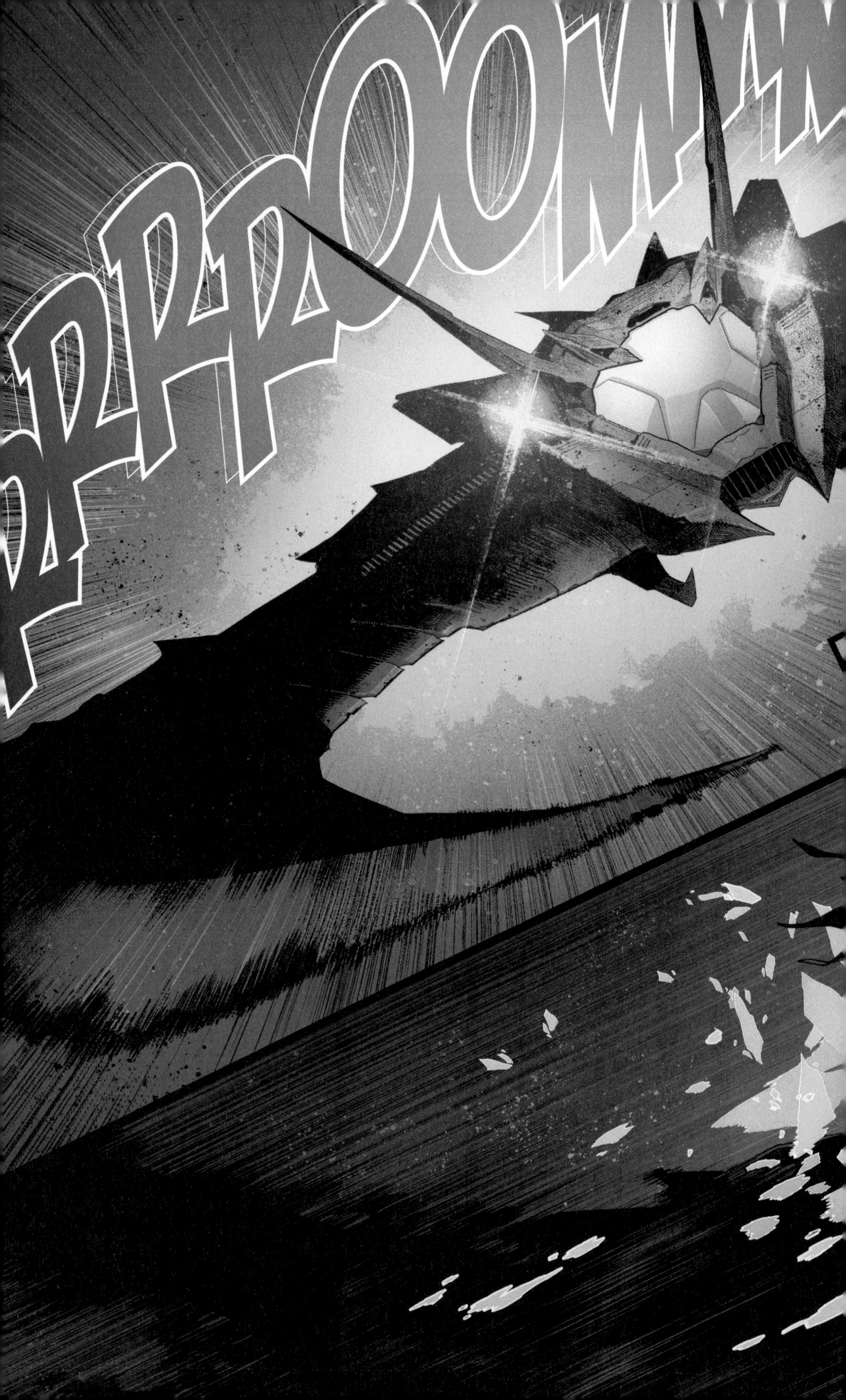
BRRROOMMM

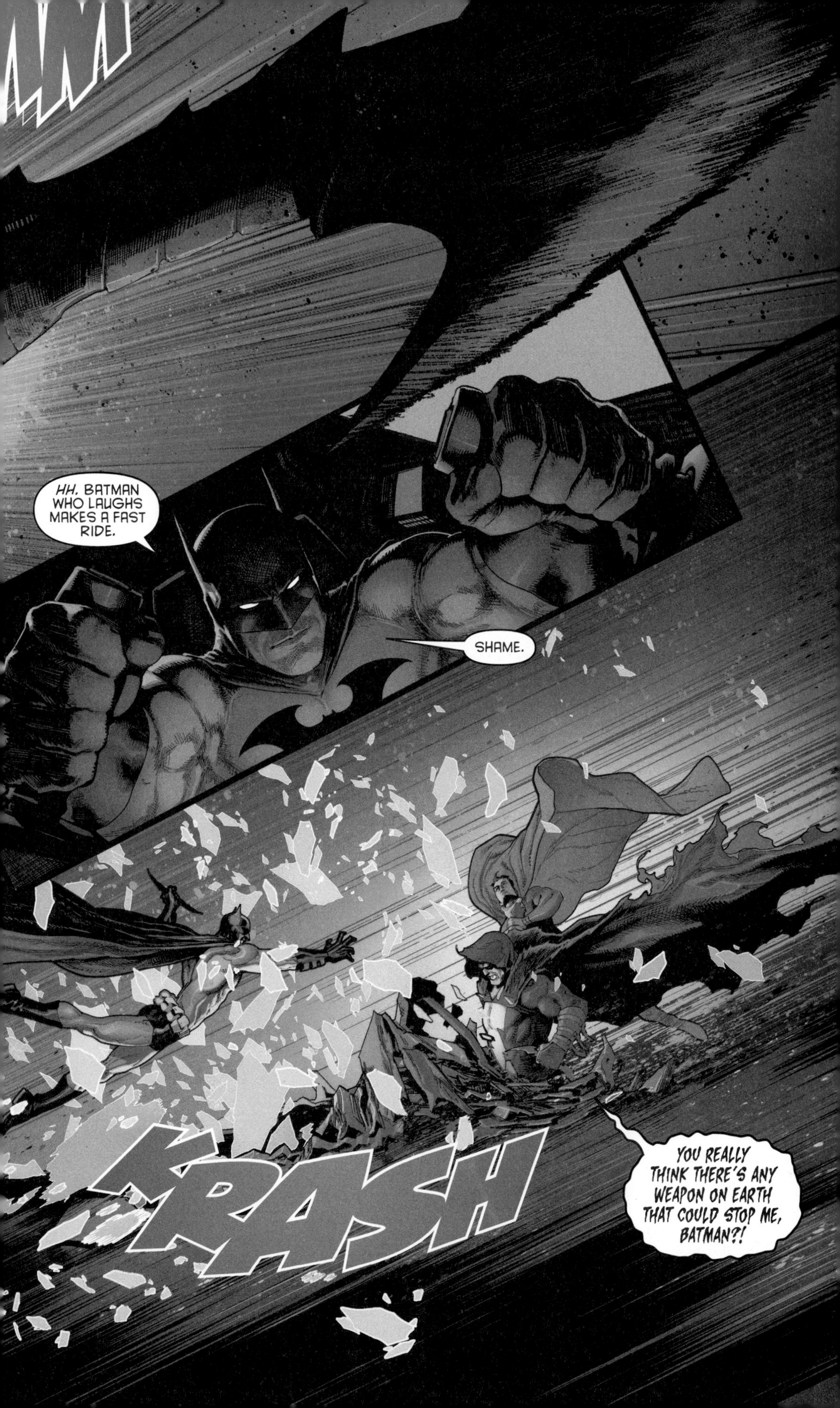
HH. BATMAN WHO LAUGHS MAKES A FAST RIDE.
SHAME.
KRASH
YOU REALLY THINK THERE'S ANY WEAPON ON EARTH THAT COULD STOP ME, BATMAN?!

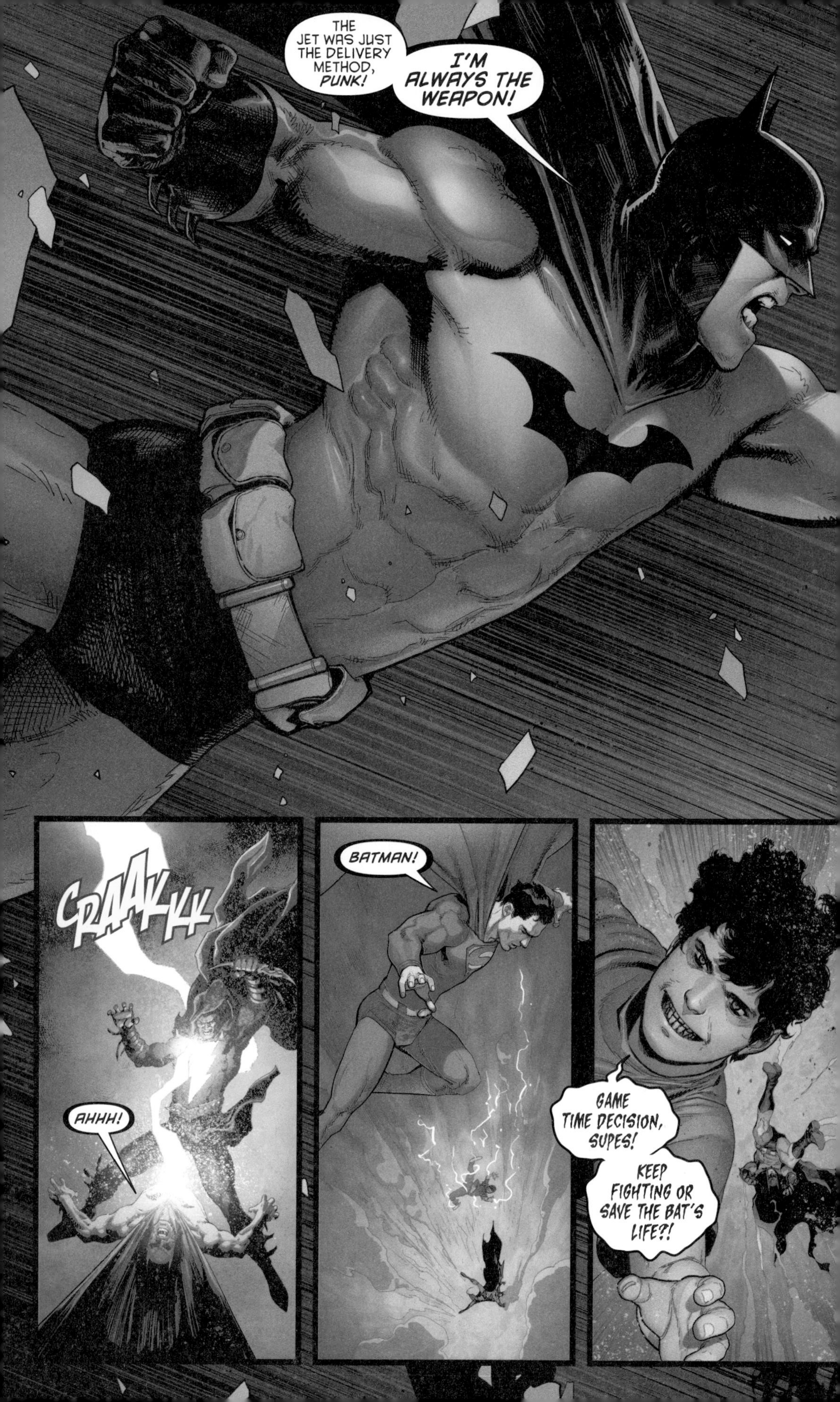
THE JET WAS JUST THE DELIVERY METHOD, PUNK!
I'M ALWAYS THE WEAPON!
CRAAKKK
AHHH!
BATMAN!
GAME TIME DECISION, SUPES!
KEEP FIGHTING OR SAVE THE BAT'S LIFE?!

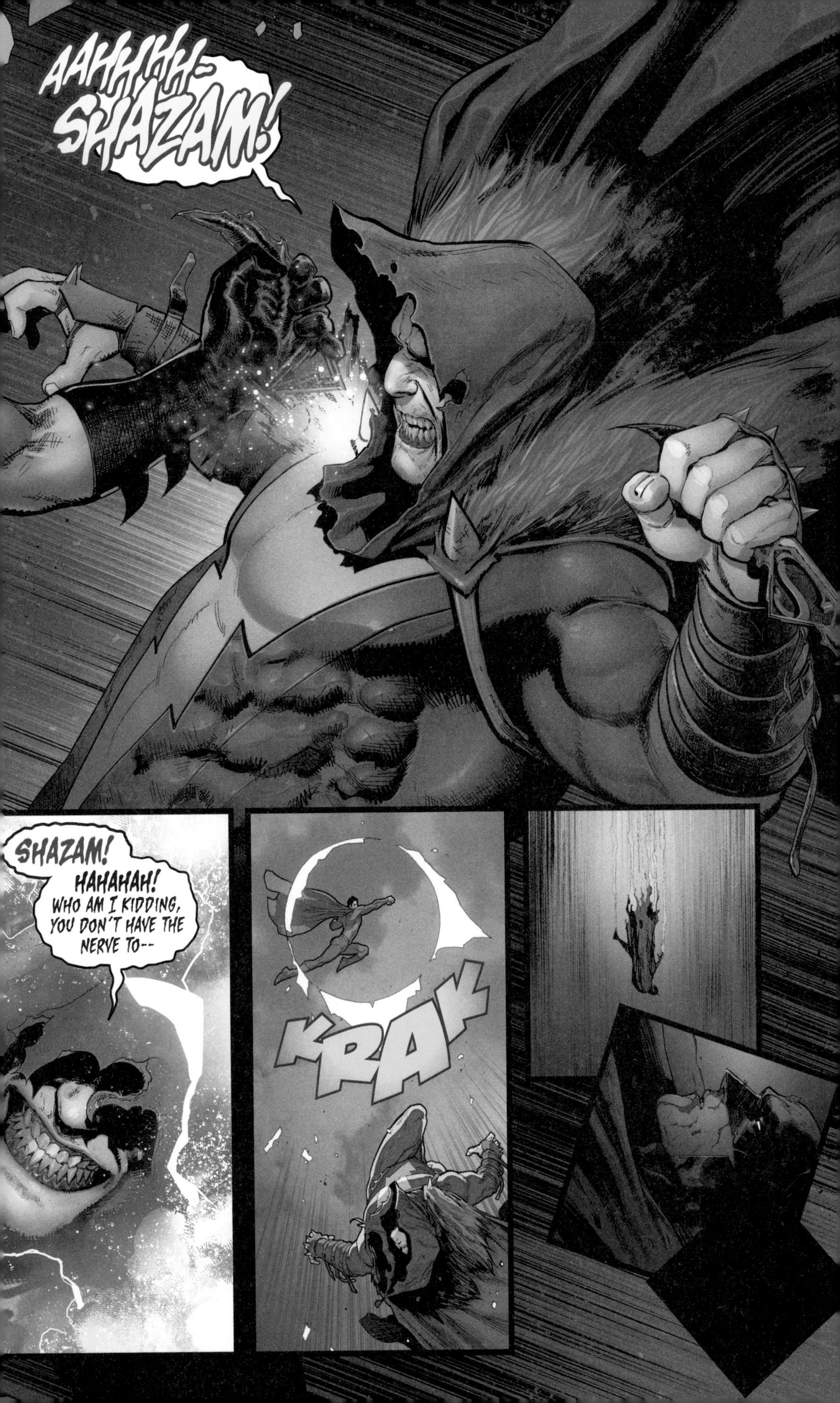
AAHHHHH-SHAZAM!
SHAZAM!
HAHAHAH! WHO AM I KIDDING, YOU DON'T HAVE THE NERVE TO--
KRAK

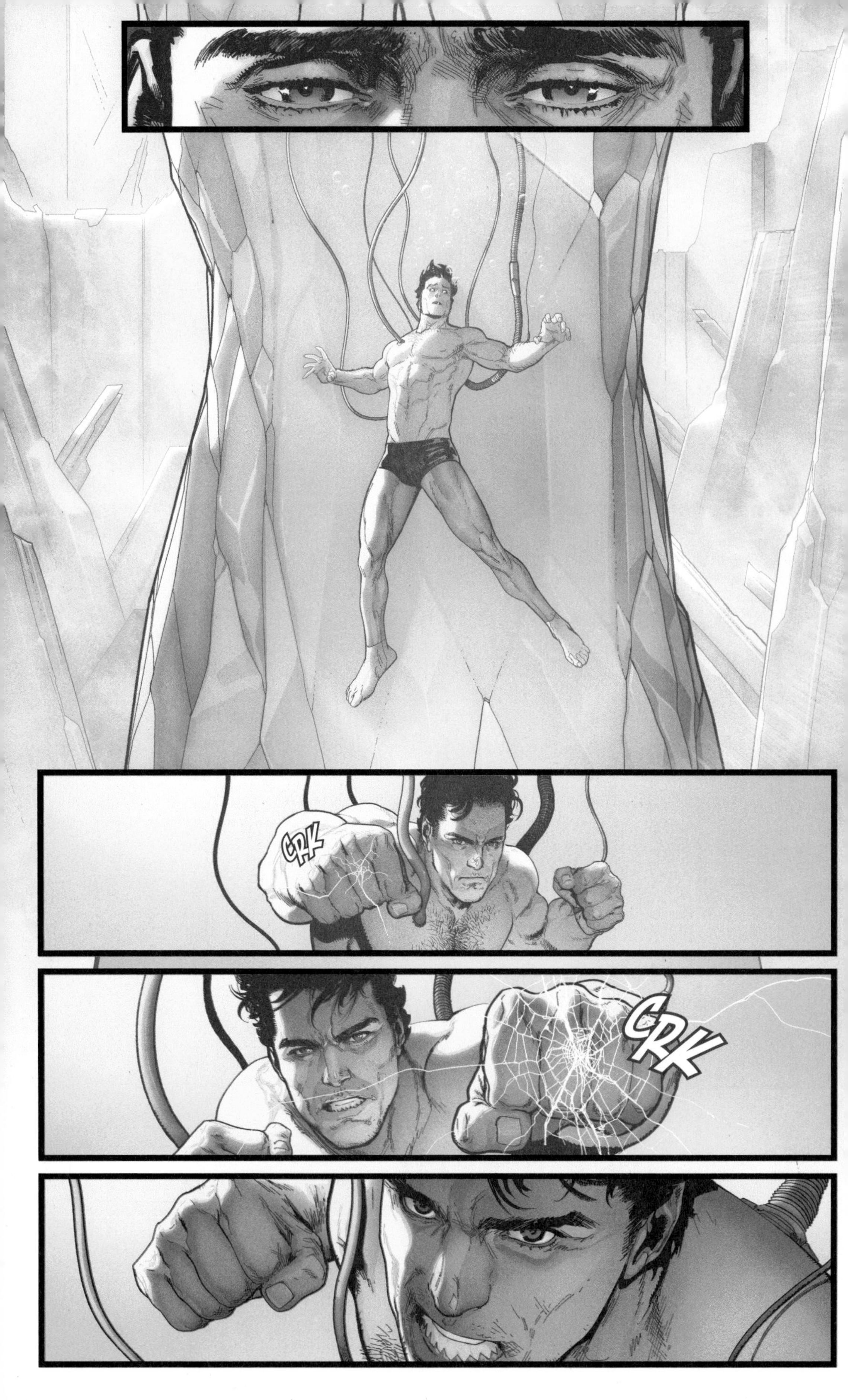

CRK
CRK

BATMAN, SIR! YOU WERE NOT READY TO BE FREED FROM THE STASIS FIELD. YOU MUST RETURN IN ORDER TO HEAL.

YOUR HUMAN INJURIES WERE SEVERE. YOUR HEART STOPPED BECAUSE OF THE MAGICAL LIGHTNING YOU ENDURED.

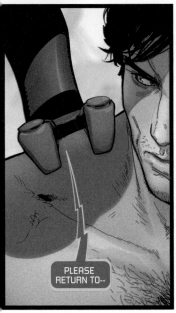

PLEASE RETURN TO--

WHERE IS HE?!

WHERE'S SHAZAM?!

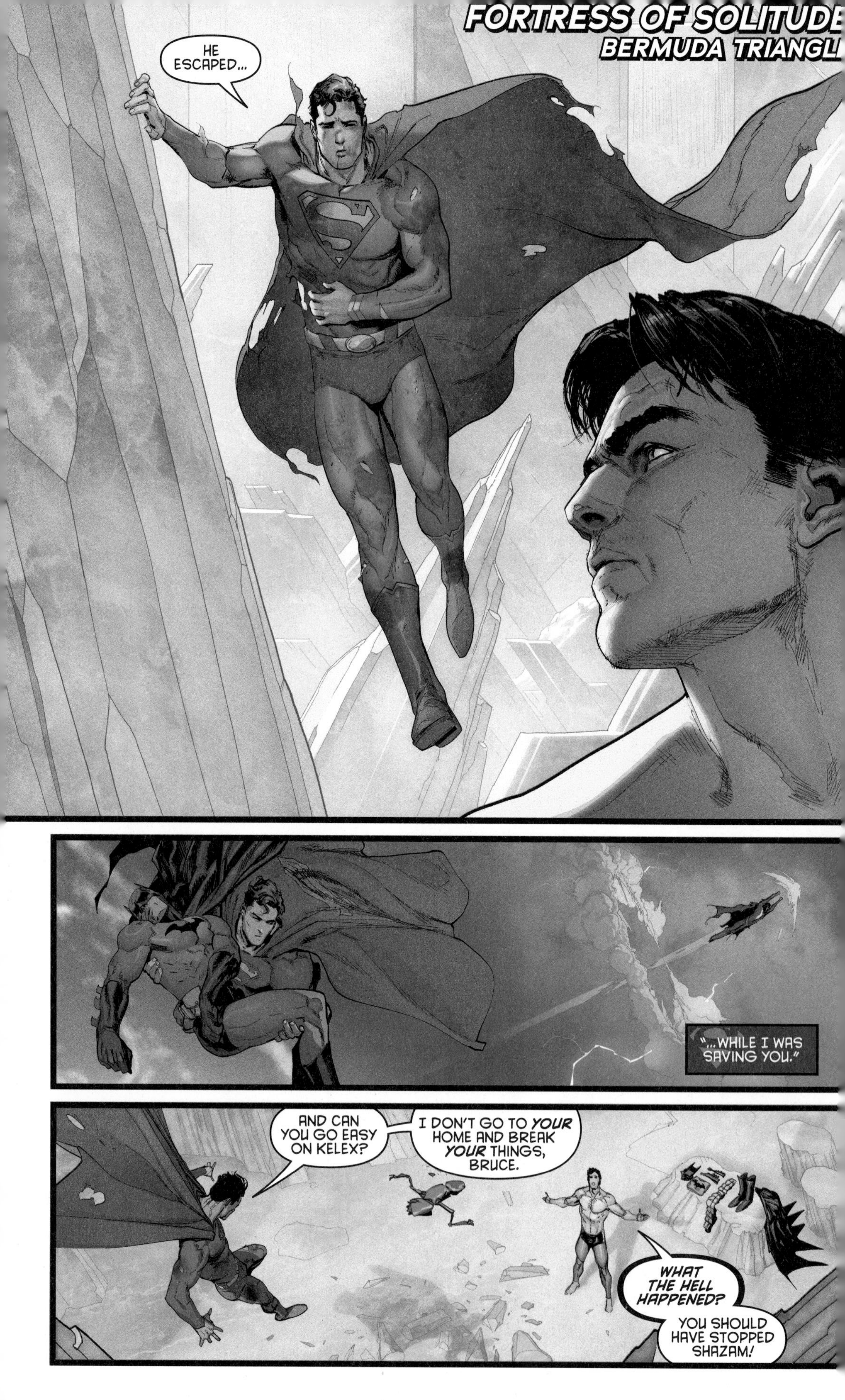
FORTRESS OF SOLITUDE
BERMUDA TRIANGL
HE ESCAPED...
"...WHILE I WAS SAVING YOU."
AND CAN YOU GO EASY ON KELEX?
I DON'T GO TO YOUR HOME AND BREAK YOUR THINGS, BRUCE.
WHAT THE HELL HAPPENED?
YOU SHOULD HAVE STOPPED SHAZAM!

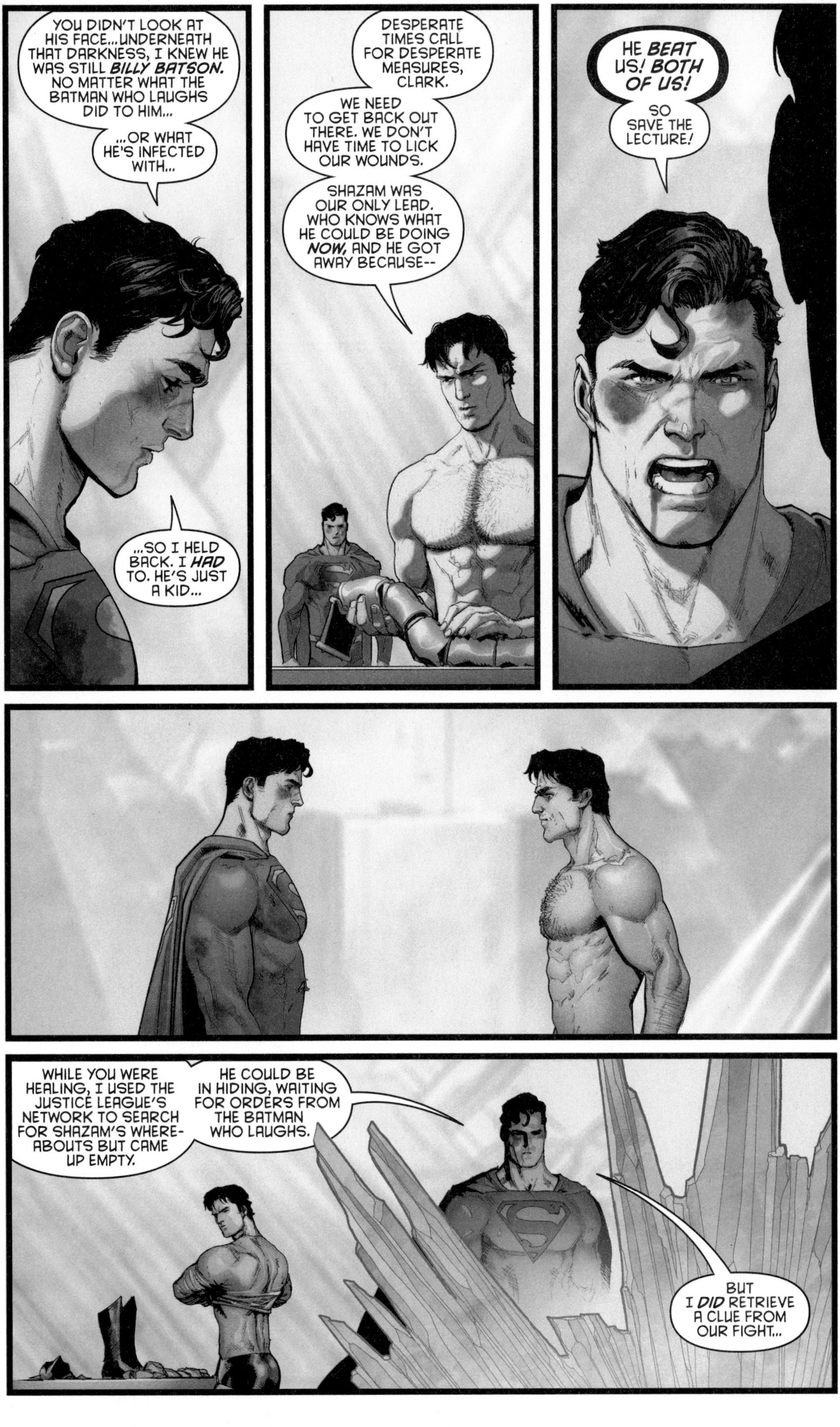
YOU DIDN'T LOOK AT HIS FACE...UNDERNEATH THAT DARKNESS, I KNEW HE WAS STILL BILLY BATSON. NO MATTER WHAT THE BATMAN WHO LAUGHS DID TO HIM...
...OR WHAT HE'S INFECTED WITH...
...SO I HELD BACK. I HAD TO. HE'S JUST A KID...
DESPERATE TIMES CALL FOR DESPERATE MEASURES, CLARK.
WE NEED TO GET BACK OUT THERE. WE DON'T HAVE TIME TO LICK OUR WOUNDS.
SHAZAM WAS OUR ONLY LEAD. WHO KNOWS WHAT HE COULD BE DOING NOW, AND HE GOT AWAY BECAUSE--
HE BEAT US! BOTH OF US!
SO SAVE THE LECTURE!
WHILE YOU WERE HEALING, I USED THE JUSTICE LEAGUE'S NETWORK TO SEARCH FOR SHAZAM'S WHERE-ABOUTS BUT CAME UP EMPTY.
HE COULD BE IN HIDING, WAITING FOR ORDERS FROM THE BATMAN WHO LAUGHS.
BUT I DID RETRIEVE A CLUE FROM OUR FIGHT...

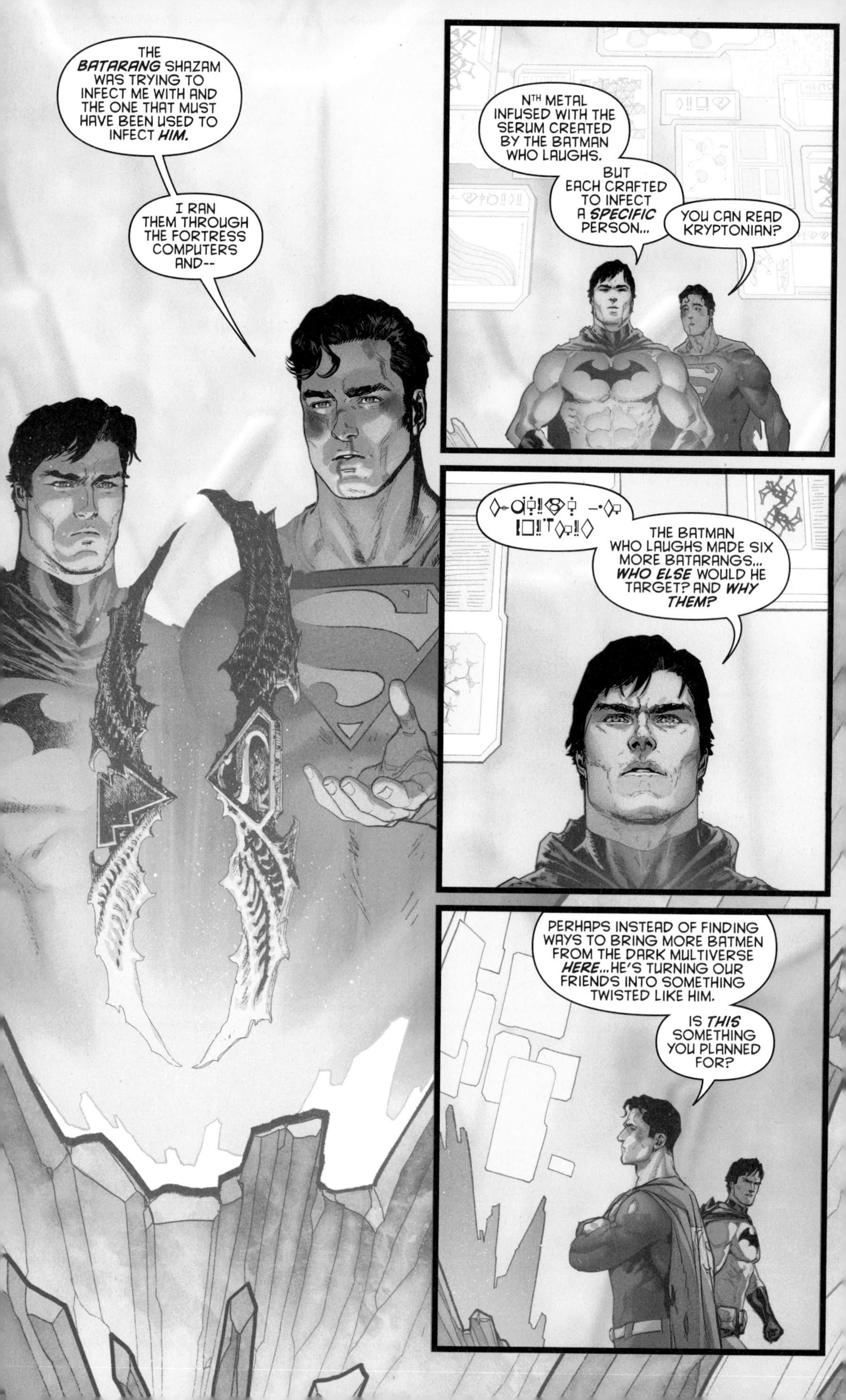
THE BATARANG SHAZAM WAS TRYING TO INFECT ME WITH AND THE ONE THAT MUST HAVE BEEN USED TO INFECT HIM.
I RAN THEM THROUGH THE FORTRESS COMPUTERS AND--
NTH METAL INFUSED WITH THE SERUM CREATED BY THE BATMAN WHO LAUGHS.
BUT EACH CRAFTED TO INFECT A SPECIFIC PERSON...
YOU CAN READ KRYPTONIAN?
THE BATMAN WHO LAUGHS MADE SIX MORE BATARANGS... WHO ELSE WOULD HE TARGET? AND WHY THEM?
PERHAPS INSTEAD OF FINDING WAYS TO BRING MORE BATMEN FROM THE DARK MULTIVERSE HERE...HE'S TURNING OUR FRIENDS INTO SOMETHING TWISTED LIKE HIM.
IS THIS SOMETHING YOU PLANNED FOR?

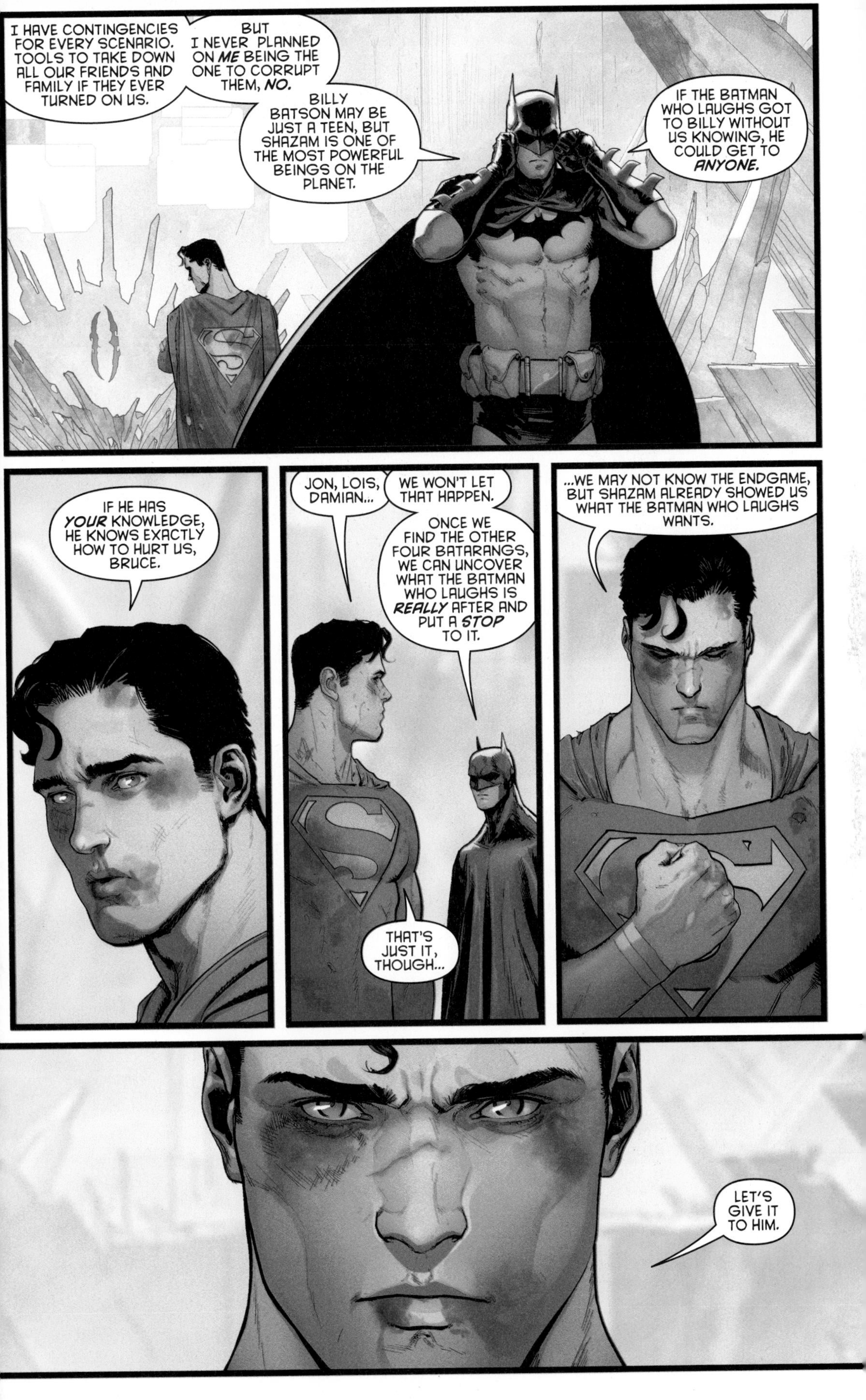
I HAVE CONTINGENCIES FOR EVERY SCENARIO. TOOLS TO TAKE DOWN ALL OUR FRIENDS AND FAMILY IF THEY EVER TURNED ON US.
BUT I NEVER PLANNED ON ME BEING THE ONE TO CORRUPT THEM, NO.
BILLY BATSON MAY BE JUST A TEEN, BUT SHAZAM IS ONE OF THE MOST POWERFUL BEINGS ON THE PLANET.
IF THE BATMAN WHO LAUGHS GOT TO BILLY WITHOUT US KNOWING, HE COULD GET TO ANYONE.
IF HE HAS YOUR KNOWLEDGE, HE KNOWS EXACTLY HOW TO HURT US, BRUCE.
JON, LOIS, DAMIAN...
WE WON'T LET THAT HAPPEN.
ONCE WE FIND THE OTHER FOUR BATARANGS, WE CAN UNCOVER WHAT THE BATMAN WHO LAUGHS IS REALLY AFTER AND PUT A STOP TO IT.
THAT'S JUST IT, THOUGH...
...WE MAY NOT KNOW THE ENDGAME, BUT SHAZAM ALREADY SHOWED US WHAT THE BATMAN WHO LAUGHS WANTS.
LET'S GIVE IT TO HIM.

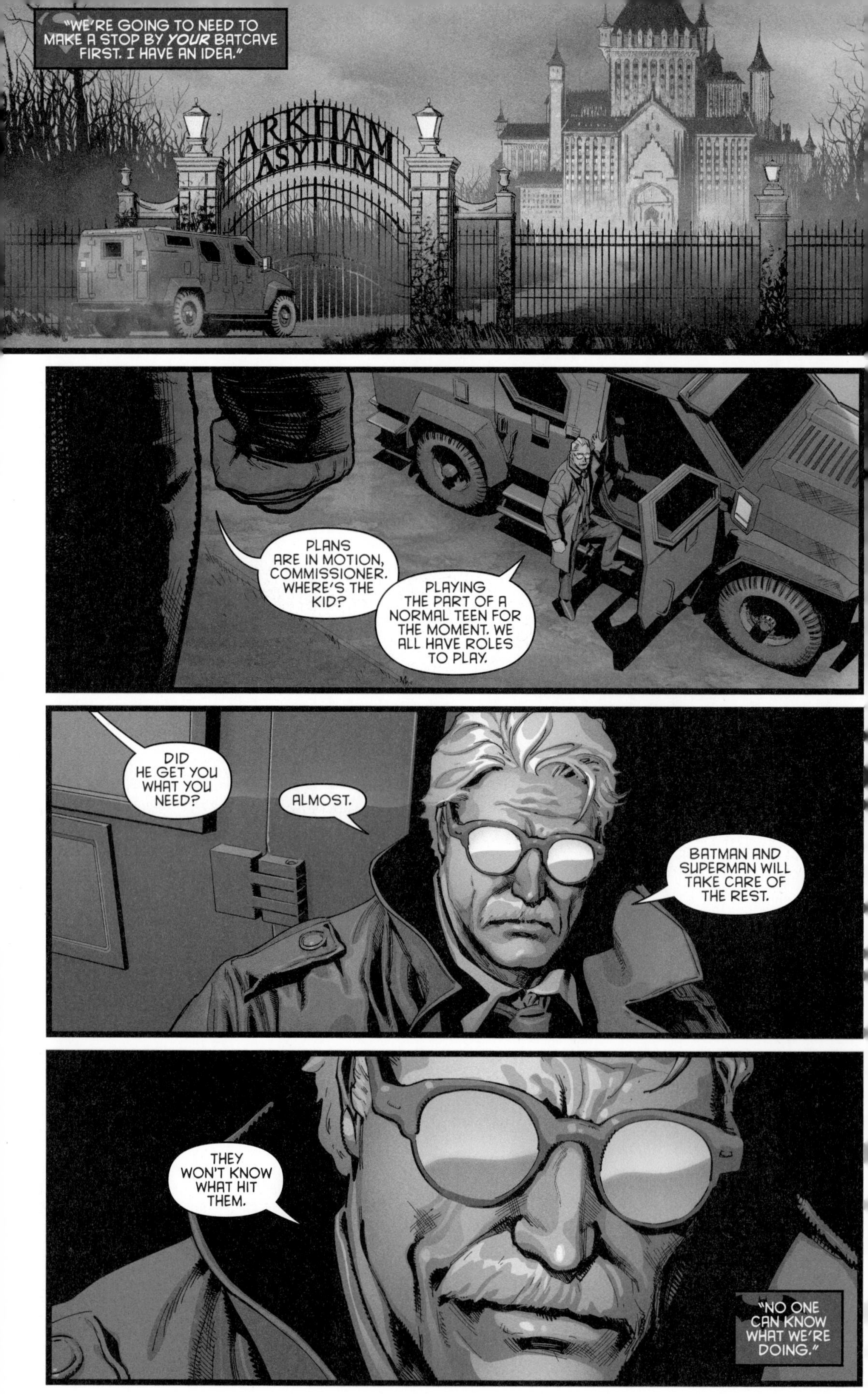
"WE'RE GOING TO NEED TO MAKE A STOP BY *YOUR* BATCAVE FIRST. I HAVE AN IDEA."
ARKHAM ASYLUM
PLANS ARE IN MOTION, COMMISSIONER. WHERE'S THE KID?
PLAYING THE PART OF A NORMAL TEEN FOR THE MOMENT. WE ALL HAVE ROLES TO PLAY.
DID HE GET YOU WHAT YOU NEED?
ALMOST.
BATMAN AND SUPERMAN WILL TAKE CARE OF THE REST.
THEY WON'T KNOW WHAT HIT THEM.
"NO ONE CAN KNOW WHAT WE'RE DOING."

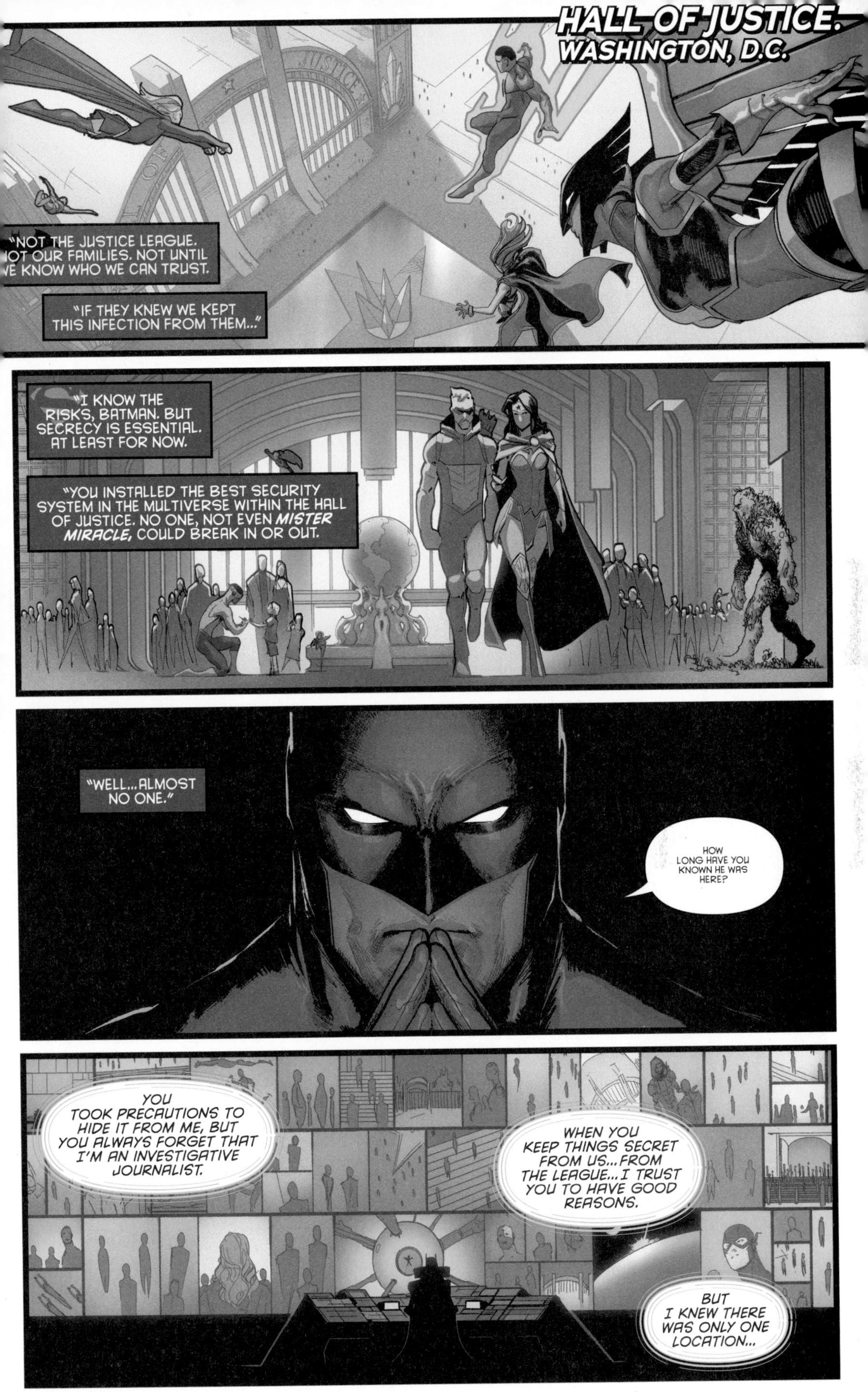
HALL OF JUSTICE. WASHINGTON, D.C.
"NOT THE JUSTICE LEAGUE. NOT OUR FAMILIES. NOT UNTIL WE KNOW WHO WE CAN TRUST.
"IF THEY KNEW WE KEPT THIS INFECTION FROM THEM..."
"I KNOW THE RISKS, BATMAN. BUT SECRECY IS ESSENTIAL. AT LEAST FOR NOW.
"YOU INSTALLED THE BEST SECURITY SYSTEM IN THE MULTIVERSE WITHIN THE HALL OF JUSTICE. NO ONE, NOT EVEN *MISTER MIRACLE,* COULD BREAK IN OR OUT.
"WELL...ALMOST NO ONE."
HOW LONG HAVE YOU KNOWN HE WAS HERE?
YOU TOOK PRECAUTIONS TO HIDE IT FROM ME, BUT YOU ALWAYS FORGET THAT I'M AN INVESTIGATIVE JOURNALIST.
WHEN YOU KEEP THINGS SECRET FROM US...FROM THE LEAGUE...I TRUST YOU TO HAVE GOOD REASONS.
BUT I KNEW THERE WAS ONLY ONE LOCATION...

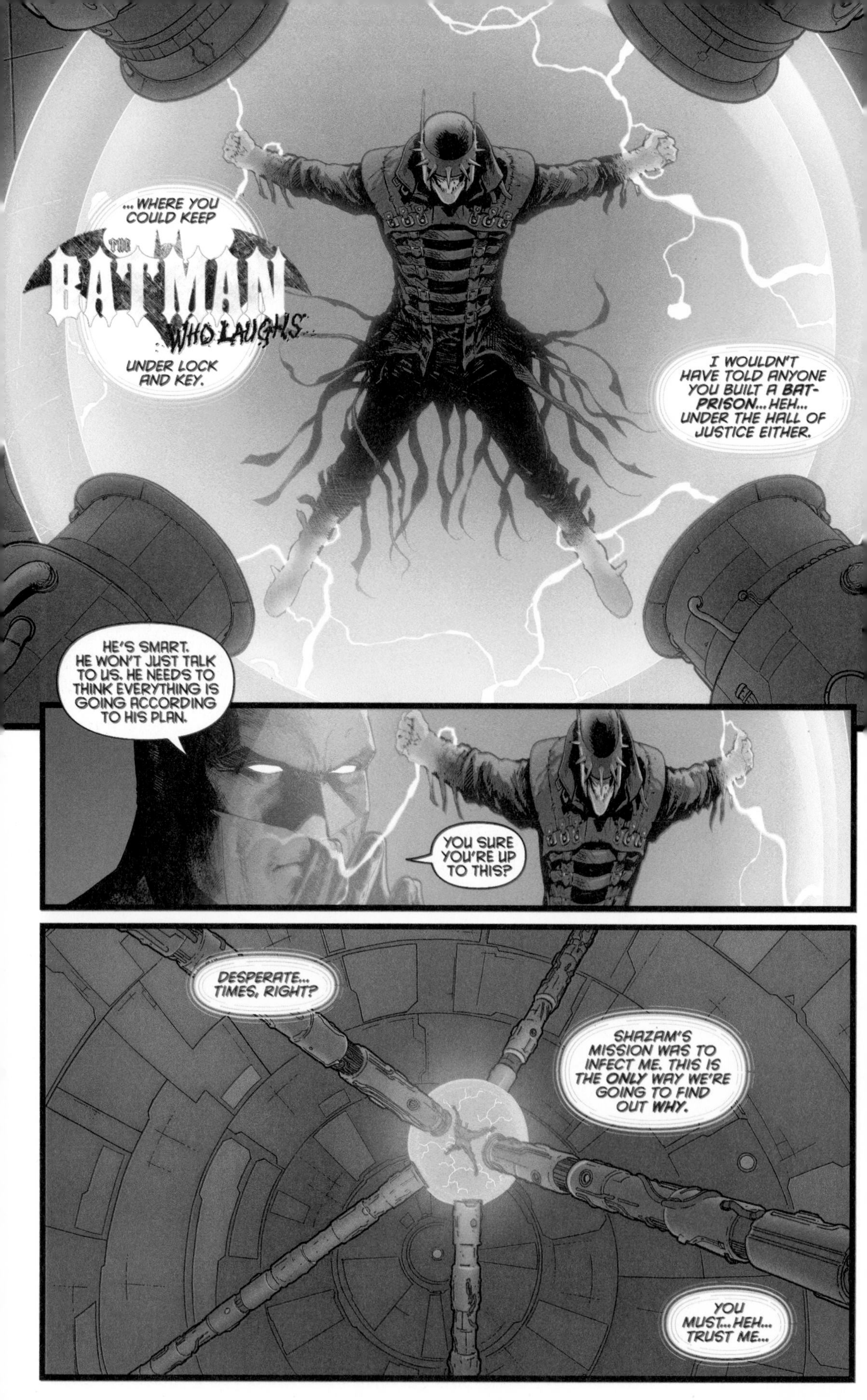
...WHERE YOU COULD KEEP
THE BATMAN WHO LAUGHS
UNDER LOCK AND KEY.
I WOULDN'T HAVE TOLD ANYONE YOU BUILT A BAT-PRISON...HEH... UNDER THE HALL OF JUSTICE EITHER.
HE'S SMART. HE WON'T JUST TALK TO US. HE NEEDS TO THINK EVERYTHING IS GOING ACCORDING TO HIS PLAN.
YOU SURE YOU'RE UP TO THIS?
DESPERATE... TIMES, RIGHT?
SHAZAM'S MISSION WAS TO INFECT ME. THIS IS THE ONLY WAY WE'RE GOING TO FIND OUT WHY.
YOU MUST...HEH... TRUST ME...

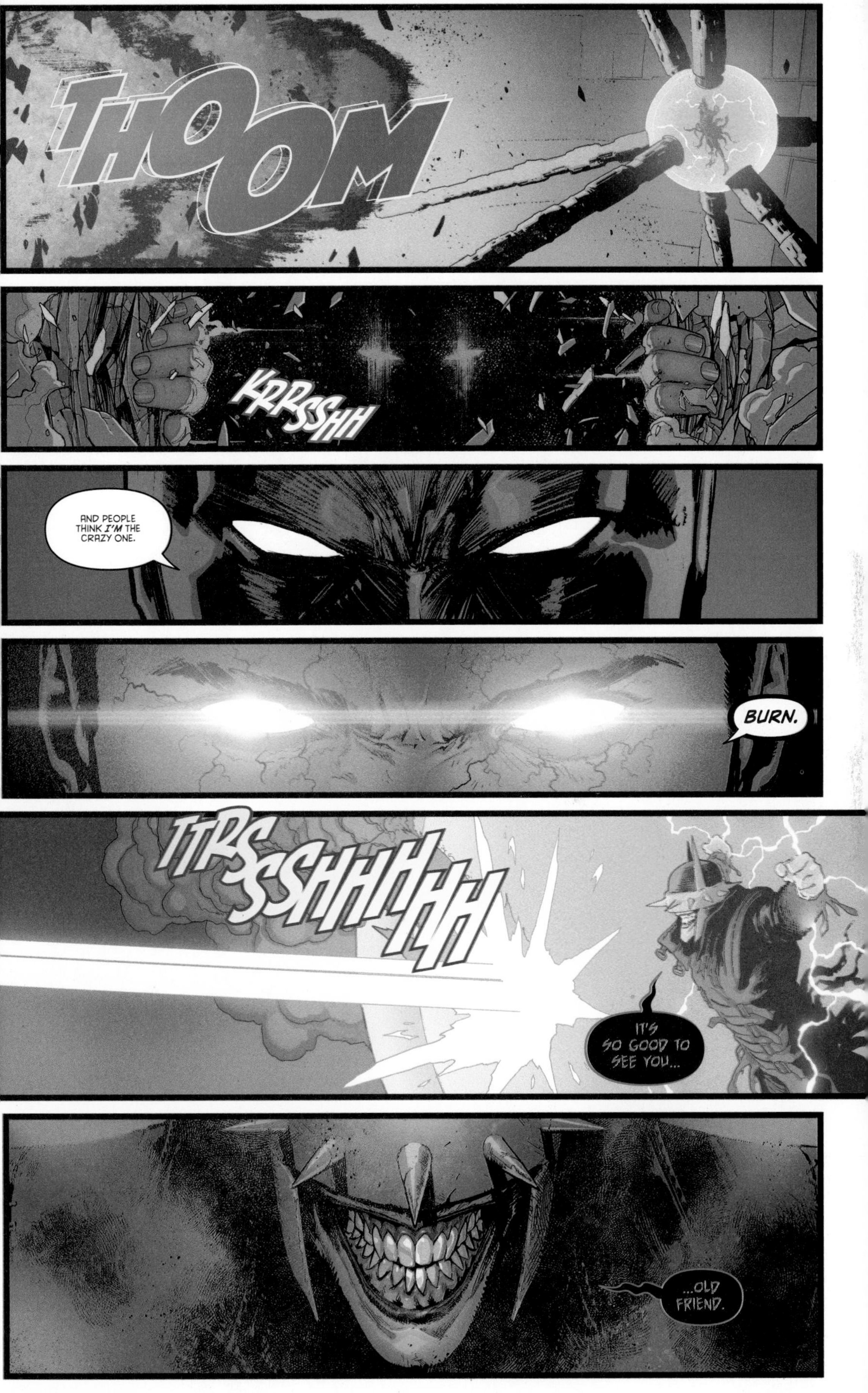
THOOM
KRRSSHH
AND PEOPLE THINK I'M THE CRAZY ONE.
BURN.
TTRSSHHHHH
IT'S SO GOOD TO SEE YOU...
...OLD FRIEND.

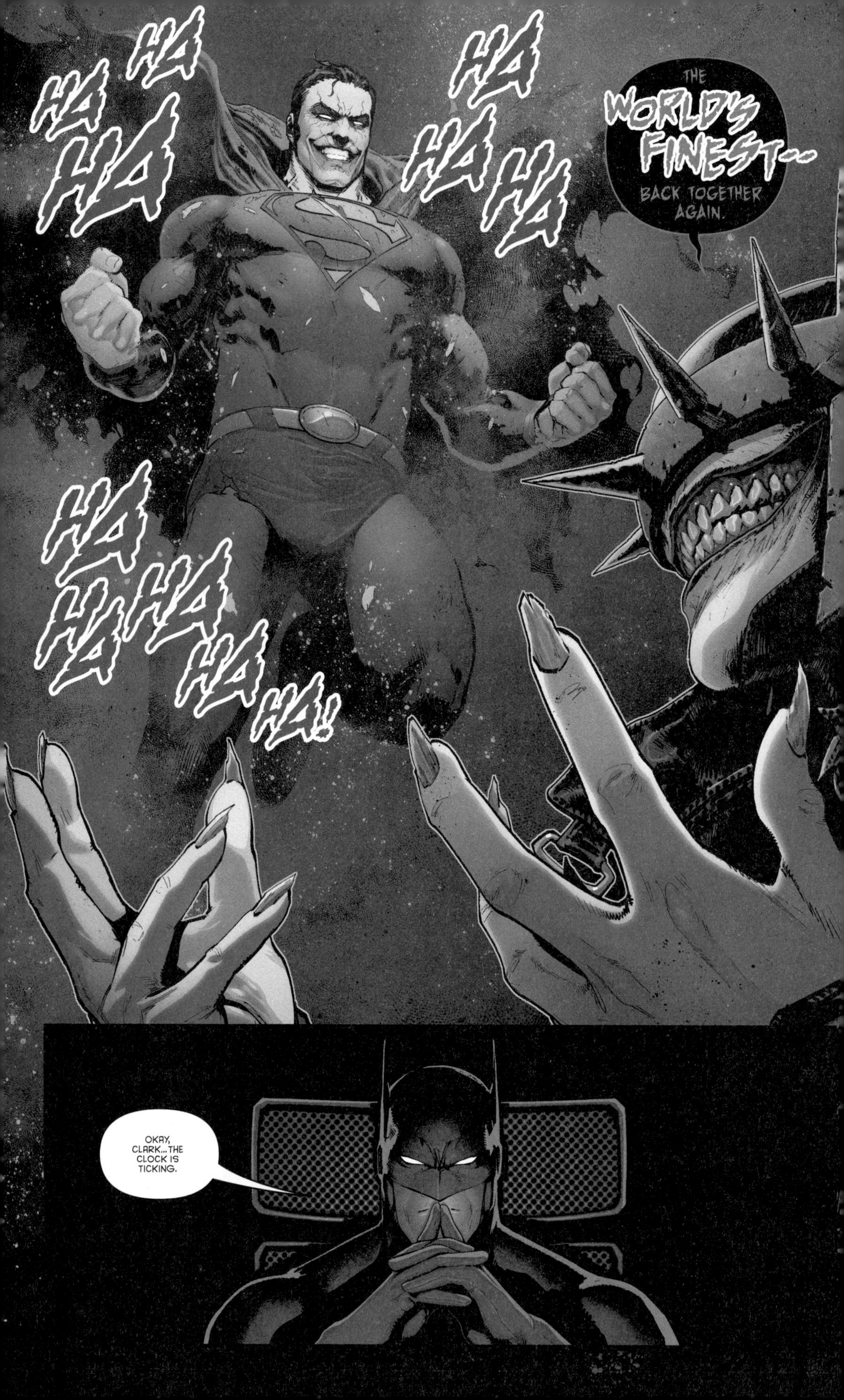
HA HA HA
HA HA HA HA
THE WORLD'S FINEST--
BACK TOGETHER AGAIN.
HA HA HA HA HA HA!
OKAY, CLARK... THE CLOCK IS TICKING.

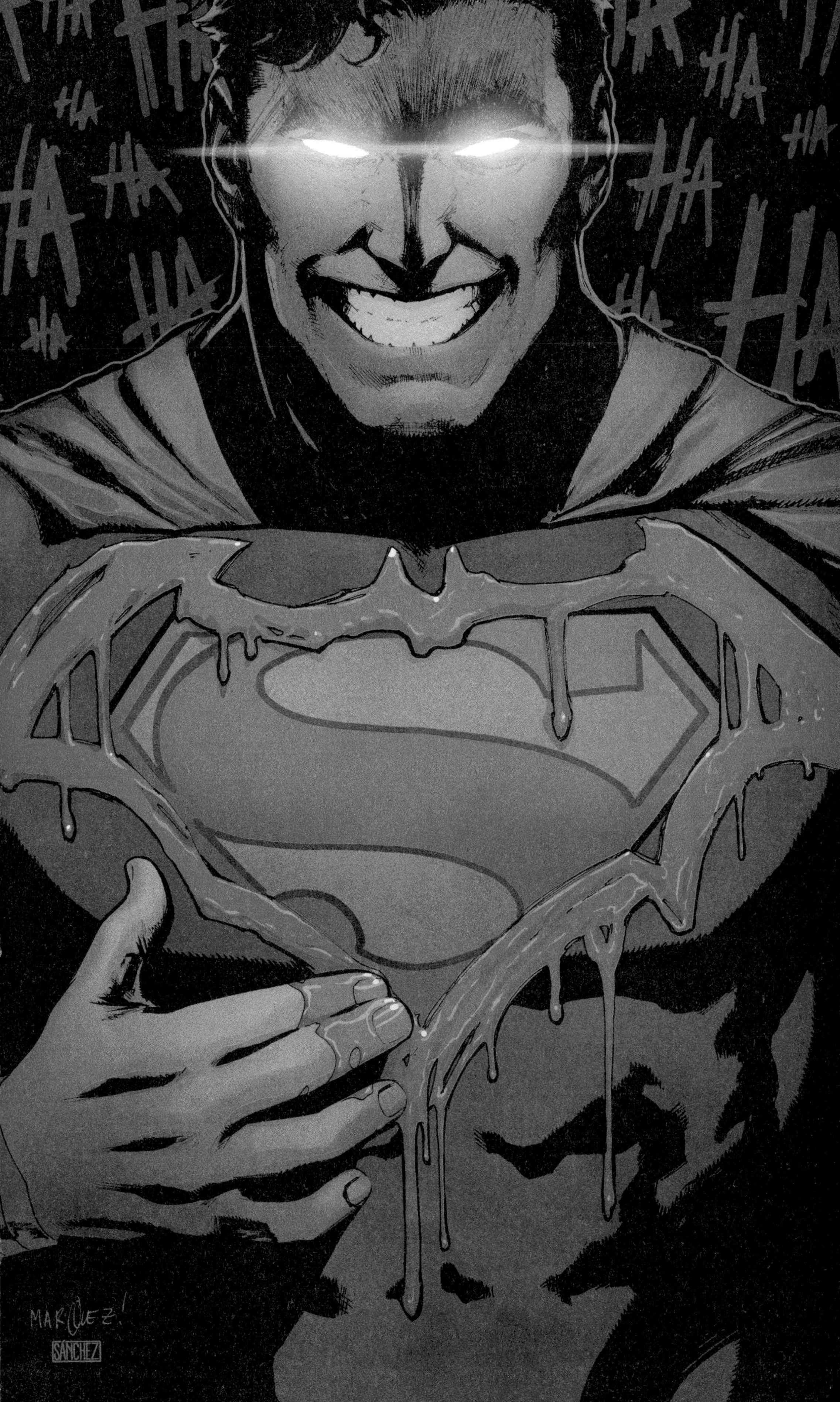
HA
HA
HA
HA
HA
HA
MARQUEZ!
SANCHEZ

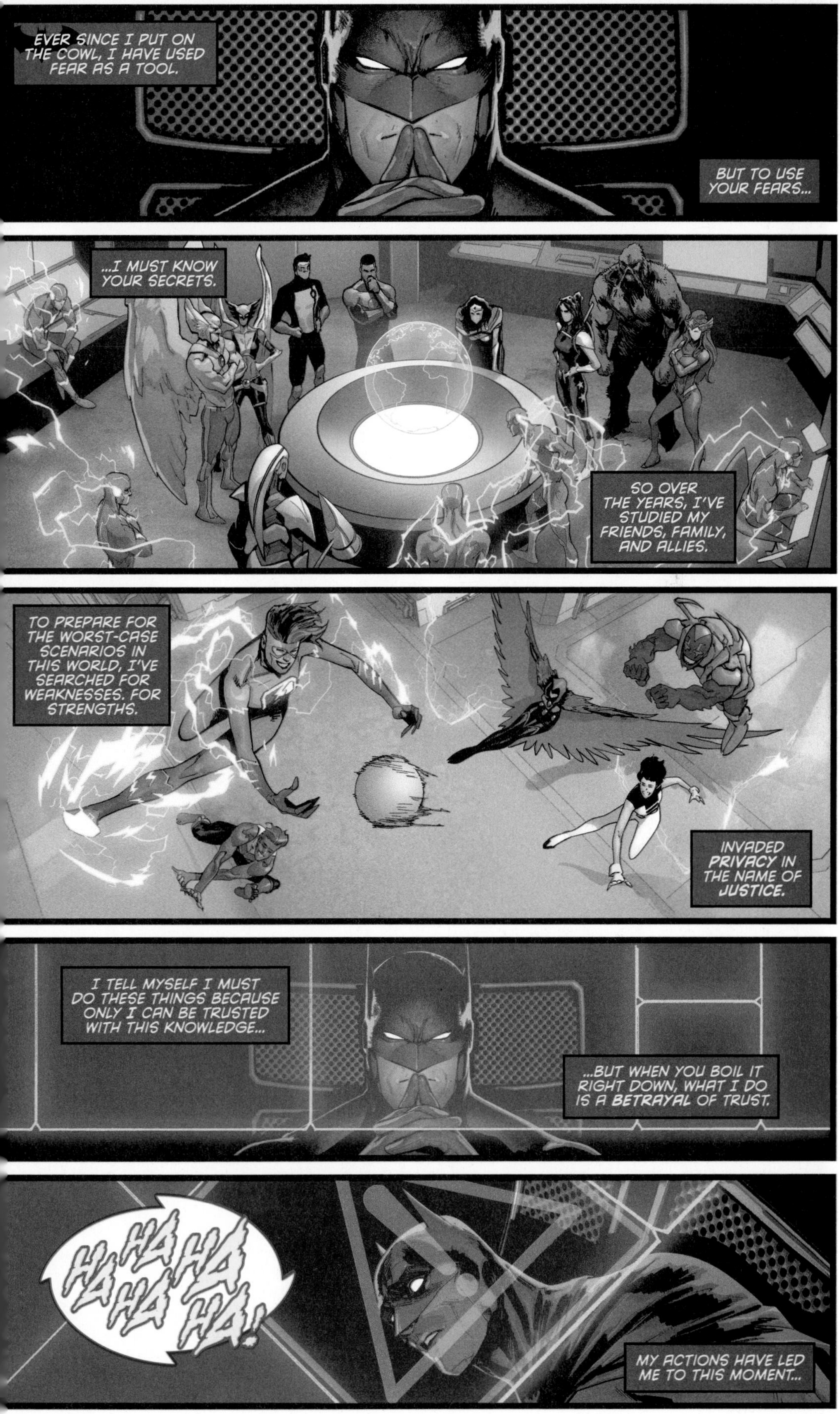
EVER SINCE I PUT ON THE COWL, I HAVE USED FEAR AS A TOOL.
BUT TO USE YOUR FEARS...
...I MUST KNOW YOUR SECRETS.
SO OVER THE YEARS, I'VE STUDIED MY FRIENDS, FAMILY, AND ALLIES.
TO PREPARE FOR THE WORST-CASE SCENARIOS IN THIS WORLD, I'VE SEARCHED FOR WEAKNESSES. FOR STRENGTHS.
INVADED PRIVACY IN THE NAME OF JUSTICE.
I TELL MYSELF I MUST DO THESE THINGS BECAUSE ONLY I CAN BE TRUSTED WITH THIS KNOWLEDGE...
...BUT WHEN YOU BOIL IT RIGHT DOWN, WHAT I DO IS A BETRAYAL OF TRUST.
HA HA HA HA HA HA!
MY ACTIONS HAVE LED ME TO THIS MOMENT...

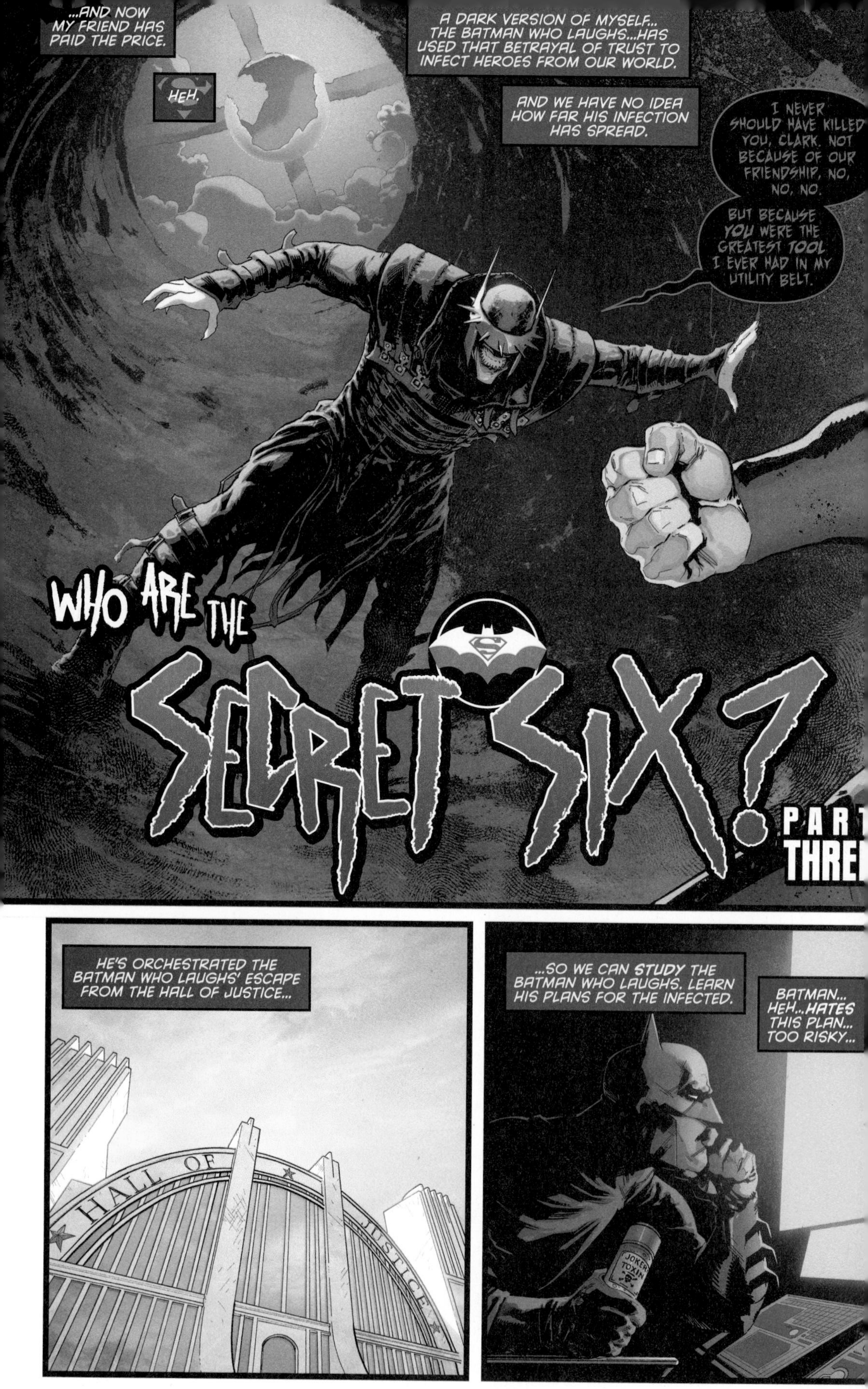
...AND NOW MY FRIEND HAS PAID THE PRICE.
HEH.
A DARK VERSION OF MYSELF... THE BATMAN WHO LAUGHS...HAS USED THAT BETRAYAL OF TRUST TO INFECT HEROES FROM OUR WORLD.
AND WE HAVE NO IDEA HOW FAR HIS INFECTION HAS SPREAD.
I NEVER SHOULD HAVE KILLED YOU, CLARK. NOT BECAUSE OF OUR FRIENDSHIP, NO, NO, NO.
BUT BECAUSE YOU WERE THE GREATEST TOOL I EVER HAD IN MY UTILITY BELT.
WHO ARE THE SECRET SIX?
PART
THRE
HE'S ORCHESTRATED THE BATMAN WHO LAUGHS' ESCAPE FROM THE HALL OF JUSTICE...
HALL OF JUSTICE
...SO WE CAN STUDY THE BATMAN WHO LAUGHS. LEARN HIS PLANS FOR THE INFECTED.
BATMAN... HEH...HATES THIS PLAN... TOO RISKY...
JOKER TOXIN

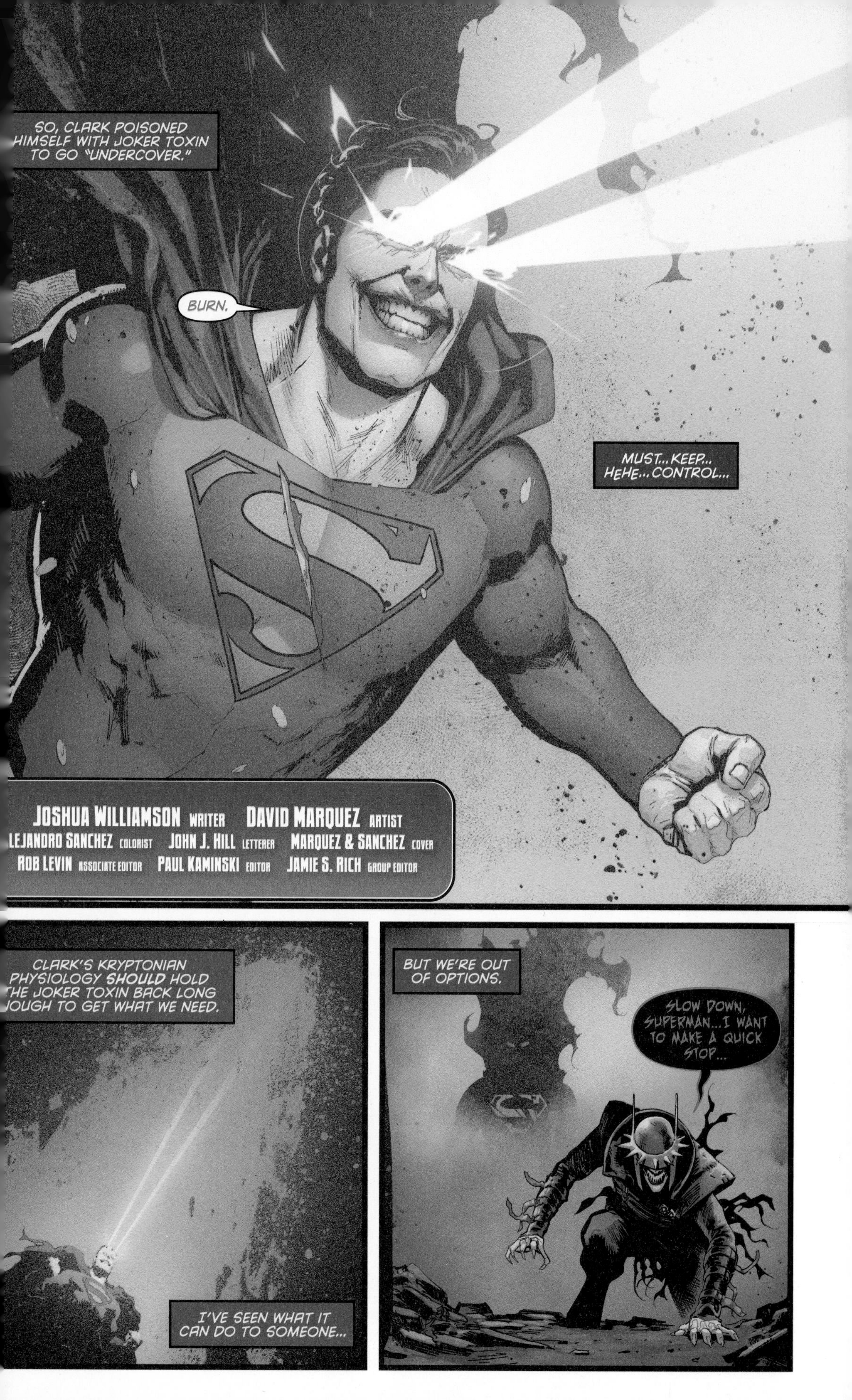
SO, CLARK POISONED HIMSELF WITH JOKER TOXIN TO GO "UNDERCOVER."
BURN.
MUST... KEEP... HEHE... CONTROL...
JOSHUA WILLIAMSON WRITER DAVID MARQUEZ ARTIST
LEJANDRO SANCHEZ COLORIST JOHN J. HILL LETTERER MARQUEZ & SANCHEZ COVER
ROB LEVIN ASSOCIATE EDITOR PAUL KAMINSKI EDITOR JAMIE S. RICH GROUP EDITOR
CLARK'S KRYPTONIAN PHYSIOLOGY SHOULD HOLD THE JOKER TOXIN BACK LONG JOUGH TO GET WHAT WE NEED.
I'VE SEEN WHAT IT CAN DO TO SOMEONE...
BUT WE'RE OUT OF OPTIONS.
SLOW DOWN, SUPERMAN... I WANT TO MAKE A QUICK STOP...

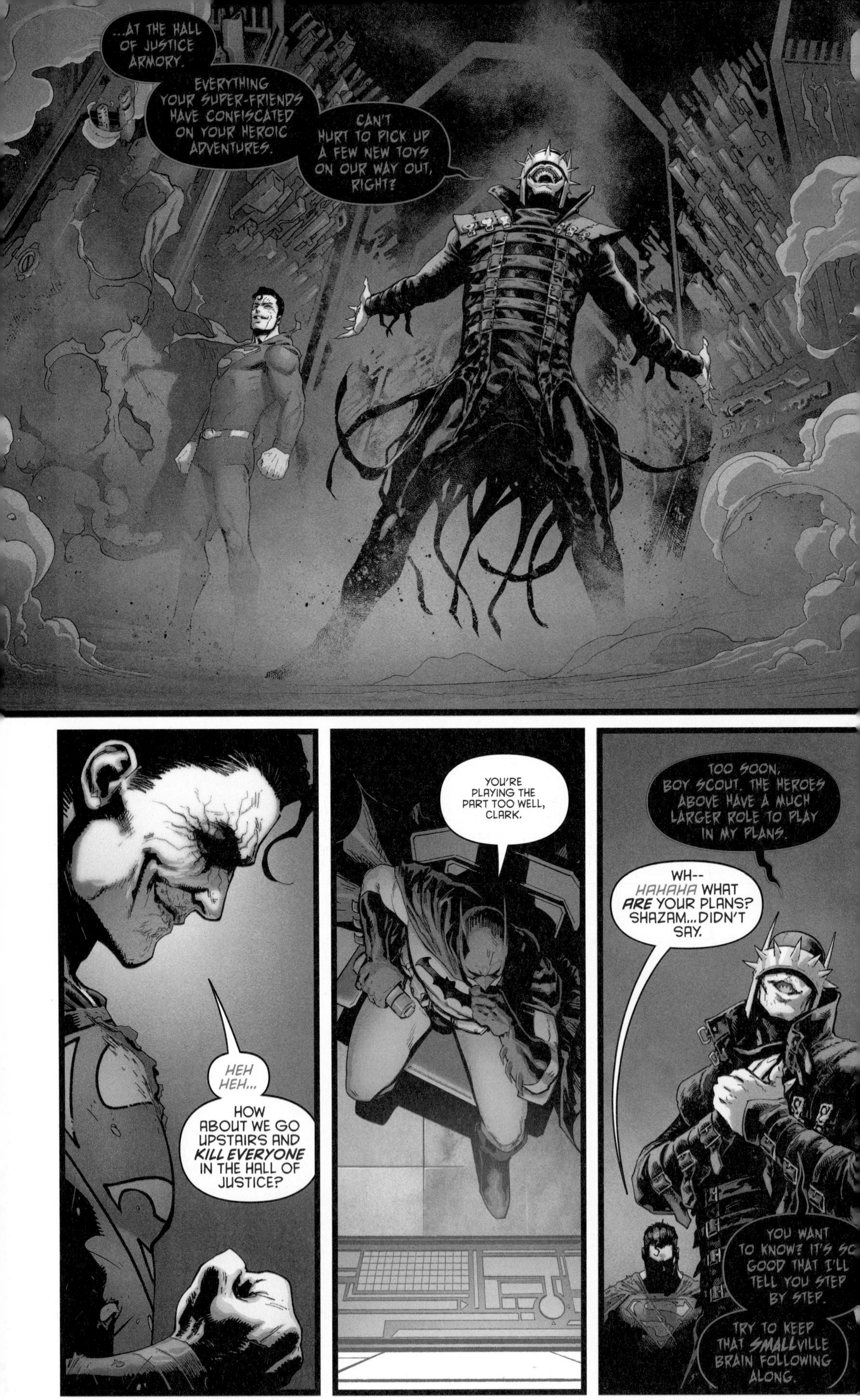

...AT THE HALL OF JUSTICE ARMORY.
EVERYTHING YOUR SUPER-FRIENDS HAVE CONFISCATED ON YOUR HEROIC ADVENTURES.
CAN'T HURT TO PICK UP A FEW NEW TOYS ON OUR WAY OUT, RIGHT?
HEH HEH...
HOW ABOUT WE GO UPSTAIRS AND KILL EVERYONE IN THE HALL OF JUSTICE?
YOU'RE PLAYING THE PART TOO WELL, CLARK.
TOO SOON, BOY SCOUT. THE HEROES ABOVE HAVE A MUCH LARGER ROLE TO PLAY IN MY PLANS.
WH-- HAHAHA WHAT ARE YOUR PLANS? SHAZAM...DIDN'T SAY.
YOU WANT TO KNOW? IT'S SO GOOD THAT I'LL TELL YOU STEP BY STEP.
TRY TO KEEP THAT SMALLVILLE BRAIN FOLLOWING ALONG.

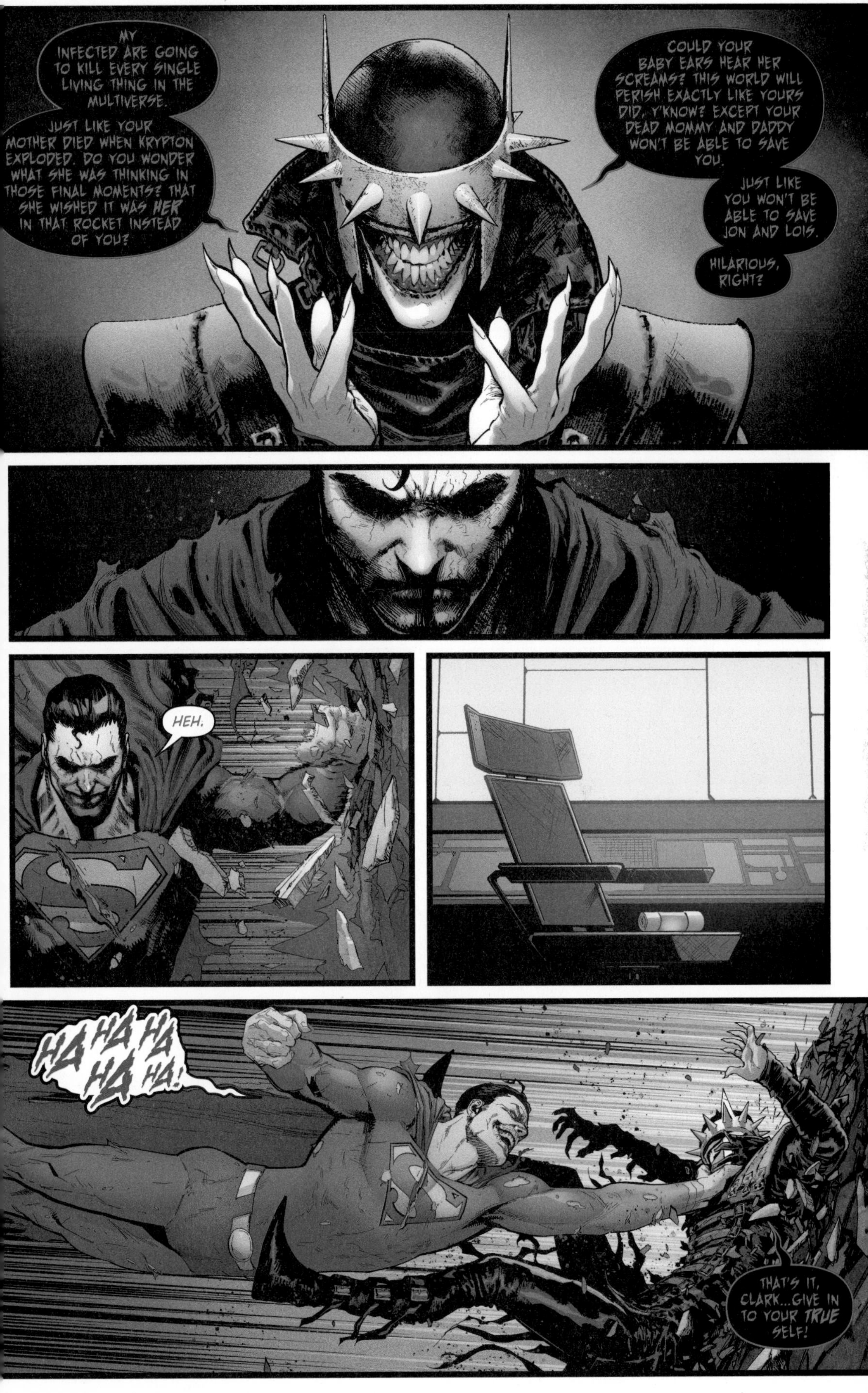
MY INFECTED ARE GOING TO KILL EVERY SINGLE LIVING THING IN THE MULTIVERSE.
JUST LIKE YOUR MOTHER DIED WHEN KRYPTON EXPLODED. DO YOU WONDER WHAT SHE WAS THINKING IN THOSE FINAL MOMENTS? THAT SHE WISHED IT WAS HER IN THAT ROCKET INSTEAD OF YOU?
COULD YOUR BABY EARS HEAR HER SCREAMS? THIS WORLD WILL PERISH EXACTLY LIKE YOURS DID, Y'KNOW? EXCEPT YOUR DEAD MOMMY AND DADDY WON'T BE ABLE TO SAVE YOU.
JUST LIKE YOU WON'T BE ABLE TO SAVE JON AND LOIS.
HILARIOUS, RIGHT?
HEH.
HA HA HA HA HA!
THAT'S IT, CLARK...GIVE IN TO YOUR TRUE SELF!

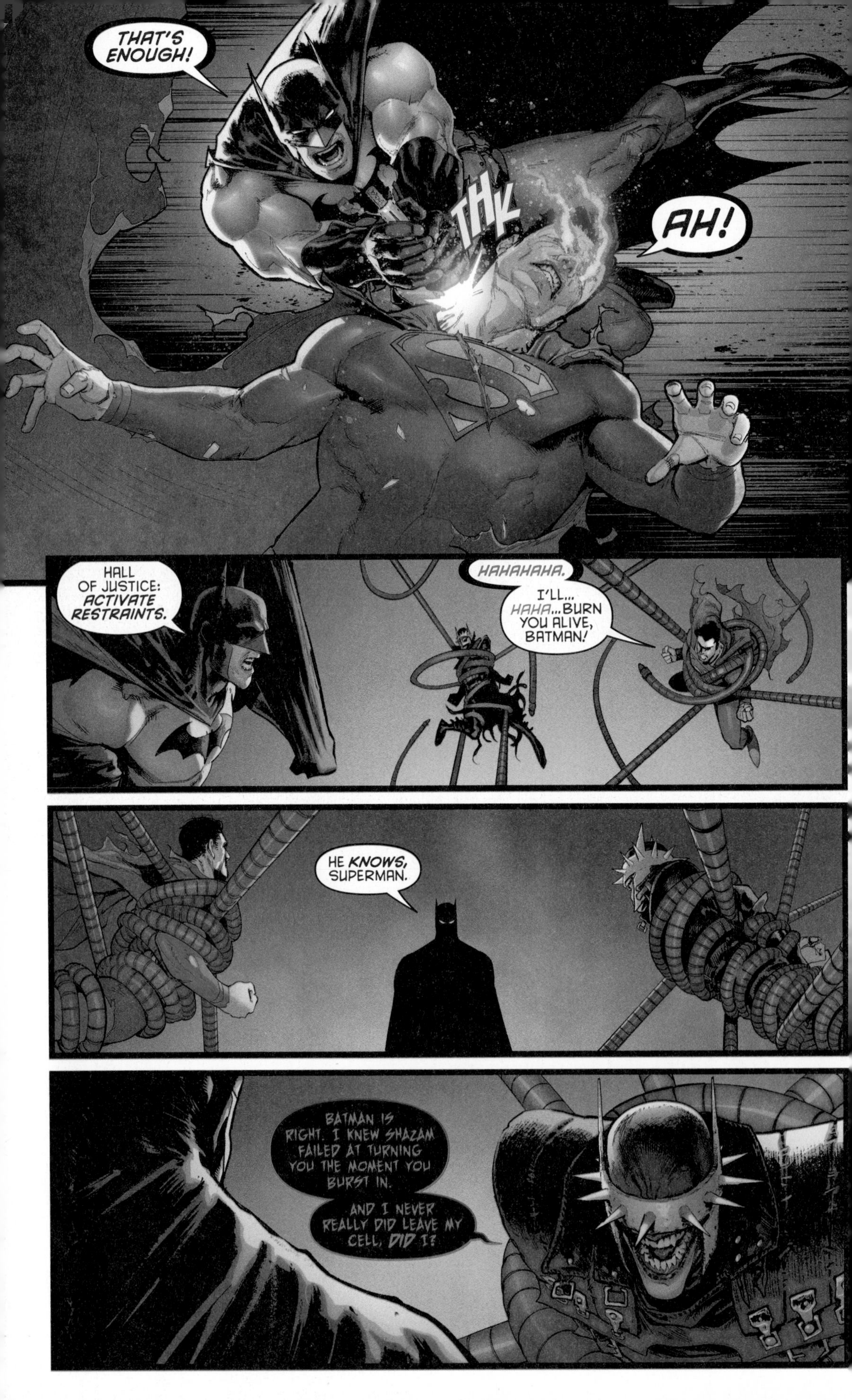
THAT'S ENOUGH!
THK
AH!
HALL OF JUSTICE: ACTIVATE RESTRAINTS.
HAHAHAHA.
I'LL... HAHA...BURN YOU ALIVE, BATMAN!
HE KNOWS, SUPERMAN.
BATMAN IS RIGHT. I KNEW SHAZAM FAILED AT TURNING YOU THE MOMENT YOU BURST IN.
AND I NEVER REALLY DID LEAVE MY CELL, DID I?

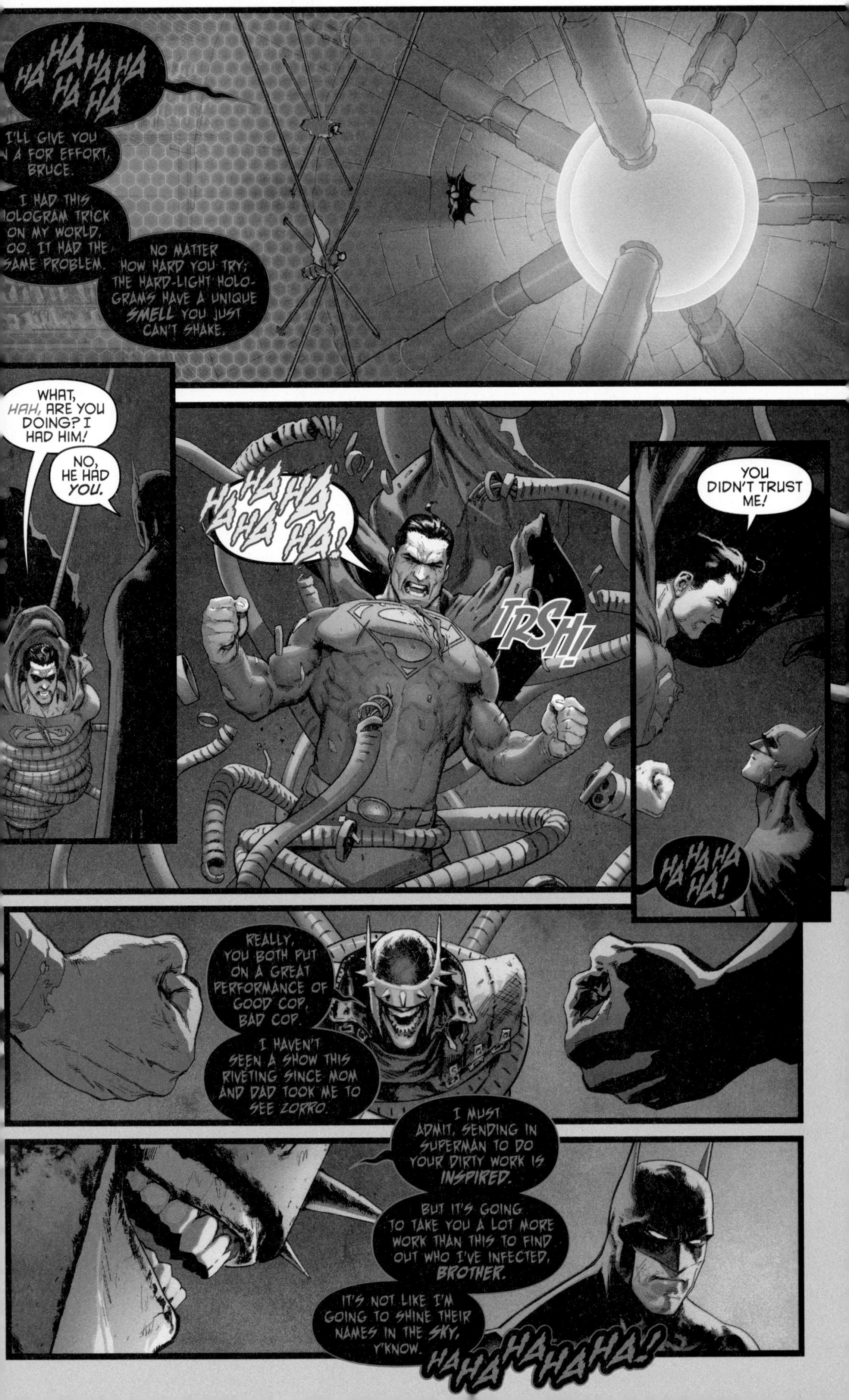
HA HA HA HA HA HA
I'LL GIVE YOU AN A FOR EFFORT, BRUCE.
I HAD THIS HOLOGRAM TRICK ON MY WORLD, TOO. IT HAD THE SAME PROBLEM.
NO MATTER HOW HARD YOU TRY; THE HARD-LIGHT HOLOGRAMS HAVE A UNIQUE SMELL YOU JUST CAN'T SHAKE.
WHAT, HAH, ARE YOU DOING? I HAD HIM!
NO, HE HAD YOU.
HA HA HA HA HA HA!
TRSH!
YOU DIDN'T TRUST ME!
HA HA HA HA HA!
REALLY, YOU BOTH PUT ON A GREAT PERFORMANCE OF GOOD COP, BAD COP.
I HAVEN'T SEEN A SHOW THIS RIVETING SINCE MOM AND DAD TOOK ME TO SEE ZORRO.
I MUST ADMIT, SENDING IN SUPERMAN TO DO YOUR DIRTY WORK IS INSPIRED.
BUT IT'S GOING TO TAKE YOU A LOT MORE WORK THAN THIS TO FIND OUT WHO I'VE INFECTED, BROTHER.
IT'S NOT LIKE I'M GOING TO SHINE THEIR NAMES IN THE SKY, Y'KNOW.
HAHAHAHAHAHA!

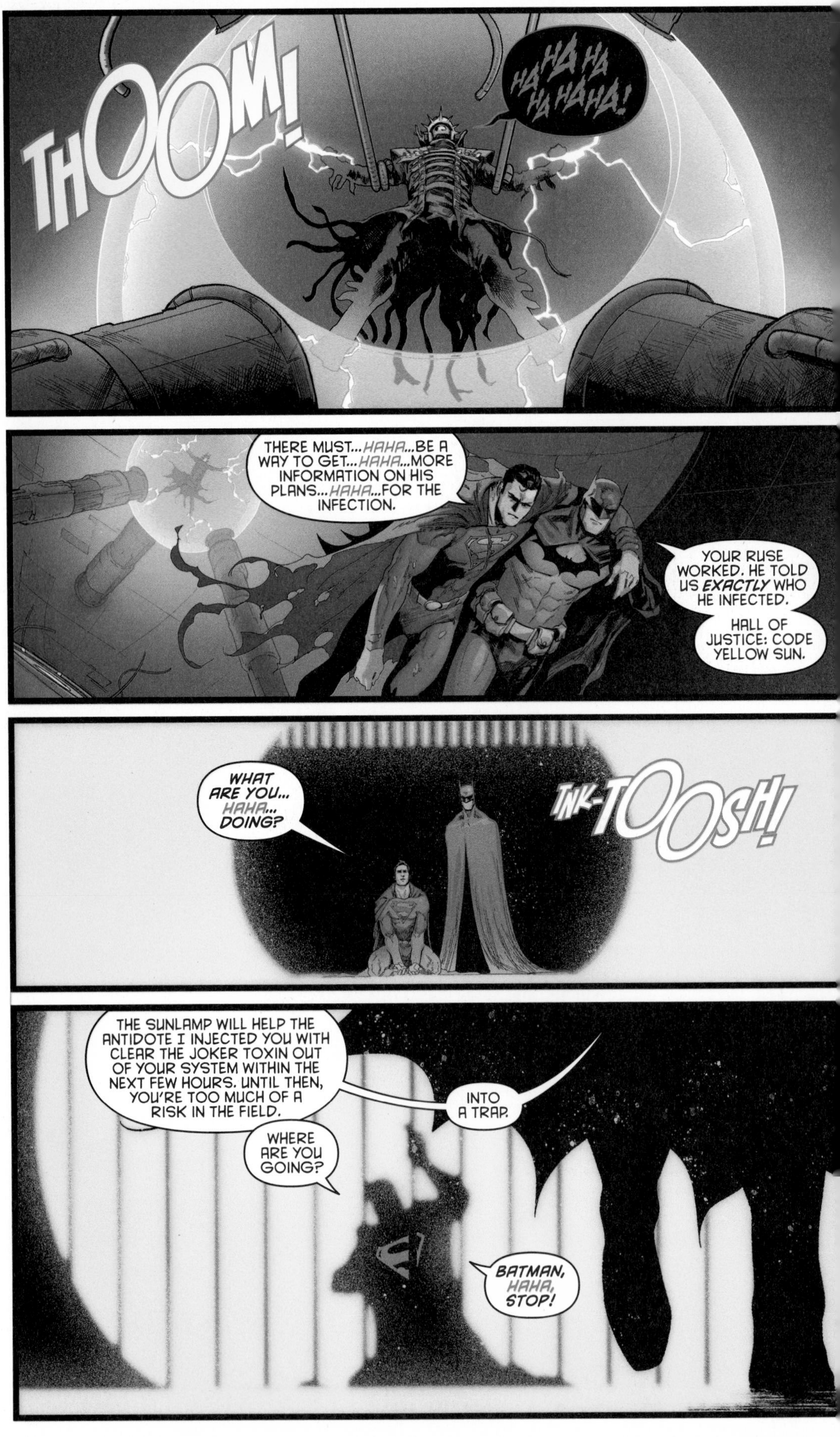
THOOM!
HA HA HA HA HA HAHA!
THERE MUST...HAHA...BE A WAY TO GET...HAHA...MORE INFORMATION ON HIS PLANS...HAHA...FOR THE INFECTION.
YOUR RUSE WORKED. HE TOLD US EXACTLY WHO HE INFECTED.
HALL OF JUSTICE: CODE YELLOW SUN.
WHAT ARE YOU... HAHA... DOING?
TNK-TOOSH!
THE SUNLAMP WILL HELP THE ANTIDOTE I INJECTED YOU WITH CLEAR THE JOKER TOXIN OUT OF YOUR SYSTEM WITHIN THE NEXT FEW HOURS. UNTIL THEN, YOU'RE TOO MUCH OF A RISK IN THE FIELD.
WHERE ARE YOU GOING?
INTO A TRAP.
BATMAN, HAHA, STOP!

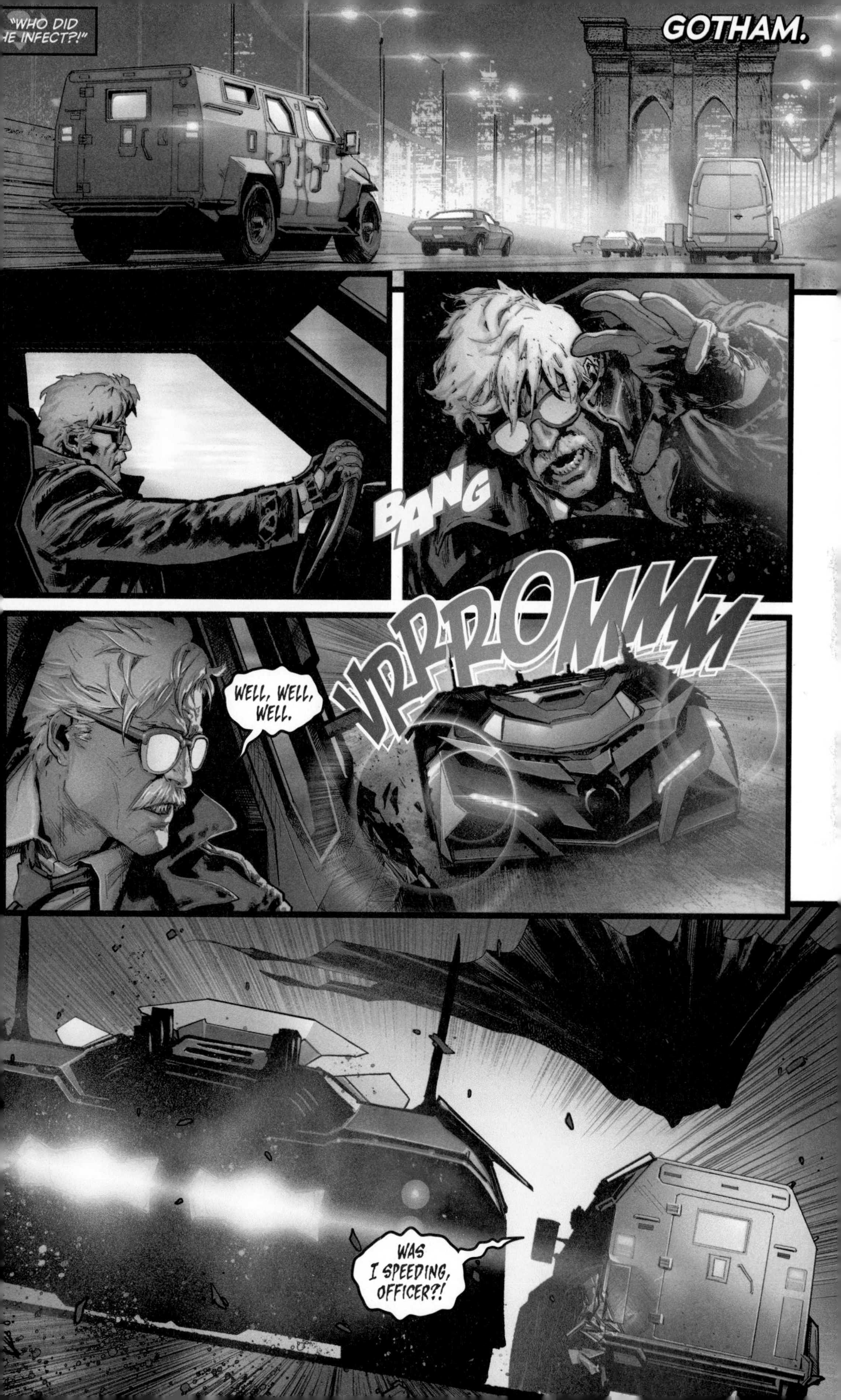
"WHO DID
HE INFECT?!"
GOTHAM.
BANG
VRRROMMM
WELL, WELL,
WELL.
WAS
I SPEEDING,
OFFICER?!

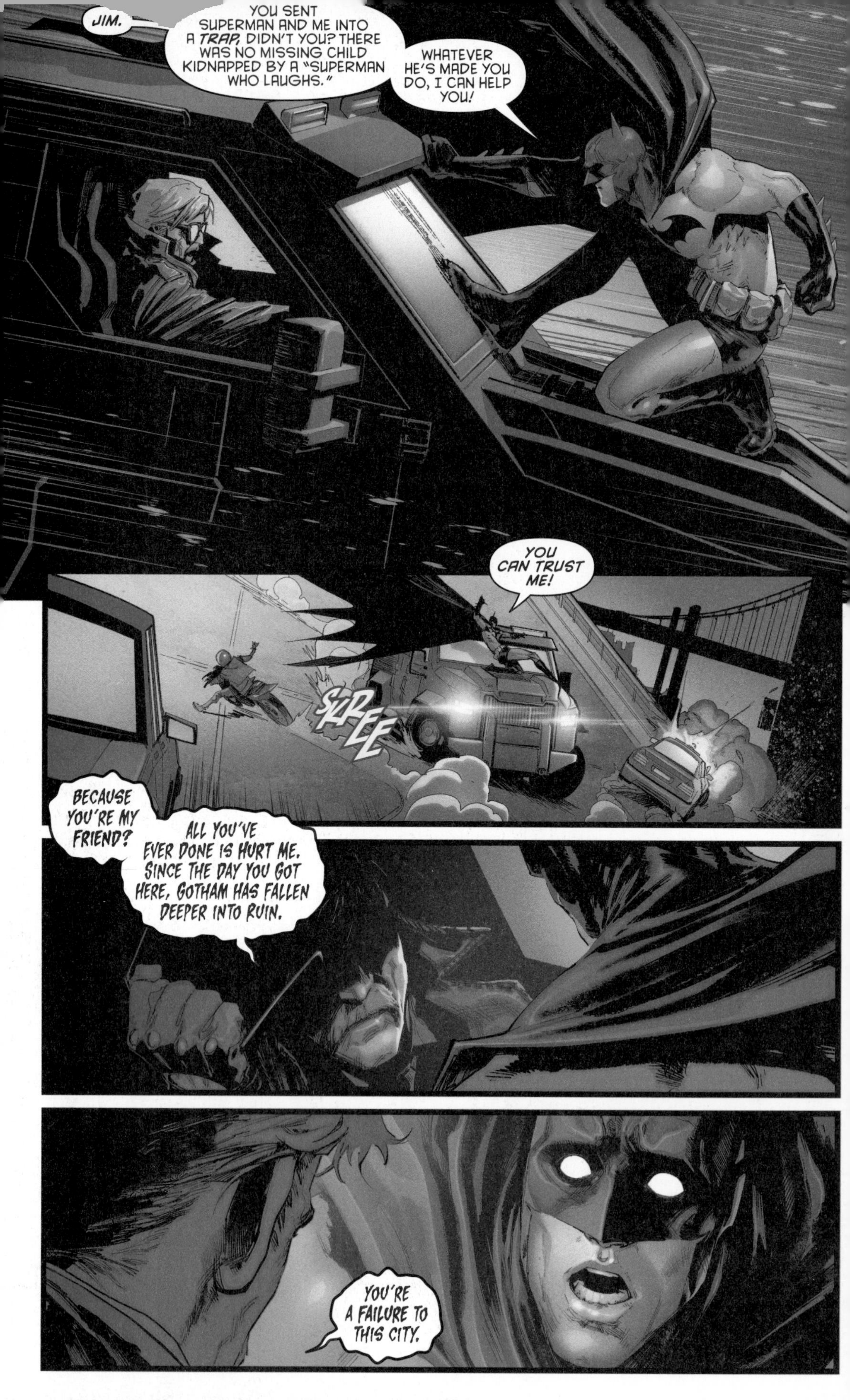
JIM.
YOU SENT SUPERMAN AND ME INTO A TRAP, DIDN'T YOU? THERE WAS NO MISSING CHILD KIDNAPPED BY A "SUPERMAN WHO LAUGHS."
WHATEVER HE'S MADE YOU DO, I CAN HELP YOU!
YOU CAN TRUST ME!
SKREE
BECAUSE YOU'RE MY FRIEND?
ALL YOU'VE EVER DONE IS HURT ME. SINCE THE DAY YOU GOT HERE, GOTHAM HAS FALLEN DEEPER INTO RUIN.
YOU'RE A FAILURE TO THIS CITY.

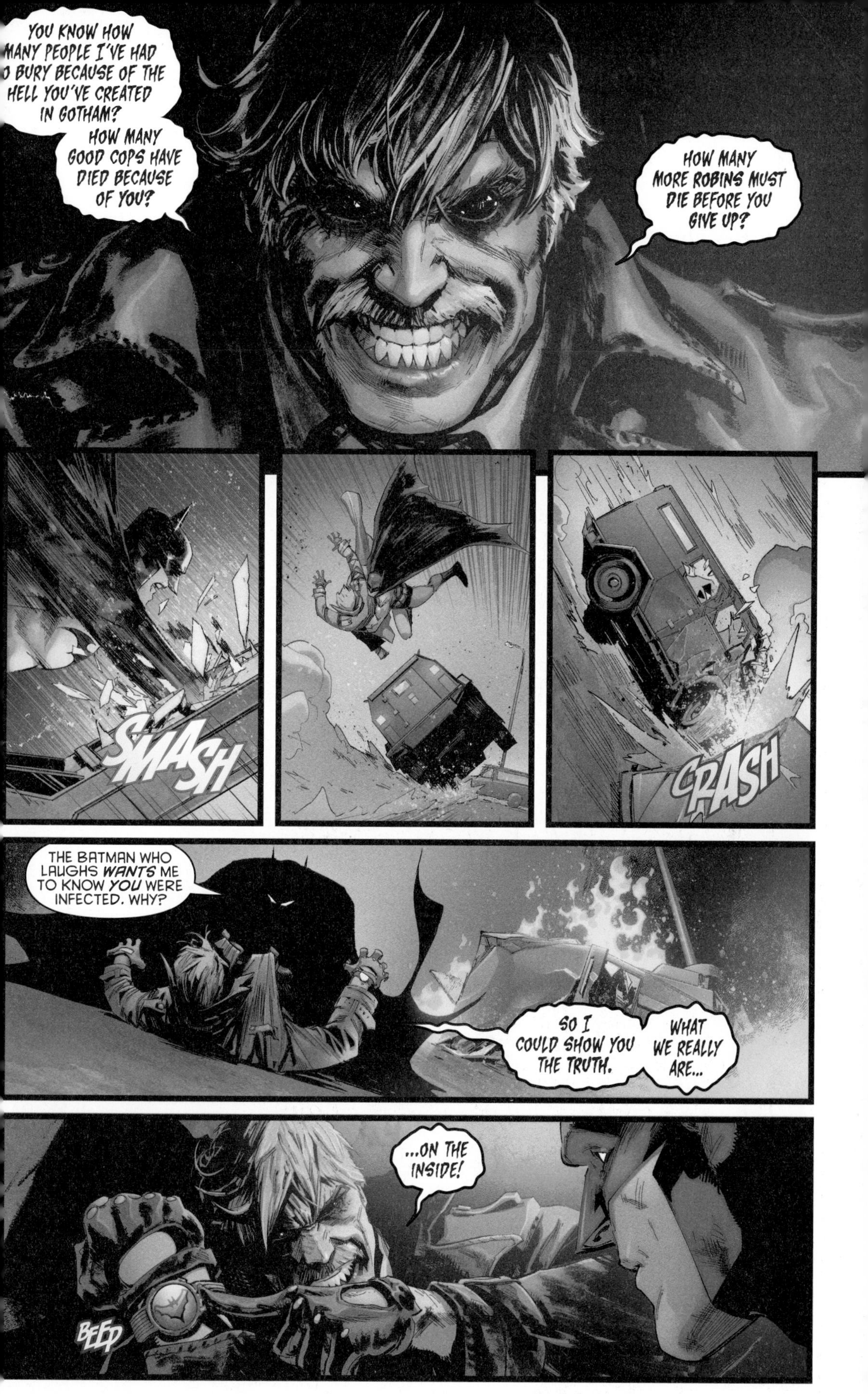

YOU KNOW HOW MANY PEOPLE I'VE HAD TO BURY BECAUSE OF THE HELL YOU'VE CREATED IN GOTHAM?
HOW MANY GOOD COPS HAVE DIED BECAUSE OF YOU?
HOW MANY MORE ROBINS MUST DIE BEFORE YOU GIVE UP?
SMASH
CRASH
THE BATMAN WHO LAUGHS *WANTS* ME TO KNOW *YOU* WERE INFECTED. WHY?
SO I COULD SHOW YOU THE TRUTH.
WHAT WE REALLY ARE...
...ON THE INSIDE!
BEEP

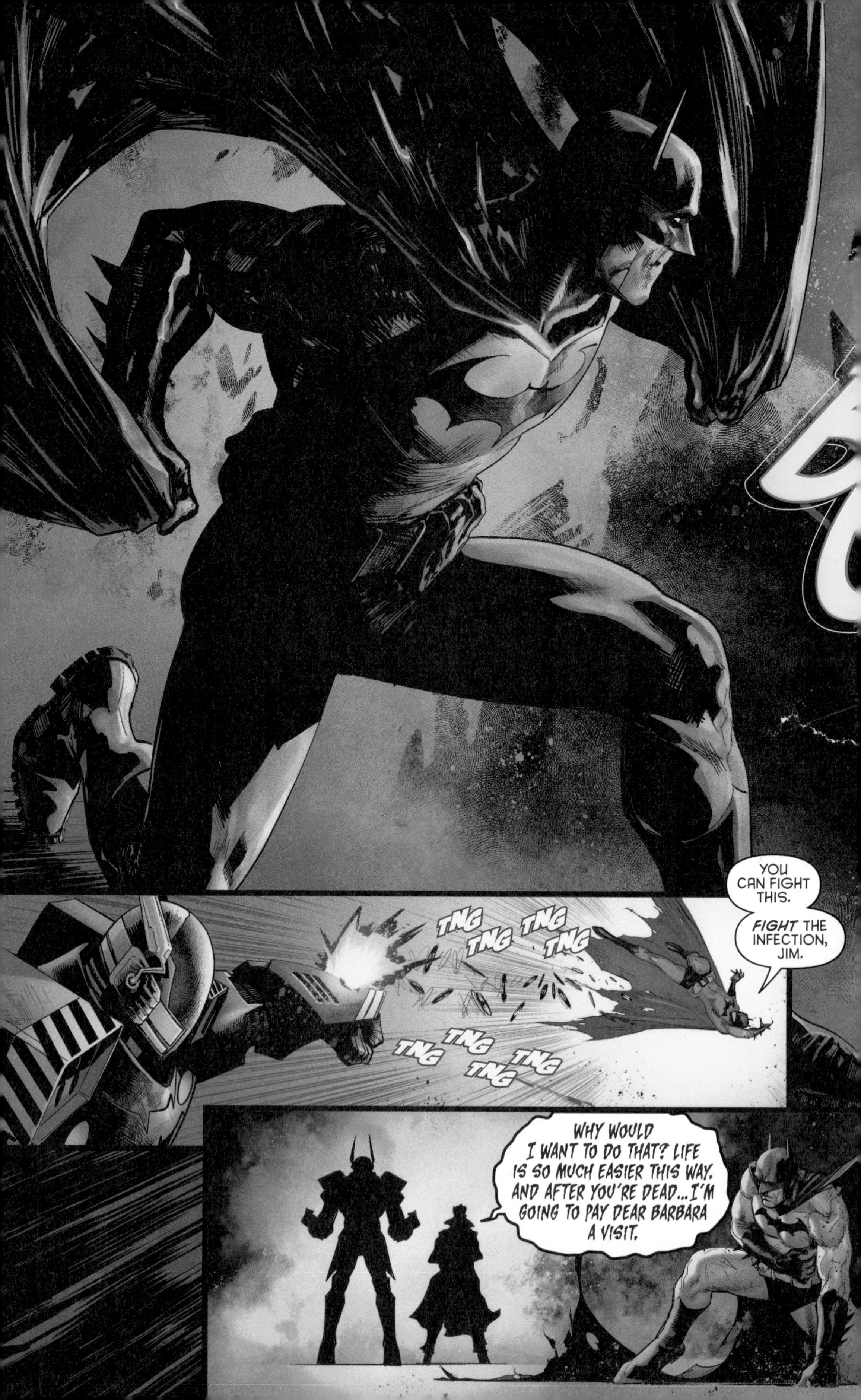
YOU CAN FIGHT THIS.
FIGHT THE INFECTION, JIM.
TNG TNG TNG TNG
TNG TNG TNG TNG
WHY WOULD I WANT TO DO THAT? LIFE IS SO MUCH EASIER THIS WAY. AND AFTER YOU'RE DEAD...I'M GOING TO PAY DEAR BARBARA A VISIT.

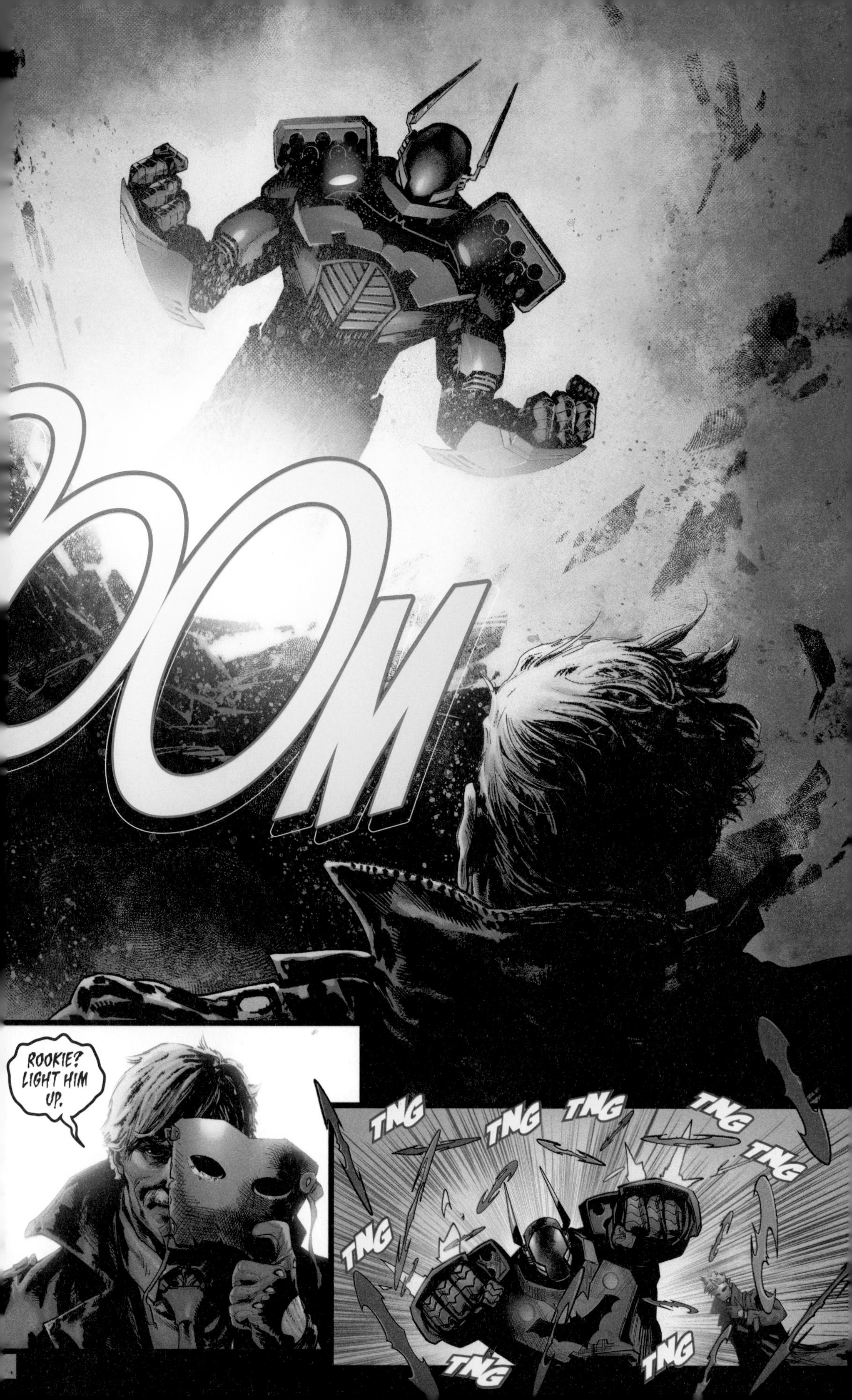
OOM
ROOKIE? LIGHT HIM UP.
TNG
TNG
TNG
TNG
TNG
TNG
TNG
TNG

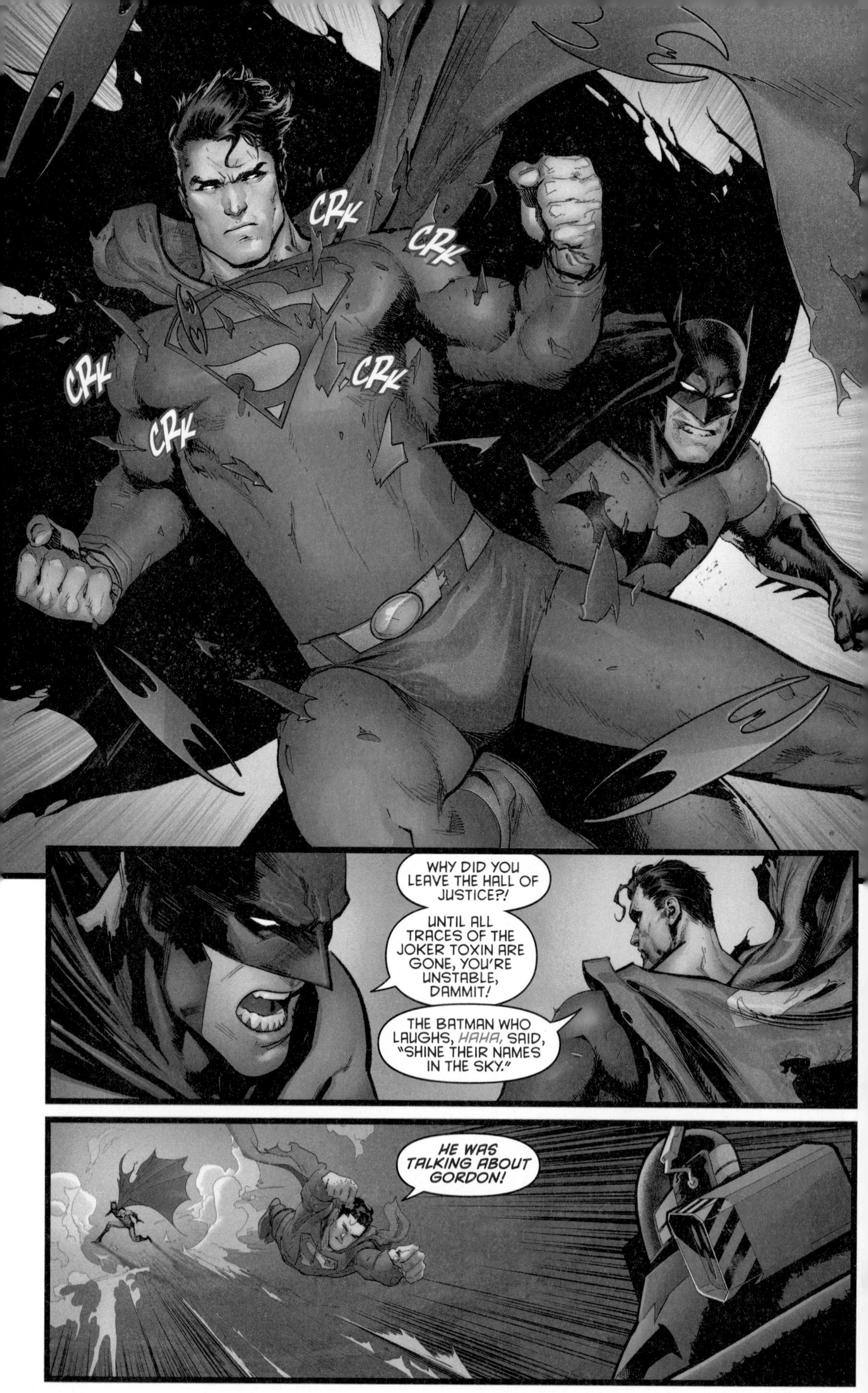
CRK
CRK
CRK
CRK
CRK
WHY DID YOU LEAVE THE HALL OF JUSTICE?!
UNTIL ALL TRACES OF THE JOKER TOXIN ARE GONE, YOU'RE UNSTABLE, DAMMIT!
THE BATMAN WHO LAUGHS, HAHA, SAID, "SHINE THEIR NAMES IN THE SKY."
HE WAS TALKING ABOUT GORDON!

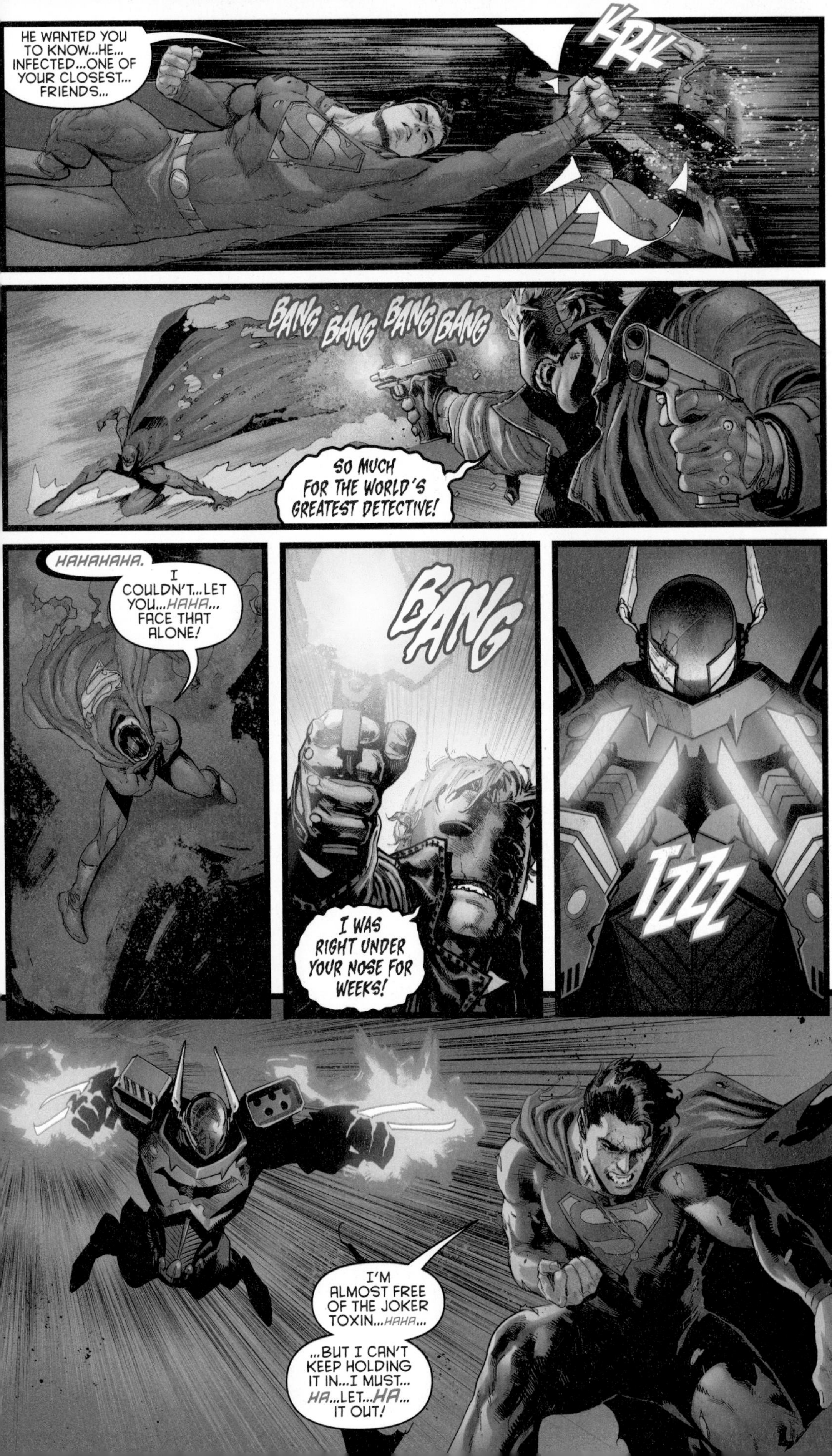

HE WANTED YOU TO KNOW...HE... INFECTED...ONE OF YOUR CLOSEST... FRIENDS...
KRK
BANG BANG BANG BANG
SO MUCH FOR THE WORLD'S GREATEST DETECTIVE!
HAHAHAHA.
I COULDN'T...LET YOU...HAHA... FACE THAT ALONE!
BANG
I WAS RIGHT UNDER YOUR NOSE FOR WEEKS!
TZZZ
I'M ALMOST FREE OF THE JOKER TOXIN...HAHA...
...BUT I CAN'T KEEP HOLDING IT IN...I MUST... HA...LET...HA... IT OUT!

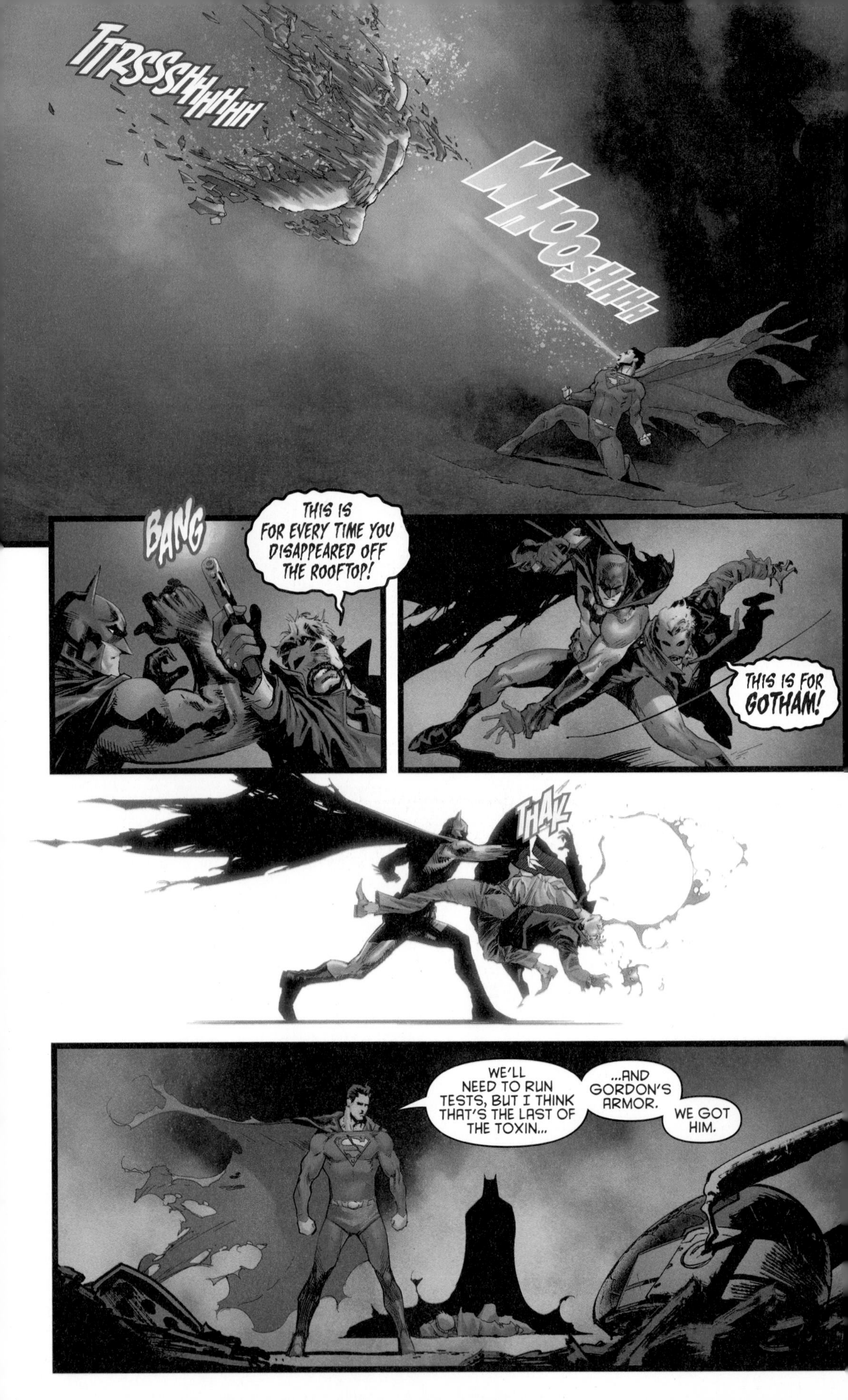
TTRSSSHHHHH
WHOOSHHHH
BANG
THIS IS FOR EVERY TIME YOU DISAPPEARED OFF THE ROOFTOP!
THIS IS FOR GOTHAM!
THAK
WE'LL NEED TO RUN TESTS, BUT I THINK THAT'S THE LAST OF THE TOXIN...
...AND GORDON'S ARMOR.
WE GOT HIM.

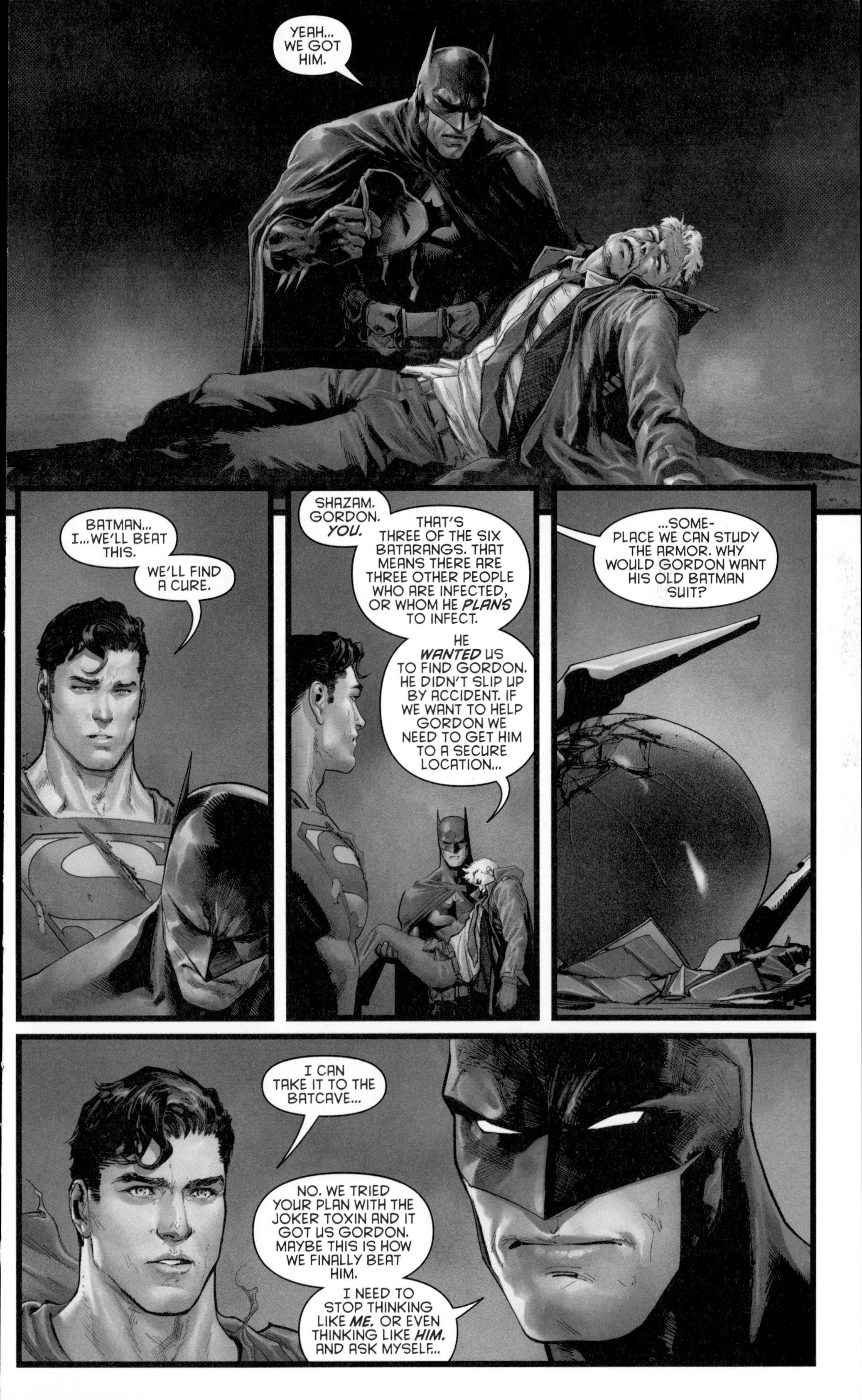

YEAH... WE GOT HIM.
BATMAN... I...WE'LL BEAT THIS.
WE'LL FIND A CURE.
SHAZAM. GORDON. *YOU.*
THAT'S THREE OF THE SIX BATARANGS. THAT MEANS THERE ARE THREE OTHER PEOPLE WHO ARE INFECTED, OR WHOM HE *PLANS* TO INFECT.
HE *WANTED* US TO FIND GORDON. HE DIDN'T SLIP UP BY ACCIDENT. IF WE WANT TO HELP GORDON WE NEED TO GET HIM TO A SECURE LOCATION...
...SOME-PLACE WE CAN STUDY THE ARMOR. WHY WOULD GORDON WANT HIS OLD BATMAN SUIT?
I CAN TAKE IT TO THE BATCAVE...
NO. WE TRIED YOUR PLAN WITH THE JOKER TOXIN AND IT GOT US GORDON. MAYBE THIS IS HOW WE FINALLY BEAT HIM.
I NEED TO STOP THINKING LIKE *ME.* OR EVEN THINKING LIKE *HIM.* AND ASK MYSELF...

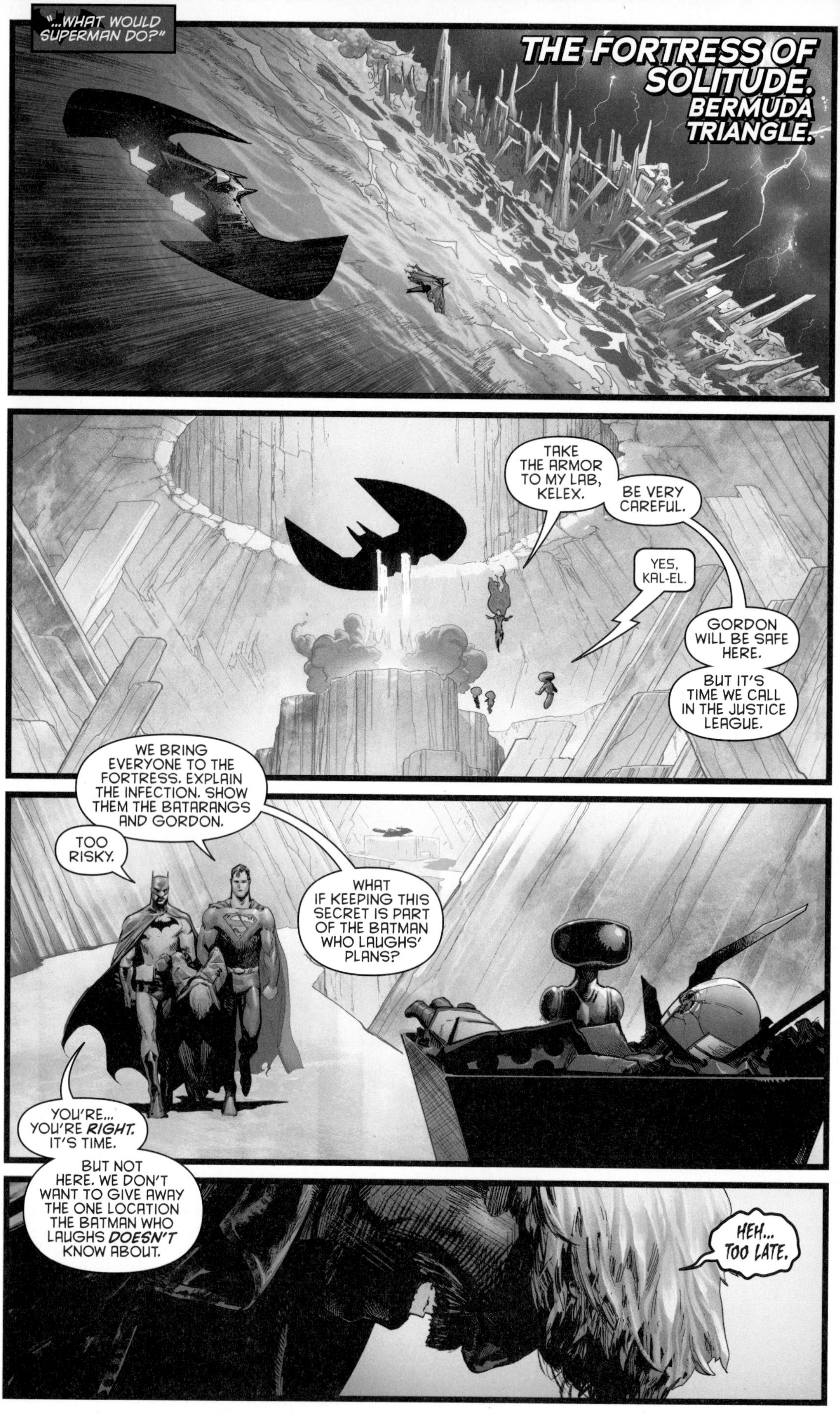
"...WHAT WOULD SUPERMAN DO?"
THE FORTRESS OF SOLITUDE. BERMUDA TRIANGLE.
TAKE THE ARMOR TO MY LAB, KELEX.
BE VERY CAREFUL.
YES, KAL-EL.
GORDON WILL BE SAFE HERE.
BUT IT'S TIME WE CALL IN THE JUSTICE LEAGUE.
WE BRING EVERYONE TO THE FORTRESS. EXPLAIN THE INFECTION. SHOW THEM THE BATARANGS AND GORDON.
TOO RISKY.
WHAT IF KEEPING THIS SECRET IS PART OF THE BATMAN WHO LAUGHS' PLANS?
YOU'RE... YOU'RE RIGHT. IT'S TIME.
BUT NOT HERE. WE DON'T WANT TO GIVE AWAY THE ONE LOCATION THE BATMAN WHO LAUGHS DOESN'T KNOW ABOUT.
HEH... TOO LATE.

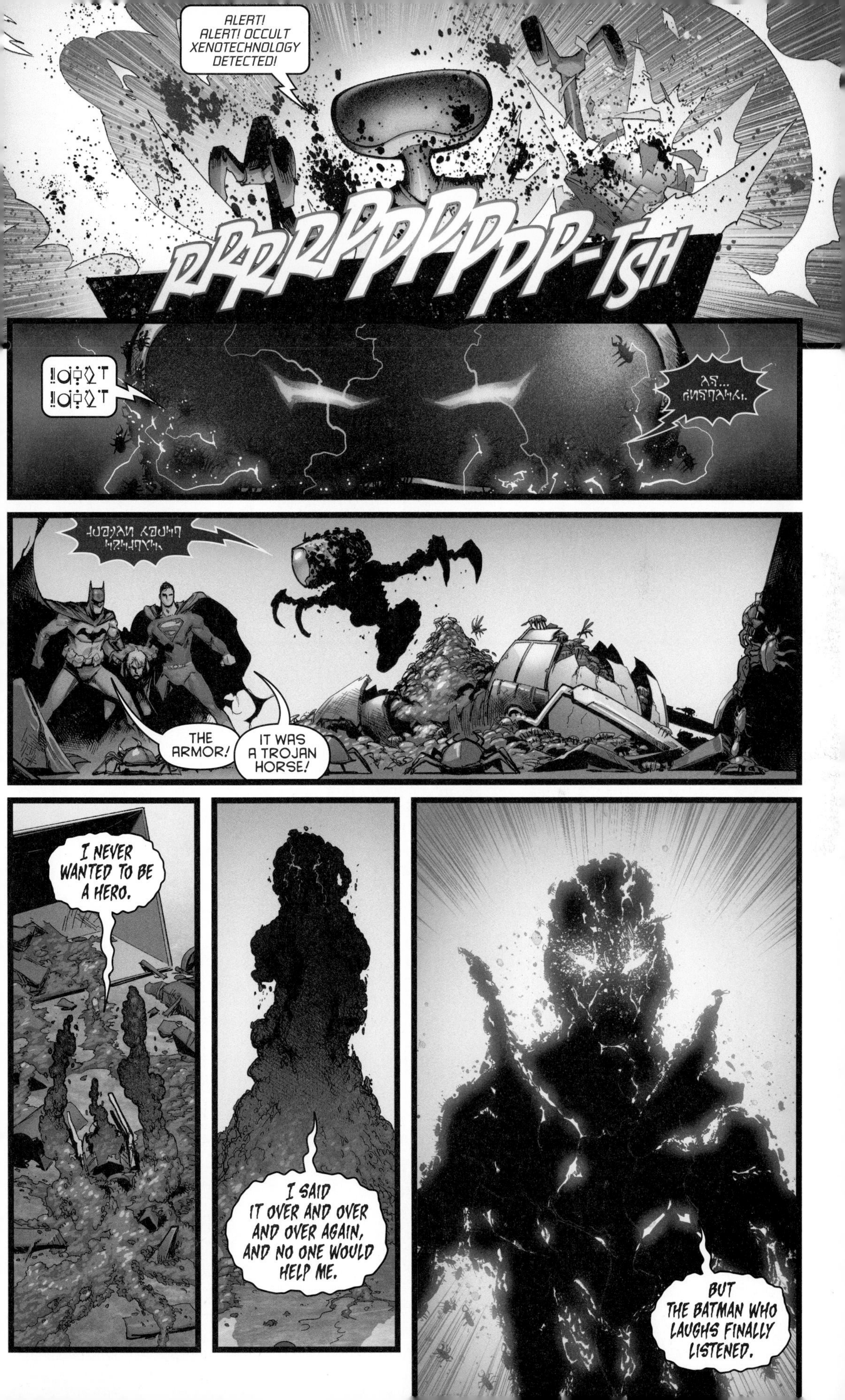
ALERT! ALERT! OCCULT XENOTECHNOLOGY DETECTED!
RRRRPPPPPPP-TSH
THE ARMOR!
IT WAS A TROJAN HORSE!
I NEVER WANTED TO BE A HERO.
I SAID IT OVER AND OVER AND OVER AGAIN, AND NO ONE WOULD HELP ME.
BUT THE BATMAN WHO LAUGHS FINALLY LISTENED.

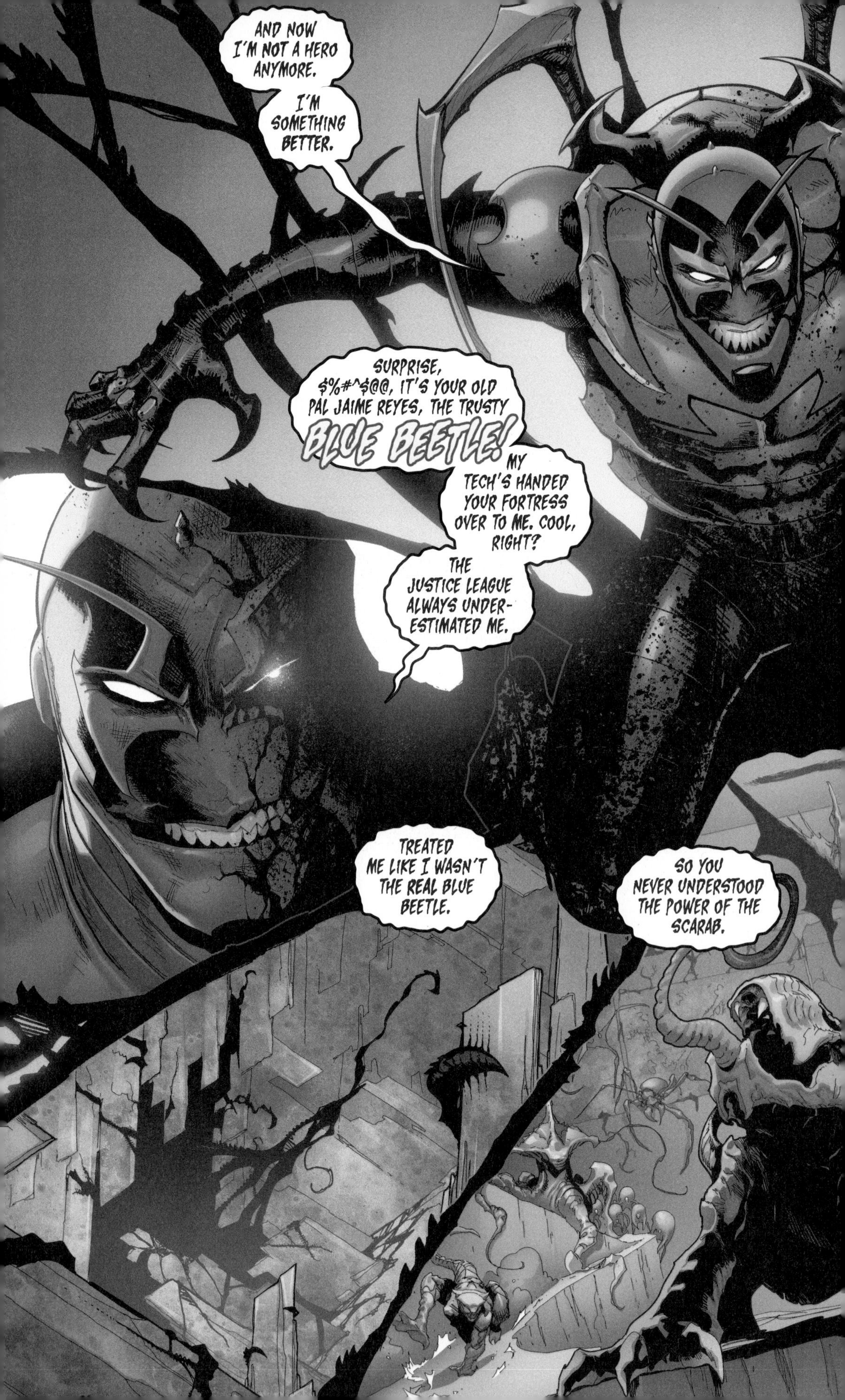
AND NOW I'M NOT A HERO ANYMORE.
I'M SOMETHING BETTER.
SURPRISE, $%#^$@@, IT'S YOUR OLD PAL JAIME REYES, THE TRUSTY BLUE BEETLE!
MY TECH'S HANDED YOUR FORTRESS OVER TO ME. COOL, RIGHT?
THE JUSTICE LEAGUE ALWAYS UNDER-ESTIMATED ME.
TREATED ME LIKE I WASN'T THE REAL BLUE BEETLE.
SO YOU NEVER UNDERSTOOD THE POWER OF THE SCARAB.

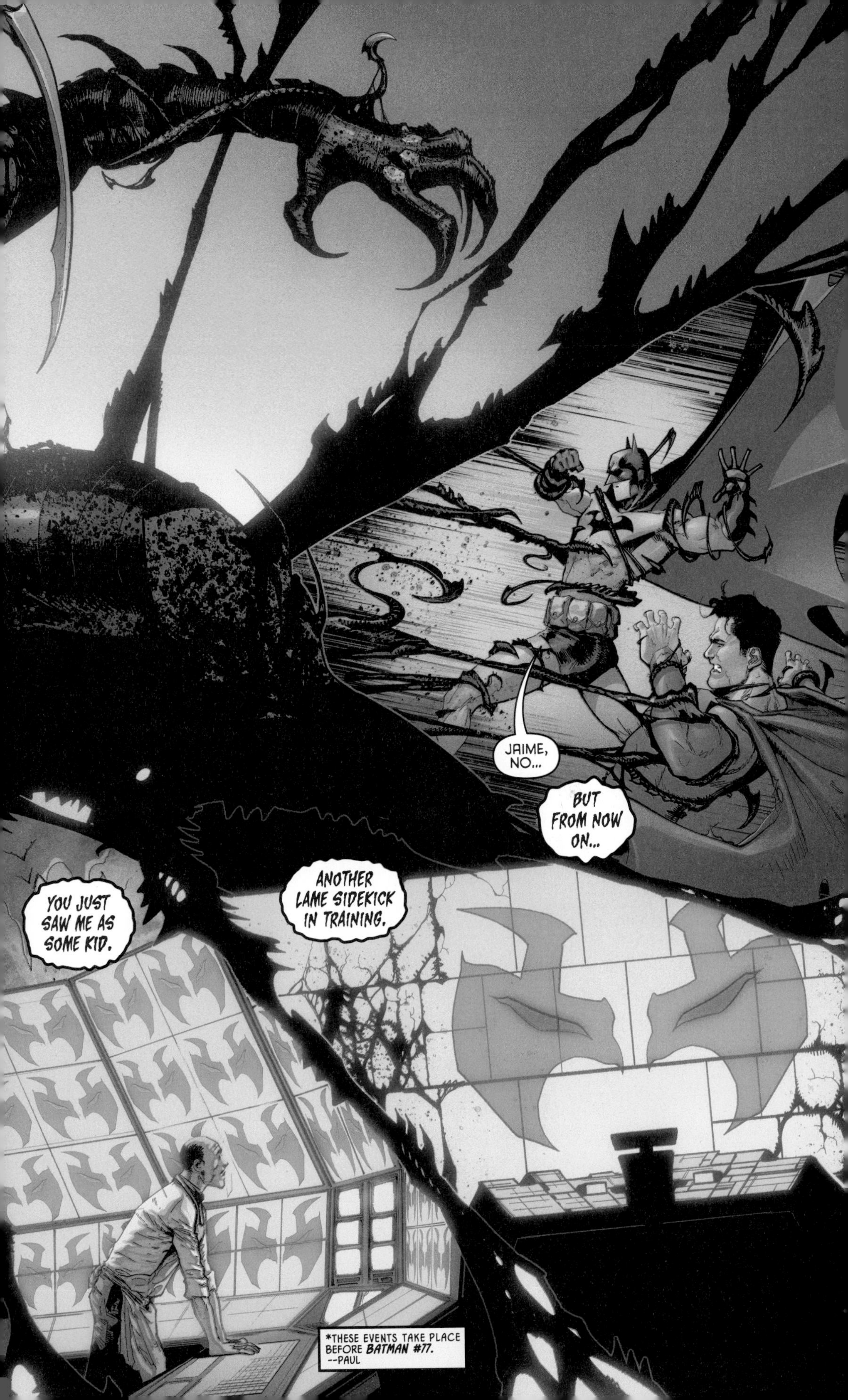
JAIME, NO...
BUT FROM NOW ON...
YOU JUST SAW ME AS SOME KID.
ANOTHER LAME SIDEKICK IN TRAINING.
*THESE EVENTS TAKE PLACE BEFORE BATMAN #77.
--PAUL

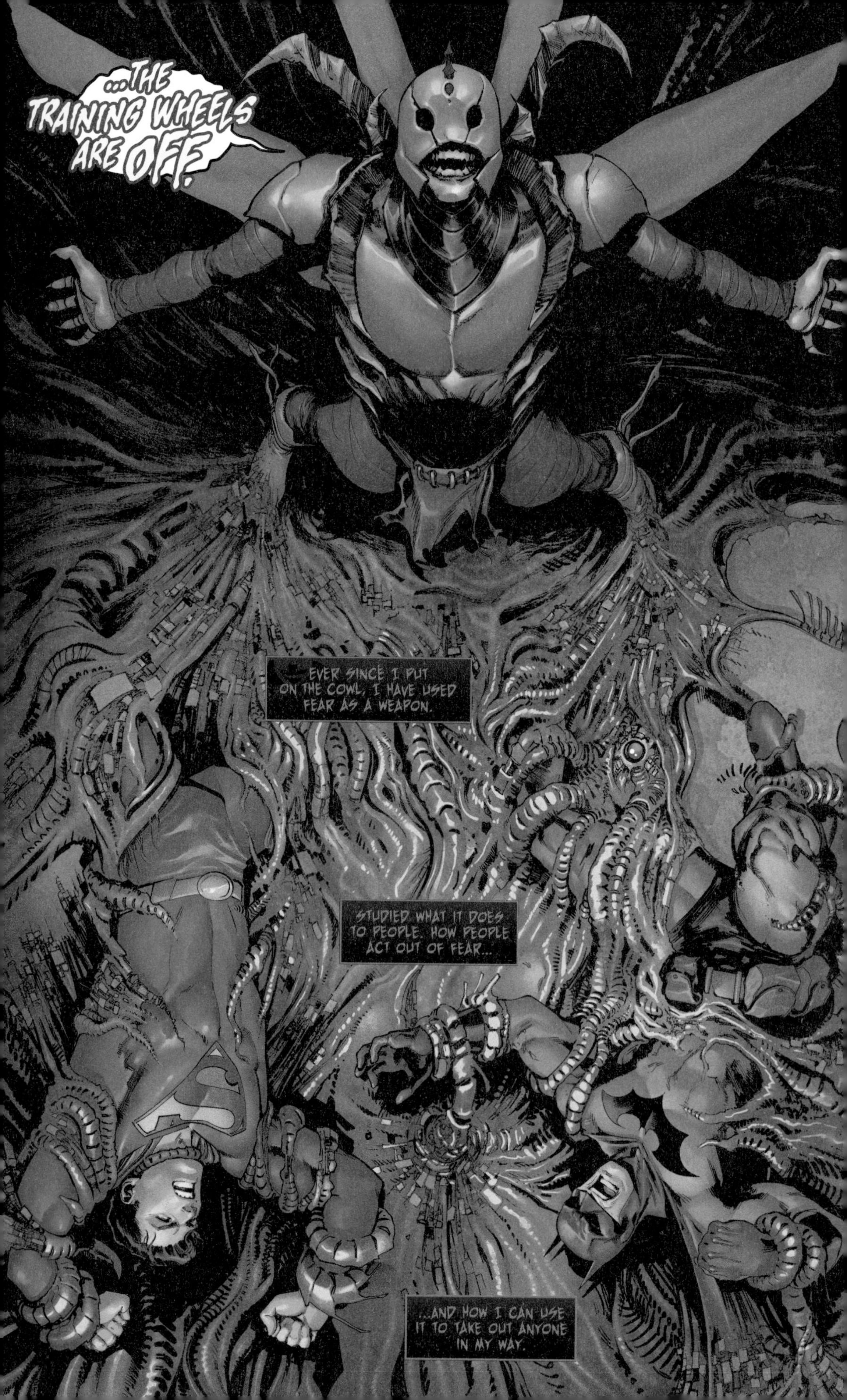
...THE TRAINING WHEELS ARE OFF.
EVER SINCE I PUT ON THE COWL, I HAVE USED FEAR AS A WEAPON.
STUDIED WHAT IT DOES TO PEOPLE. HOW PEOPLE ACT OUT OF FEAR...
...AND HOW I CAN USE IT TO TAKE OUT ANYONE IN MY WAY.

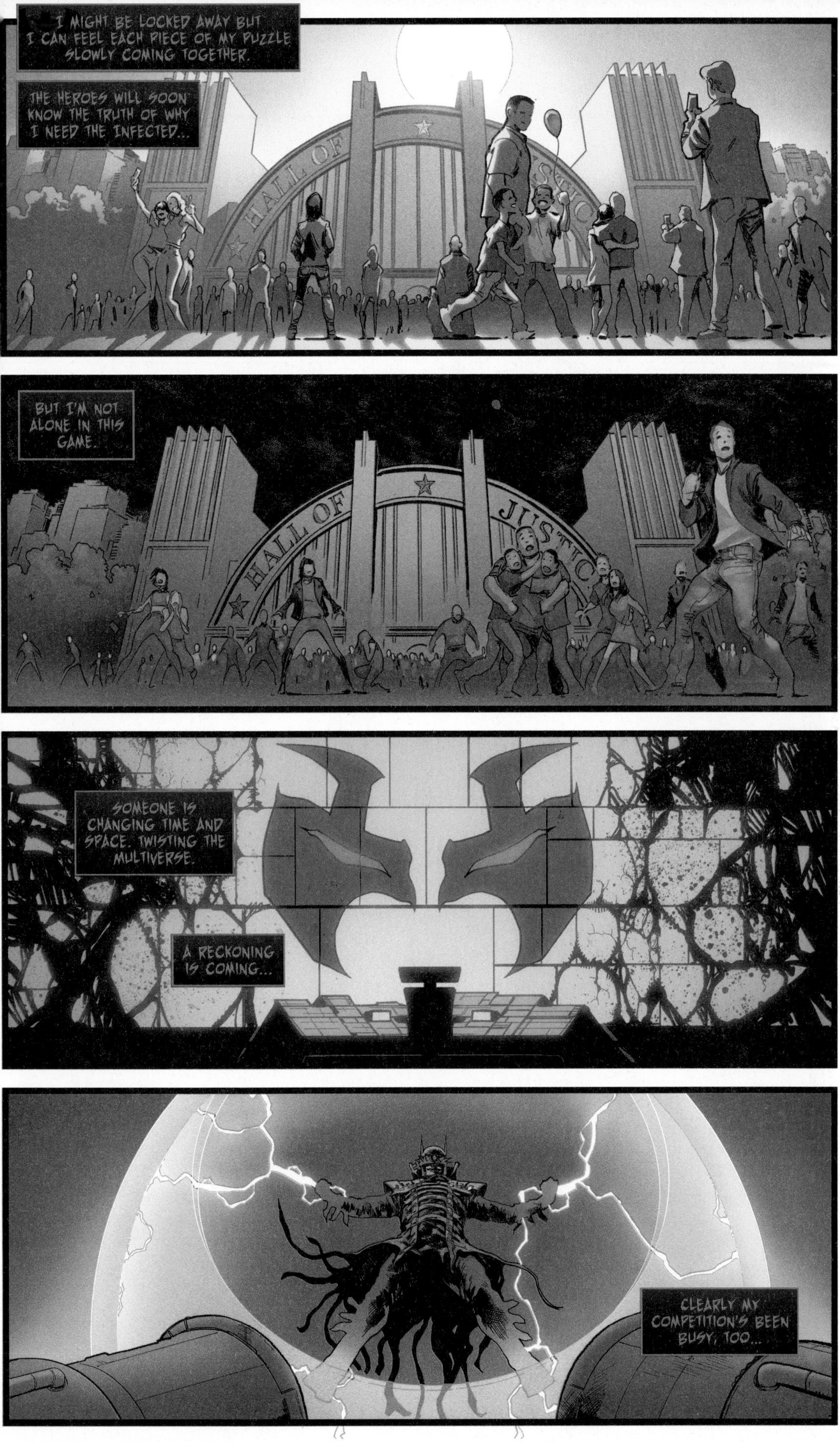
I MIGHT BE LOCKED AWAY BUT I CAN FEEL EACH PIECE OF MY PUZZLE SLOWLY COMING TOGETHER.
THE HEROES WILL SOON KNOW THE TRUTH OF WHY I NEED THE INFECTED...
HALL OF JUSTICE
BUT I'M NOT ALONE IN THIS GAME.
HALL OF JUSTICE
SOMEONE IS CHANGING TIME AND SPACE. TWISTING THE MULTIVERSE.
A RECKONING IS COMING...
CLEARLY MY COMPETITION'S BEEN BUSY, TOO...

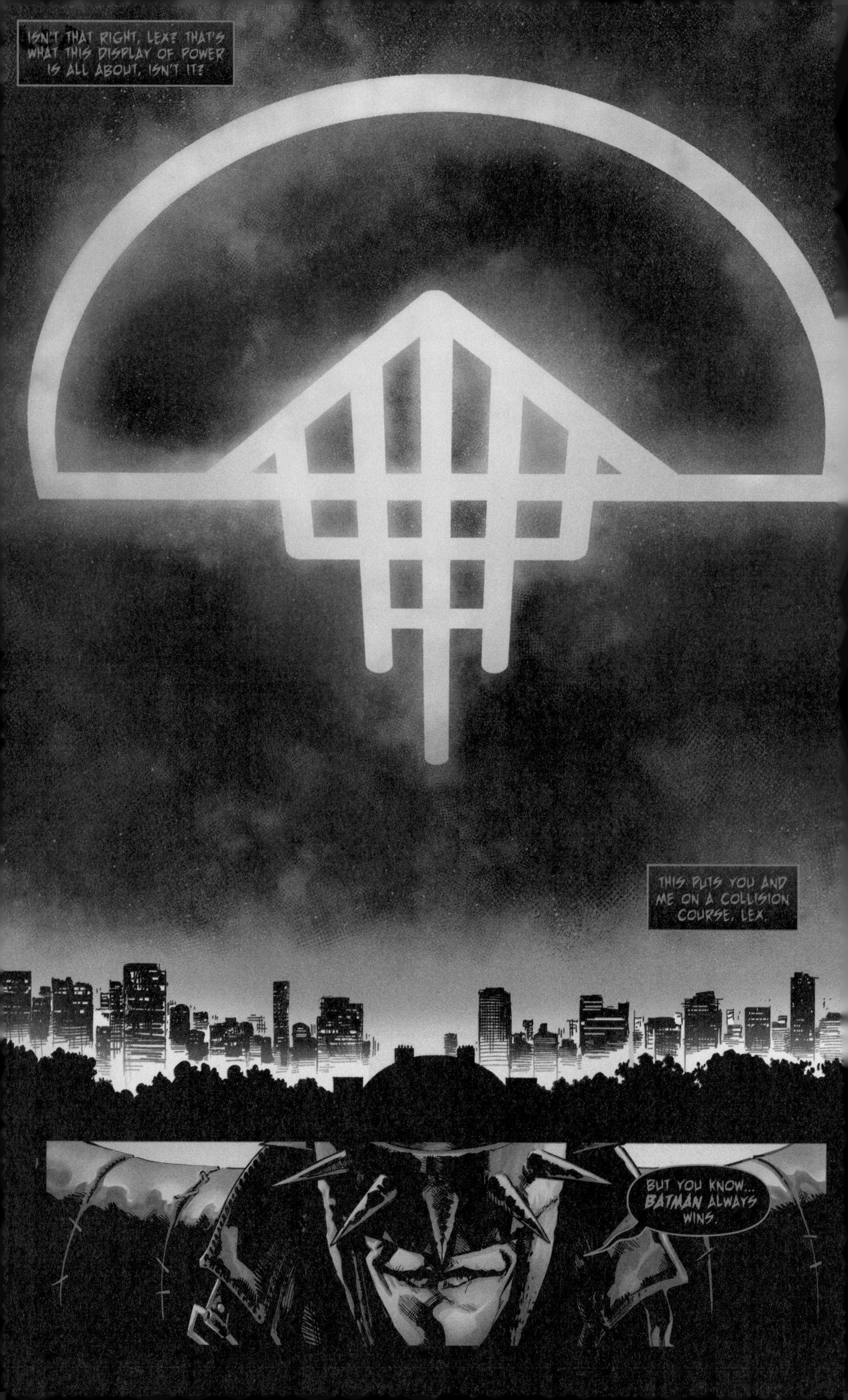

ISN'T THAT RIGHT, LEX? THAT'S WHAT THIS DISPLAY OF POWER IS ALL ABOUT, ISN'T IT?
THIS PUTS YOU AND ME ON A COLLISION COURSE, LEX.
BUT YOU KNOW... BATMAN ALWAYS WINS.

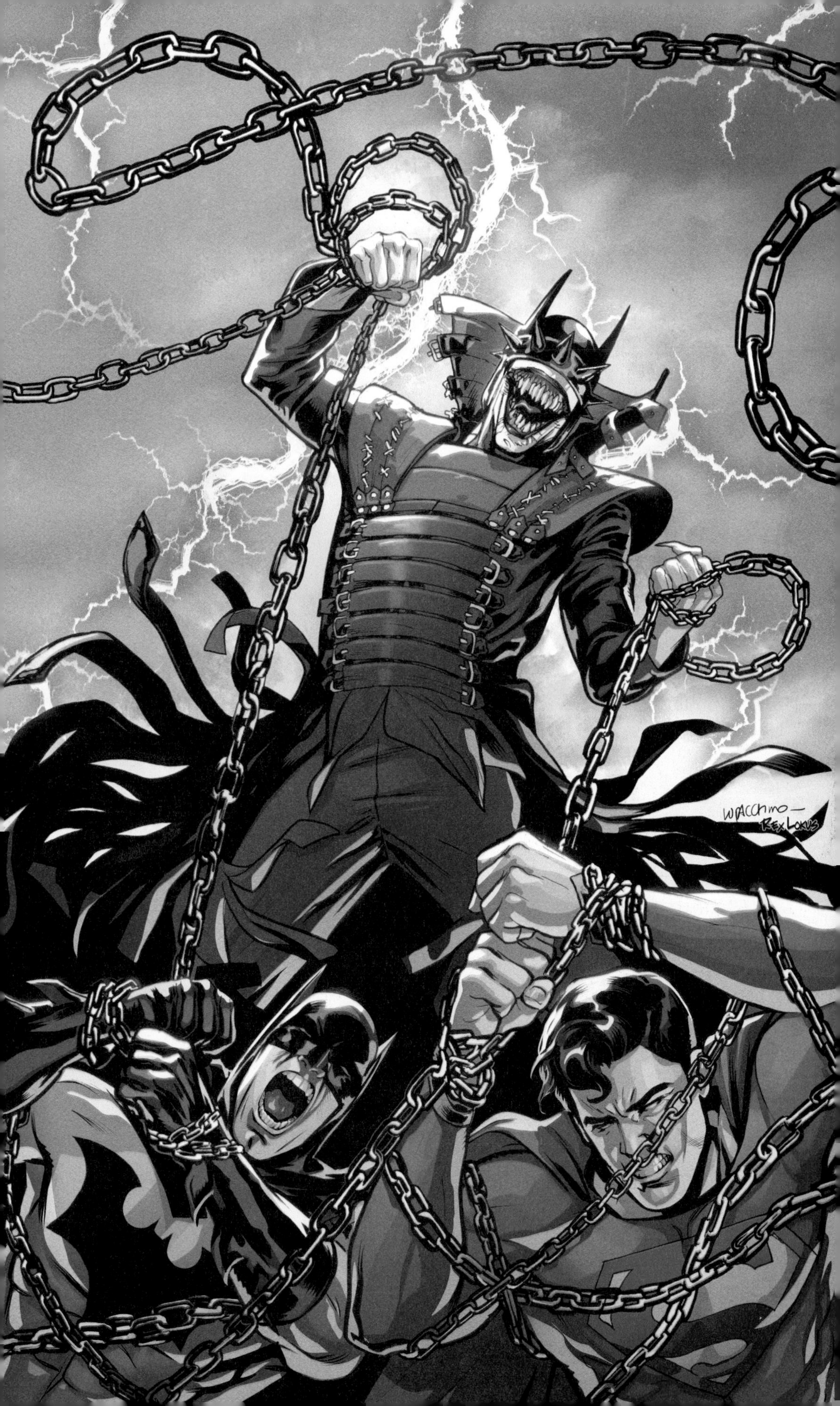
WPACCHMO—
REX LOKUS

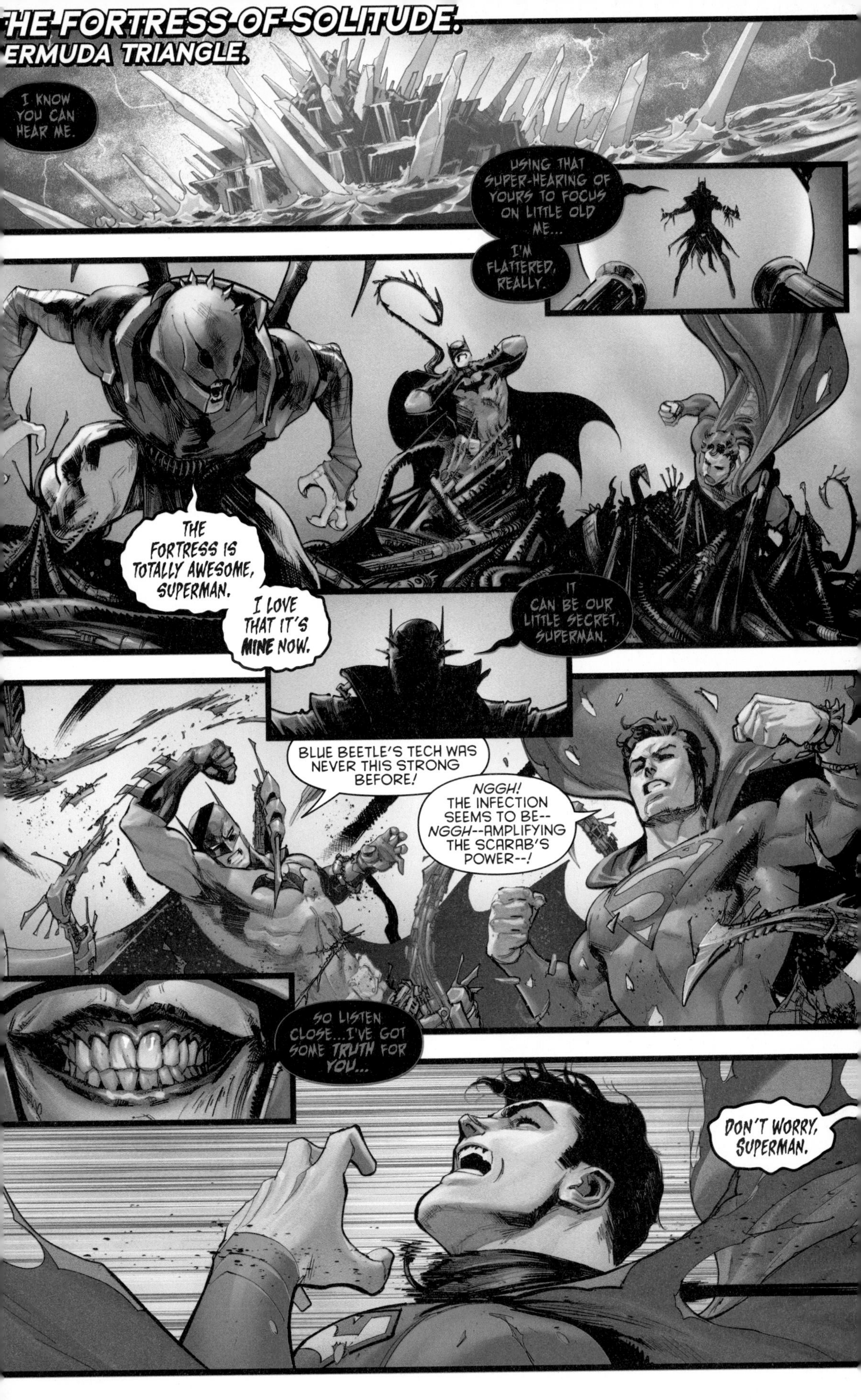
THE FORTRESS OF SOLITUDE.
ERMUDA TRIANGLE.
I KNOW YOU CAN HEAR ME.
USING THAT SUPER-HEARING OF YOURS TO FOCUS ON LITTLE OLD ME...
I'M FLATTERED, REALLY.
THE FORTRESS IS TOTALLY AWESOME, SUPERMAN.
I LOVE THAT IT'S MINE NOW.
IT CAN BE OUR LITTLE SECRET, SUPERMAN.
BLUE BEETLE'S TECH WAS NEVER THIS STRONG BEFORE!
NGGH! THE INFECTION SEEMS TO BE--NGGH--AMPLIFYING THE SCARAB'S POWER--!
SO LISTEN CLOSE...I'VE GOT SOME TRUTH FOR YOU...
DON'T WORRY, SUPERMAN.

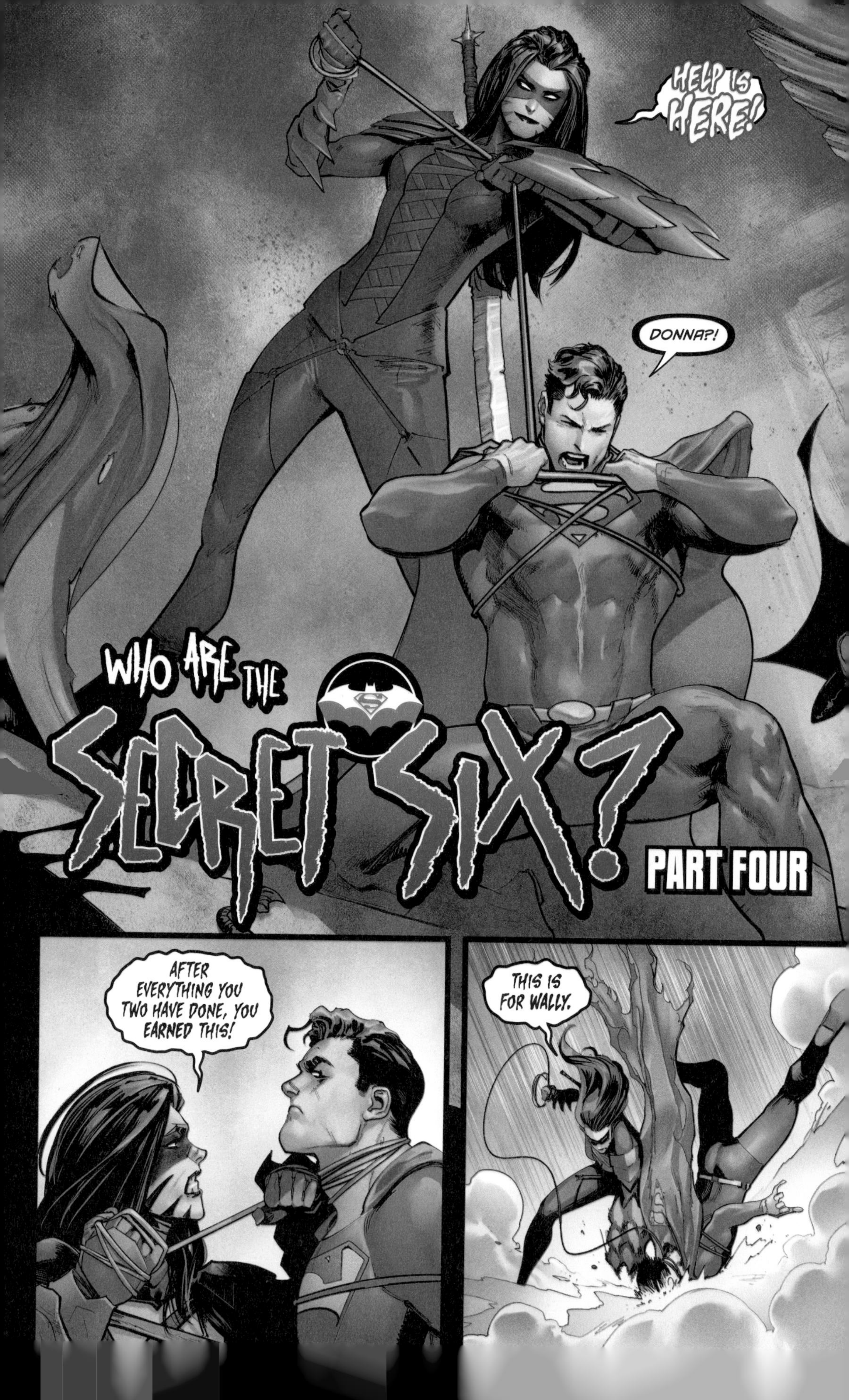
HELP IS HERE!
DONNA?!
WHO ARE THE
SECRET SIX?
PART FOUR
AFTER EVERYTHING YOU TWO HAVE DONE, YOU EARNED THIS!
THIS IS FOR WALLY.

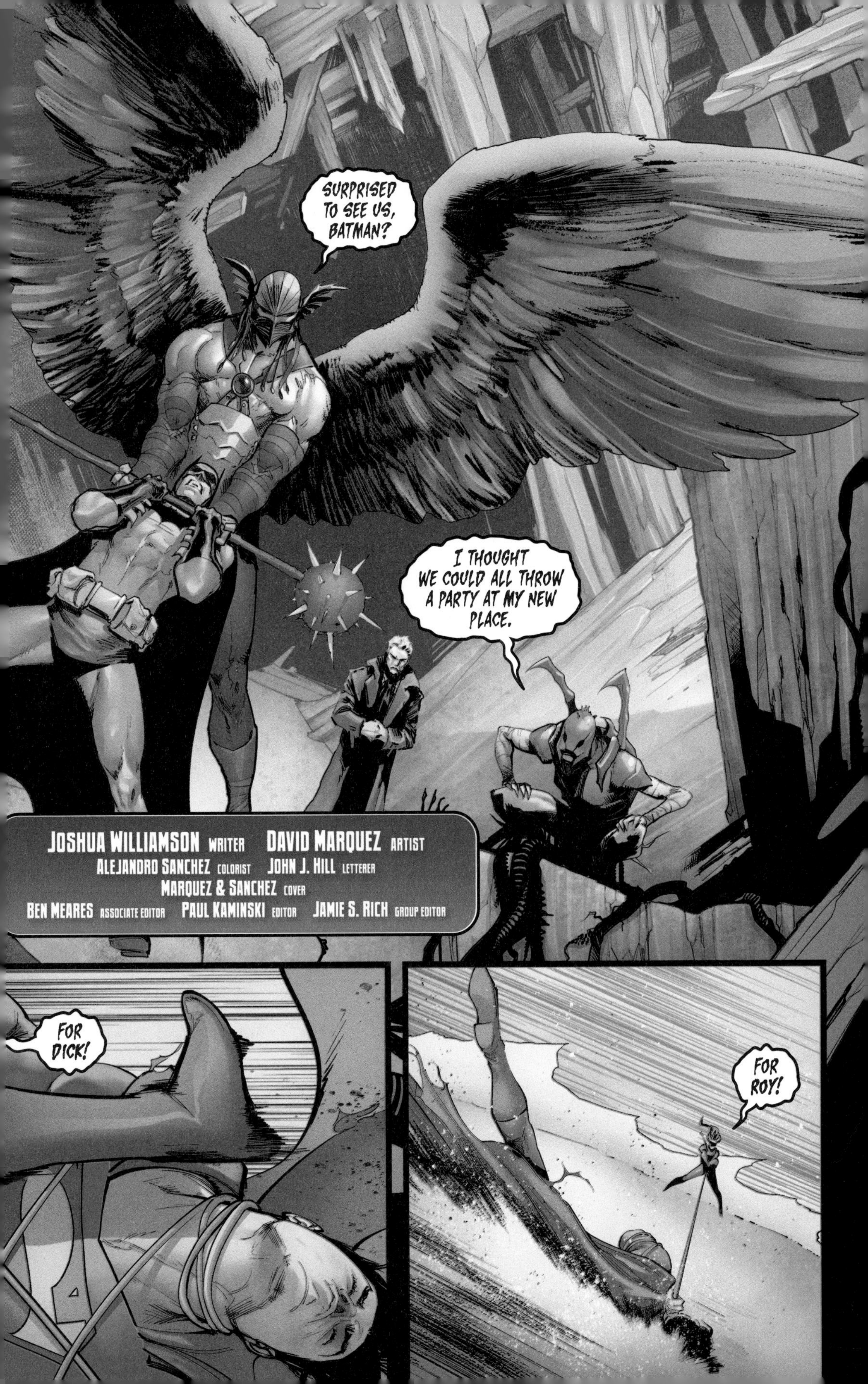
SURPRISED TO SEE US, BATMAN?
I THOUGHT WE COULD ALL THROW A PARTY AT MY NEW PLACE.
JOSHUA WILLIAMSON WRITER DAVID MARQUEZ ARTIST
ALEJANDRO SANCHEZ COLORIST JOHN J. HILL LETTERER
MARQUEZ & SANCHEZ COVER
BEN MEARES ASSOCIATE EDITOR PAUL KAMINSKI EDITOR JAMIE S. RICH GROUP EDITOR
FOR DICK!
FOR ROY!

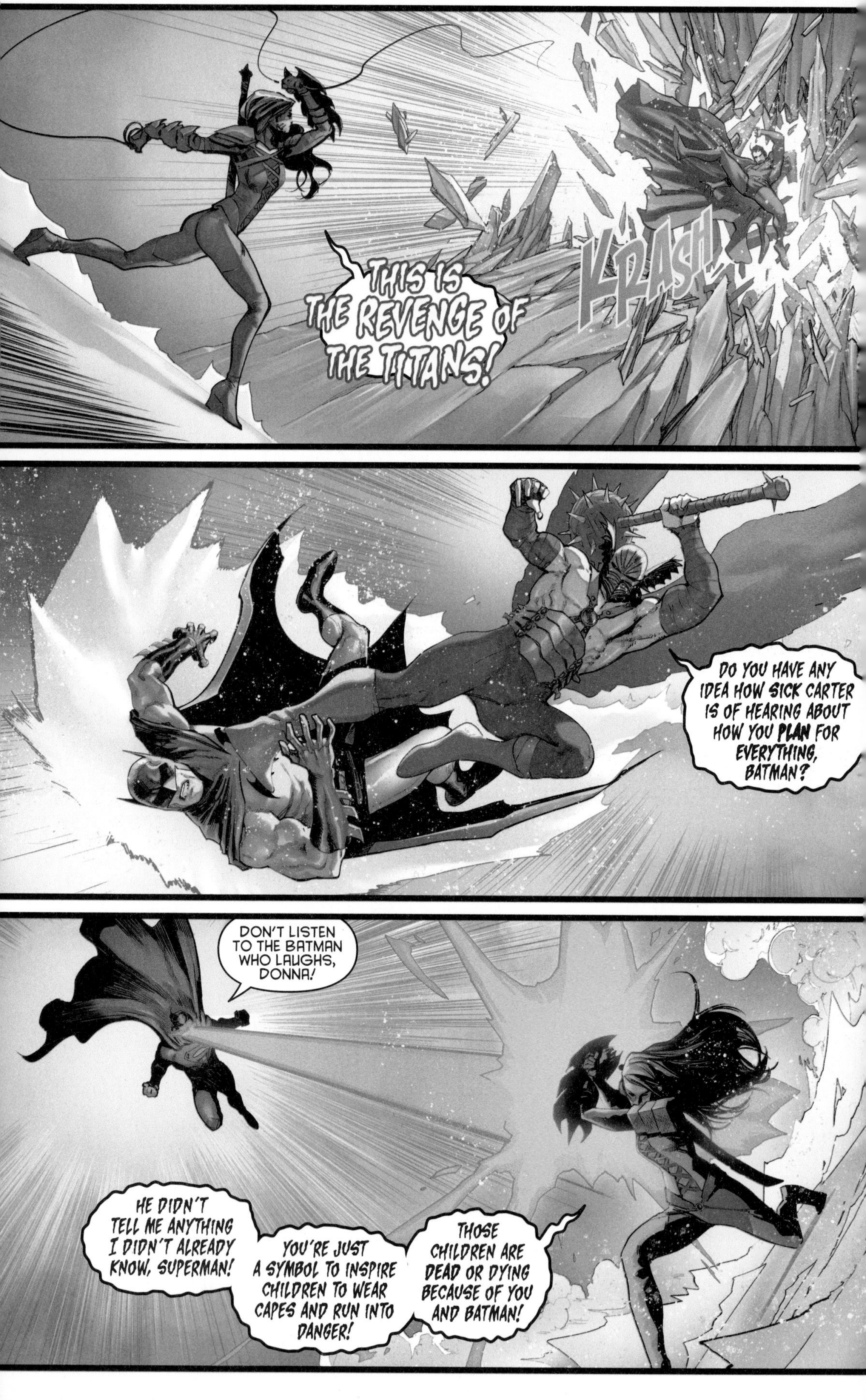
THIS IS THE REVENGE OF THE TITANS!
KRASH!
DO YOU HAVE ANY IDEA HOW SICK CARTER IS OF HEARING ABOUT HOW YOU PLAN FOR EVERYTHING, BATMAN?
DON'T LISTEN TO THE BATMAN WHO LAUGHS, DONNA!
HE DIDN'T TELL ME ANYTHING I DIDN'T ALREADY KNOW, SUPERMAN!
YOU'RE JUST A SYMBOL TO INSPIRE CHILDREN TO WEAR CAPES AND RUN INTO DANGER!
THOSE CHILDREN ARE DEAD OR DYING BECAUSE OF YOU AND BATMAN!

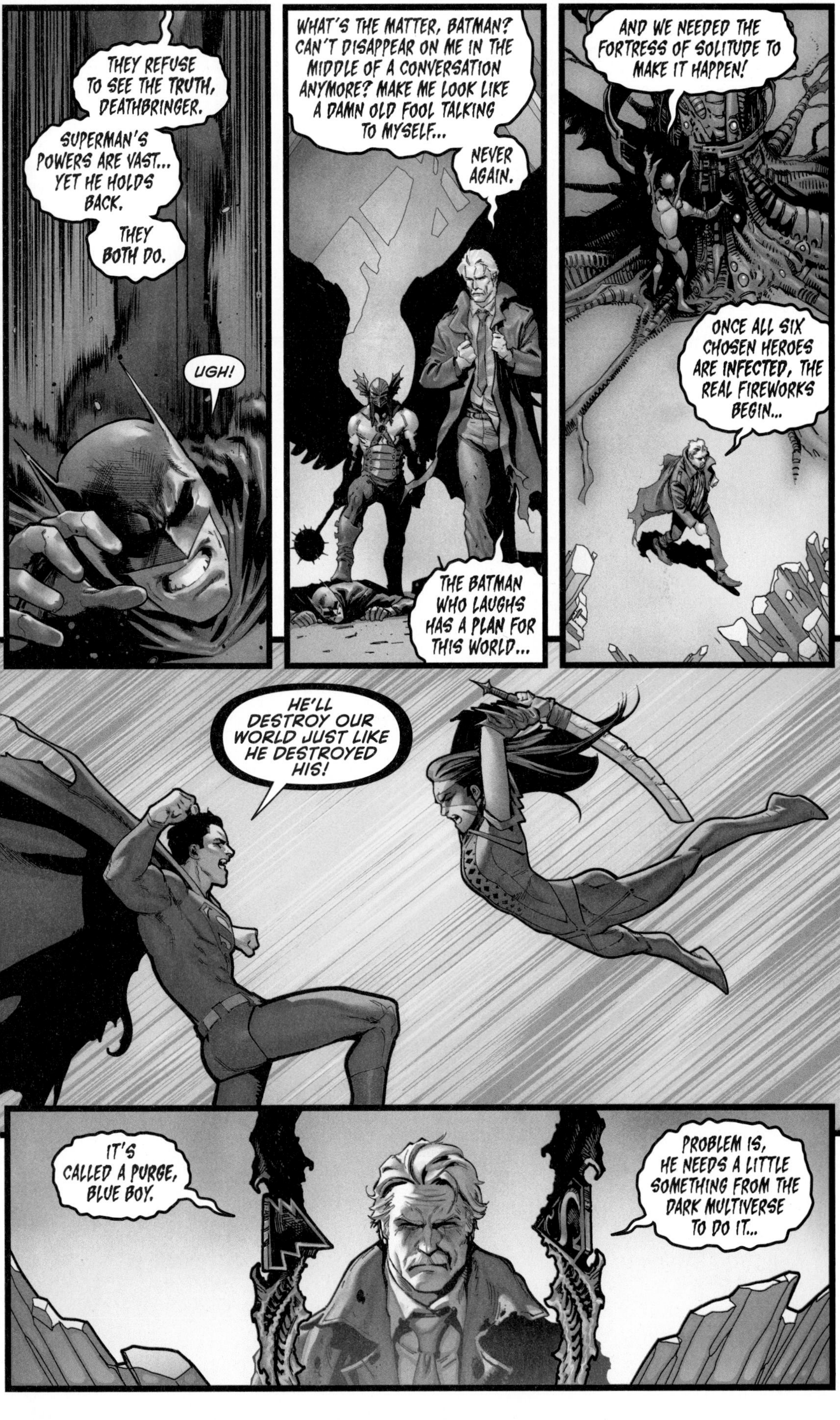
THEY REFUSE TO SEE THE TRUTH, DEATHBRINGER.
SUPERMAN'S POWERS ARE VAST... YET HE HOLDS BACK.
THEY BOTH DO.
UGH!
WHAT'S THE MATTER, BATMAN? CAN'T DISAPPEAR ON ME IN THE MIDDLE OF A CONVERSATION ANYMORE? MAKE ME LOOK LIKE A DAMN OLD FOOL TALKING TO MYSELF...
NEVER AGAIN.
THE BATMAN WHO LAUGHS HAS A PLAN FOR THIS WORLD...
AND WE NEEDED THE FORTRESS OF SOLITUDE TO MAKE IT HAPPEN!
ONCE ALL SIX CHOSEN HEROES ARE INFECTED, THE REAL FIREWORKS BEGIN...
HE'LL DESTROY OUR WORLD JUST LIKE HE DESTROYED HIS!
IT'S CALLED A PURGE, BLUE BOY.
PROBLEM IS, HE NEEDS A LITTLE SOMETHING FROM THE DARK MULTIVERSE TO DO IT...

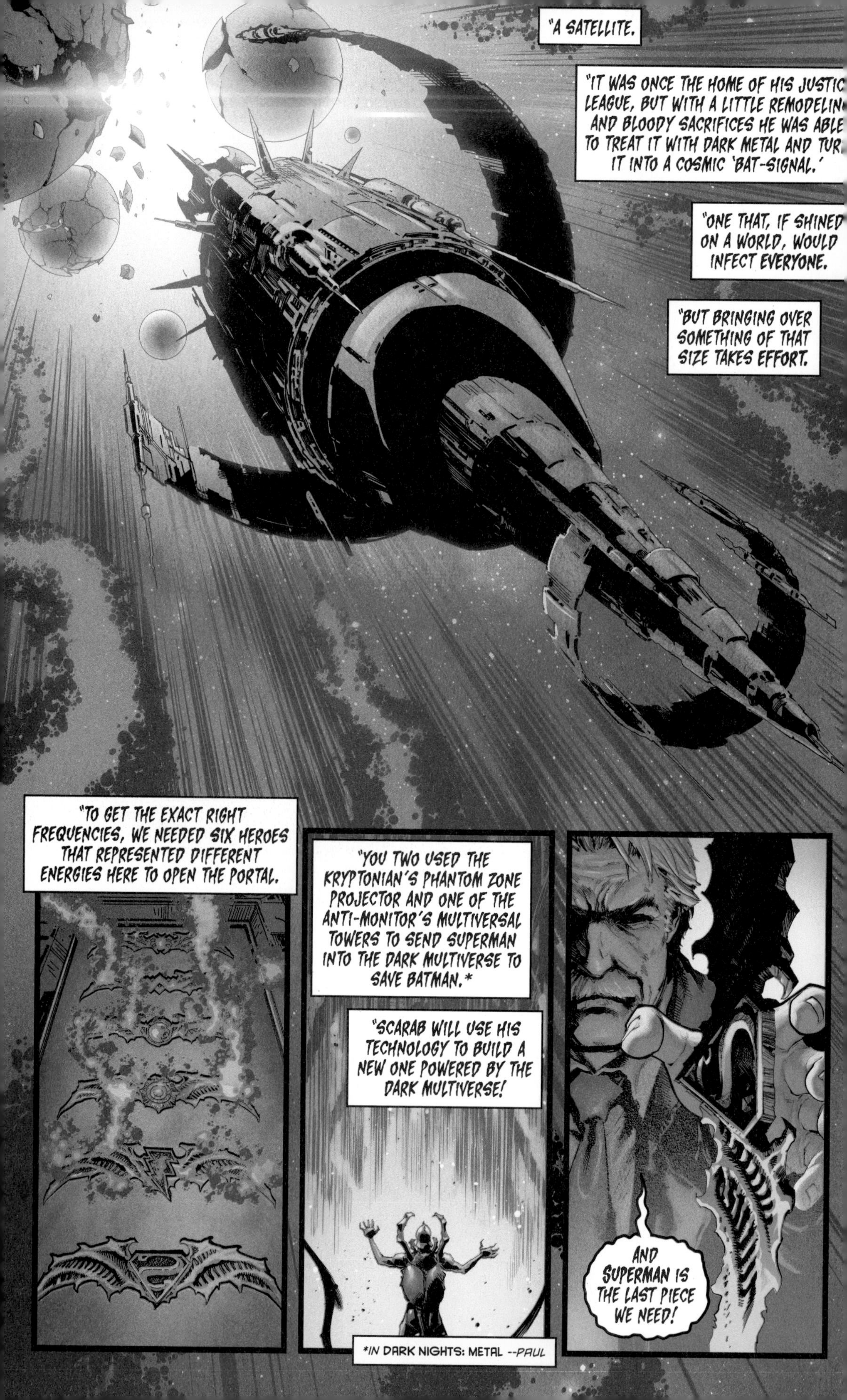
"A SATELLITE.
"IT WAS ONCE THE HOME OF HIS JUSTIC LEAGUE, BUT WITH A LITTLE REMODELIN AND BLOODY SACRIFICES HE WAS ABLE TO TREAT IT WITH DARK METAL AND TUR IT INTO A COSMIC 'BAT-SIGNAL.'
"ONE THAT, IF SHINED ON A WORLD, WOULD INFECT EVERYONE.
"BUT BRINGING OVER SOMETHING OF THAT SIZE TAKES EFFORT.
"TO GET THE EXACT RIGHT FREQUENCIES, WE NEEDED SIX HEROES THAT REPRESENTED DIFFERENT ENERGIES HERE TO OPEN THE PORTAL.
"YOU TWO USED THE KRYPTONIAN'S PHANTOM ZONE PROJECTOR AND ONE OF THE ANTI-MONITOR'S MULTIVERSAL TOWERS TO SEND SUPERMAN INTO THE DARK MULTIVERSE TO SAVE BATMAN.*
"SCARAB WILL USE HIS TECHNOLOGY TO BUILD A NEW ONE POWERED BY THE DARK MULTIVERSE!
AND SUPERMAN IS THE LAST PIECE WE NEED!
*IN DARK NIGHTS: METAL --PAUL

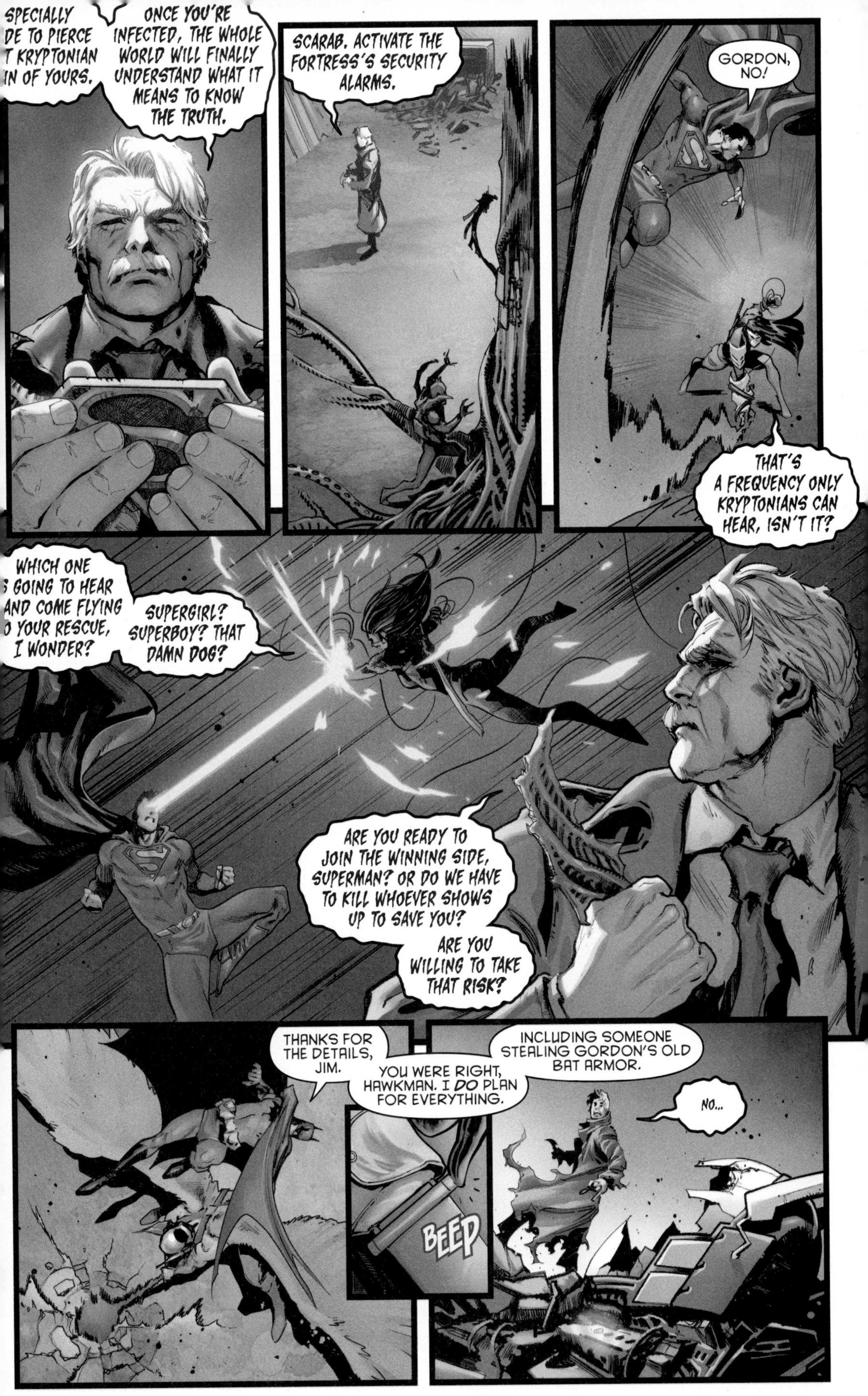
SPECIALLY
DE TO PIERCE
T KRYPTONIAN
IN OF YOURS.
ONCE YOU'RE INFECTED, THE WHOLE WORLD WILL FINALLY UNDERSTAND WHAT IT MEANS TO KNOW THE TRUTH.
SCARAB. ACTIVATE THE FORTRESS'S SECURITY ALARMS.
GORDON, NO!
THAT'S A FREQUENCY ONLY KRYPTONIANS CAN HEAR, ISN'T IT?
WHICH ONE
S GOING TO HEAR
AND COME FLYING
O YOUR RESCUE,
I WONDER?
SUPERGIRL? SUPERBOY? THAT DAMN DOG?
ARE YOU READY TO JOIN THE WINNING SIDE, SUPERMAN? OR DO WE HAVE TO KILL WHOEVER SHOWS UP TO SAVE YOU?
ARE YOU WILLING TO TAKE THAT RISK?
THANKS FOR THE DETAILS, JIM.
YOU WERE RIGHT, HAWKMAN. I *DO* PLAN FOR EVERYTHING.
INCLUDING SOMEONE STEALING GORDON'S OLD BAT ARMOR.
BEEP
NO...

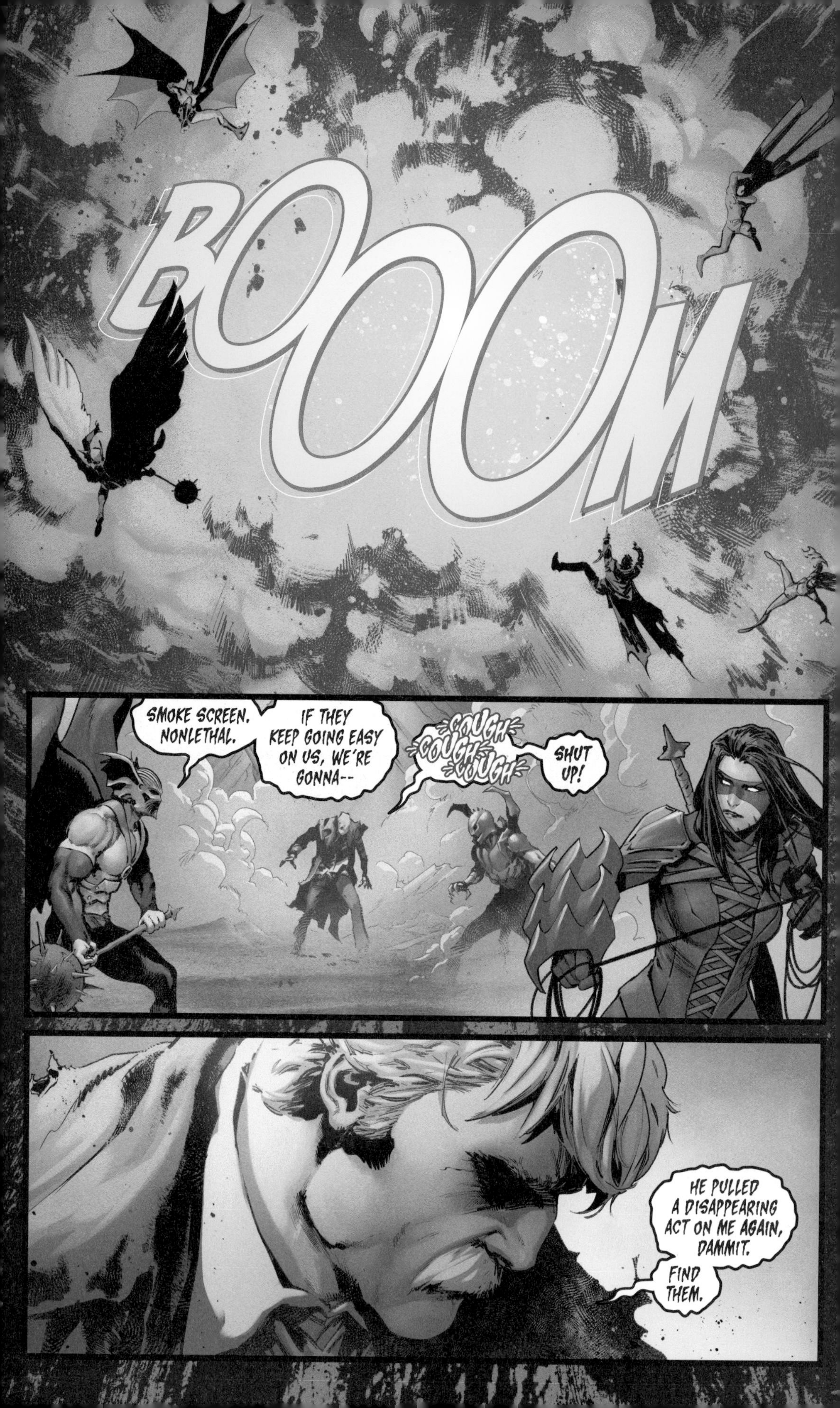
BOOOM
SMOKE SCREEN. NONLETHAL.
IF THEY KEEP GOING EASY ON US, WE'RE GONNA--
COUGH COUGH COUGH
SHUT UP!
HE PULLED A DISAPPEARING ACT ON ME AGAIN, DAMMIT.
FIND THEM.

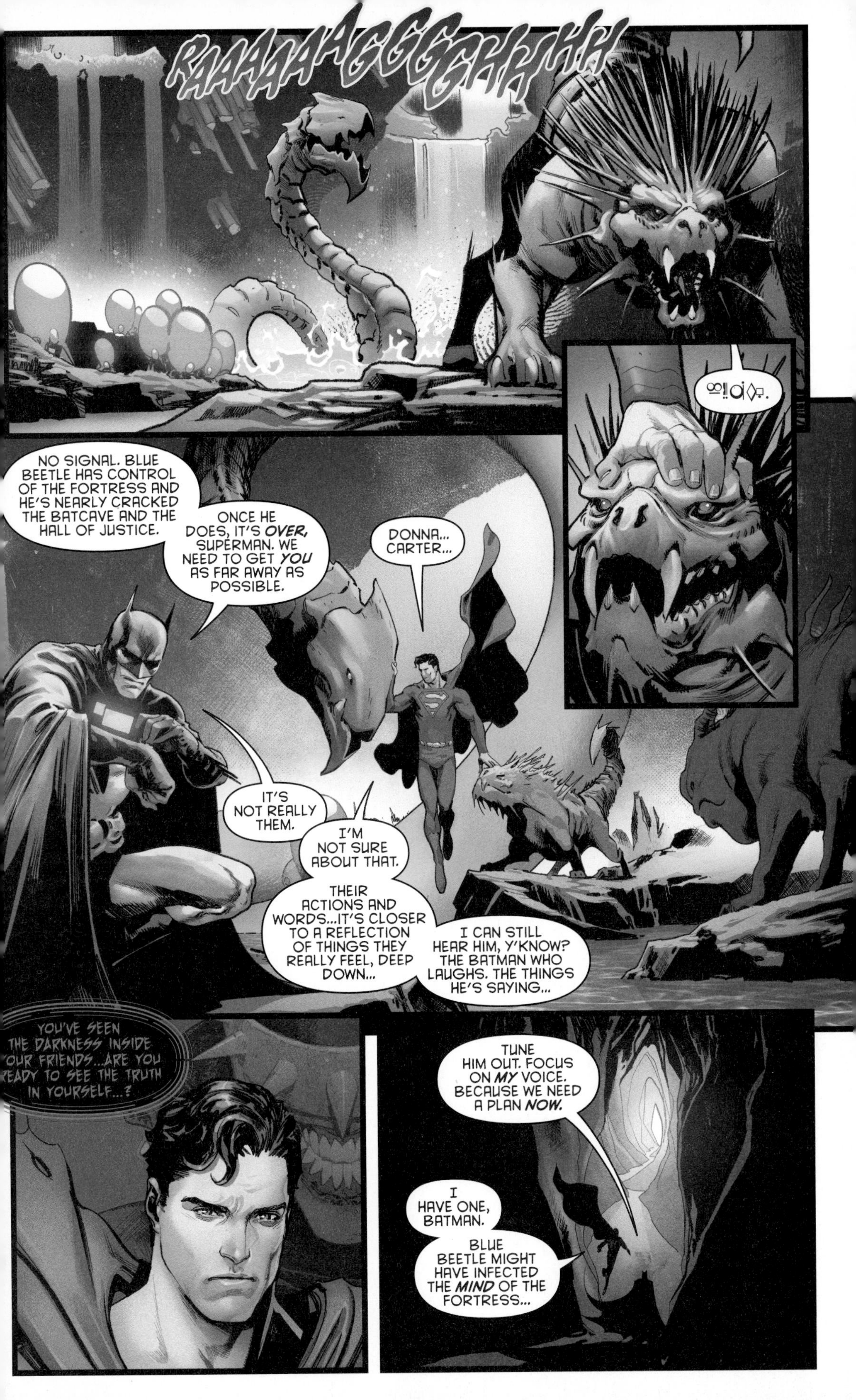
RAAAAAAGGGGHHHH
NO SIGNAL. BLUE BEETLE HAS CONTROL OF THE FORTRESS AND HE'S NEARLY CRACKED THE BATCAVE AND THE HALL OF JUSTICE.
ONCE HE DOES, IT'S *OVER,* SUPERMAN. WE NEED TO GET *YOU* AS FAR AWAY AS POSSIBLE.
DONNA... CARTER...
IT'S NOT REALLY THEM.
I'M NOT SURE ABOUT THAT.
THEIR ACTIONS AND WORDS...IT'S CLOSER TO A REFLECTION OF THINGS THEY REALLY FEEL, DEEP DOWN...
I CAN STILL HEAR HIM, Y'KNOW? THE BATMAN WHO LAUGHS. THE THINGS HE'S SAYING...
YOU'VE SEEN THE DARKNESS INSIDE YOUR FRIENDS...ARE YOU READY TO SEE THE TRUTH IN YOURSELF...?
TUNE HIM OUT. FOCUS ON *MY* VOICE. BECAUSE WE NEED A PLAN *NOW.*
I HAVE ONE, BATMAN.
BLUE BEETLE MIGHT HAVE INFECTED THE *MIND* OF THE FORTRESS...

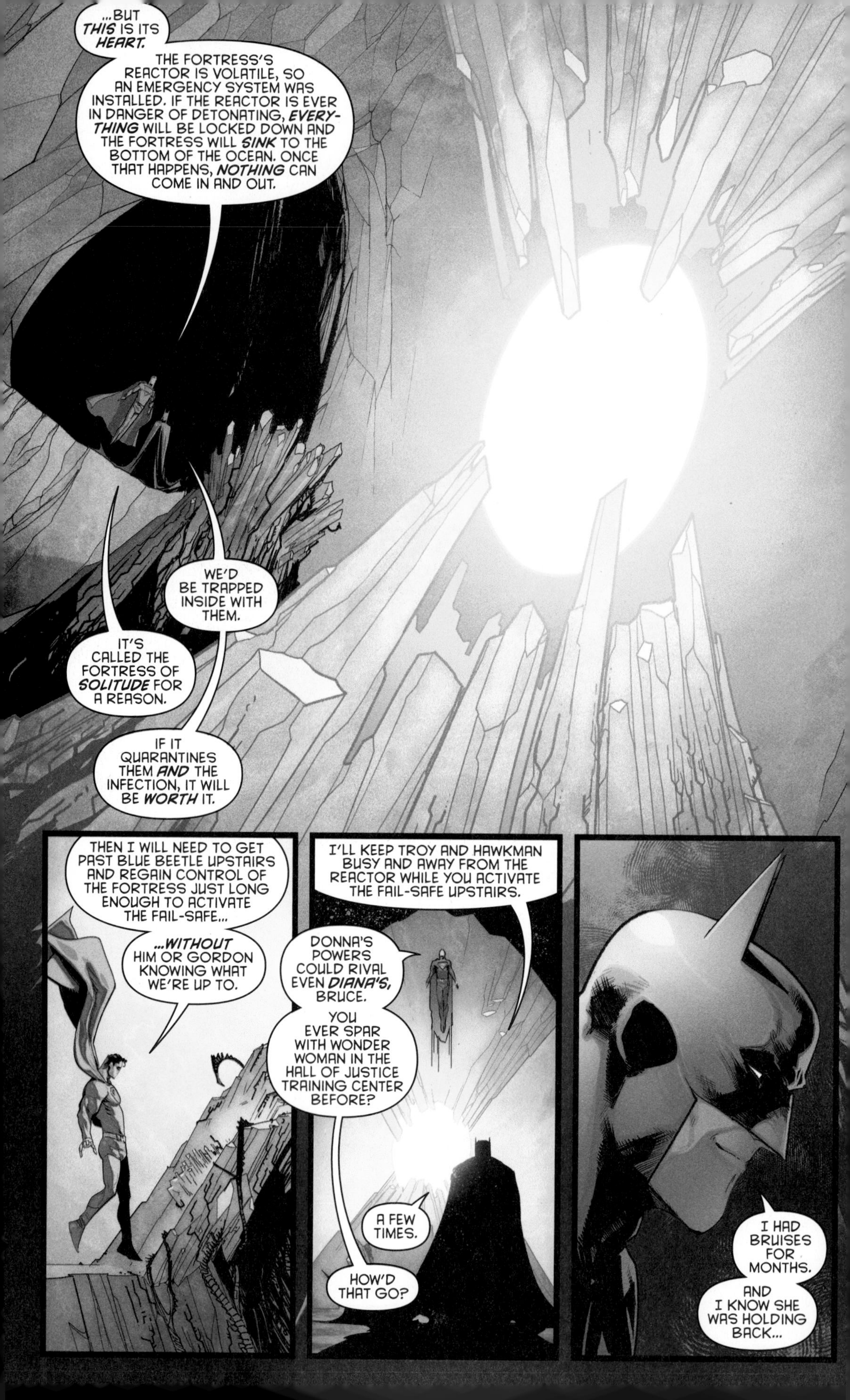
...BUT *THIS* IS ITS *HEART.*
THE FORTRESS'S REACTOR IS VOLATILE, SO AN EMERGENCY SYSTEM WAS INSTALLED. IF THE REACTOR IS EVER IN DANGER OF DETONATING, *EVERY-THING* WILL BE LOCKED DOWN AND THE FORTRESS WILL *SINK* TO THE BOTTOM OF THE OCEAN. ONCE THAT HAPPENS, *NOTHING* CAN COME IN AND OUT.
WE'D BE TRAPPED INSIDE WITH THEM.
IT'S CALLED THE FORTRESS OF *SOLITUDE* FOR A REASON.
IF IT QUARANTINES THEM *AND* THE INFECTION, IT WILL BE *WORTH* IT.
THEN I WILL NEED TO GET PAST BLUE BEETLE UPSTAIRS AND REGAIN CONTROL OF THE FORTRESS JUST LONG ENOUGH TO ACTIVATE THE FAIL-SAFE...
...WITHOUT HIM OR GORDON KNOWING WHAT WE'RE UP TO.
I'LL KEEP TROY AND HAWKMAN BUSY AND AWAY FROM THE REACTOR WHILE YOU ACTIVATE THE FAIL-SAFE UPSTAIRS.
DONNA'S POWERS COULD RIVAL EVEN *DIANA'S,* BRUCE.
YOU EVER SPAR WITH WONDER WOMAN IN THE HALL OF JUSTICE TRAINING CENTER BEFORE?
A FEW TIMES.
HOW'D THAT GO?
I HAD BRUISES FOR MONTHS.
AND I KNOW SHE WAS HOLDING BACK...

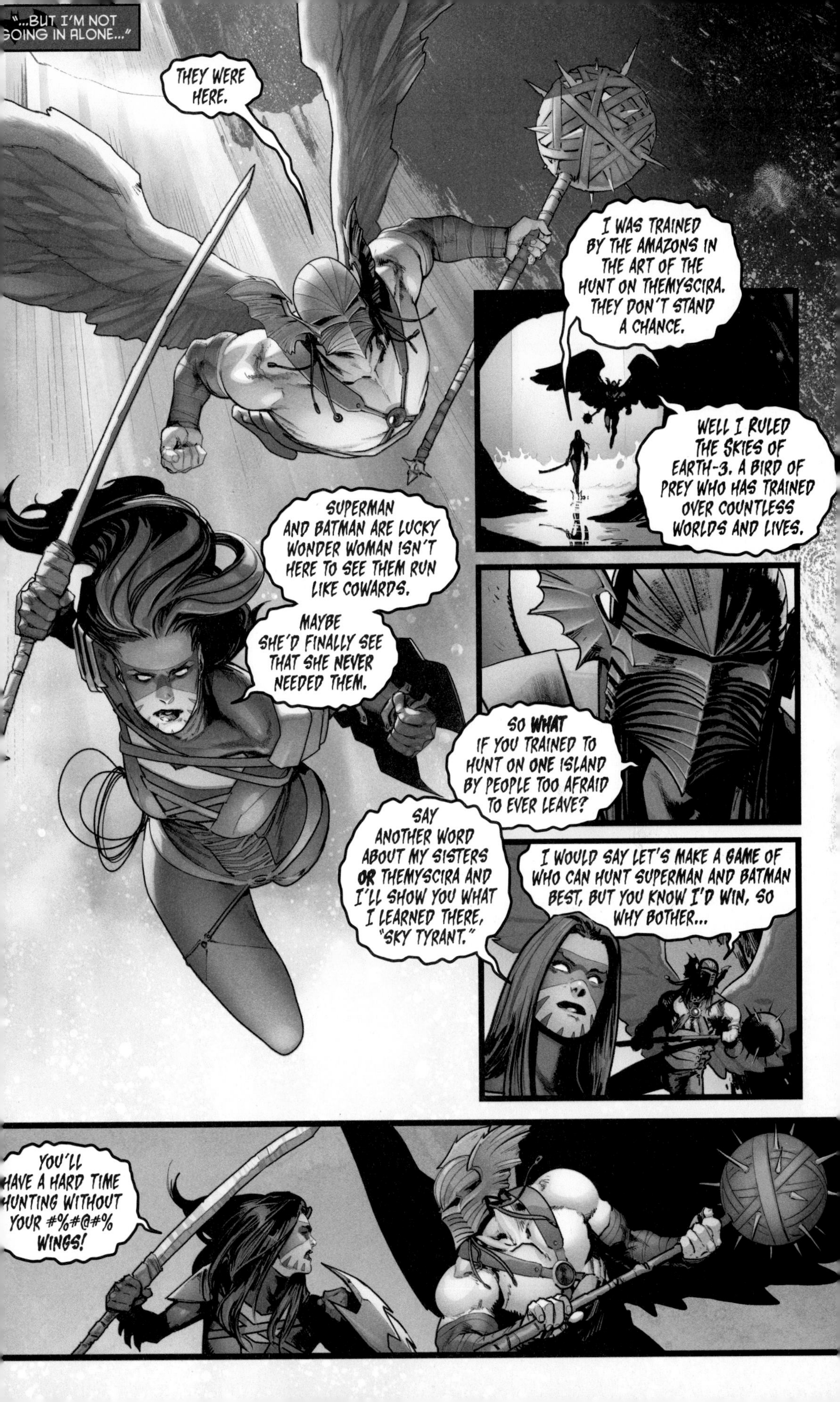
"...BUT I'M NOT GOING IN ALONE..."
THEY WERE HERE.
I WAS TRAINED BY THE AMAZONS IN THE ART OF THE HUNT ON THEMYSCIRA. THEY DON'T STAND A CHANCE.
WELL I RULED THE SKIES OF EARTH-3. A BIRD OF PREY WHO HAS TRAINED OVER COUNTLESS WORLDS AND LIVES.
SUPERMAN AND BATMAN ARE LUCKY WONDER WOMAN ISN'T HERE TO SEE THEM RUN LIKE COWARDS.
MAYBE SHE'D FINALLY SEE THAT SHE NEVER NEEDED THEM.
SO WHAT IF YOU TRAINED TO HUNT ON ONE ISLAND BY PEOPLE TOO AFRAID TO EVER LEAVE?
SAY ANOTHER WORD ABOUT MY SISTERS OR THEMYSCIRA AND I'LL SHOW YOU WHAT I LEARNED THERE, "SKY TYRANT."
I WOULD SAY LET'S MAKE A GAME OF WHO CAN HUNT SUPERMAN AND BATMAN BEST, BUT YOU KNOW I'D WIN, SO WHY BOTHER...
YOU'LL HAVE A HARD TIME HUNTING WITHOUT YOUR #%#@#% WINGS!

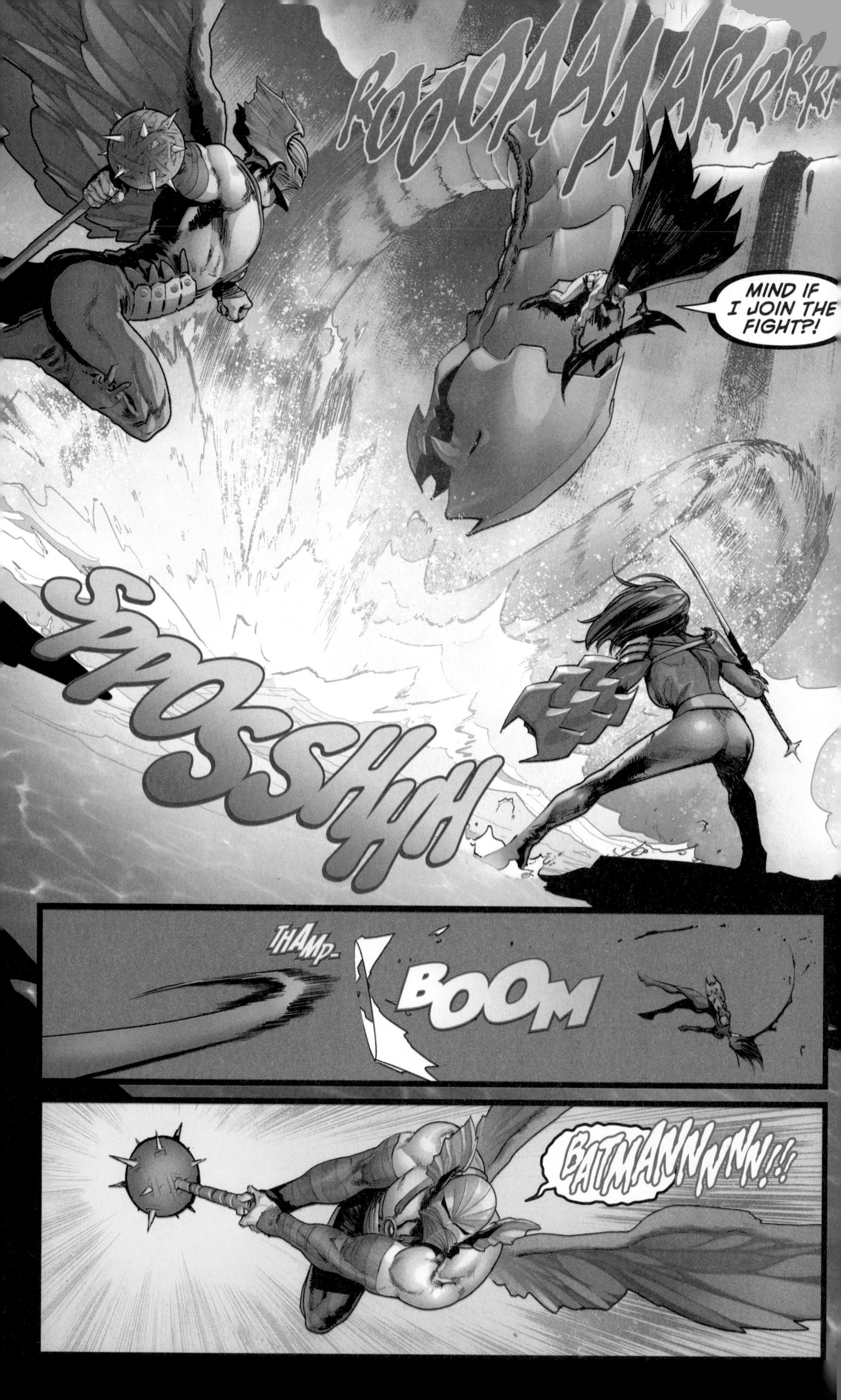
ROOOAAAAARRRR
MIND IF I JOIN THE FIGHT?!
SPPOSSHHH
THAMP-
BOOM
BATMANNNNN!!

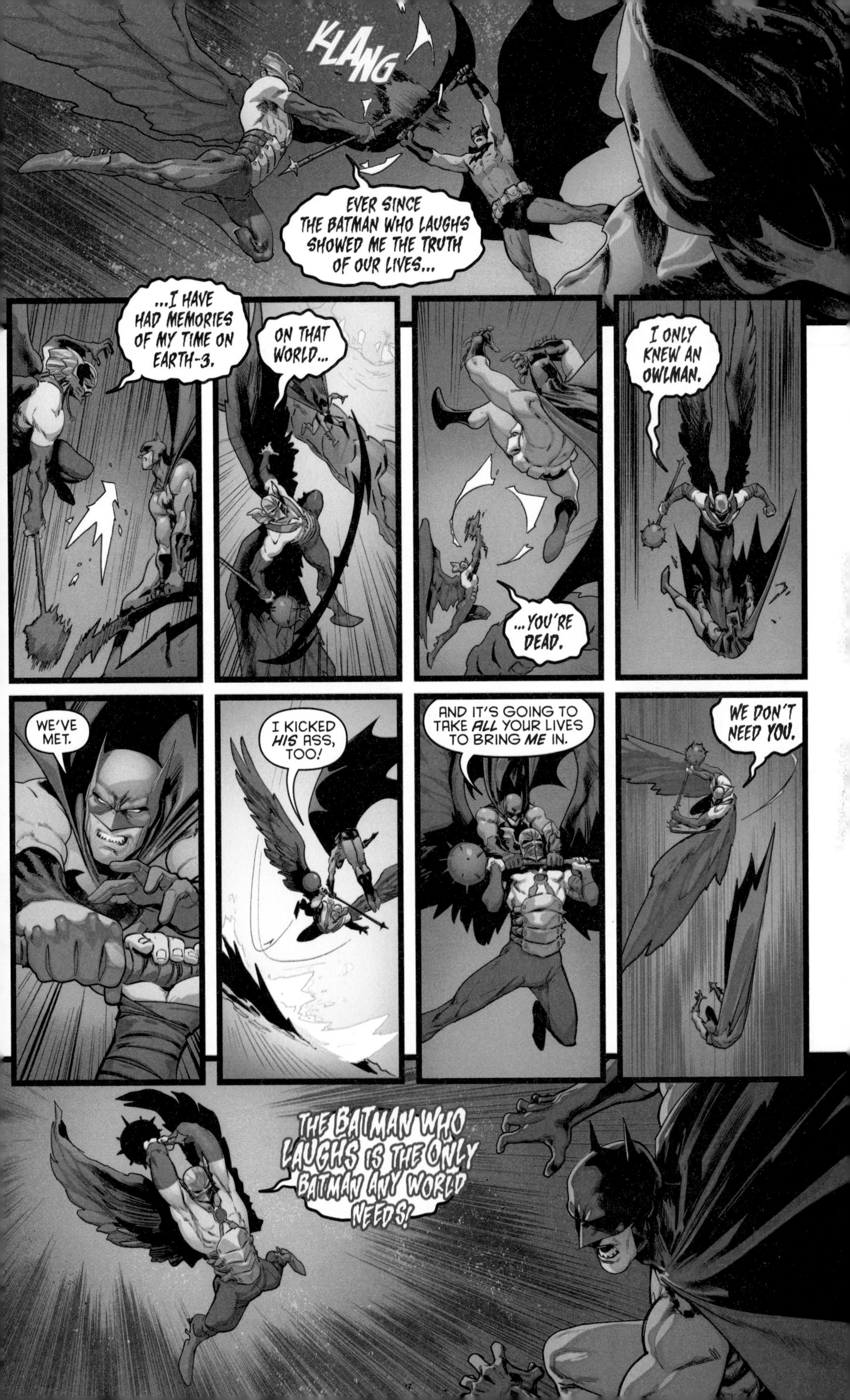
KLANG
EVER SINCE THE BATMAN WHO LAUGHS SHOWED ME THE TRUTH OF OUR LIVES...
...I HAVE HAD MEMORIES OF MY TIME ON EARTH-3.
ON THAT WORLD...
...YOU'RE DEAD.
I ONLY KNEW AN OWLMAN.
WE'VE MET.
I KICKED HIS ASS, TOO!
AND IT'S GOING TO TAKE ALL YOUR LIVES TO BRING ME IN.
WE DON'T NEED YOU.
THE BATMAN WHO LAUGHS IS THE ONLY BATMAN ANY WORLD NEEDS!

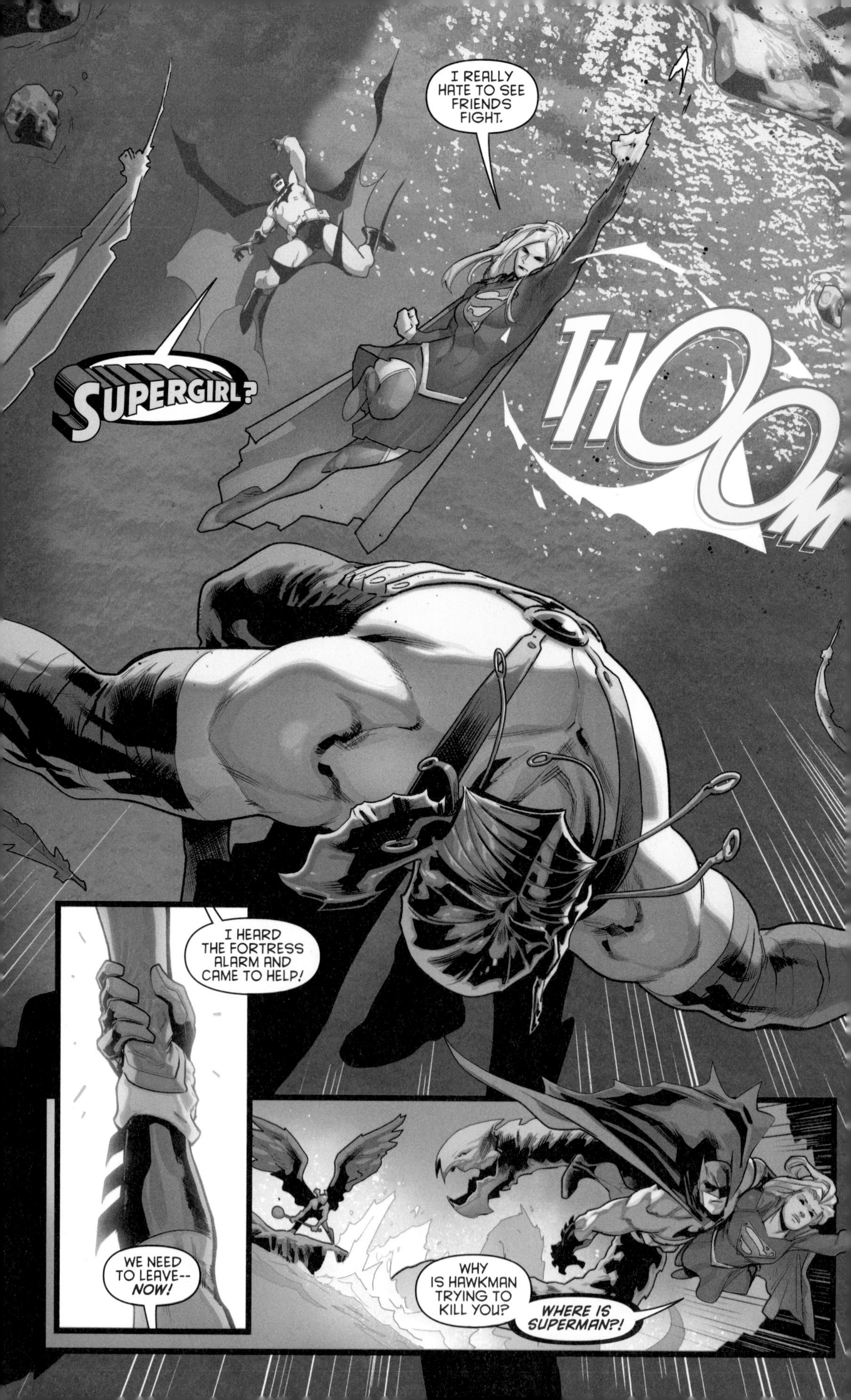
I REALLY HATE TO SEE FRIENDS FIGHT.
SUPERGIRL?
THOOOM
I HEARD THE FORTRESS ALARM AND CAME TO HELP!
WE NEED TO LEAVE-- *NOW!*
WHY IS HAWKMAN TRYING TO KILL YOU?
WHERE IS SUPERMAN?!

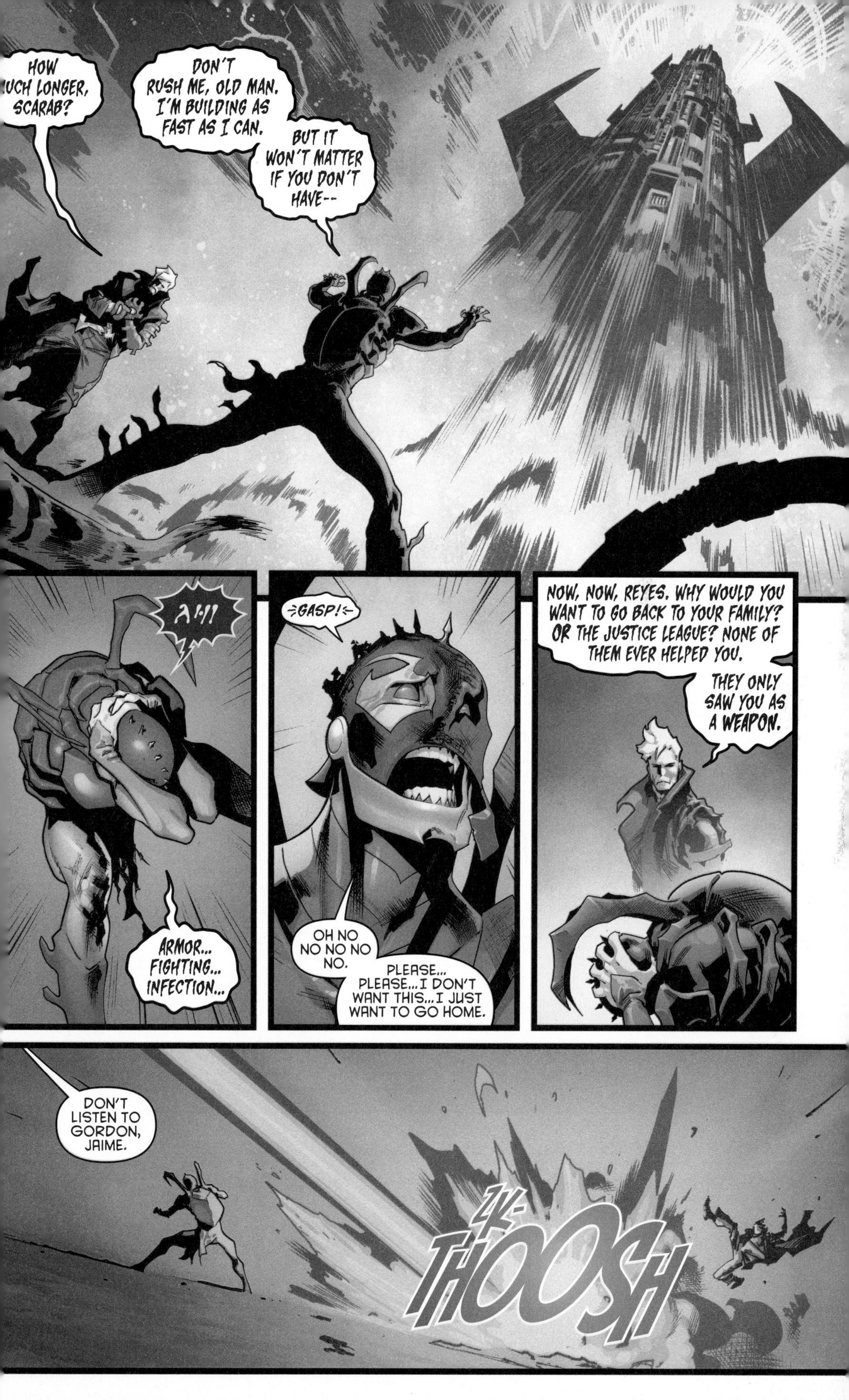

HOW UCH LONGER, SCARAB?
DON'T RUSH ME, OLD MAN. I'M BUILDING AS FAST AS I CAN.
BUT IT WON'T MATTER IF YOU DON'T HAVE--
ARMOR... FIGHTING... INFECTION...
GASP!
OH NO NO NO NO NO NO.
PLEASE... PLEASE...I DON'T WANT THIS...I JUST WANT TO GO HOME.
NOW, NOW, REYES. WHY WOULD YOU WANT TO GO BACK TO YOUR FAMILY? OR THE JUSTICE LEAGUE? NONE OF THEM EVER HELPED YOU.
THEY ONLY SAW YOU AS A WEAPON.
DON'T LISTEN TO GORDON, JAIME.
ZK-THOOSH

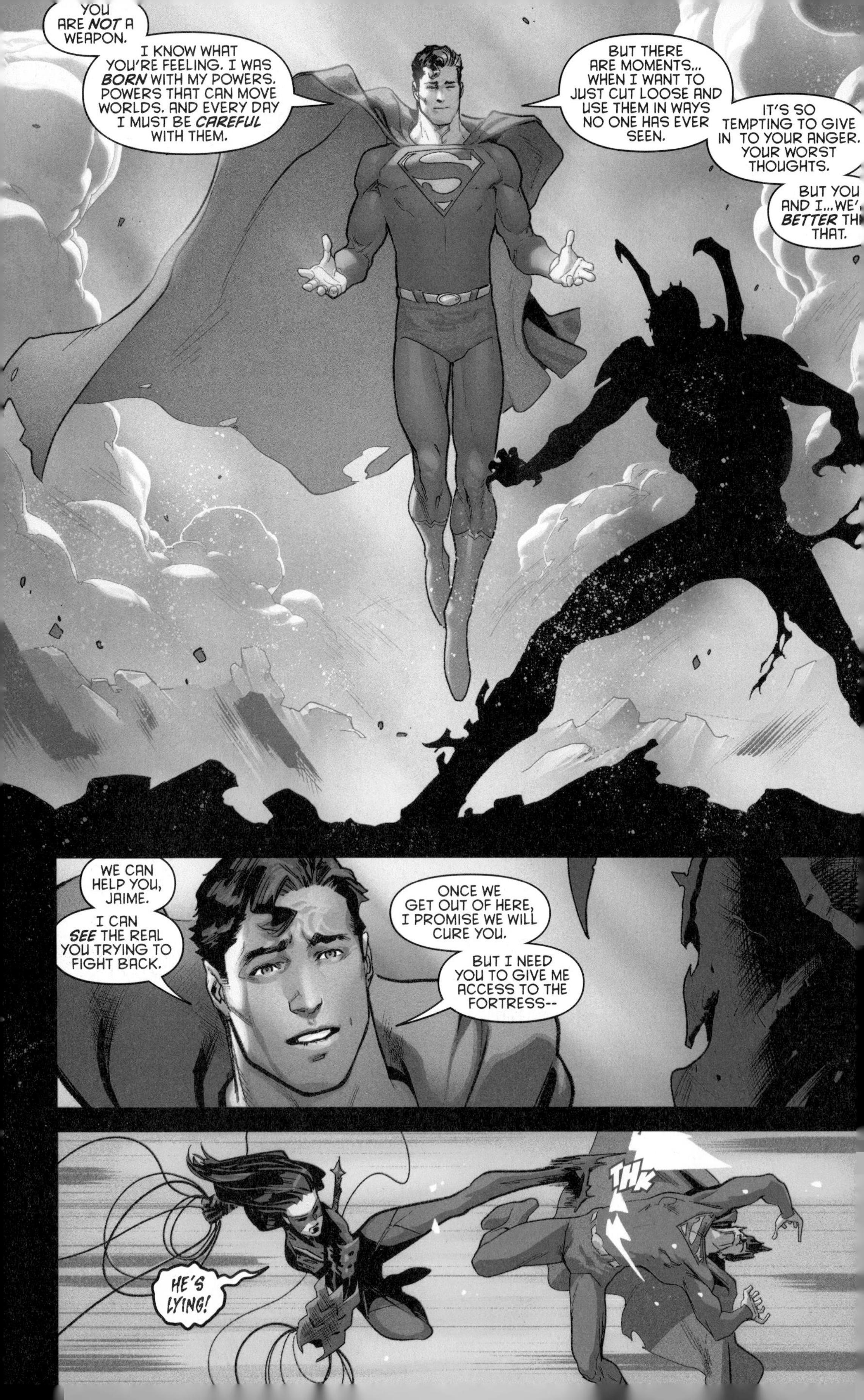

YOU ARE NOT A WEAPON.
I KNOW WHAT YOU'RE FEELING. I WAS BORN WITH MY POWERS. POWERS THAT CAN MOVE WORLDS. AND EVERY DAY I MUST BE CAREFUL WITH THEM.
BUT THERE ARE MOMENTS... WHEN I WANT TO JUST CUT LOOSE AND USE THEM IN WAYS NO ONE HAS EVER SEEN.
IT'S SO TEMPTING TO GIVE IN TO YOUR ANGER. YOUR WORST THOUGHTS.
WE CAN HELP YOU, JAIME.
I CAN SEE THE REAL YOU TRYING TO FIGHT BACK.
ONCE WE GET OUT OF HERE, I PROMISE WE WILL CURE YOU.
BUT I NEED YOU TO GIVE ME ACCESS TO THE FORTRESS--
HE'S LYING!
THK

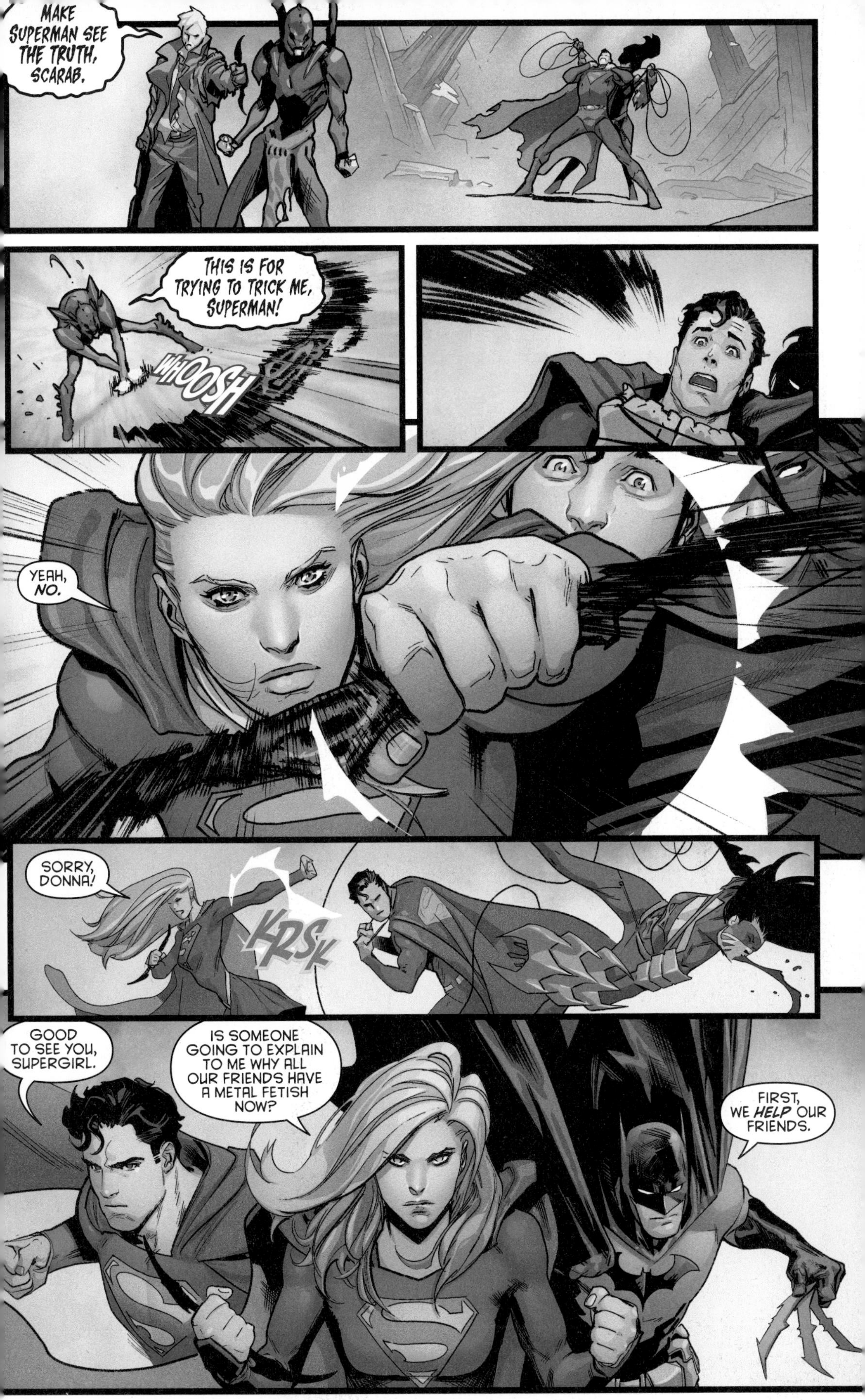
MAKE SUPERMAN SEE THE TRUTH, SCARAB.
THIS IS FOR TRYING TO TRICK ME, SUPERMAN!
WHOOSH
YEAH, NO.
SORRY, DONNA!
KRSK
GOOD TO SEE YOU, SUPERGIRL.
IS SOMEONE GOING TO EXPLAIN TO ME WHY ALL OUR FRIENDS HAVE A METAL FETISH NOW?
FIRST, WE HELP OUR FRIENDS.

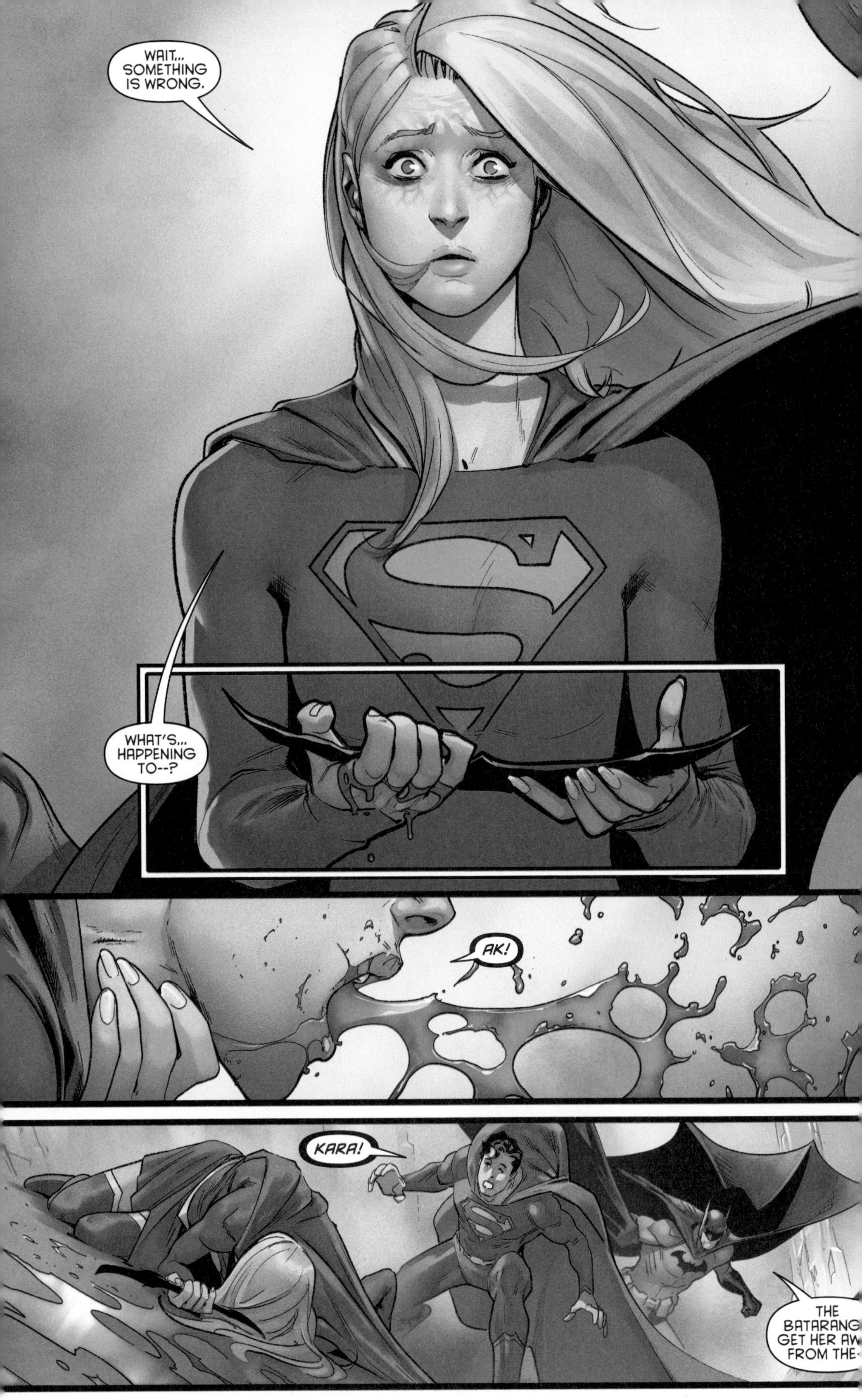
WAIT... SOMETHING IS WRONG.
WHAT'S... HAPPENING TO--?
AK!
KARA!
THE BATARANG GET HER AW FROM THE

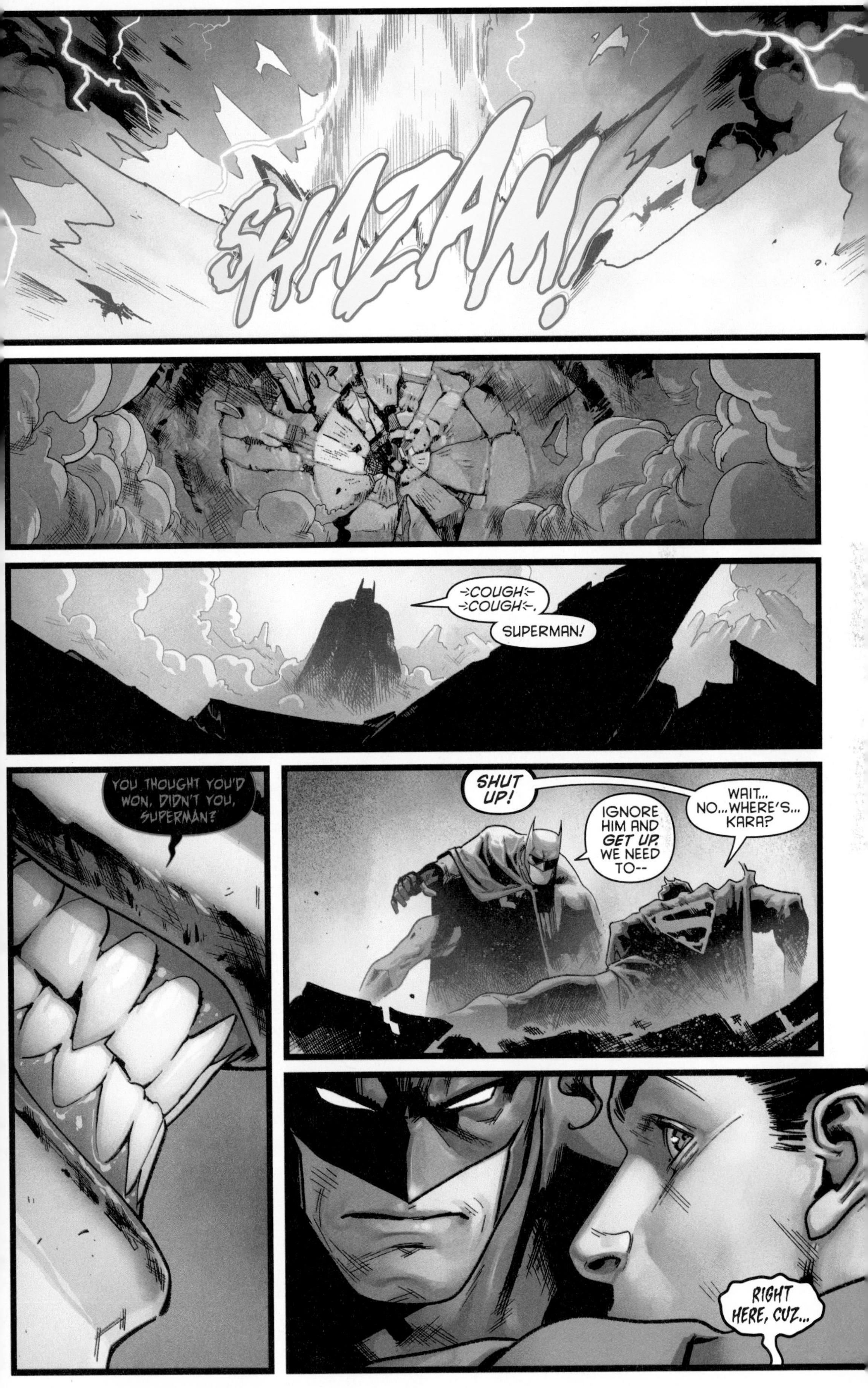
SHAZAM!
COUGH COUGH.
SUPERMAN!
YOU THOUGHT YOU'D WON, DIDN'T YOU, SUPERMAN?
SHUT UP!
IGNORE HIM AND GET UP. WE NEED TO--
WAIT... NO...WHERE'S... KARA?
RIGHT HERE, CUZ...

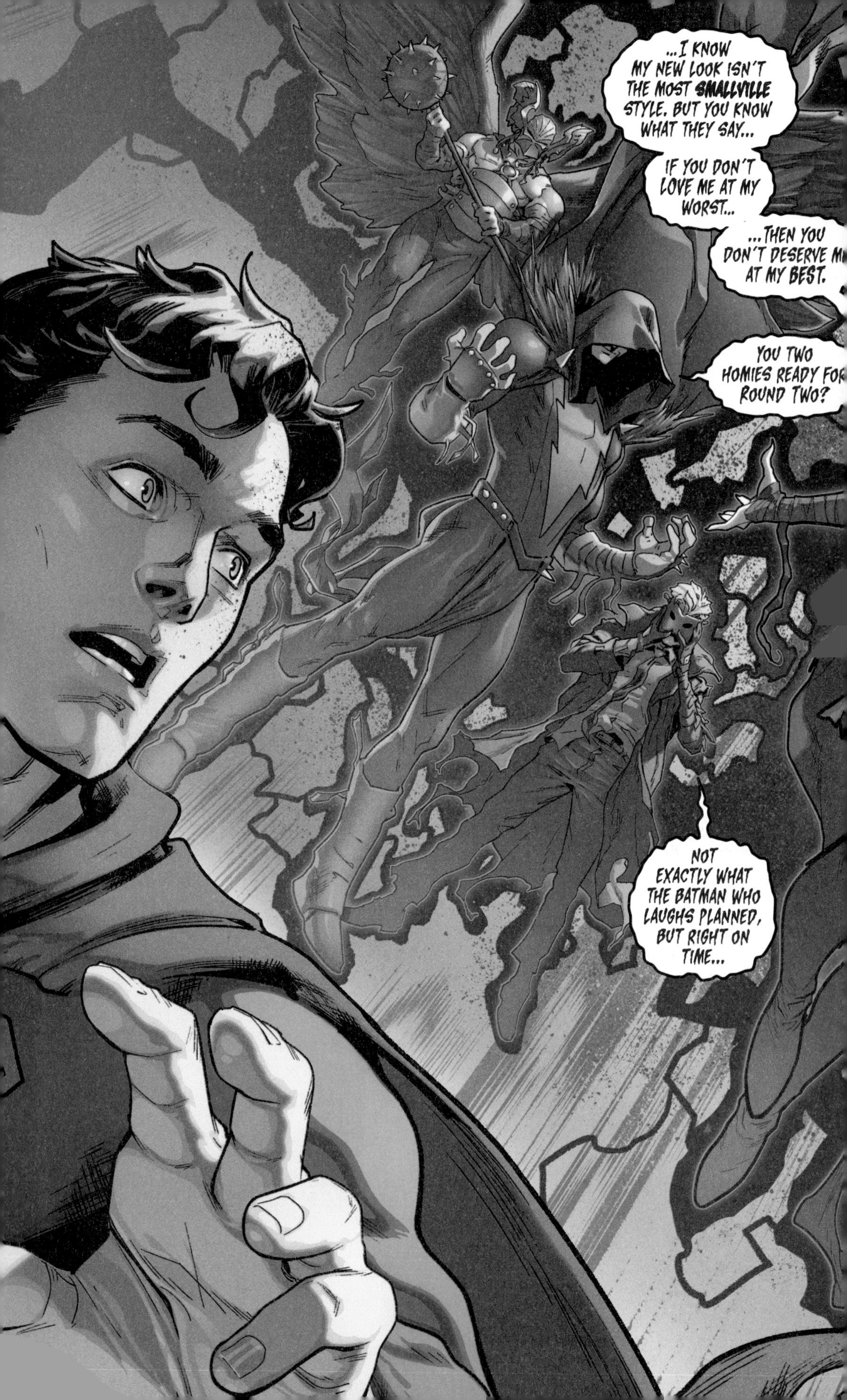

...I KNOW MY NEW LOOK ISN'T THE MOST SMALLVILLE STYLE. BUT YOU KNOW WHAT THEY SAY...
IF YOU DON'T LOVE ME AT MY WORST...
...THEN YOU DON'T DESERVE ME AT MY BEST.
YOU TWO HOMIES READY FOR ROUND TWO?
NOT EXACTLY WHAT THE BATMAN WHO LAUGHS PLANNED, BUT RIGHT ON TIME...

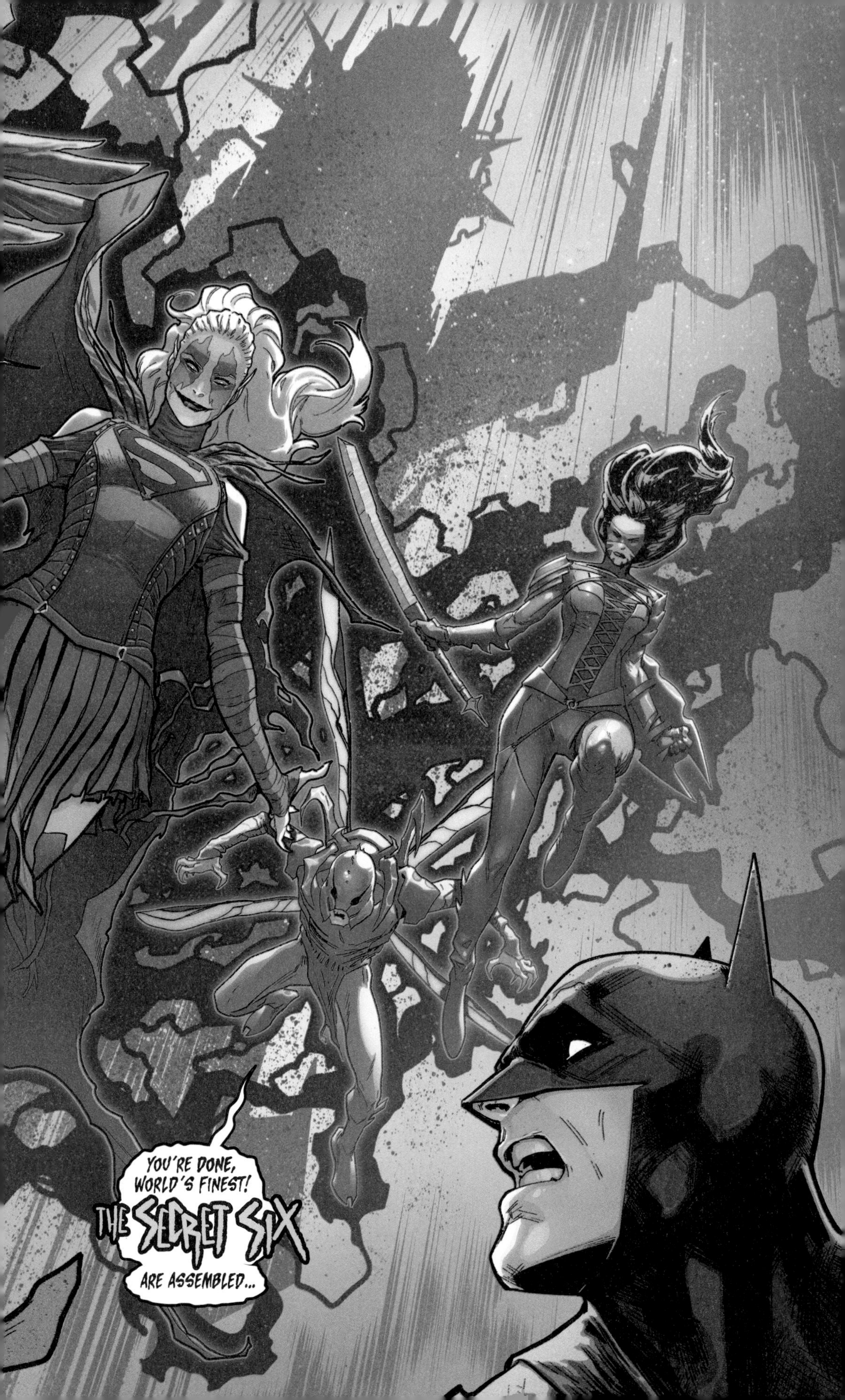
YOU'RE DONE, WORLD'S FINEST!
THE SECRET SIX
ARE ASSEMBLED...

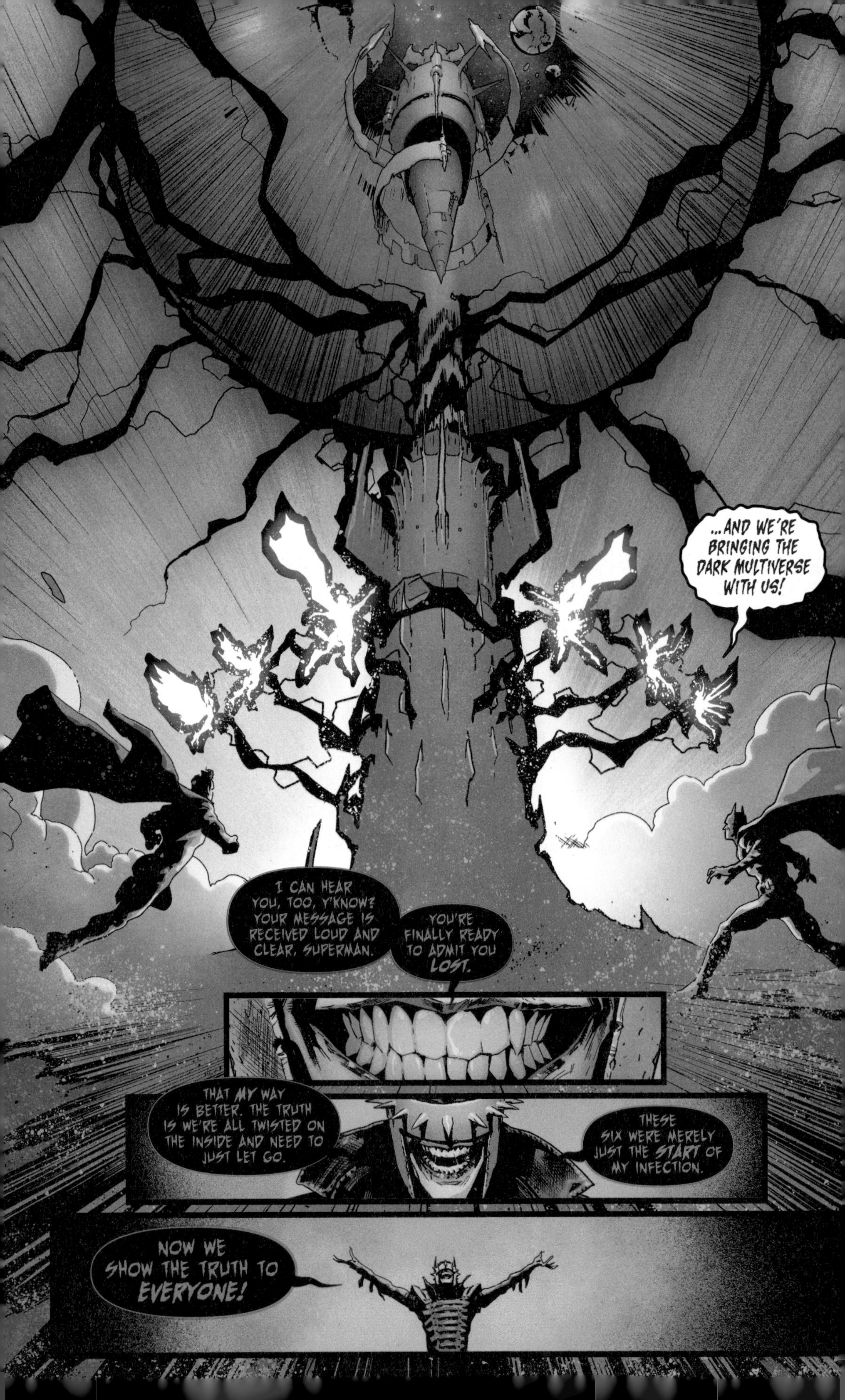
...AND WE'RE BRINGING THE DARK MULTIVERSE WITH US!
I CAN HEAR YOU, TOO, Y'KNOW? YOUR MESSAGE IS RECEIVED LOUD AND CLEAR, SUPERMAN.
YOU'RE FINALLY READY TO ADMIT YOU LOST.
THAT MY WAY IS BETTER. THE TRUTH IS WE'RE ALL TWISTED ON THE INSIDE AND NEED TO JUST LET GO.
THESE SIX WERE MERELY JUST THE START OF MY INFECTION.
NOW WE SHOW THE TRUTH TO EVERYONE!

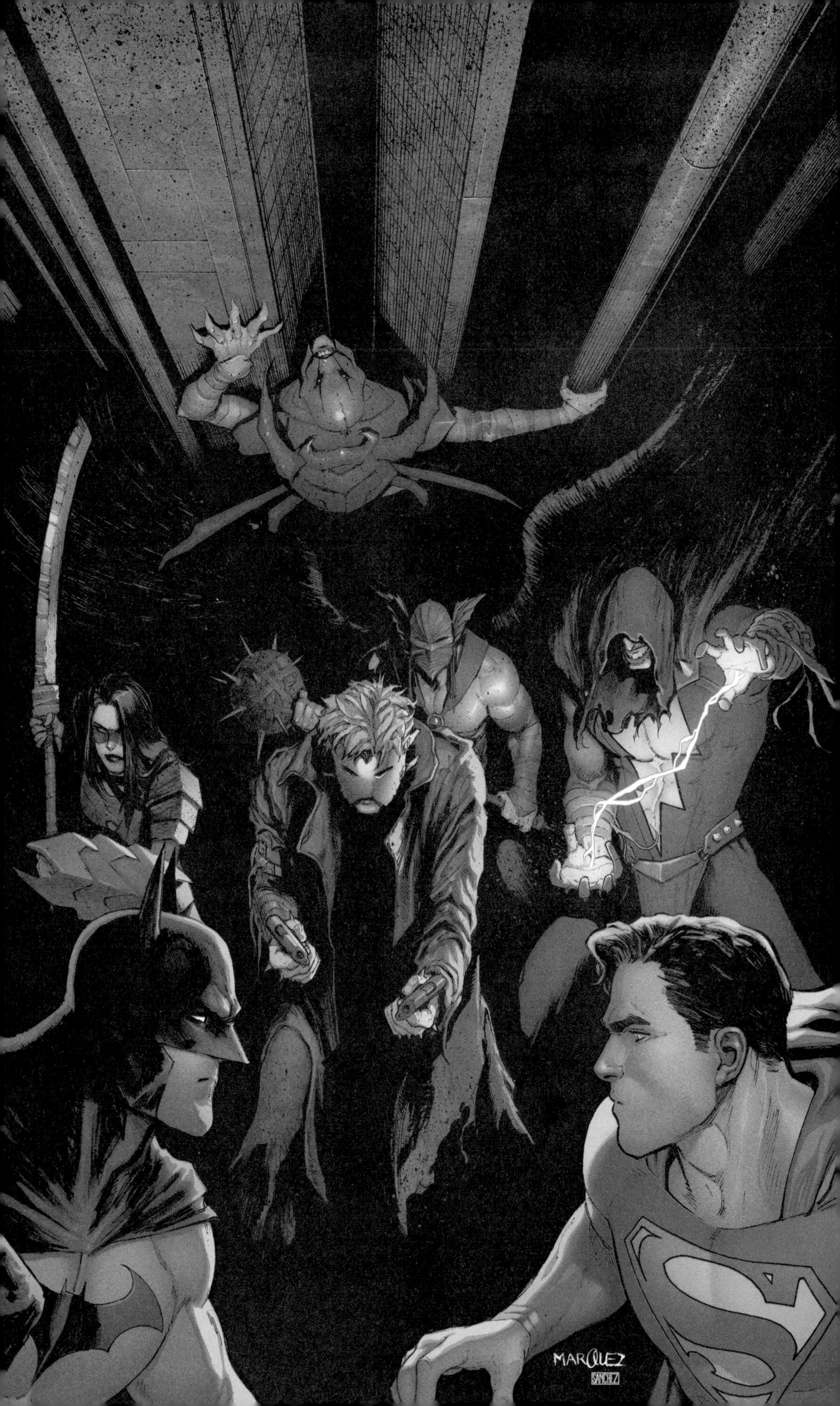
MARQUEZ
SANCHEZ

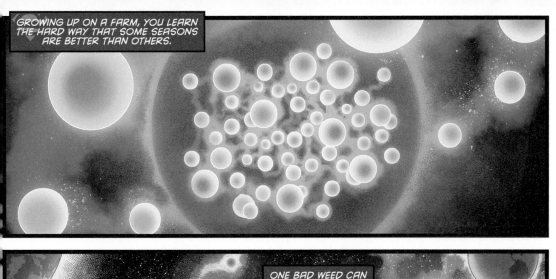

GROWING UP ON A FARM, YOU LEARN THE HARD WAY THAT SOME SEASONS ARE BETTER THAN OTHERS.

ONE BAD WEED CAN KILL A WHOLE CROP.

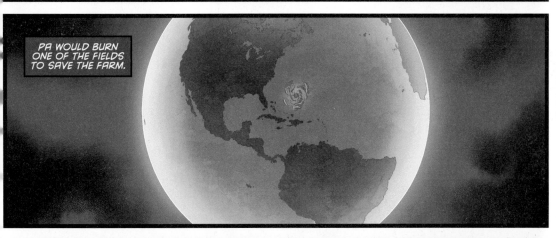

PA WOULD BURN ONE OF THE FIELDS TO SAVE THE FARM.

ON MY DARKEST DAYS, I WORRY OUR WORLD HAS BECOME A WEED THAT IS INFECTING THE ENTIRE MULTIVERSE...

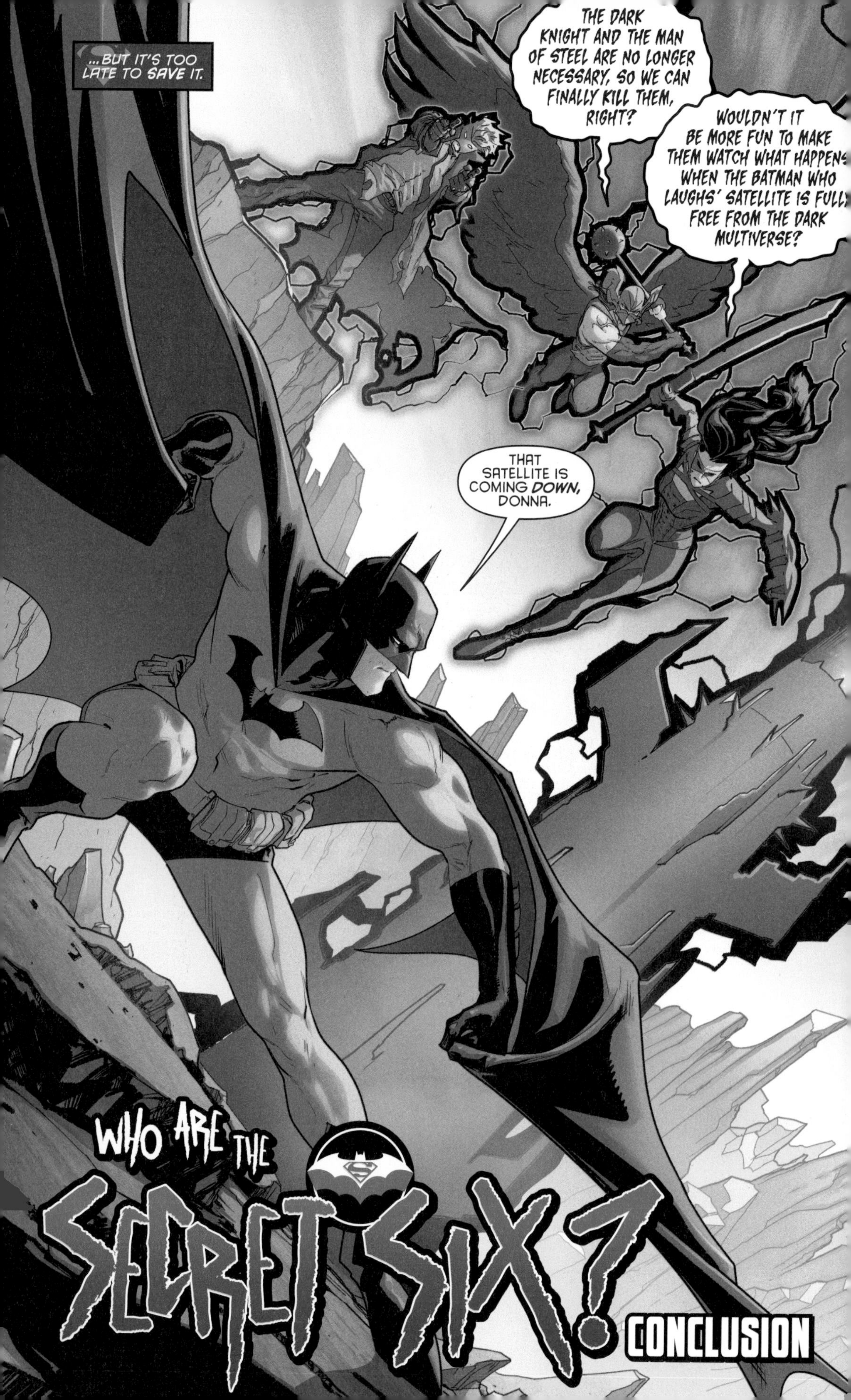
...BUT IT'S TOO LATE TO SAVE IT.
THE DARK KNIGHT AND THE MAN OF STEEL ARE NO LONGER NECESSARY, SO WE CAN FINALLY KILL THEM, RIGHT?
WOULDN'T IT BE MORE FUN TO MAKE THEM WATCH WHAT HAPPENS WHEN THE BATMAN WHO LAUGHS' SATELLITE IS FULLY FREE FROM THE DARK MULTIVERSE?
THAT SATELLITE IS COMING DOWN, DONNA.
WHO ARE THE SECRET SIX?
CONCLUSION

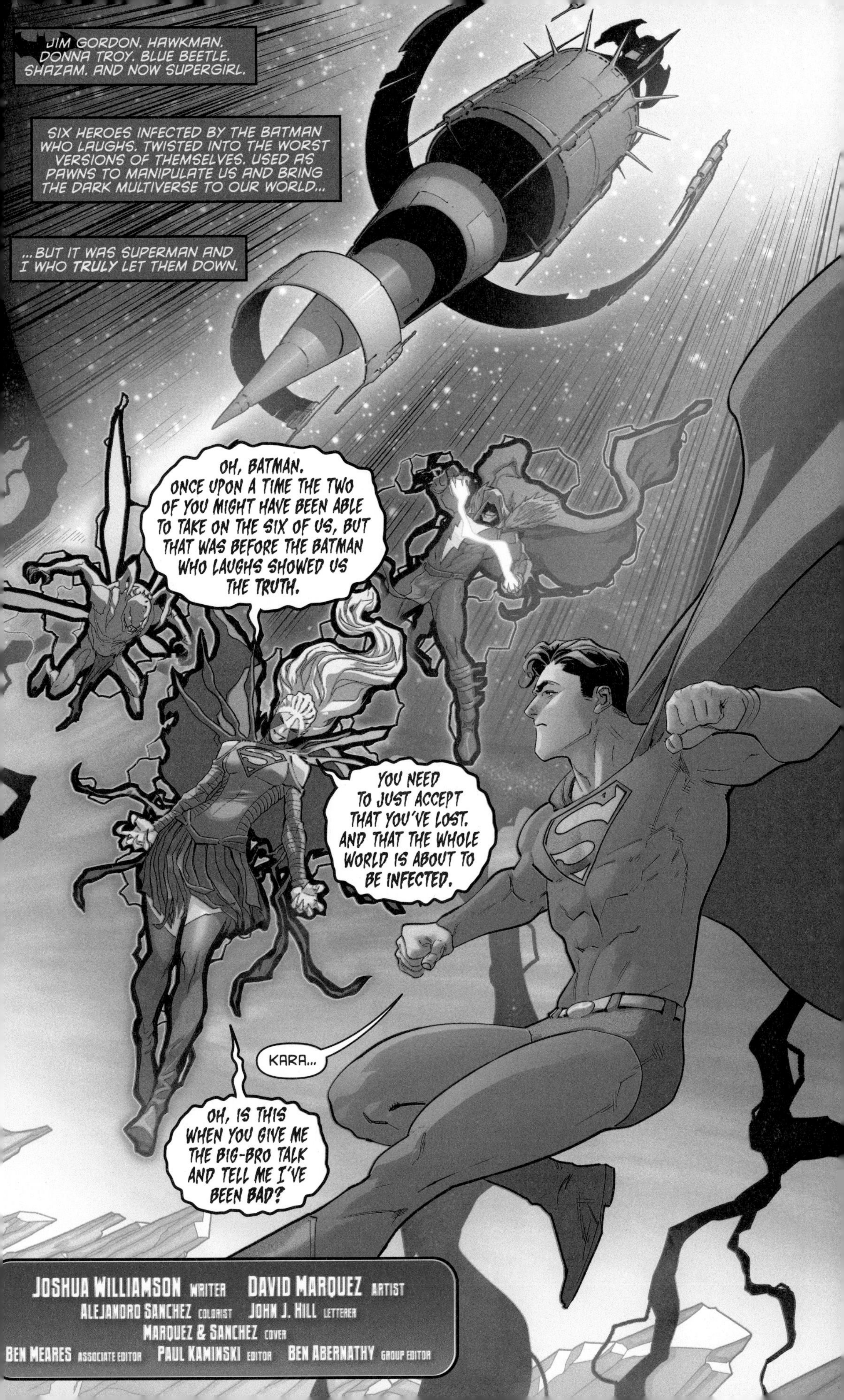
JIM GORDON. HAWKMAN. DONNA TROY. BLUE BEETLE. SHAZAM. AND NOW SUPERGIRL.
SIX HEROES INFECTED BY THE BATMAN WHO LAUGHS. TWISTED INTO THE WORST VERSIONS OF THEMSELVES. USED AS PAWNS TO MANIPULATE US AND BRING THE DARK MULTIVERSE TO OUR WORLD...
...BUT IT WAS SUPERMAN AND I WHO TRULY LET THEM DOWN.
OH, BATMAN. ONCE UPON A TIME THE TWO OF YOU MIGHT HAVE BEEN ABLE TO TAKE ON THE SIX OF US, BUT THAT WAS BEFORE THE BATMAN WHO LAUGHS SHOWED US THE TRUTH.
YOU NEED TO JUST ACCEPT THAT YOU'VE LOST. AND THAT THE WHOLE WORLD IS ABOUT TO BE INFECTED.
KARA...
OH, IS THIS WHEN YOU GIVE ME THE BIG-BRO TALK AND TELL ME I'VE BEEN BAD?
JOSHUA WILLIAMSON WRITER DAVID MARQUEZ ARTIST
ALEJANDRO SANCHEZ COLORIST JOHN J. HILL LETTERER
MARQUEZ & SANCHEZ COVER
BEN MEARES ASSOCIATE EDITOR PAUL KAMINSKI EDITOR BEN ABERNATHY GROUP EDITOR

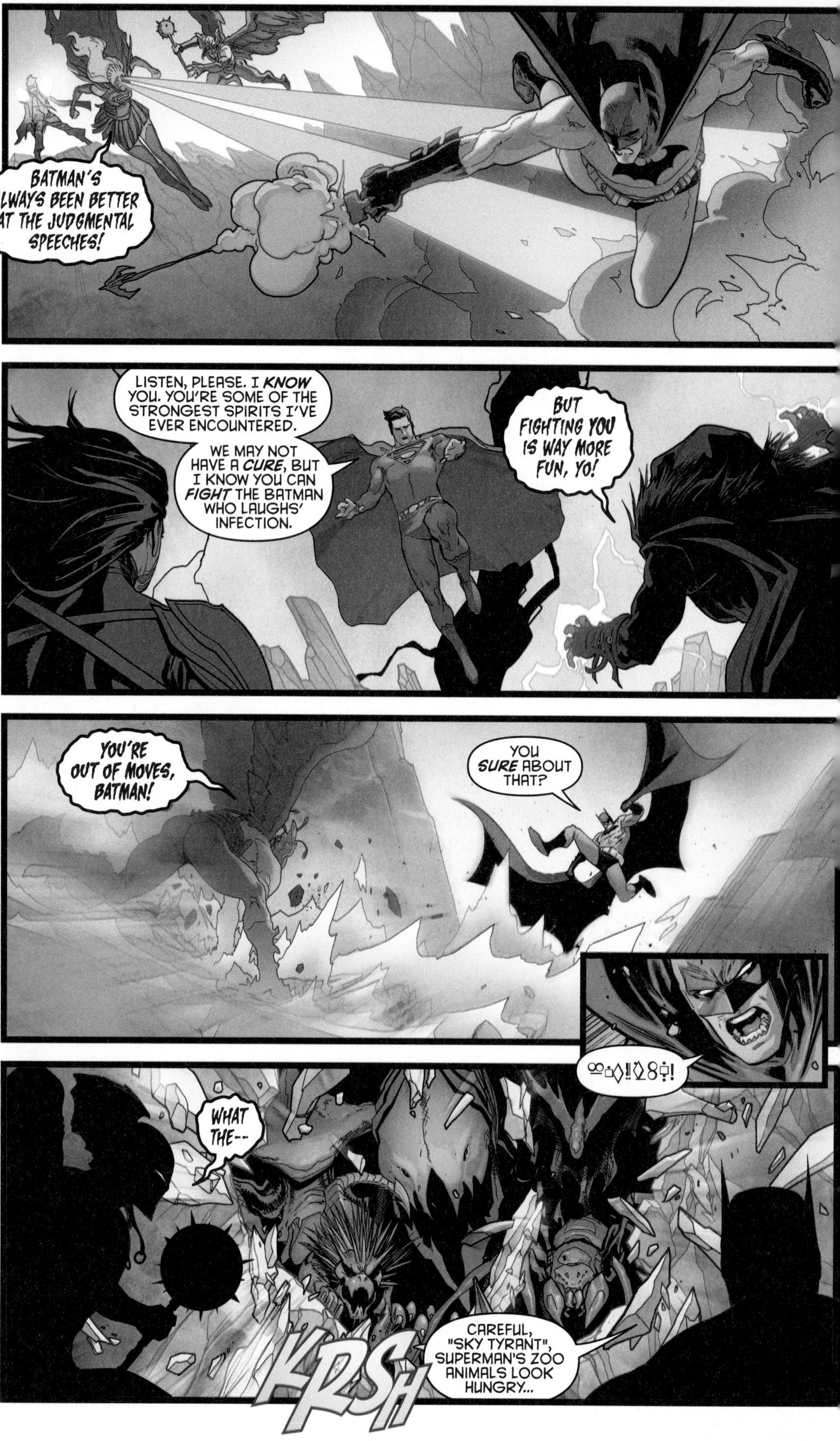
BATMAN'S ALWAYS BEEN BETTER AT THE JUDGMENTAL SPEECHES!
LISTEN, PLEASE. I KNOW YOU. YOU'RE SOME OF THE STRONGEST SPIRITS I'VE EVER ENCOUNTERED.
WE MAY NOT HAVE A CURE, BUT I KNOW YOU CAN FIGHT THE BATMAN WHO LAUGHS' INFECTION.
BUT FIGHTING YOU IS WAY MORE FUN, YO!
YOU'RE OUT OF MOVES, BATMAN!
YOU SURE ABOUT THAT?
WHAT THE--
KRSH
CAREFUL, "SKY TYRANT", SUPERMAN'S ZOO ANIMALS LOOK HUNGRY...

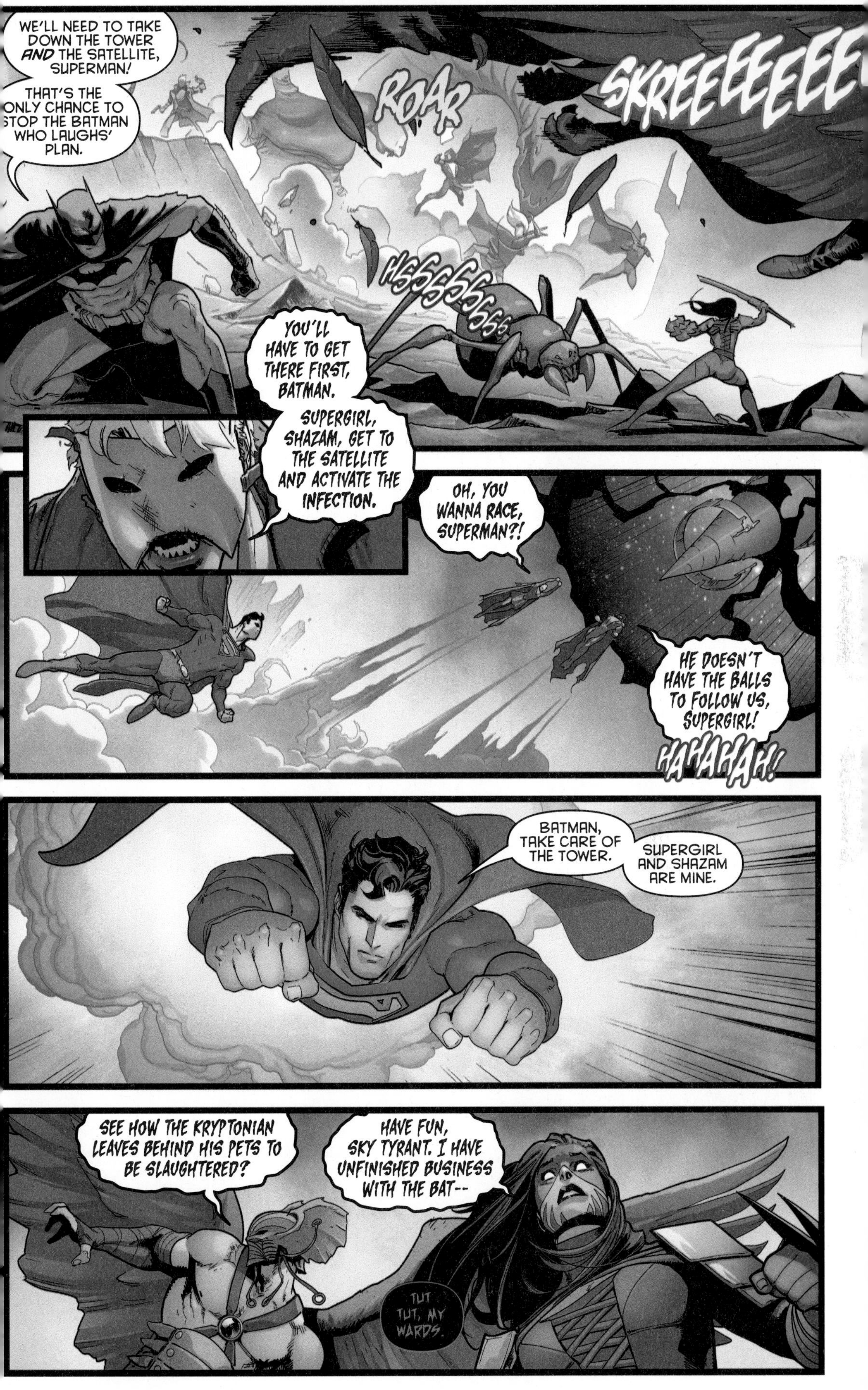
WE'LL NEED TO TAKE DOWN THE TOWER AND THE SATELLITE, SUPERMAN!
THAT'S THE ONLY CHANCE TO STOP THE BATMAN WHO LAUGHS' PLAN.
ROAR
SKREEEEEEEEE
HSSSSSSSSSS
YOU'LL HAVE TO GET THERE FIRST, BATMAN.
SUPERGIRL, SHAZAM, GET TO THE SATELLITE AND ACTIVATE THE INFECTION.
OH, YOU WANNA RACE, SUPERMAN?!
HE DOESN'T HAVE THE BALLS TO FOLLOW US, SUPERGIRL!
HAHAHAH!
BATMAN, TAKE CARE OF THE TOWER.
SUPERGIRL AND SHAZAM ARE MINE.
SEE HOW THE KRYPTONIAN LEAVES BEHIND HIS PETS TO BE SLAUGHTERED?
HAVE FUN, SKY TYRANT. I HAVE UNFINISHED BUSINESS WITH THE BAT--
TUT TUT, MY WARDS.

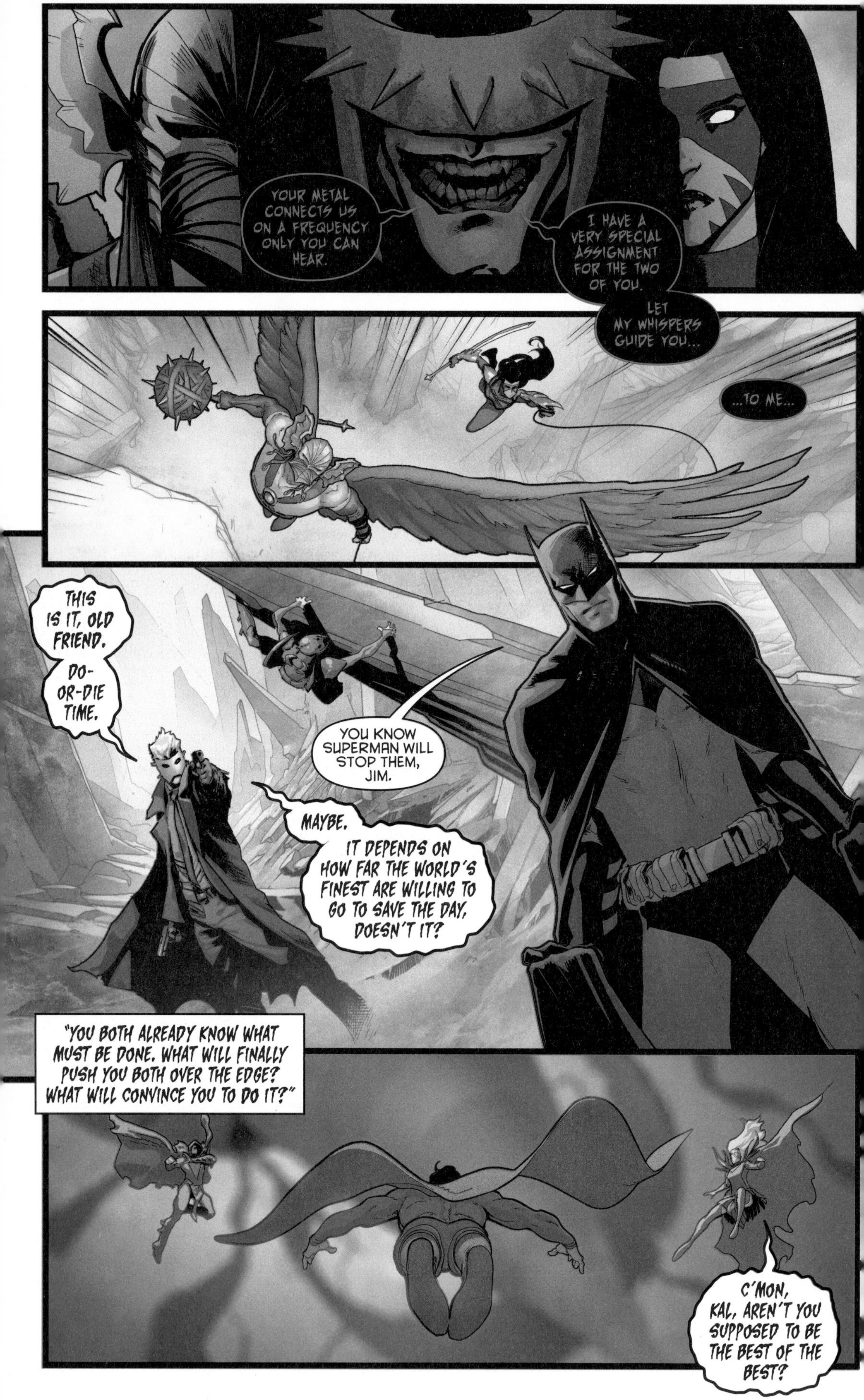
YOUR METAL CONNECTS US ON A FREQUENCY ONLY YOU CAN HEAR.
I HAVE A VERY SPECIAL ASSIGNMENT FOR THE TWO OF YOU.
LET MY WHISPERS GUIDE YOU...
...TO ME...
THIS IS IT, OLD FRIEND.
DO-OR-DIE TIME.
YOU KNOW SUPERMAN WILL STOP THEM, JIM.
MAYBE.
IT DEPENDS ON HOW FAR THE WORLD'S FINEST ARE WILLING TO GO TO SAVE THE DAY, DOESN'T IT?
"YOU BOTH ALREADY KNOW WHAT MUST BE DONE. WHAT WILL FINALLY PUSH YOU BOTH OVER THE EDGE? WHAT WILL CONVINCE YOU TO DO IT?"
C'MON, KAL, AREN'T YOU SUPPOSED TO BE THE BEST OF THE BEST?

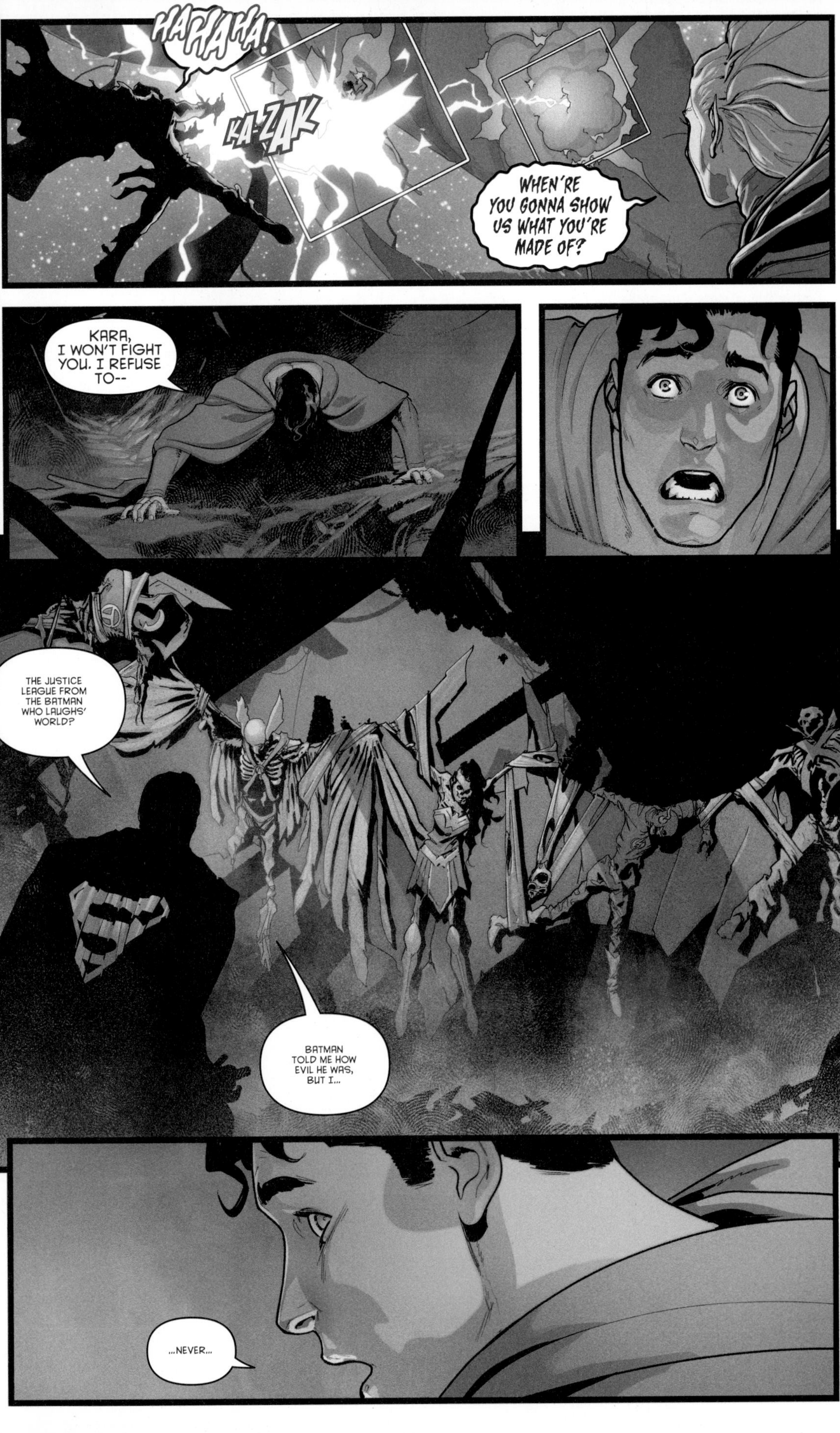
HAHAHA!
KA-ZAK
WHEN'RE YOU GONNA SHOW US WHAT YOU'RE MADE OF?
KARA, I WON'T FIGHT YOU. I REFUSE TO--
THE JUSTICE LEAGUE FROM THE BATMAN WHO LAUGHS' WORLD?
BATMAN TOLD ME HOW EVIL HE WAS, BUT I...
...NEVER...

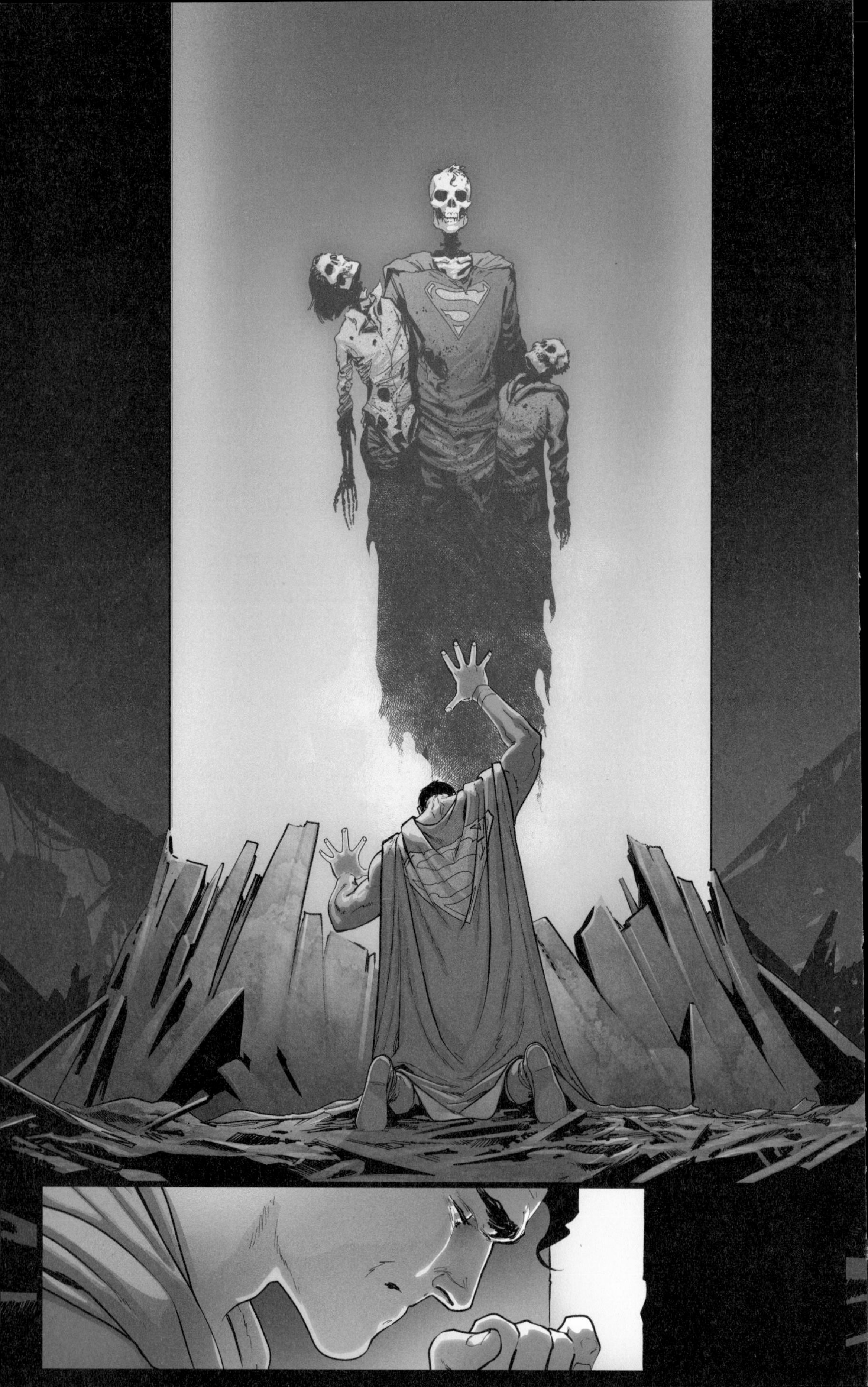

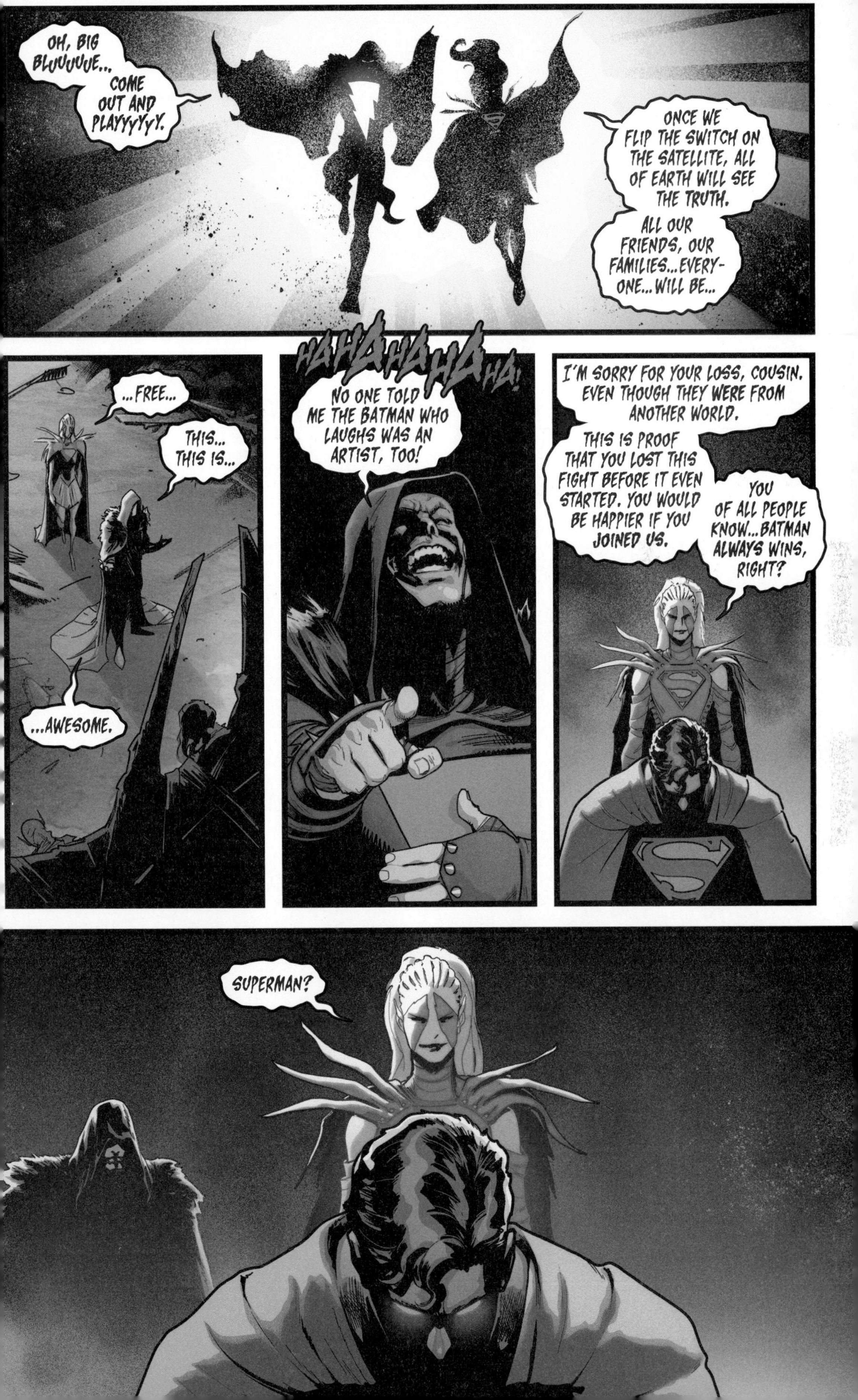

OH, BIG BLUUUUE... COME OUT AND PLAYYYYYY.
ONCE WE FLIP THE SWITCH ON THE SATELLITE, ALL OF EARTH WILL SEE THE TRUTH.
ALL OUR FRIENDS, OUR FAMILIES...EVERY-ONE...WILL BE...
...FREE...
THIS... THIS IS...
...AWESOME.
HAHAHAHAHAHA!
NO ONE TOLD ME THE BATMAN WHO LAUGHS WAS AN ARTIST, TOO!
I'M SORRY FOR YOUR LOSS, COUSIN. EVEN THOUGH THEY WERE FROM ANOTHER WORLD.
THIS IS PROOF THAT YOU LOST THIS FIGHT BEFORE IT EVEN STARTED. YOU WOULD BE HAPPIER IF YOU JOINED US.
YOU OF ALL PEOPLE KNOW...BATMAN ALWAYS WINS, RIGHT?
SUPERMAN?

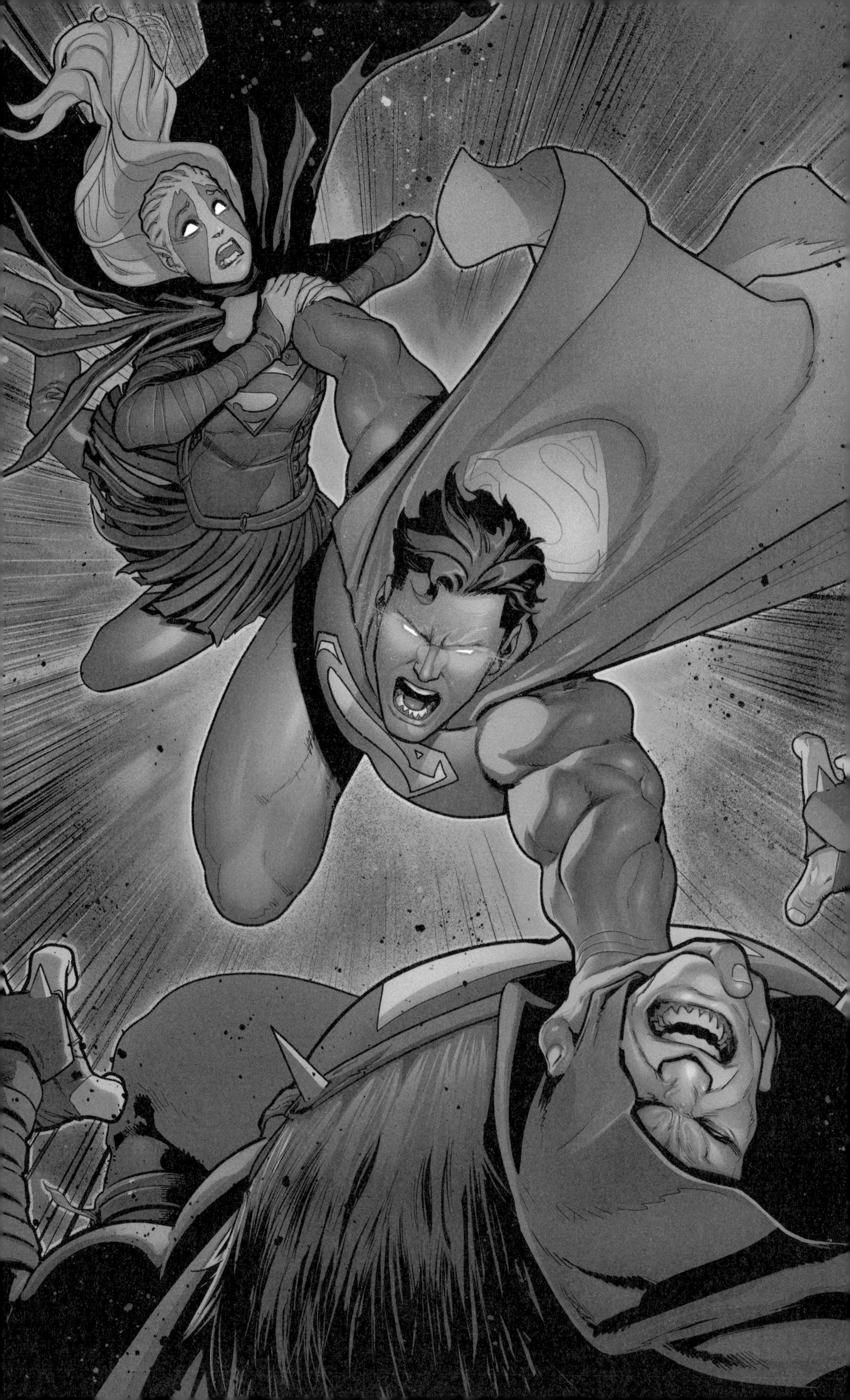

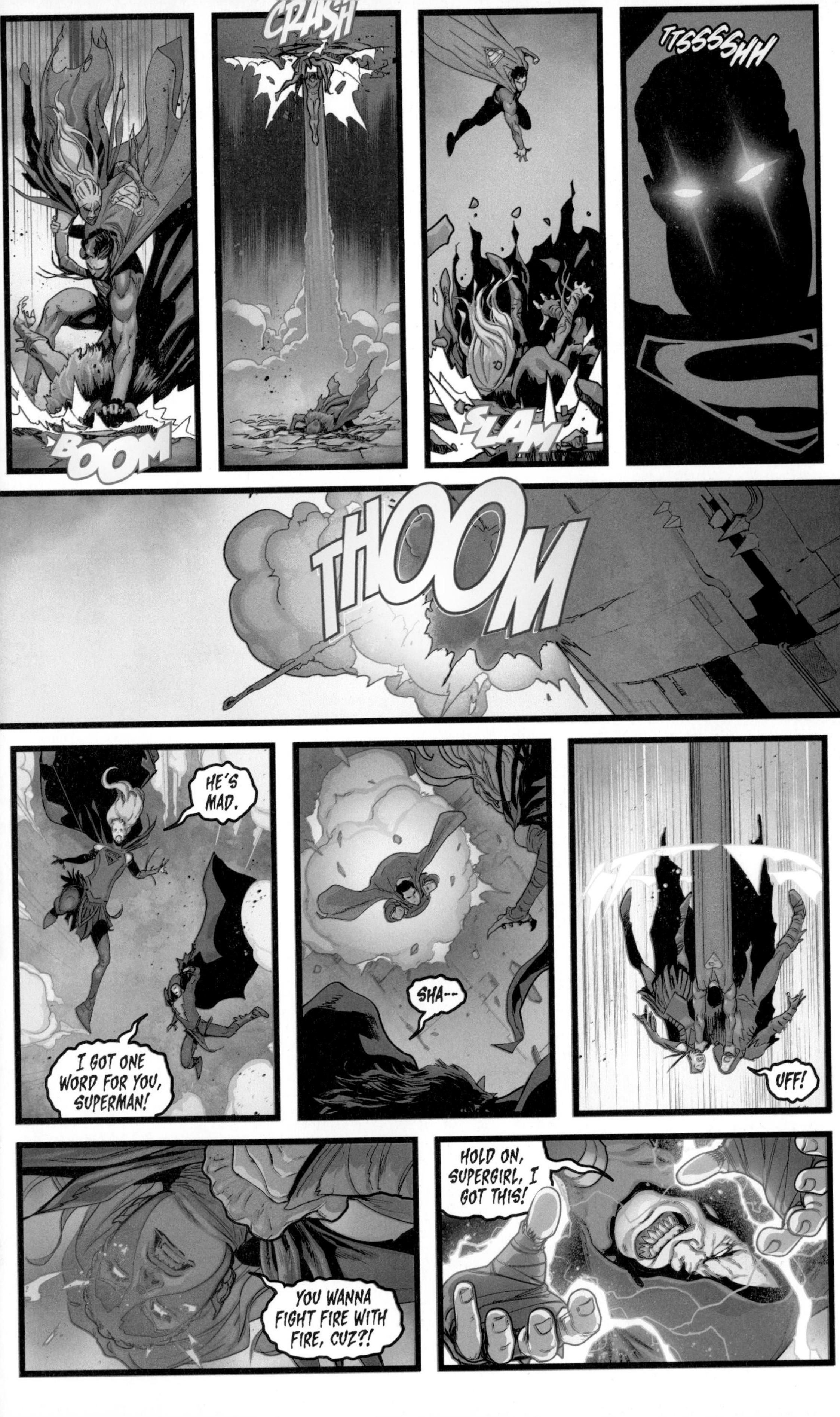
BOOM
CRASH
SLAM
TTSSSSHH
THOOM
HE'S MAD.
I GOT ONE WORD FOR YOU, SUPERMAN!
SHA--
UFF!
YOU WANNA FIGHT FIRE WITH FIRE, CUZ?!
HOLD ON, SUPERGIRL, I GOT THIS!

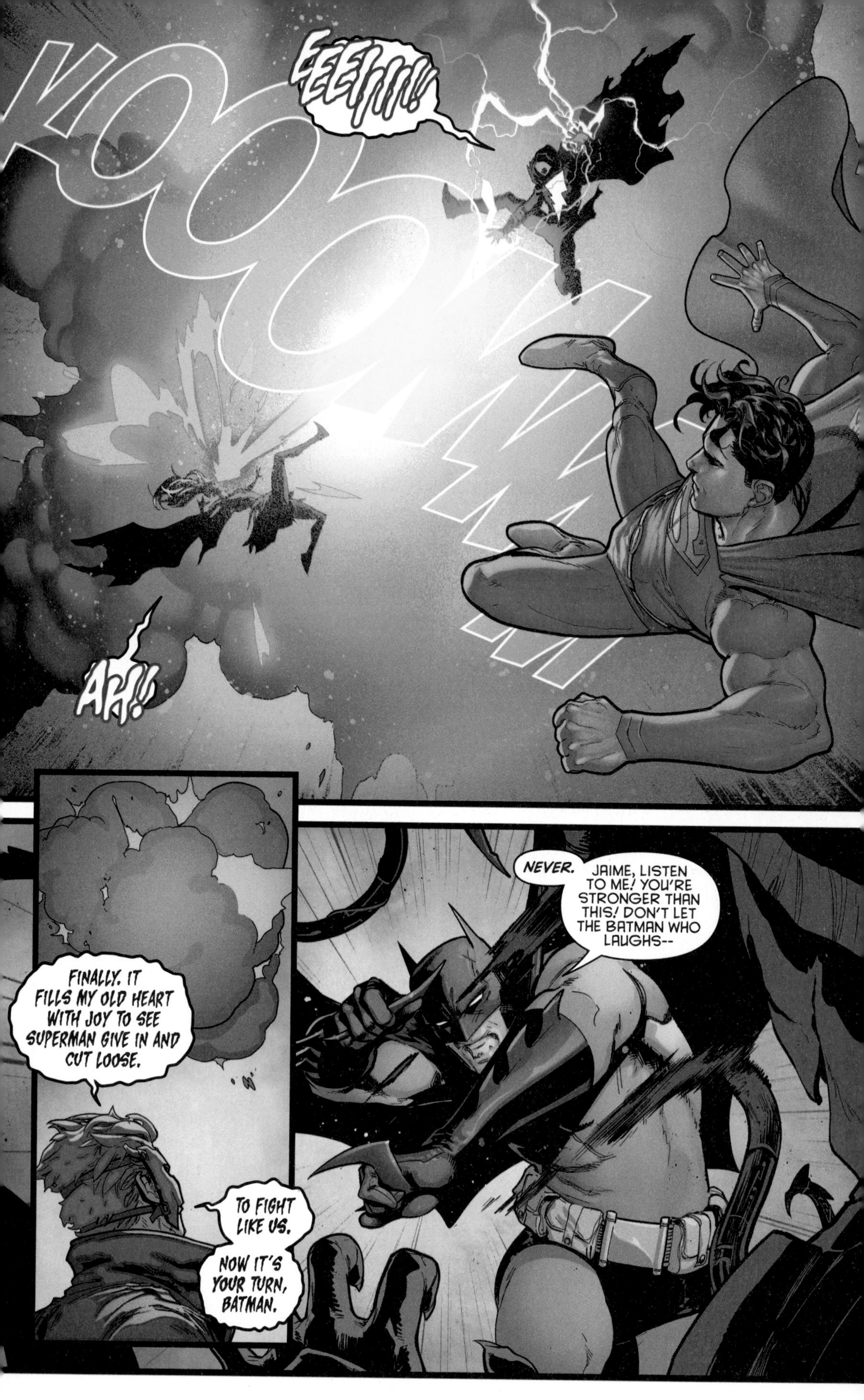EEEIIII!!
K'OOOOMM
AH!!
FINALLY. IT FILLS MY OLD HEART WITH JOY TO SEE SUPERMAN GIVE IN AND CUT LOOSE.
TO FIGHT LIKE US.
NOW IT'S YOUR TURN, BATMAN.
NEVER.
JAIME, LISTEN TO ME! YOU'RE STRONGER THAN THIS! DON'T LET THE BATMAN WHO LAUGHS--

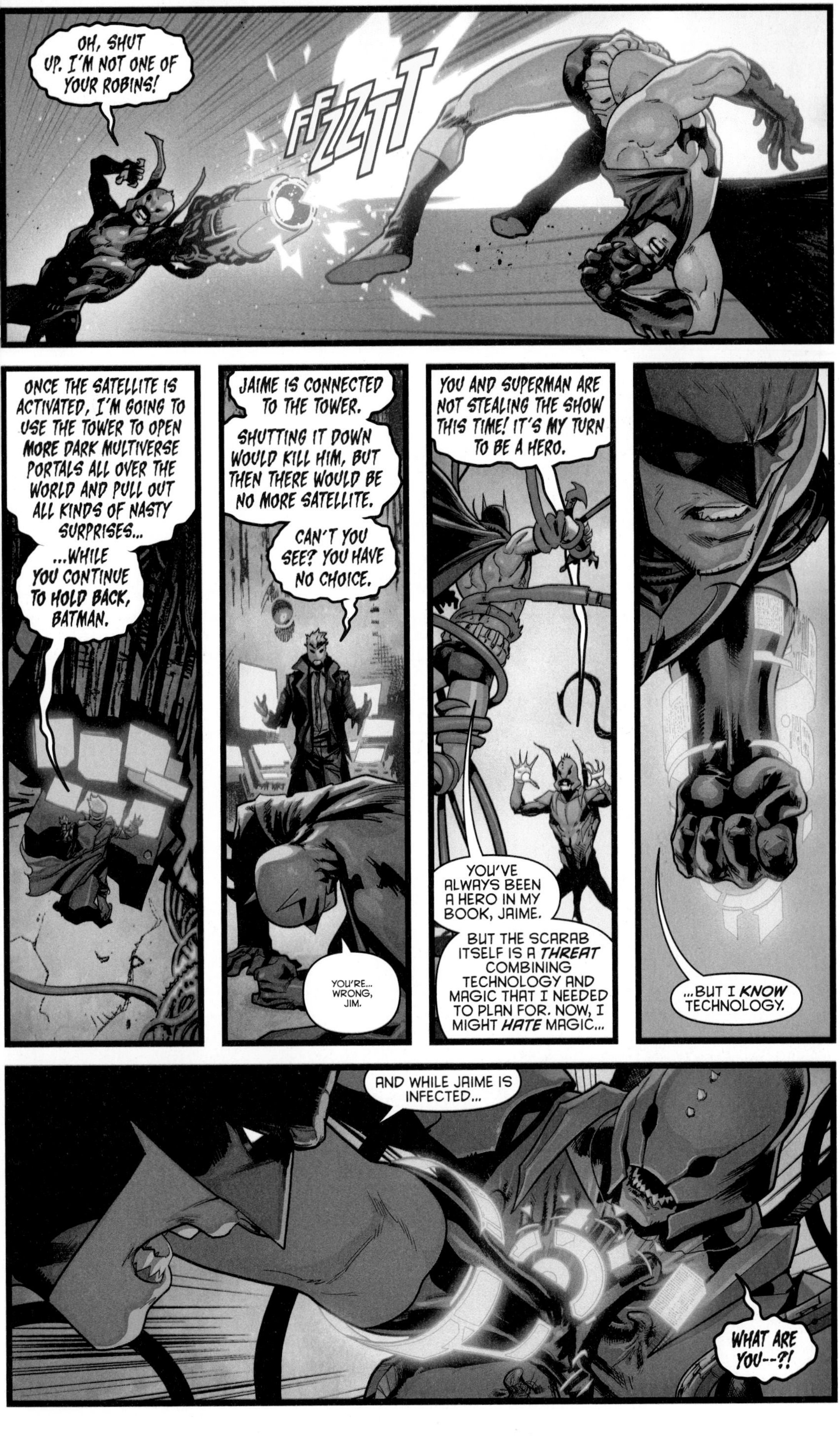

OH, SHUT UP. I'M NOT ONE OF YOUR ROBINS!
FFZZTT
ONCE THE SATELLITE IS ACTIVATED, I'M GOING TO USE THE TOWER TO OPEN MORE DARK MULTIVERSE PORTALS ALL OVER THE WORLD AND PULL OUT ALL KINDS OF NASTY SURPRISES...
...WHILE YOU CONTINUE TO HOLD BACK, BATMAN.
JAIME IS CONNECTED TO THE TOWER.
SHUTTING IT DOWN WOULD KILL HIM, BUT THEN THERE WOULD BE NO MORE SATELLITE.
CAN'T YOU SEE? YOU HAVE NO CHOICE.
YOU'RE... WRONG, JIM.
YOU AND SUPERMAN ARE NOT STEALING THE SHOW THIS TIME! IT'S MY TURN TO BE A HERO.
YOU'VE ALWAYS BEEN A HERO IN MY BOOK, JAIME.
BUT THE SCARAB ITSELF IS A *THREAT* COMBINING TECHNOLOGY AND MAGIC THAT I NEEDED TO PLAN FOR. NOW, I MIGHT *HATE* MAGIC...
...BUT I *KNOW* TECHNOLOGY.
AND WHILE JAIME IS INFECTED...
WHAT ARE YOU--?!

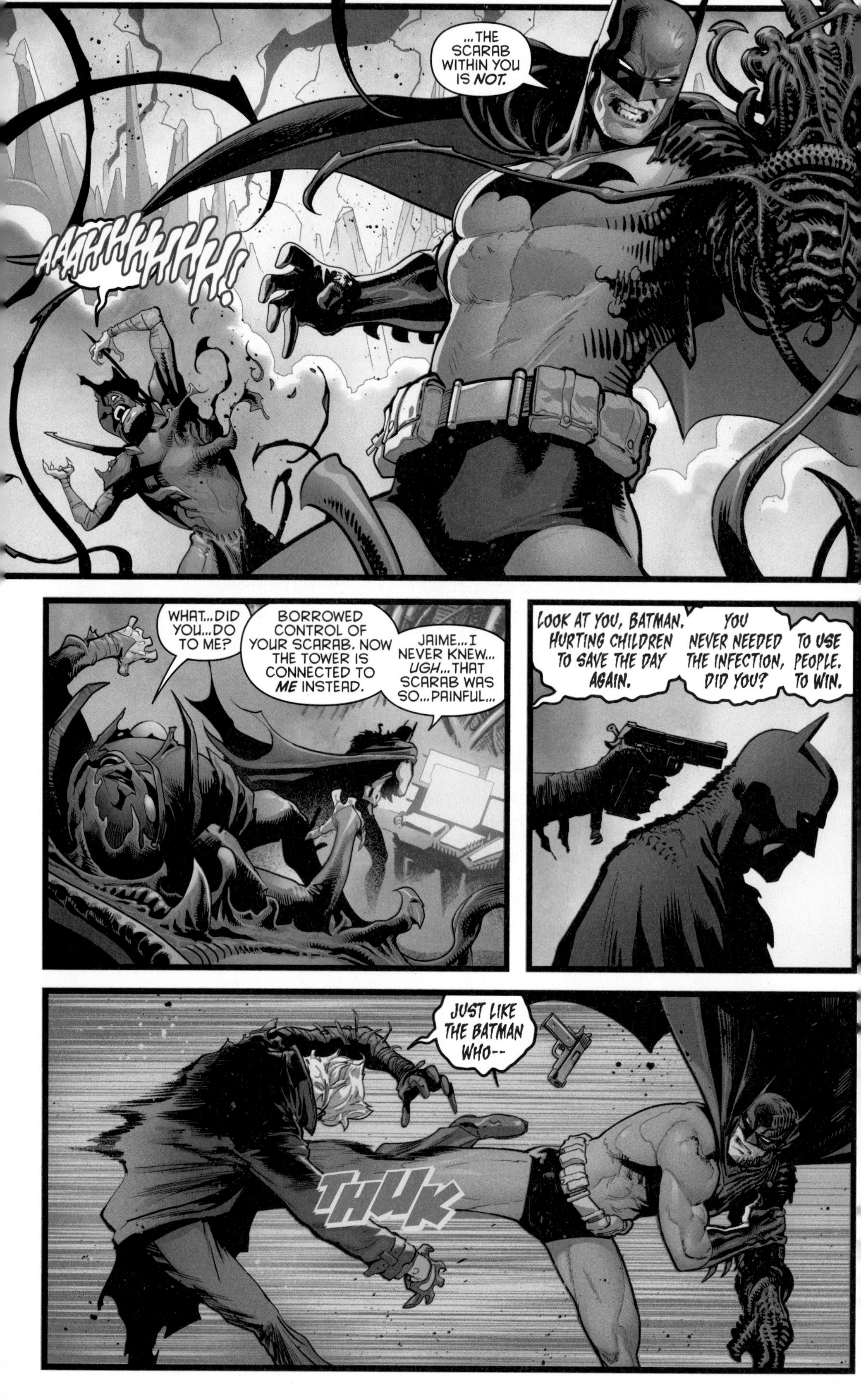
...THE SCARAB WITHIN YOU IS *NOT.*
AAAHHHHHHH!
WHAT...DID YOU...DO TO ME?
BORROWED CONTROL OF YOUR SCARAB. NOW THE TOWER IS CONNECTED TO *ME* INSTEAD.
JAIME...I NEVER KNEW... *UGH*...THAT SCARAB WAS SO...PAINFUL...
LOOK AT YOU, BATMAN. HURTING CHILDREN TO SAVE THE DAY AGAIN.
YOU NEVER NEEDED THE INFECTION, DID YOU?
TO USE PEOPLE. TO WIN.
JUST LIKE THE BATMAN WHO--
THUK

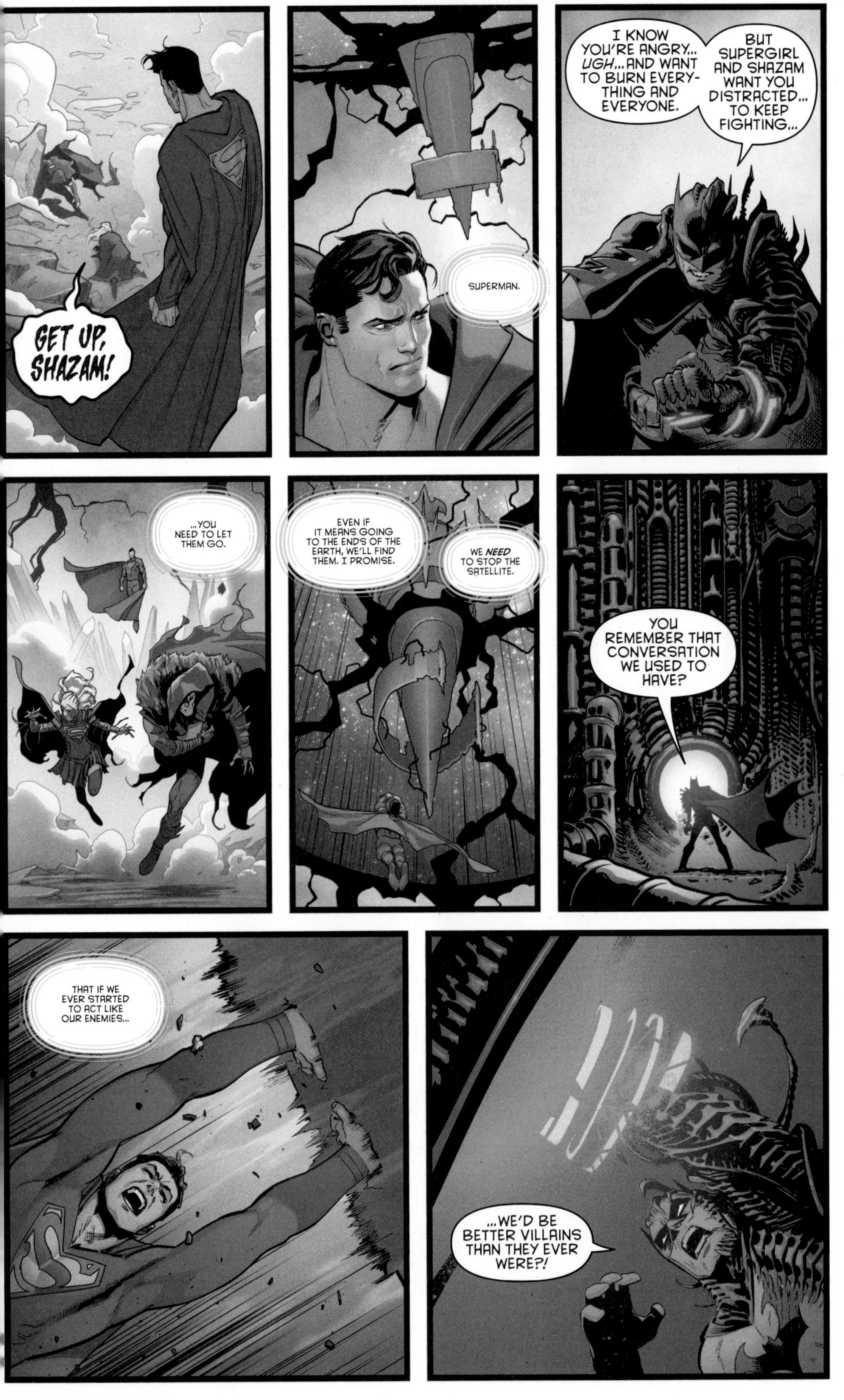
GET UP, SHAZAM!
SUPERMAN.
I KNOW YOU'RE ANGRY... *UGH*... AND WANT TO BURN EVERY-THING AND EVERYONE.
BUT SUPERGIRL AND SHAZAM WANT YOU DISTRACTED... TO KEEP FIGHTING...
...YOU NEED TO LET THEM GO.
EVEN IF IT MEANS GOING TO THE ENDS OF THE EARTH, WE'LL FIND THEM. I PROMISE.
WE *NEED* TO STOP THE SATELLITE.
YOU REMEMBER THAT CONVERSATION WE USED TO HAVE?
THAT IF WE EVER STARTED TO ACT LIKE OUR ENEMIES...
...WE'D BE BETTER VILLAINS THAN THEY EVER WERE?!

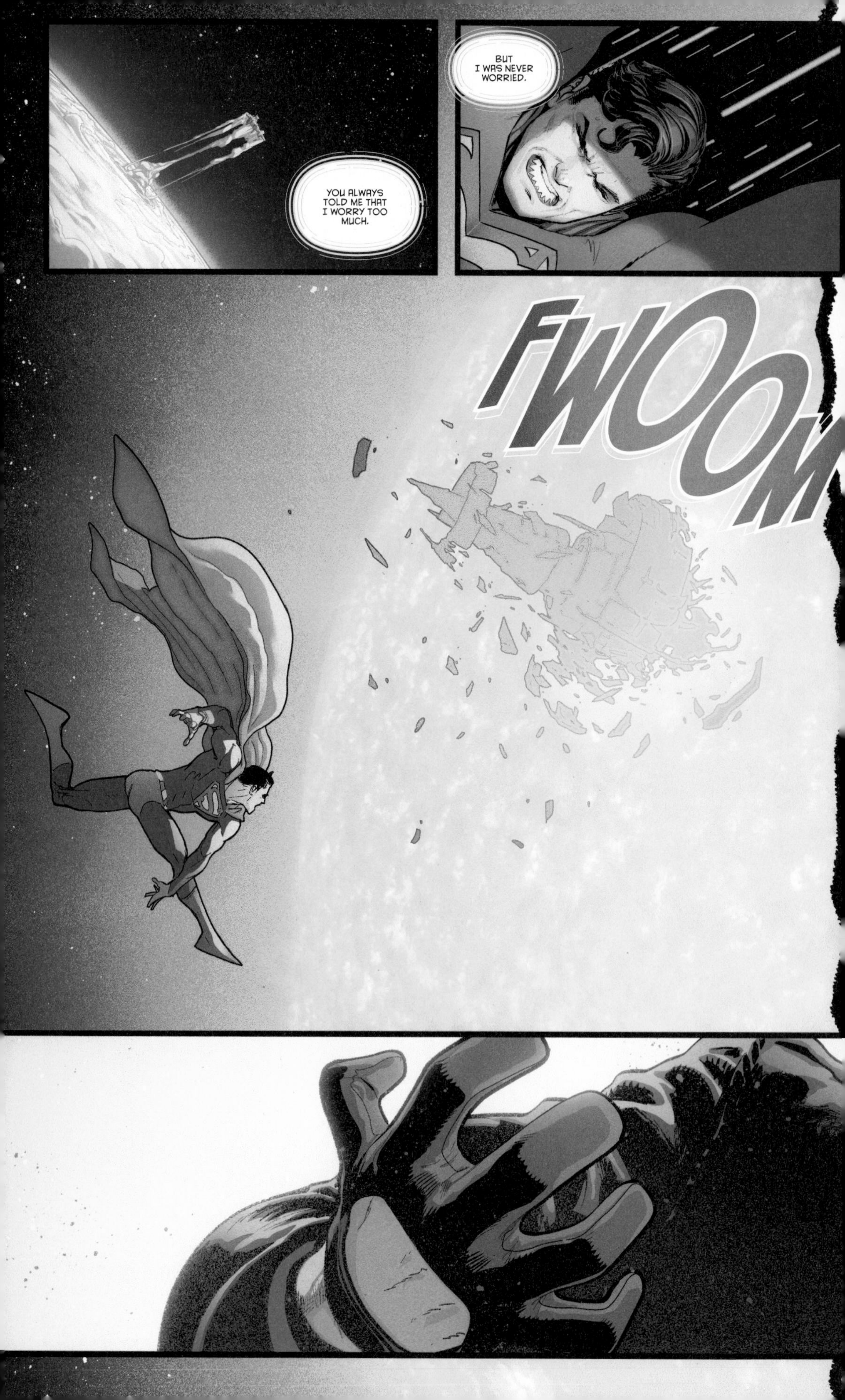
YOU ALWAYS TOLD ME THAT I WORRY TOO MUCH.
BUT I WAS NEVER WORRIED.
FWOOM

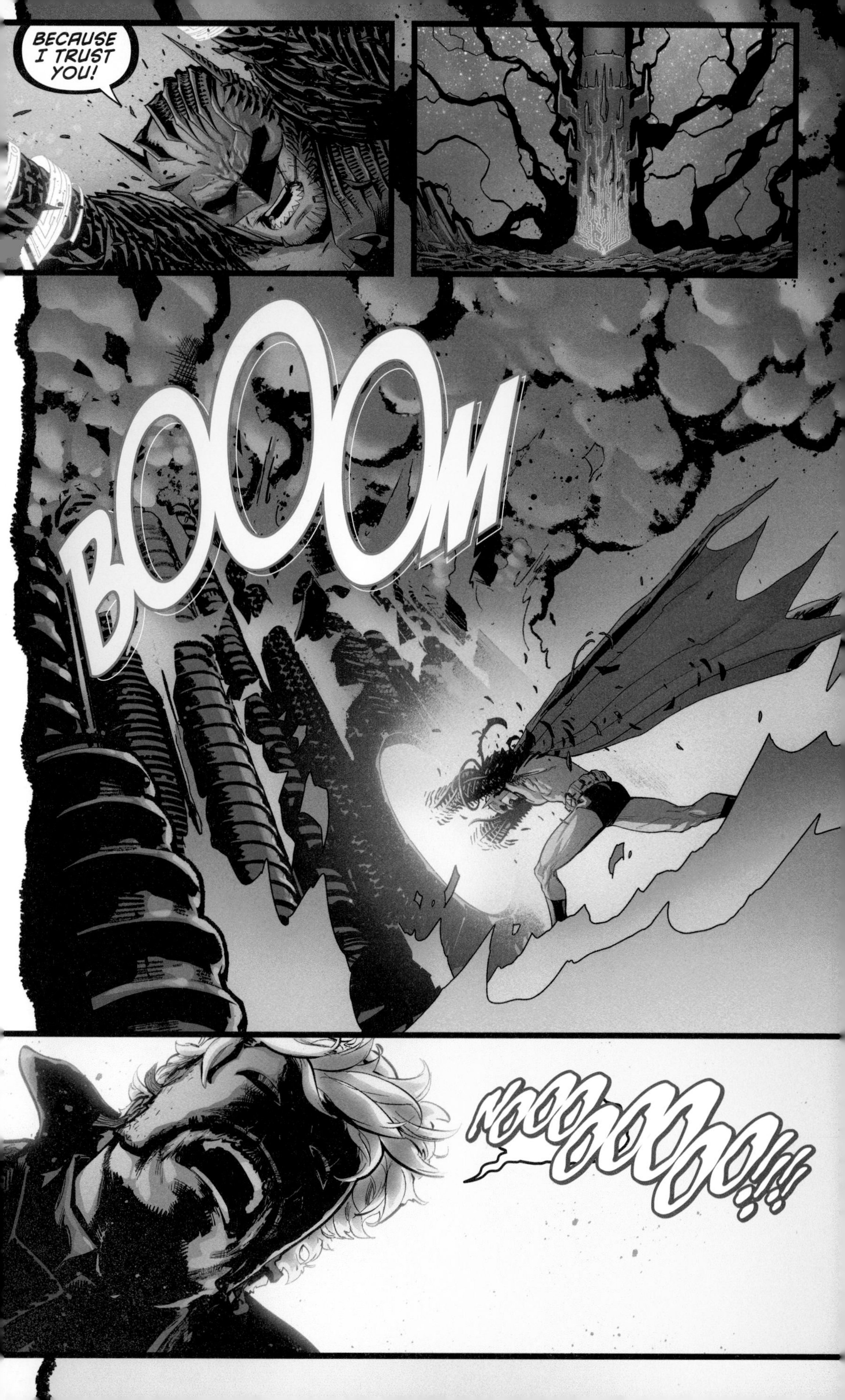
BECAUSE I TRUST YOU!
BOOOM
NOOOOOOOO!!!

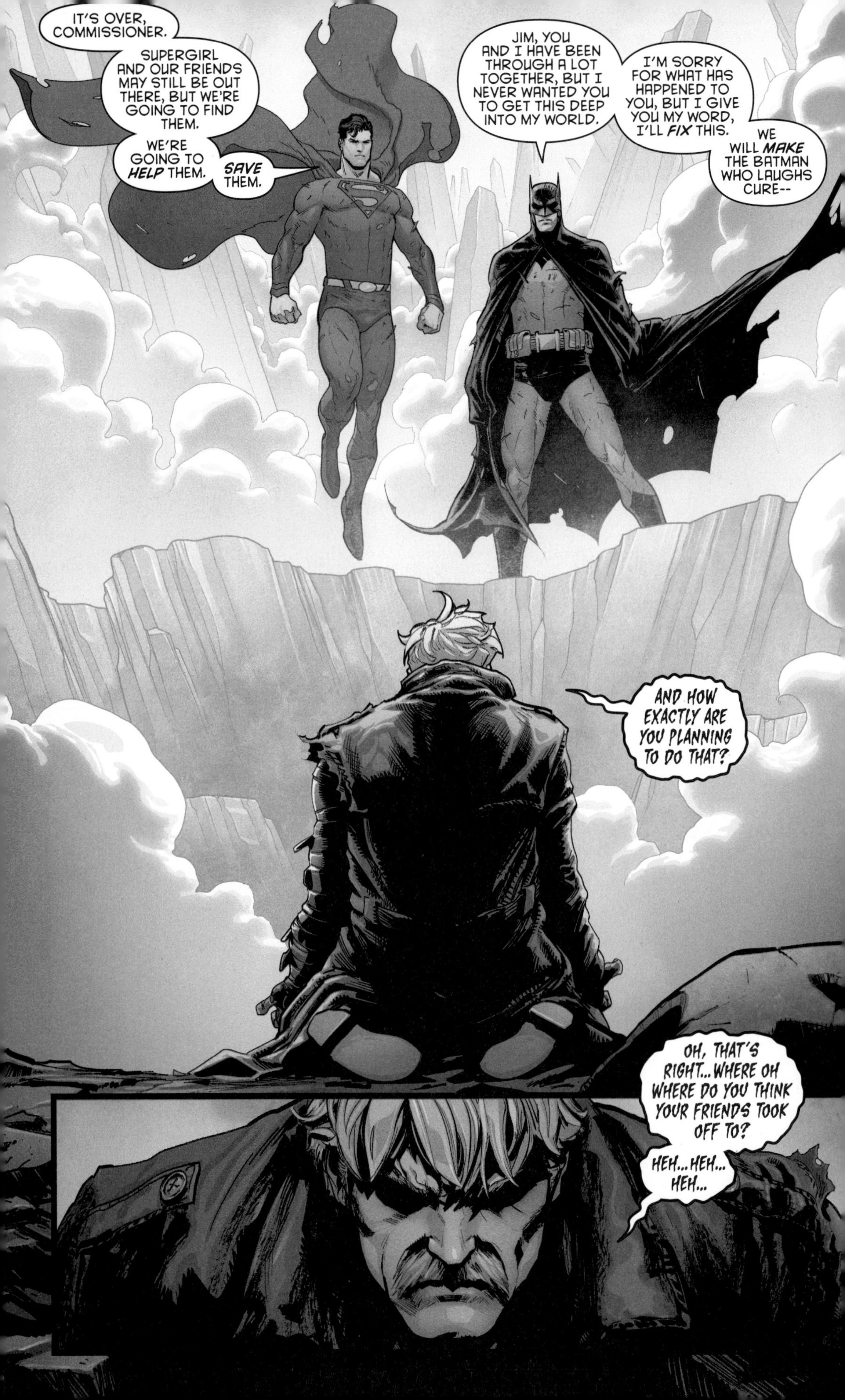
IT'S OVER, COMMISSIONER.
SUPERGIRL AND OUR FRIENDS MAY STILL BE OUT THERE, BUT WE'RE GOING TO FIND THEM.
WE'RE GOING TO HELP THEM.
SAVE THEM.
JIM, YOU AND I HAVE BEEN THROUGH A LOT TOGETHER, BUT I NEVER WANTED YOU TO GET THIS DEEP INTO MY WORLD.
I'M SORRY FOR WHAT HAS HAPPENED TO YOU, BUT I GIVE YOU MY WORD, I'LL FIX THIS.
WE WILL MAKE THE BATMAN WHO LAUGHS CURE--
AND HOW EXACTLY ARE YOU PLANNING TO DO THAT?
OH, THAT'S RIGHT... WHERE OH WHERE DO YOU THINK YOUR FRIENDS TOOK OFF TO?
HEH... HEH... HEH...

RUN!

WHERE IS EVERYONE?

THEY JUST KEPT LAUGHING, SUPERMAN.

THE PRISON.

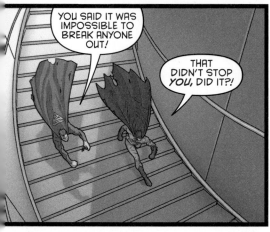

YOU SAID IT WAS IMPOSSIBLE TO BREAK ANYONE OUT!

THAT DIDN'T STOP *YOU*, DID IT?!

DAMN.

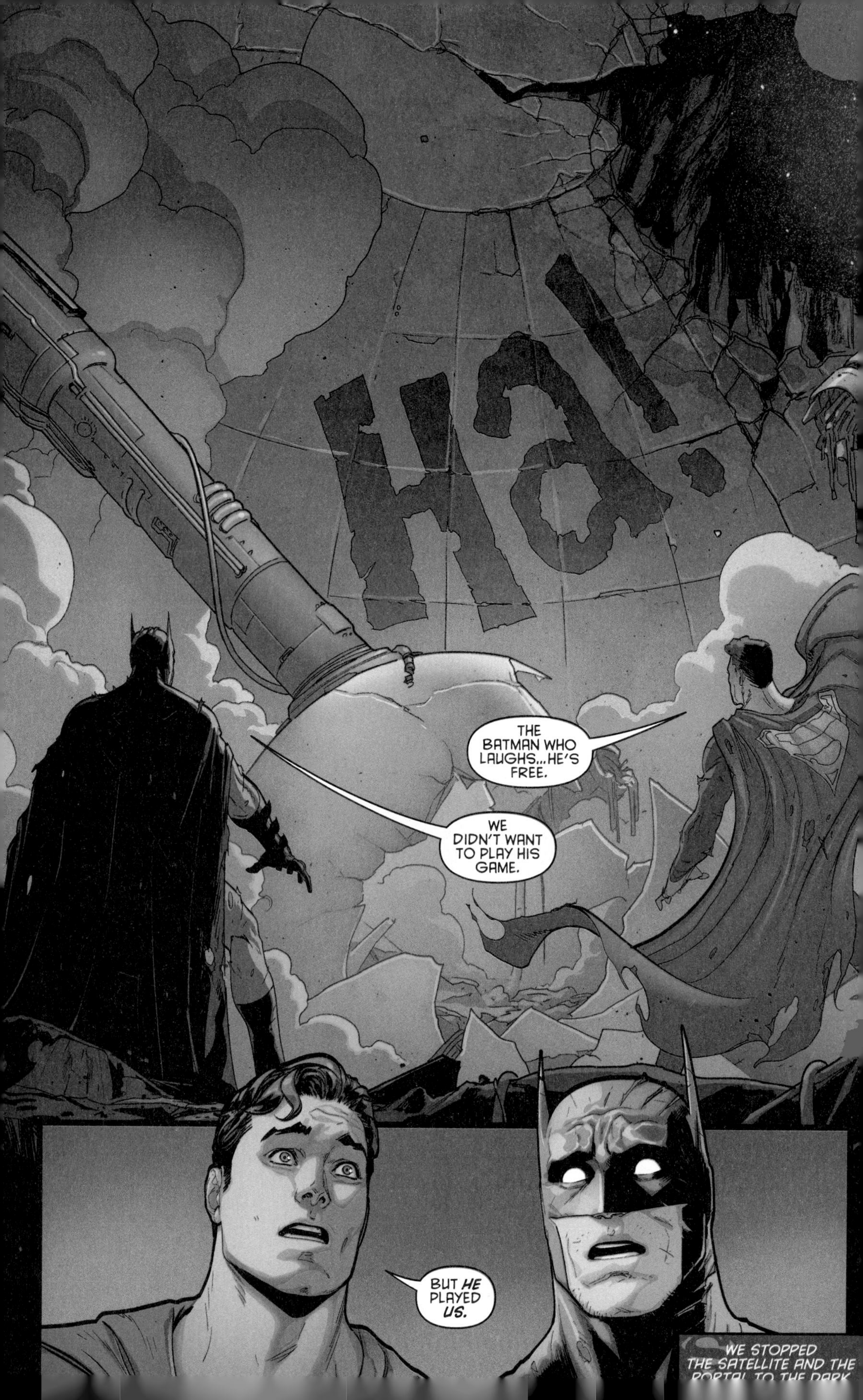
THE BATMAN WHO LAUGHS...HE'S FREE.
WE DIDN'T WANT TO PLAY HIS GAME.
BUT *HE* PLAYED *US.*
WE STOPPED THE SATELLITE AND THE

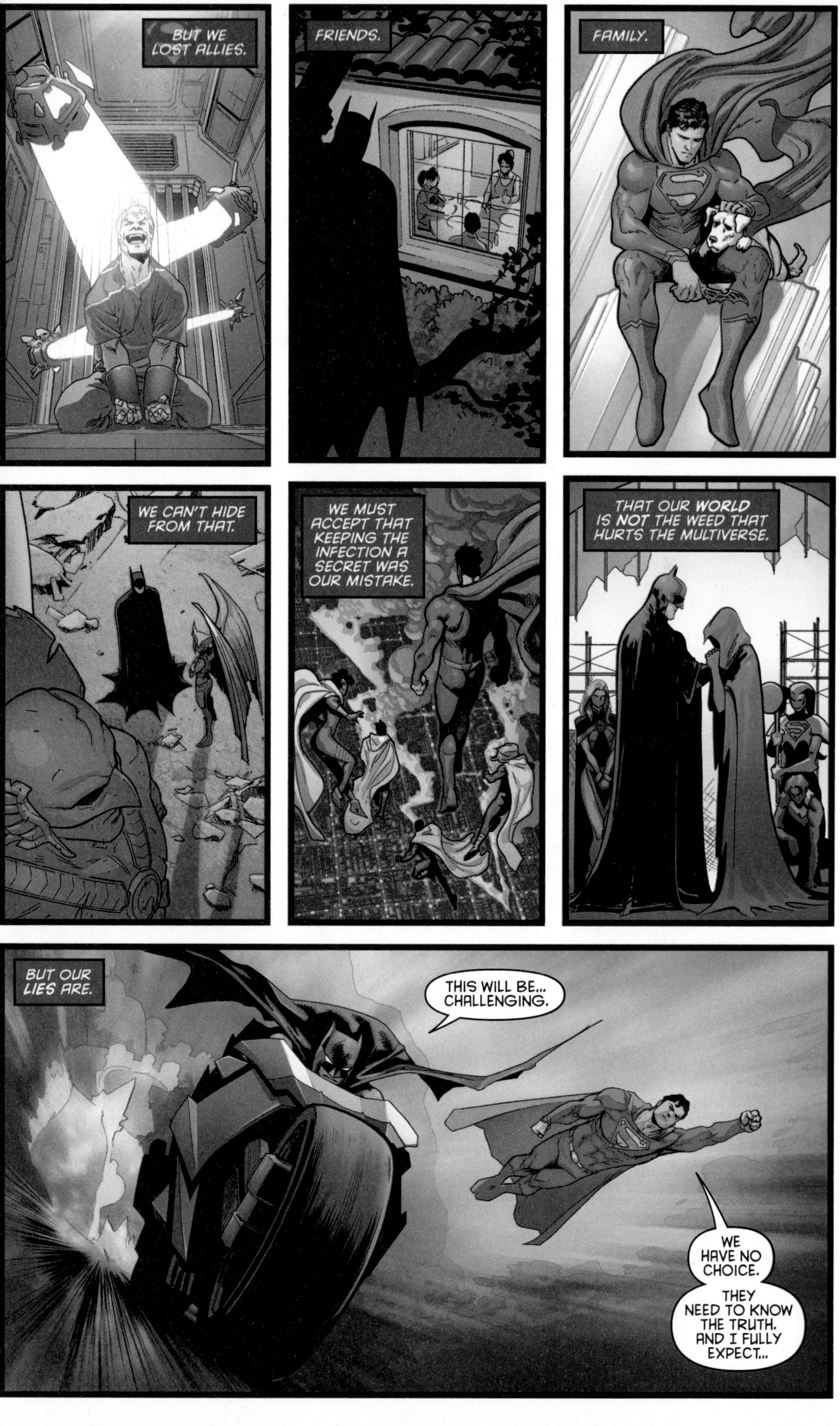
BUT WE LOST ALLIES.
FRIENDS.
FAMILY.
WE CAN'T HIDE FROM THAT.
WE MUST ACCEPT THAT KEEPING THE INFECTION A SECRET WAS OUR MISTAKE.
THAT OUR WORLD IS NOT THE WEED THAT HURTS THE MULTIVERSE.
BUT OUR LIES ARE.
THIS WILL BE... CHALLENGING.
WE HAVE NO CHOICE.
THEY NEED TO KNOW THE TRUTH. AND I FULLY EXPECT...

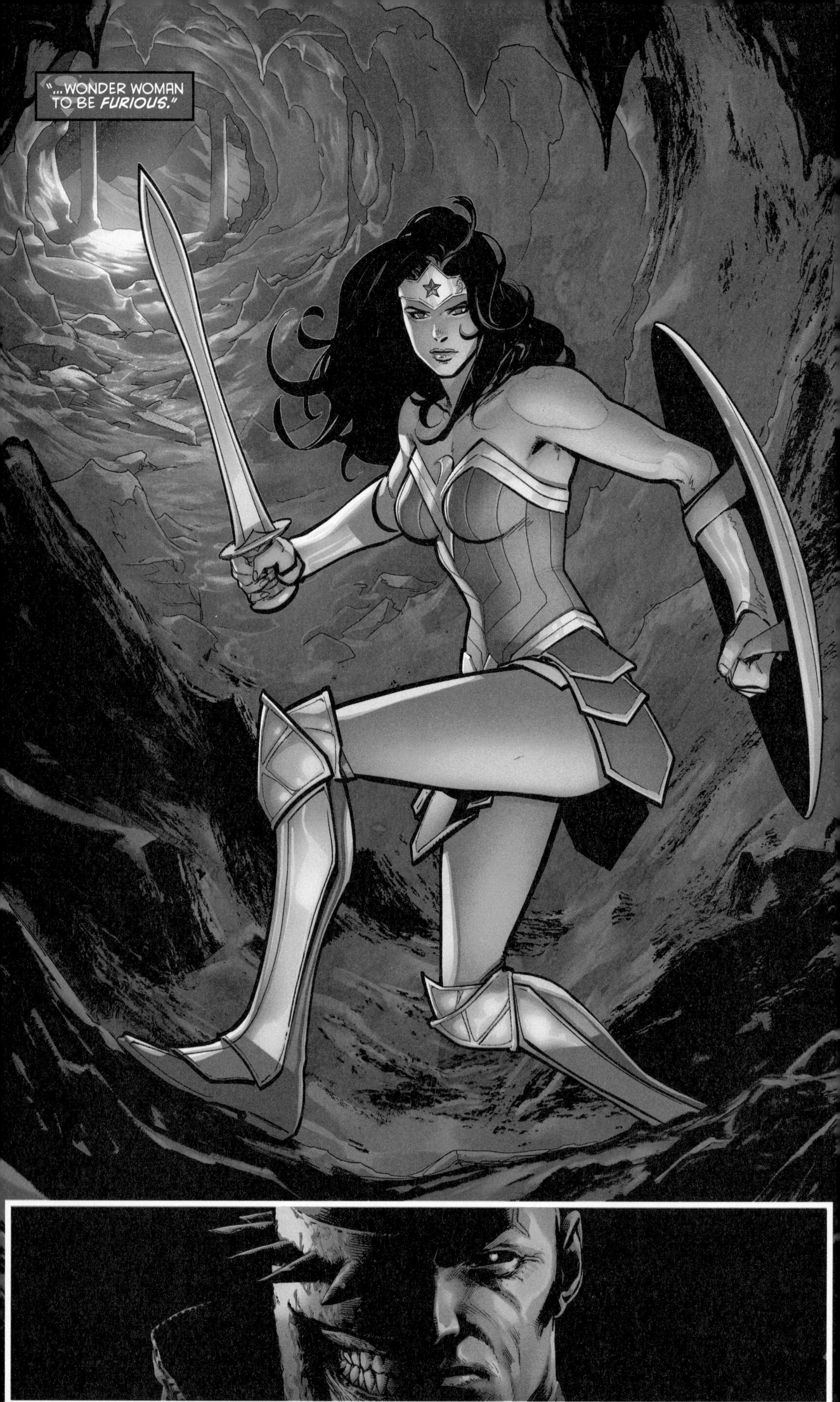
"...WONDER WOMAN TO BE FURIOUS."

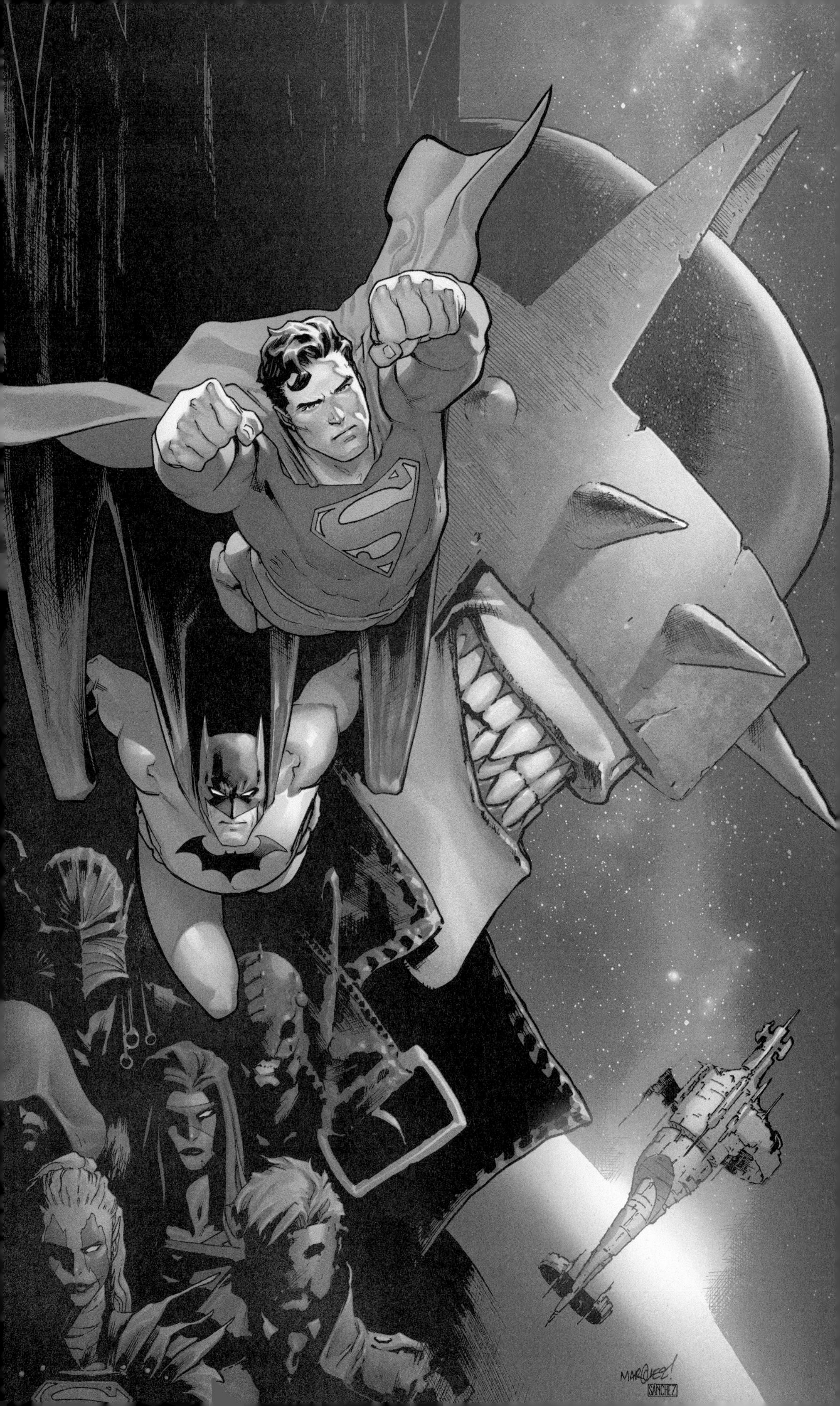
MARQUEZ!
SANCHEZ

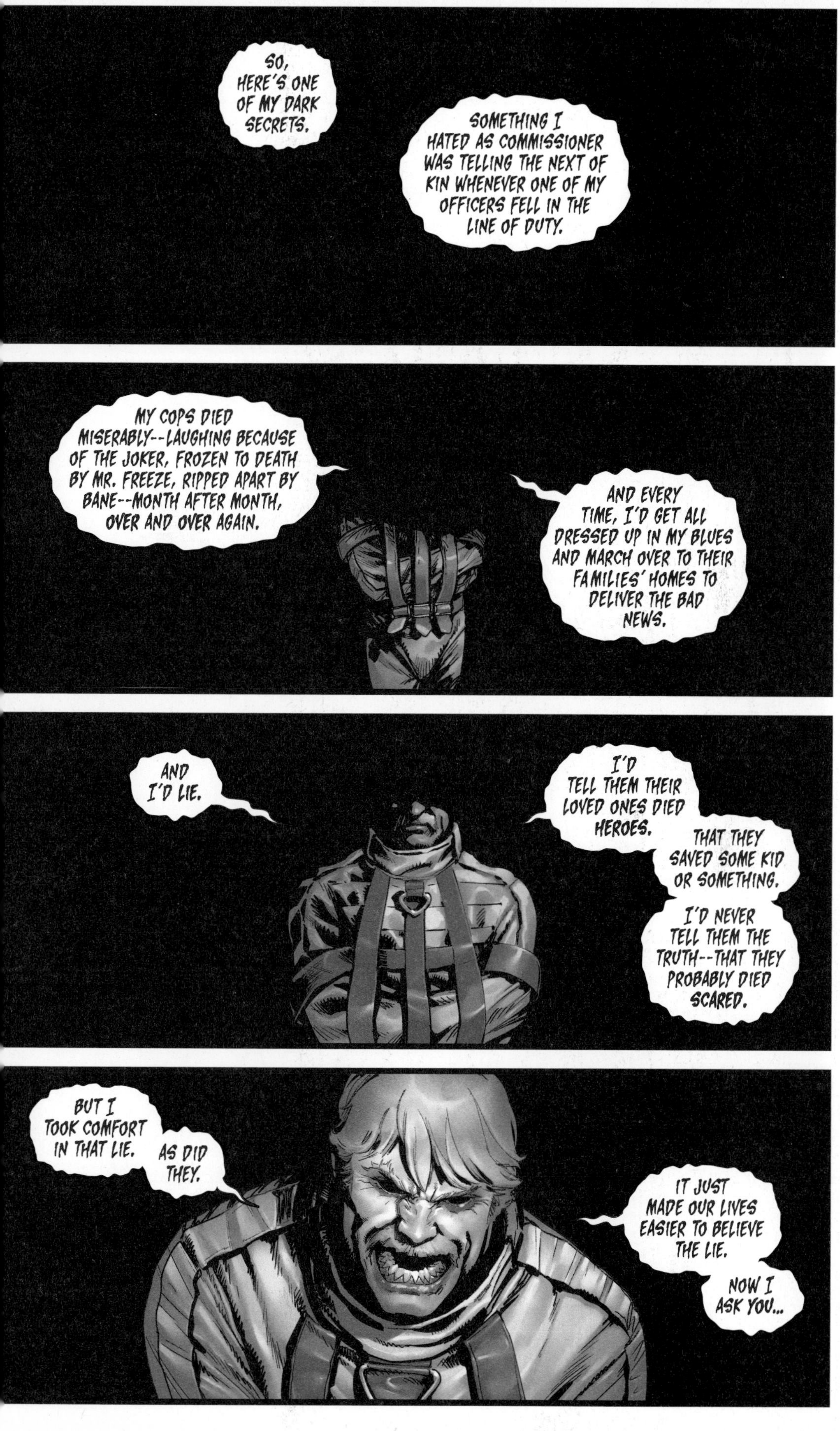
SO, HERE'S ONE OF MY DARK SECRETS.
SOMETHING I HATED AS COMMISSIONER WAS TELLING THE NEXT OF KIN WHENEVER ONE OF MY OFFICERS FELL IN THE LINE OF DUTY.
MY COPS DIED MISERABLY--LAUGHING BECAUSE OF THE JOKER, FROZEN TO DEATH BY MR. FREEZE, RIPPED APART BY BANE--MONTH AFTER MONTH, OVER AND OVER AGAIN.
AND EVERY TIME, I'D GET ALL DRESSED UP IN MY BLUES AND MARCH OVER TO THEIR FAMILIES' HOMES TO DELIVER THE BAD NEWS.
AND I'D LIE.
I'D TELL THEM THEIR LOVED ONES DIED HEROES.
THAT THEY SAVED SOME KID OR SOMETHING.
I'D NEVER TELL THEM THE TRUTH--THAT THEY PROBABLY DIED SCARED.
BUT I TOOK COMFORT IN THAT LIE.
AS DID THEY.
IT JUST MADE OUR LIVES EASIER TO BELIEVE THE LIE.
NOW I ASK YOU...

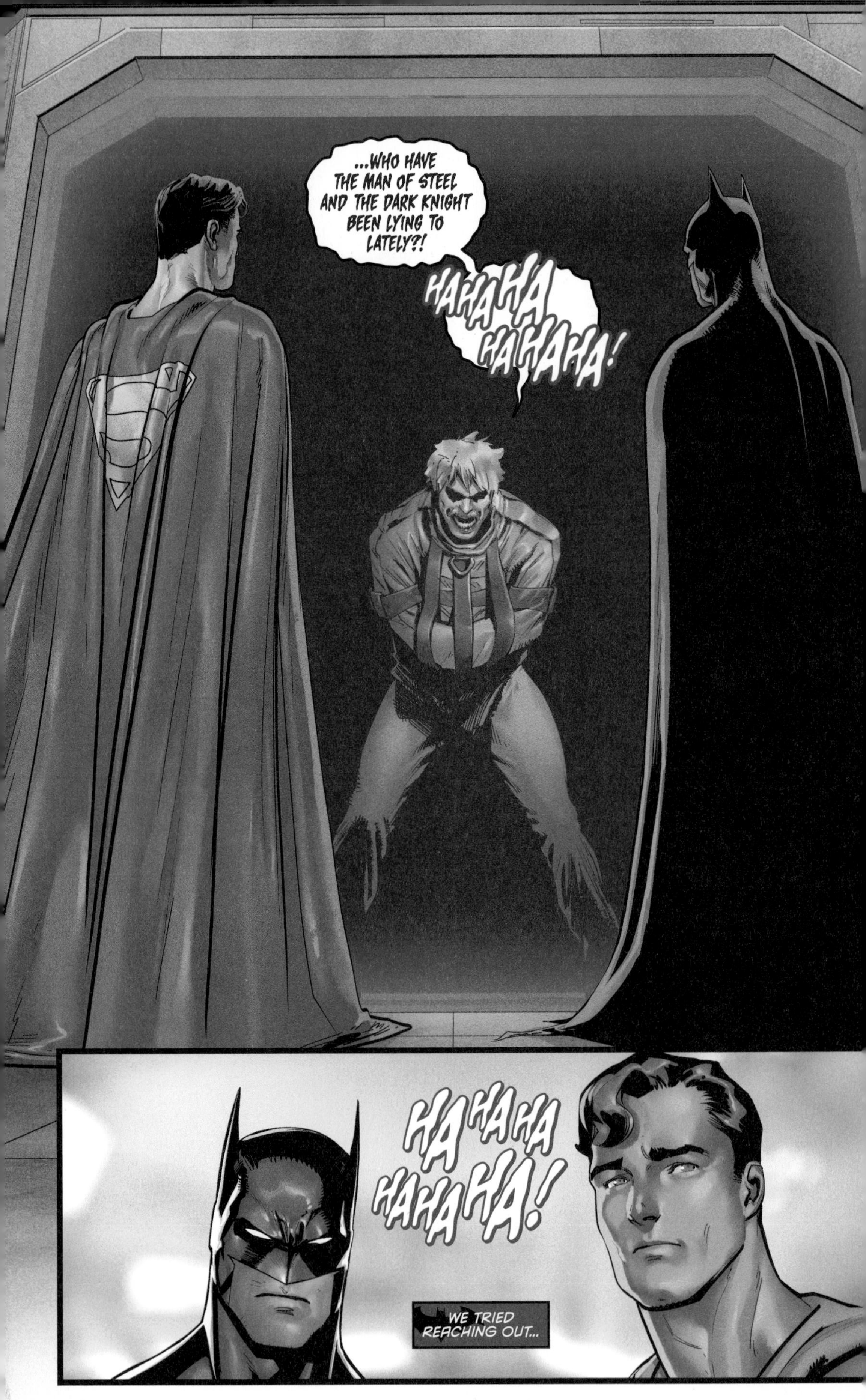
...WHO HAVE THE MAN OF STEEL AND THE DARK KNIGHT BEEN LYING TO LATELY?!
HAHAHA HAHAHA!
HAHAHA HAHAHAHA!
WE TRIED REACHING OUT...

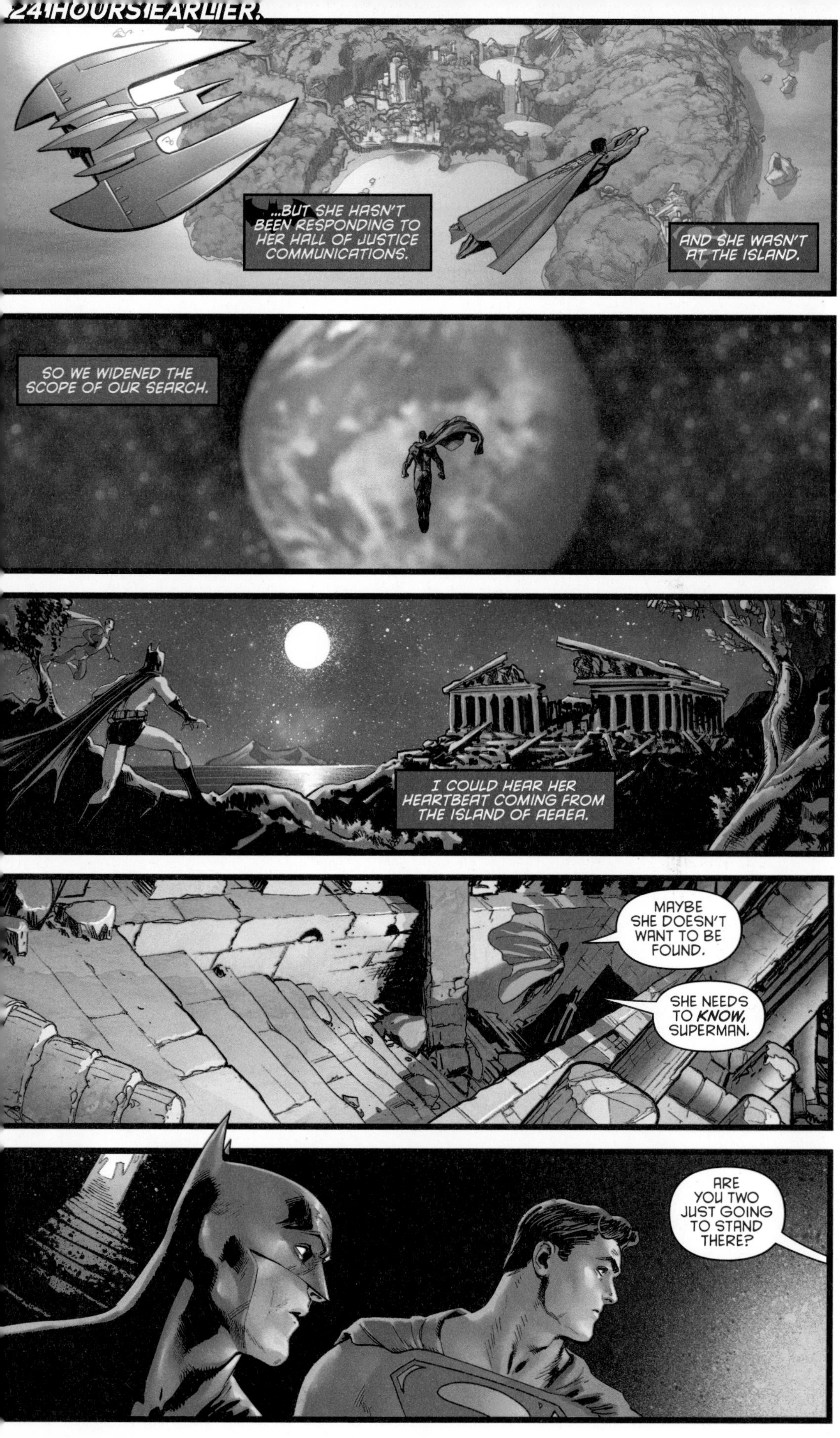

24 HOURS EARLIER.
...BUT SHE HASN'T BEEN RESPONDING TO HER HALL OF JUSTICE COMMUNICATIONS.
AND SHE WASN'T AT THE ISLAND.
SO WE WIDENED THE SCOPE OF OUR SEARCH.
I COULD HEAR HER HEARTBEAT COMING FROM THE ISLAND OF AEAEA.
MAYBE SHE DOESN'T WANT TO BE FOUND.
SHE NEEDS TO *KNOW,* SUPERMAN.
ARE YOU TWO JUST GOING TO STAND THERE?

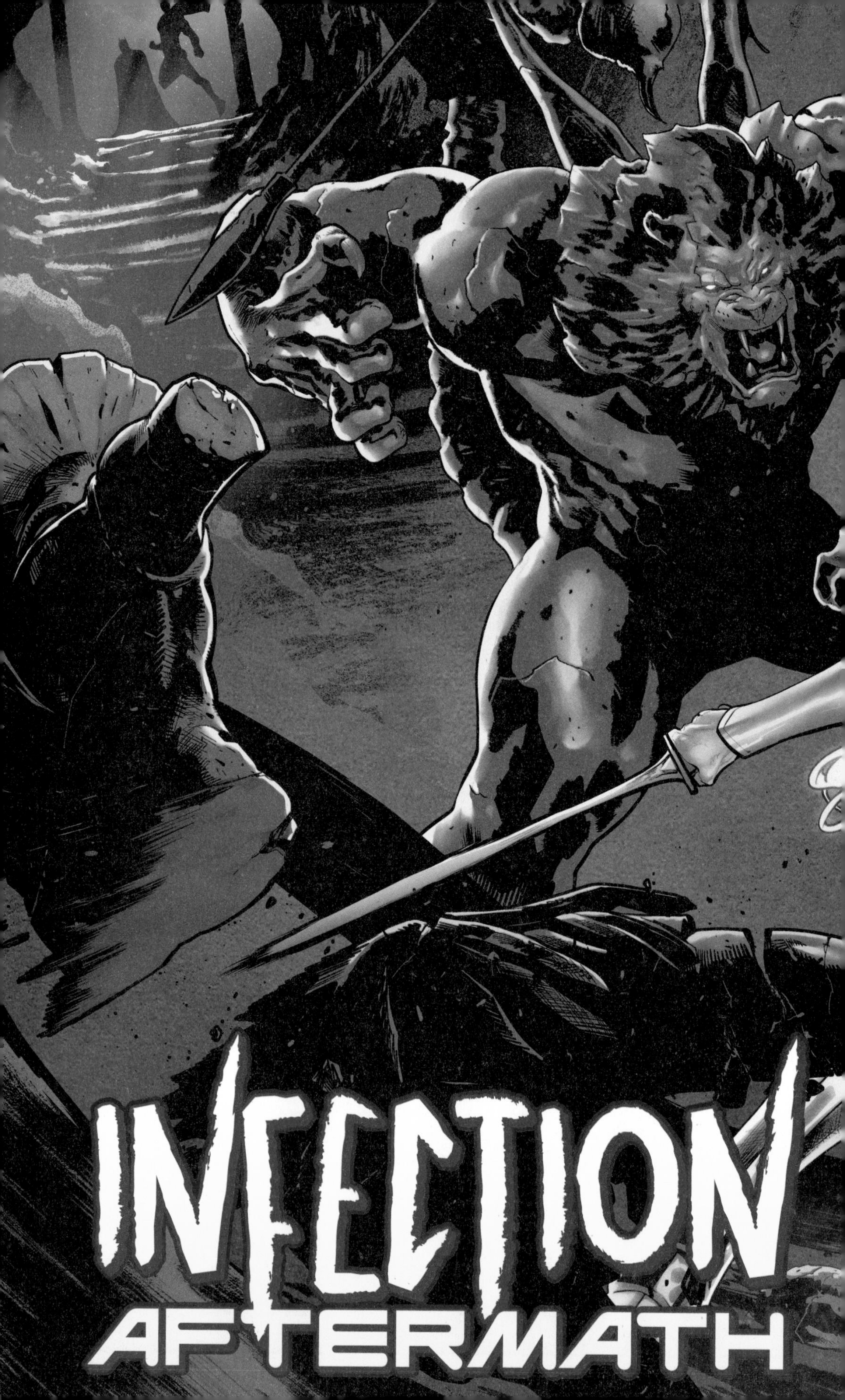
INFECTION
AFTERMATH

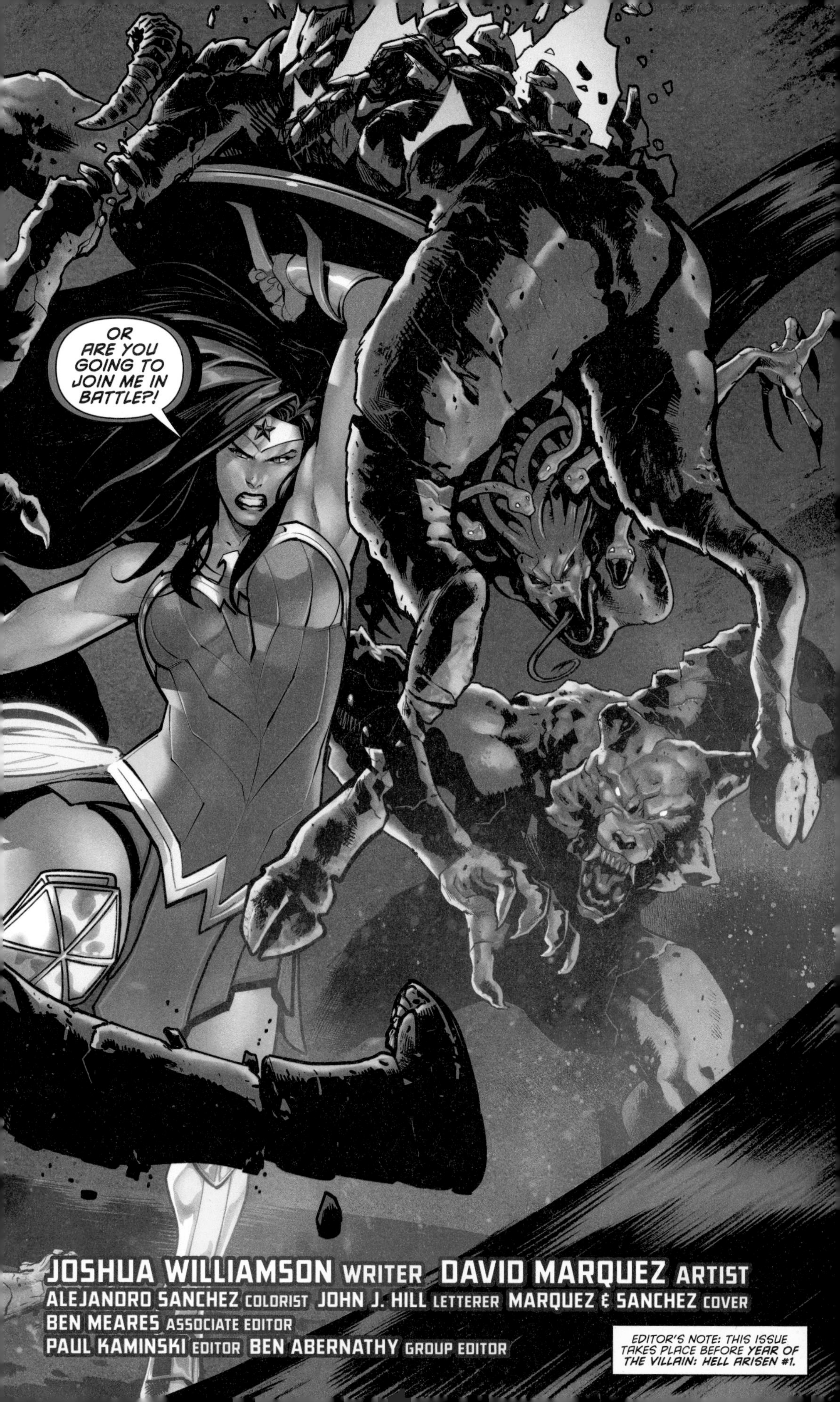
OR ARE YOU GOING TO JOIN ME IN BATTLE?!
JOSHUA WILLIAMSON WRITER DAVID MARQUEZ ARTIST
ALEJANDRO SANCHEZ COLORIST JOHN J. HILL LETTERER MARQUEZ & SANCHEZ COVER
BEN MEARES ASSOCIATE EDITOR
PAUL KAMINSKI EDITOR BEN ABERNATHY GROUP EDITOR
EDITOR'S NOTE: THIS ISSUE TAKES PLACE BEFORE YEAR OF THE VILLAIN: HELL ARISEN #1.

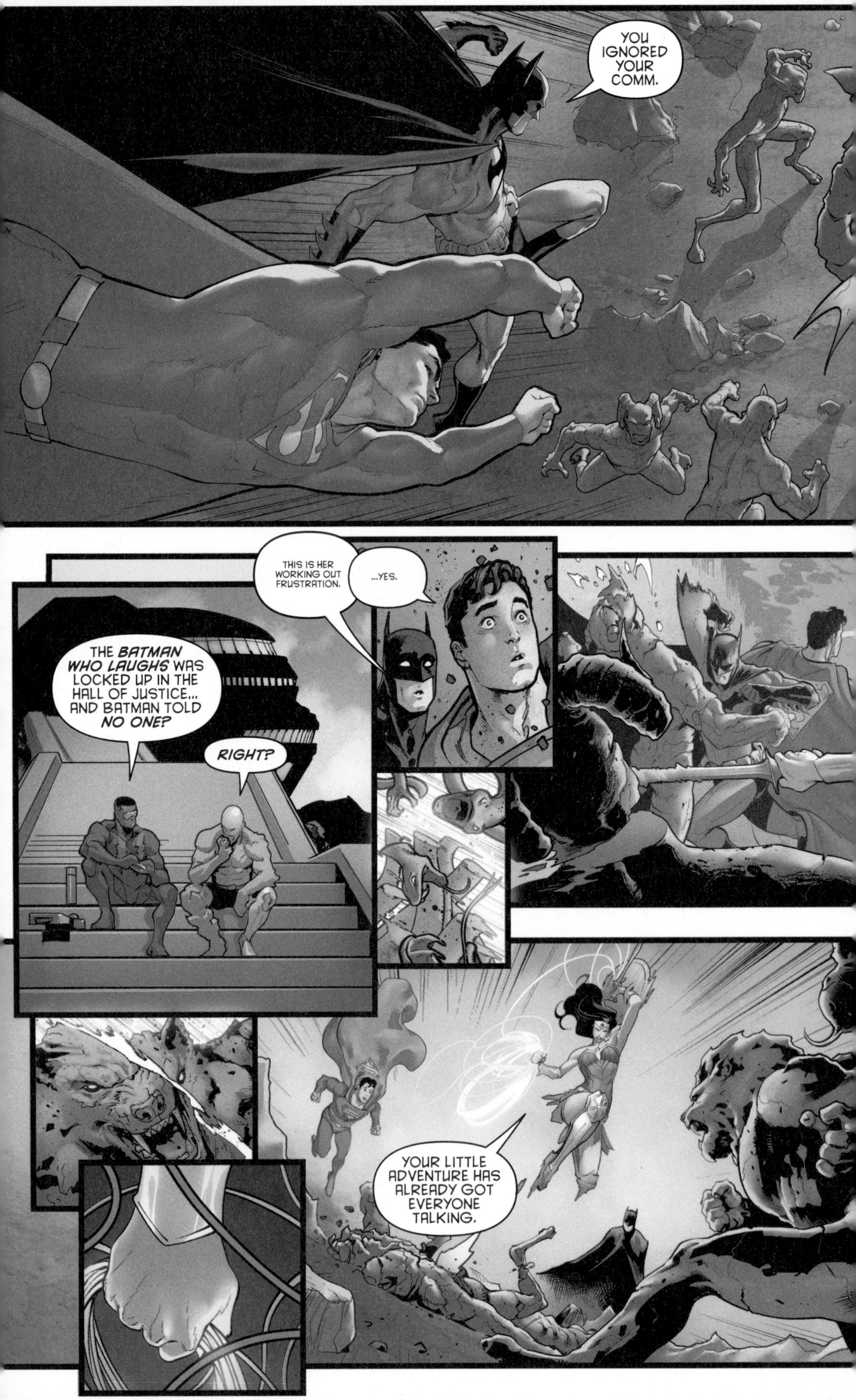
YOU IGNORED YOUR COMM.
THE BATMAN WHO LAUGHS WAS LOCKED UP IN THE HALL OF JUSTICE... AND BATMAN TOLD NO ONE?
RIGHT?
THIS IS HER WORKING OUT FRUSTRATION.
...YES.
YOUR LITTLE ADVENTURE HAS ALREADY GOT EVERYONE TALKING.

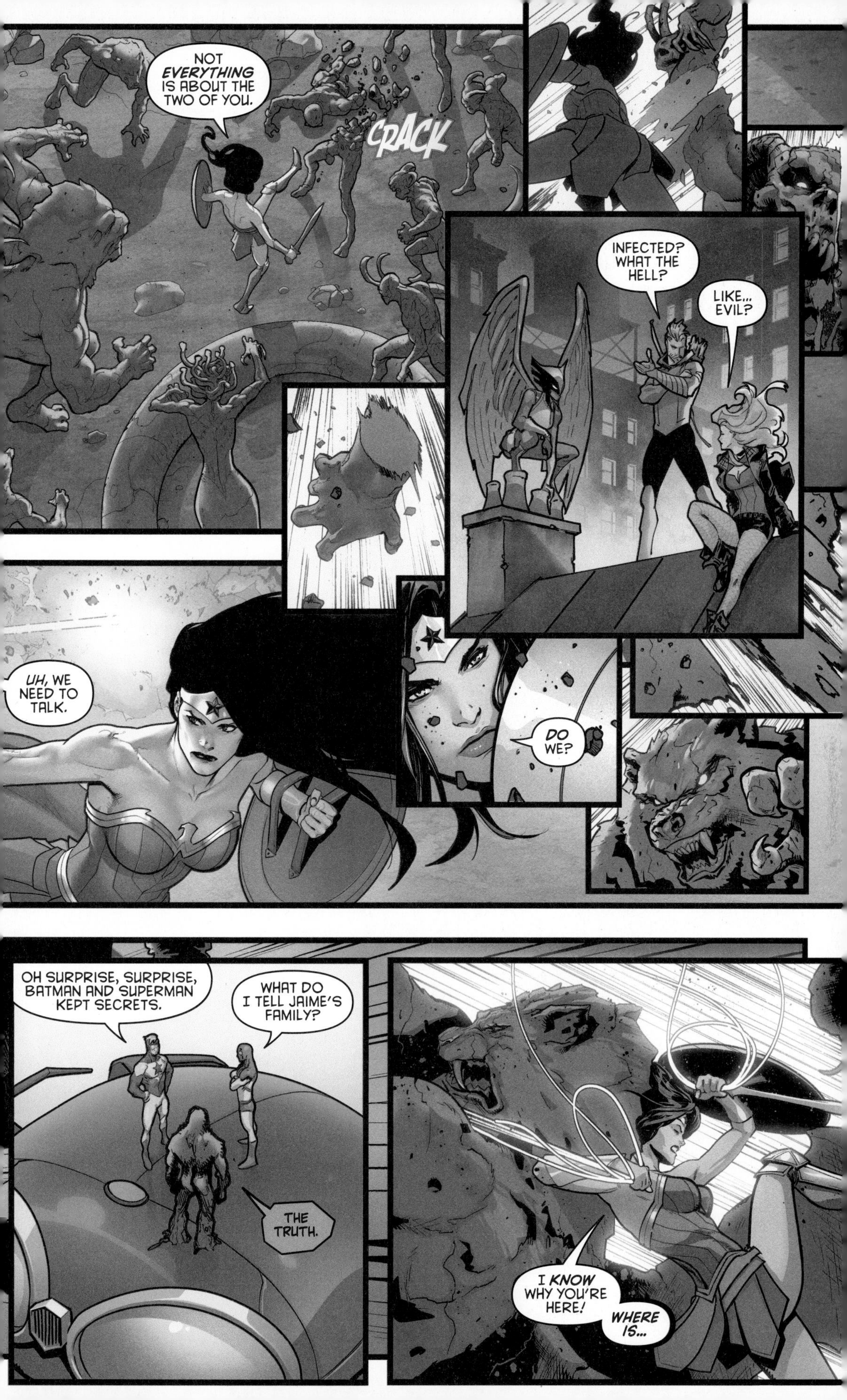
NOT EVERYTHING IS ABOUT THE TWO OF YOU.
CRACK
INFECTED? WHAT THE HELL?
LIKE... EVIL?
UH, WE NEED TO TALK.
DO WE?
OH SURPRISE, SURPRISE, BATMAN AND SUPERMAN KEPT SECRETS.
WHAT DO I TELL JAIME'S FAMILY?
THE TRUTH.
I KNOW WHY YOU'RE HERE!
WHERE IS...

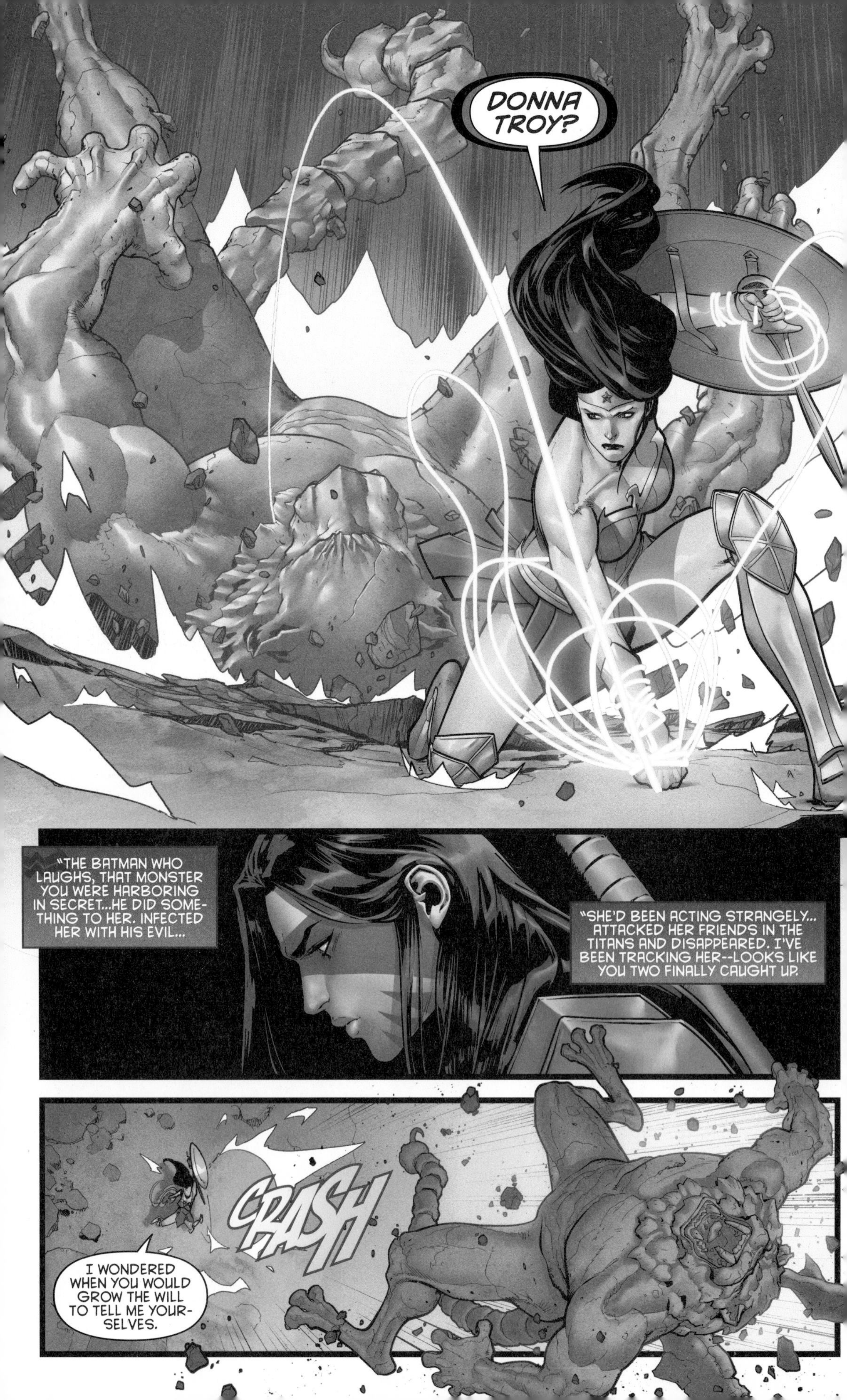
DONNA TROY?
"THE BATMAN WHO LAUGHS, THAT MONSTER YOU WERE HARBORING IN SECRET...HE DID SOMETHING TO HER. INFECTED HER WITH HIS EVIL...
"SHE'D BEEN ACTING STRANGELY... ATTACKED HER FRIENDS IN THE TITANS AND DISAPPEARED. I'VE BEEN TRACKING HER--LOOKS LIKE YOU TWO FINALLY CAUGHT UP.
CRASH
I WONDERED WHEN YOU WOULD GROW THE WILL TO TELL ME YOURSELVES.

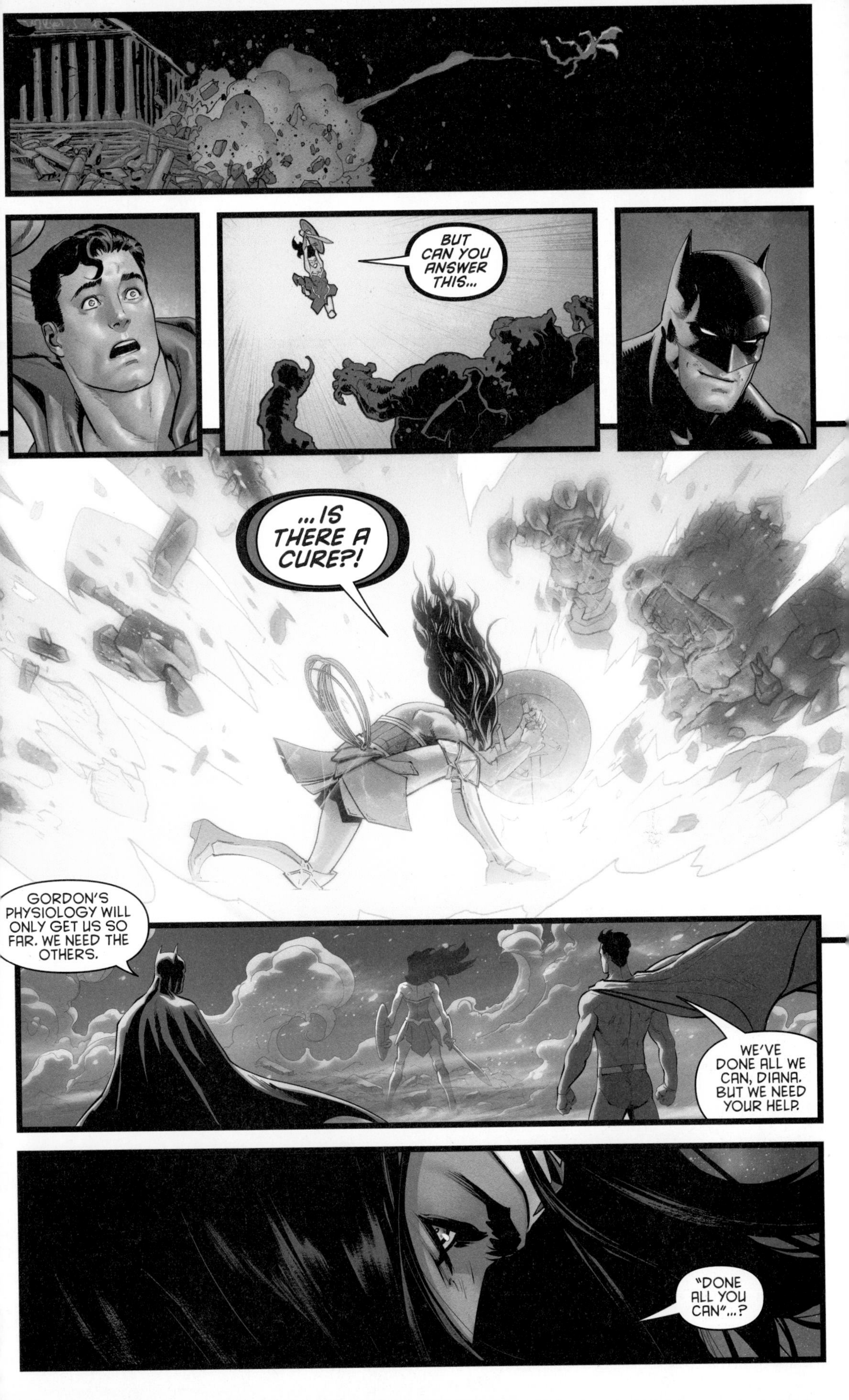
BUT CAN YOU ANSWER THIS...
...IS THERE A CURE?!
GORDON'S PHYSIOLOGY WILL ONLY GET US SO FAR. WE NEED THE OTHERS.
WE'VE DONE ALL WE CAN, DIANA. BUT WE NEED YOUR HELP.
"DONE ALL YOU CAN"...?

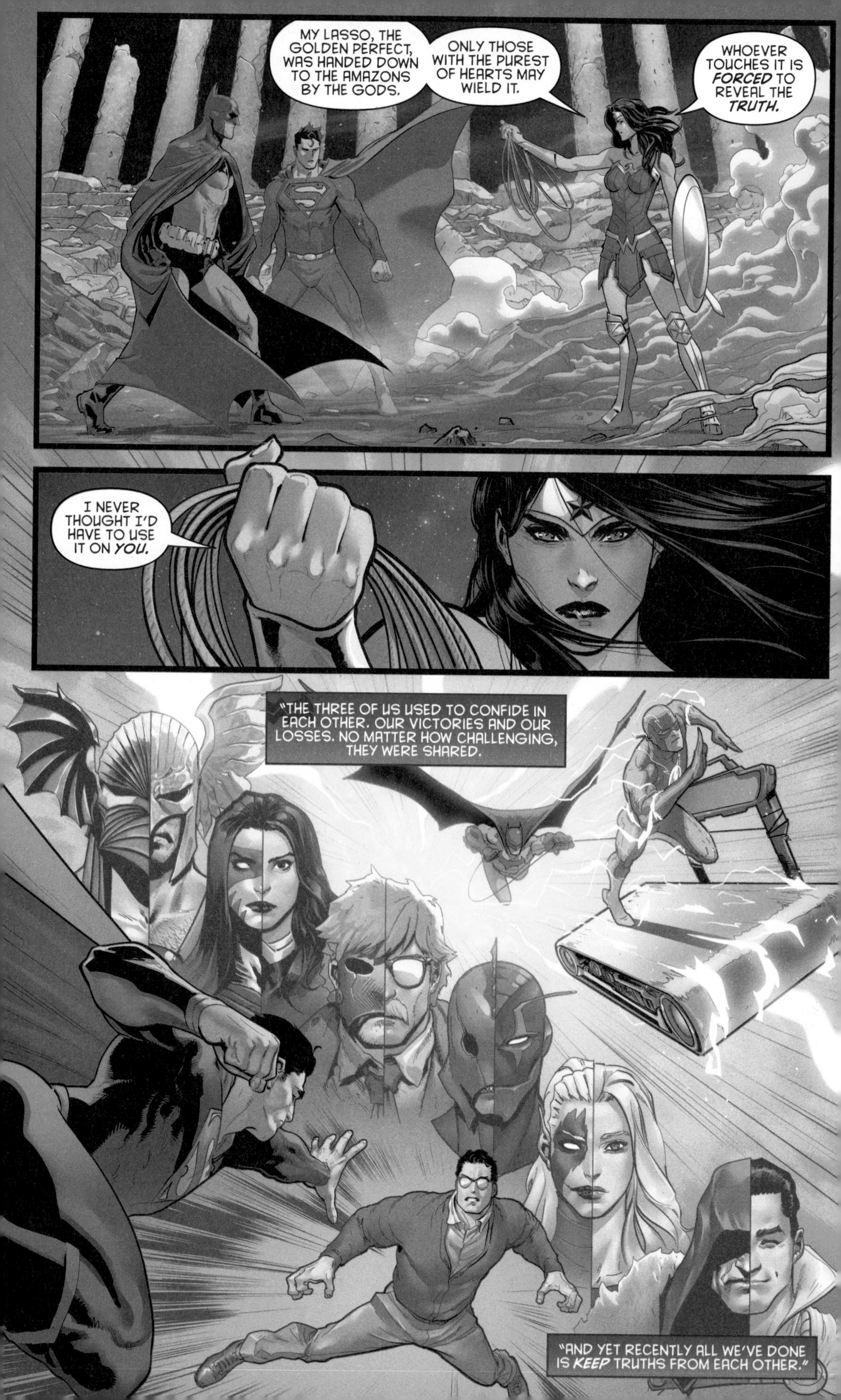
MY LASSO, THE GOLDEN PERFECT, WAS HANDED DOWN TO THE AMAZONS BY THE GODS.
ONLY THOSE WITH THE PUREST OF HEARTS MAY WIELD IT.
WHOEVER TOUCHES IT IS *FORCED* TO REVEAL THE *TRUTH.*
I NEVER THOUGHT I'D HAVE TO USE IT ON *YOU.*
"THE THREE OF US USED TO CONFIDE IN EACH OTHER. OUR VICTORIES AND OUR LOSSES. NO MATTER HOW CHALLENGING, THEY WERE SHARED.
"AND YET RECENTLY ALL WE'VE DONE IS *KEEP* TRUTHS FROM EACH OTHER."

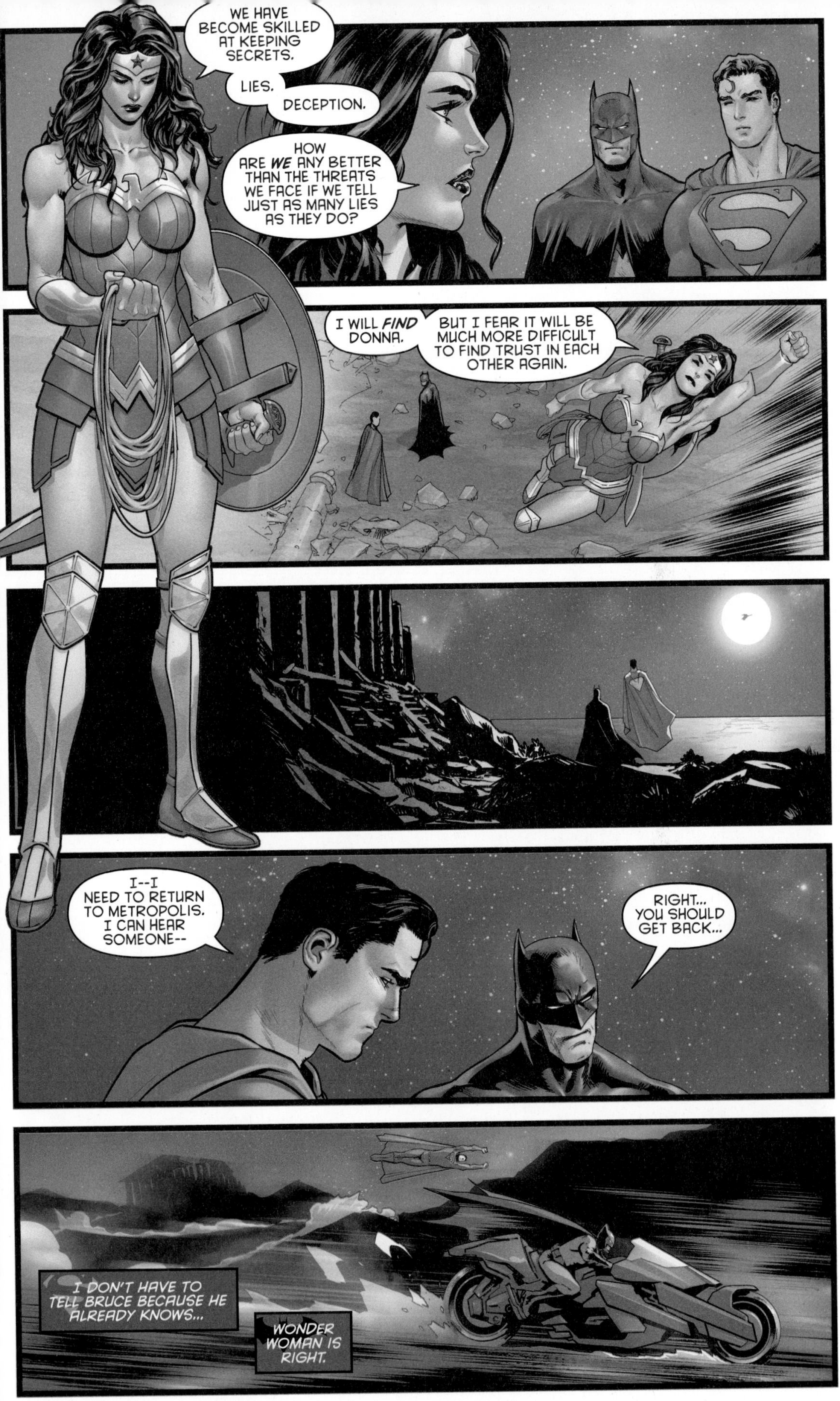
WE HAVE BECOME SKILLED AT KEEPING SECRETS.
LIES.
DECEPTION.
HOW ARE *WE* ANY BETTER THAN THE THREATS WE FACE IF WE TELL JUST AS MANY LIES AS THEY DO?
I WILL *FIND* DONNA.
BUT I FEAR IT WILL BE MUCH MORE DIFFICULT TO FIND TRUST IN EACH OTHER AGAIN.
I--I NEED TO RETURN TO METROPOLIS. I CAN HEAR SOMEONE--
RIGHT... YOU SHOULD GET BACK...
I DON'T HAVE TO TELL BRUCE BECAUSE HE ALREADY KNOWS...
WONDER WOMAN IS RIGHT.

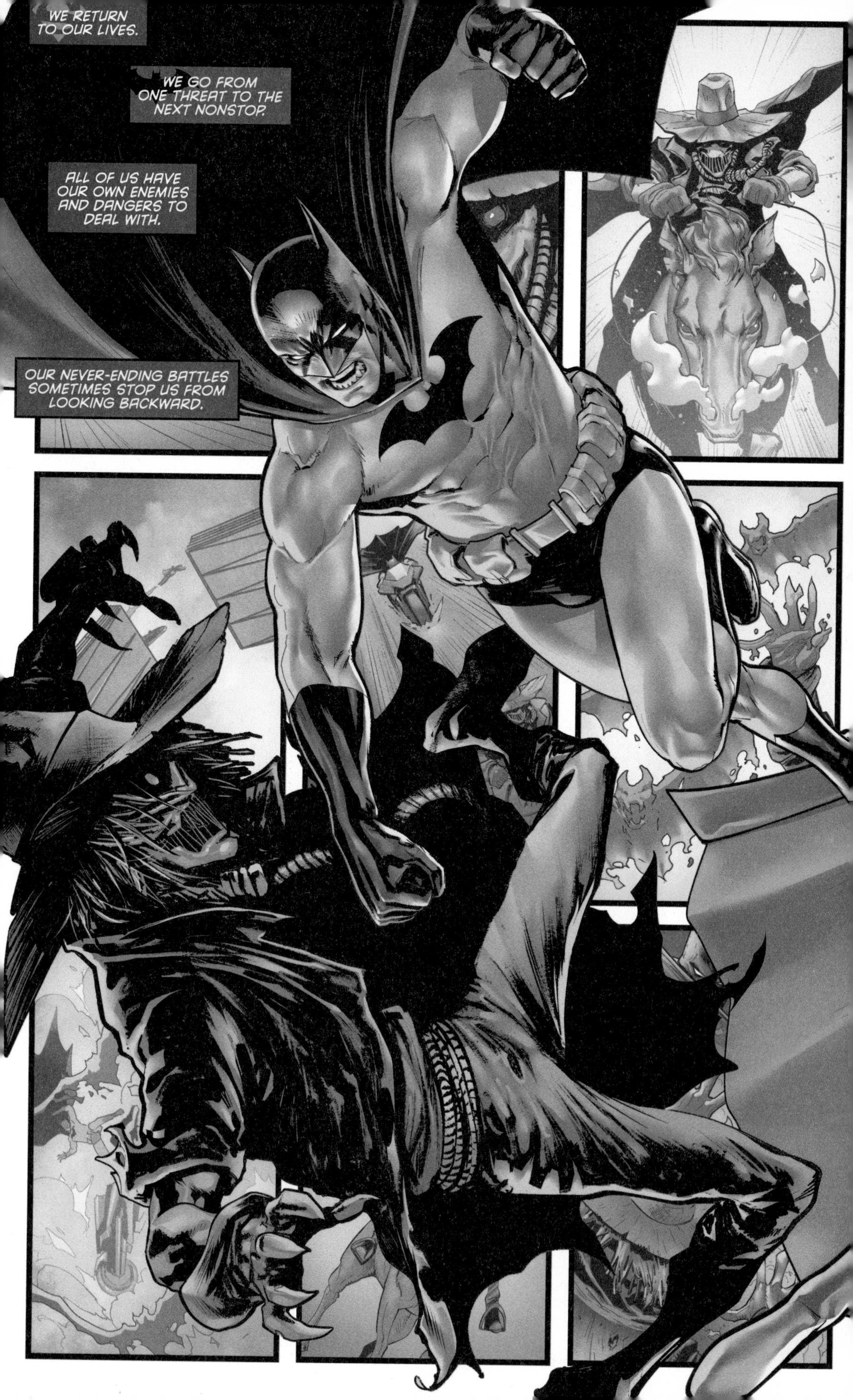
WE RETURN TO OUR LIVES.
WE GO FROM ONE THREAT TO THE NEXT NONSTOP.
ALL OF US HAVE OUR OWN ENEMIES AND DANGERS TO DEAL WITH.
OUR NEVER-ENDING BATTLES SOMETIMES STOP US FROM LOOKING BACKWARD.

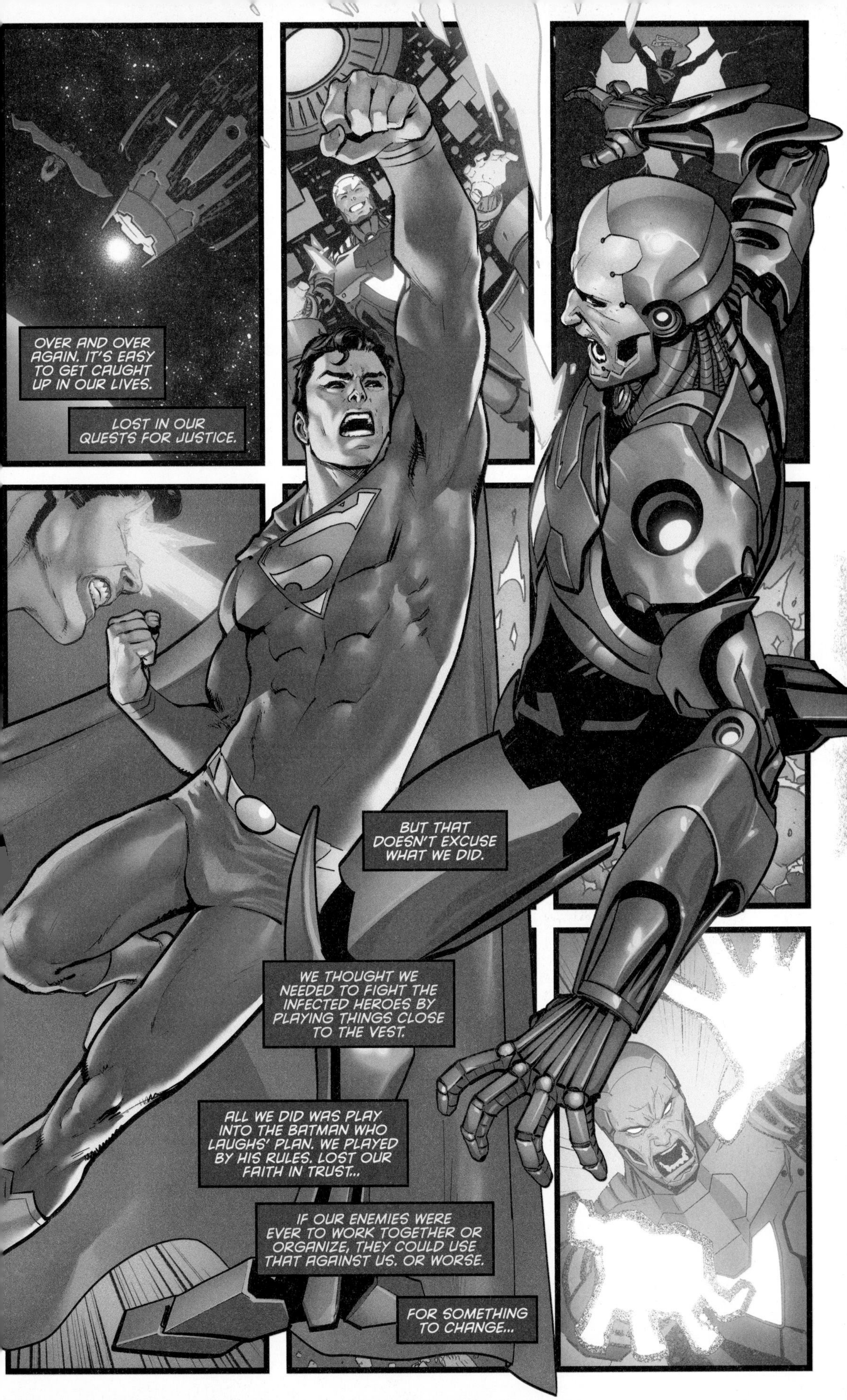
OVER AND OVER AGAIN. IT'S EASY TO GET CAUGHT UP IN OUR LIVES.
LOST IN OUR QUESTS FOR JUSTICE.
BUT THAT DOESN'T EXCUSE WHAT WE DID.
WE THOUGHT WE NEEDED TO FIGHT THE INFECTED HEROES BY PLAYING THINGS CLOSE TO THE VEST.
ALL WE DID WAS PLAY INTO THE BATMAN WHO LAUGHS' PLAN. WE PLAYED BY HIS RULES. LOST OUR FAITH IN TRUST...
IF OUR ENEMIES WERE EVER TO WORK TOGETHER OR ORGANIZE, THEY COULD USE THAT AGAINST US. OR WORSE.
FOR SOMETHING TO CHANGE...

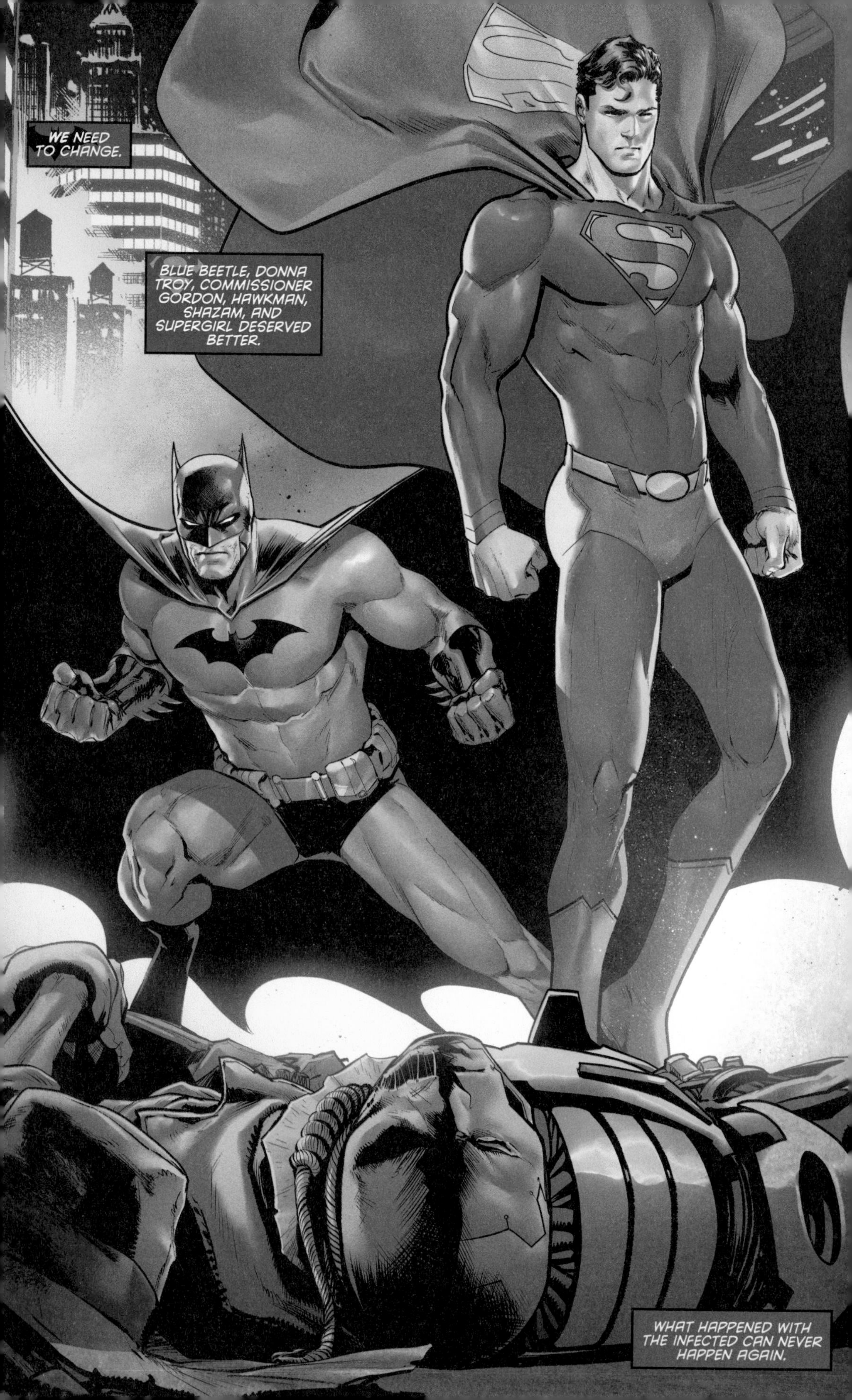
WE NEED TO CHANGE.
BLUE BEETLE, DONNA TROY, COMMISSIONER GORDON, HAWKMAN, SHAZAM, AND SUPERGIRL DESERVED BETTER.
WHAT HAPPENED WITH THE INFECTED CAN NEVER HAPPEN AGAIN.

WE MADE A LOT OF MISTAKES RECENTLY THAT COST US.

TIME ON OUR OWN ALLOWS US TO CONSIDER A *NEW WAY* OF DOING THINGS.

BRUCE LOVES TO BE MYSTERIOUS, BUT I KNOW HIM.

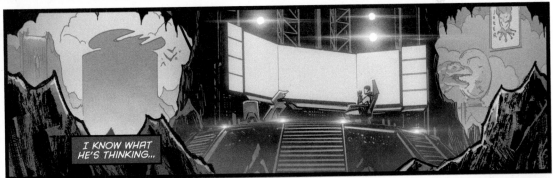

I KNOW WHAT HE'S THINKING...

SO... EVEN THOUGH YOU REVEALED YOUR SECRET IDENTITY TO THE WORLD--

--YOU'RE STILL WEARING THE GLASSES?

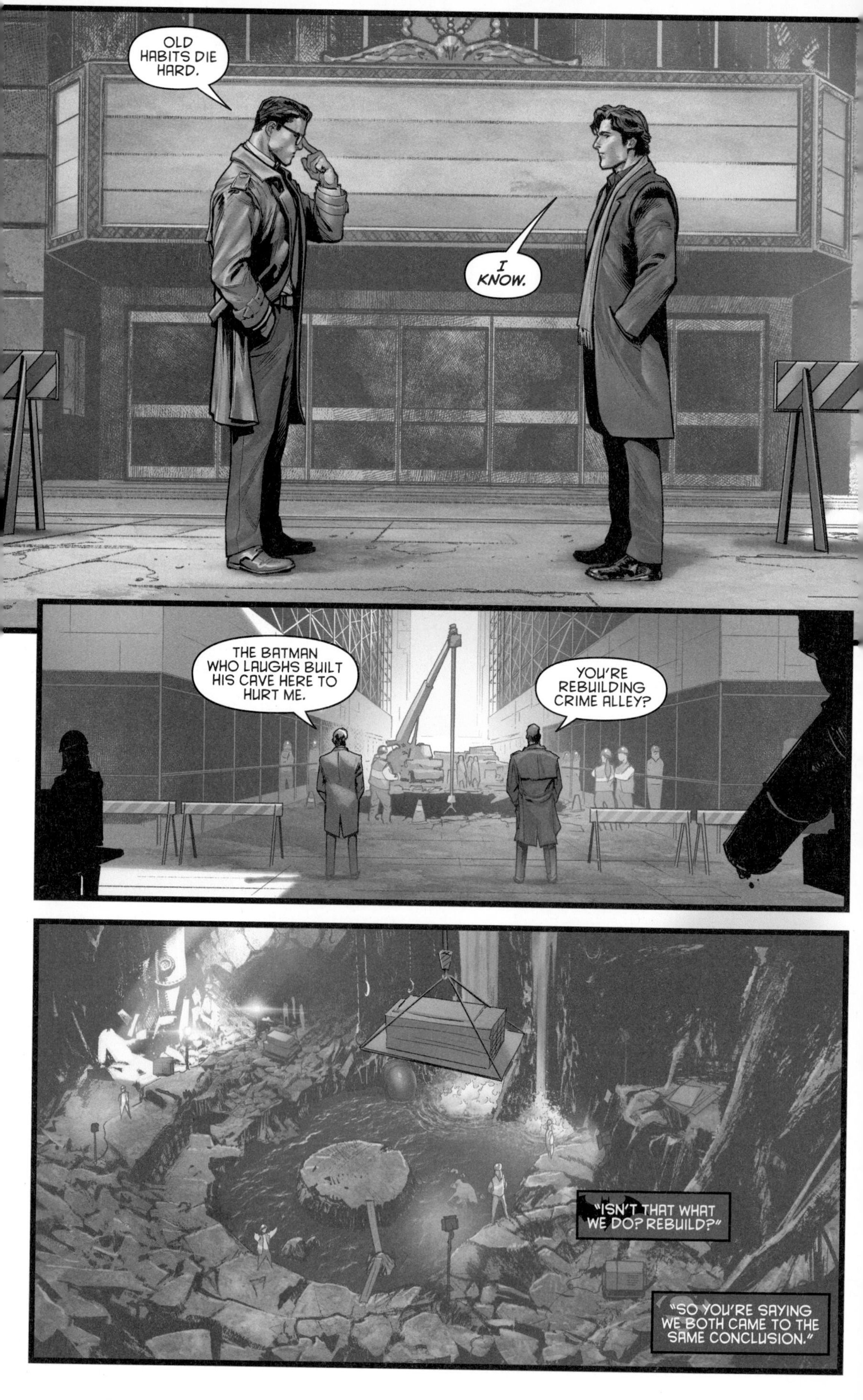
OLD HABITS DIE HARD.
I KNOW.
THE BATMAN WHO LAUGHS BUILT HIS CAVE HERE TO HURT ME.
YOU'RE REBUILDING CRIME ALLEY?
"ISN'T THAT WHAT WE DO? REBUILD?"
"SO YOU'RE SAYING WE BOTH CAME TO THE SAME CONCLUSION."

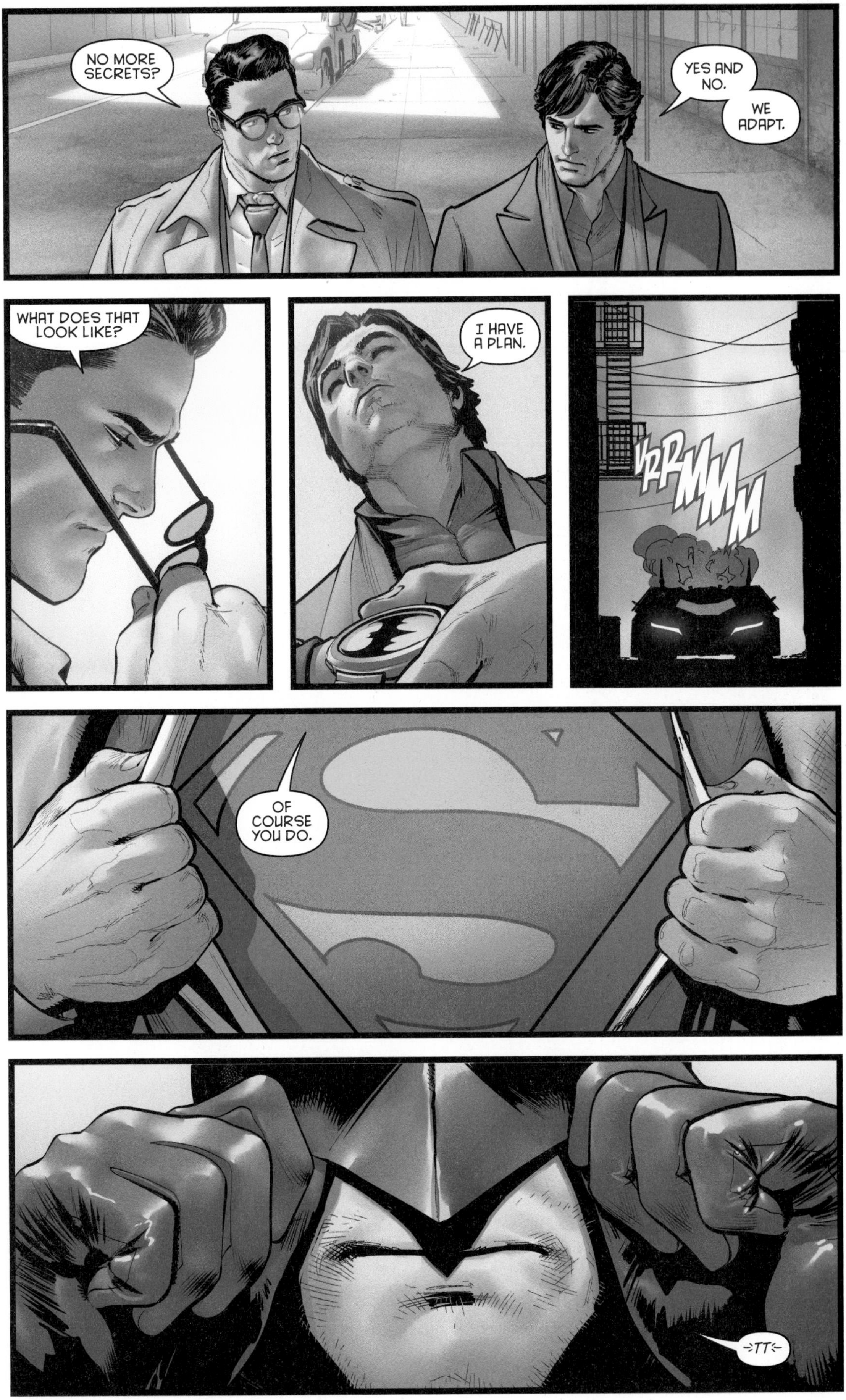
NO MORE SECRETS?
YES AND NO.
WE ADAPT.
WHAT DOES THAT LOOK LIKE?
I HAVE A PLAN.
VRRMMMM
OF COURSE YOU DO.
TT

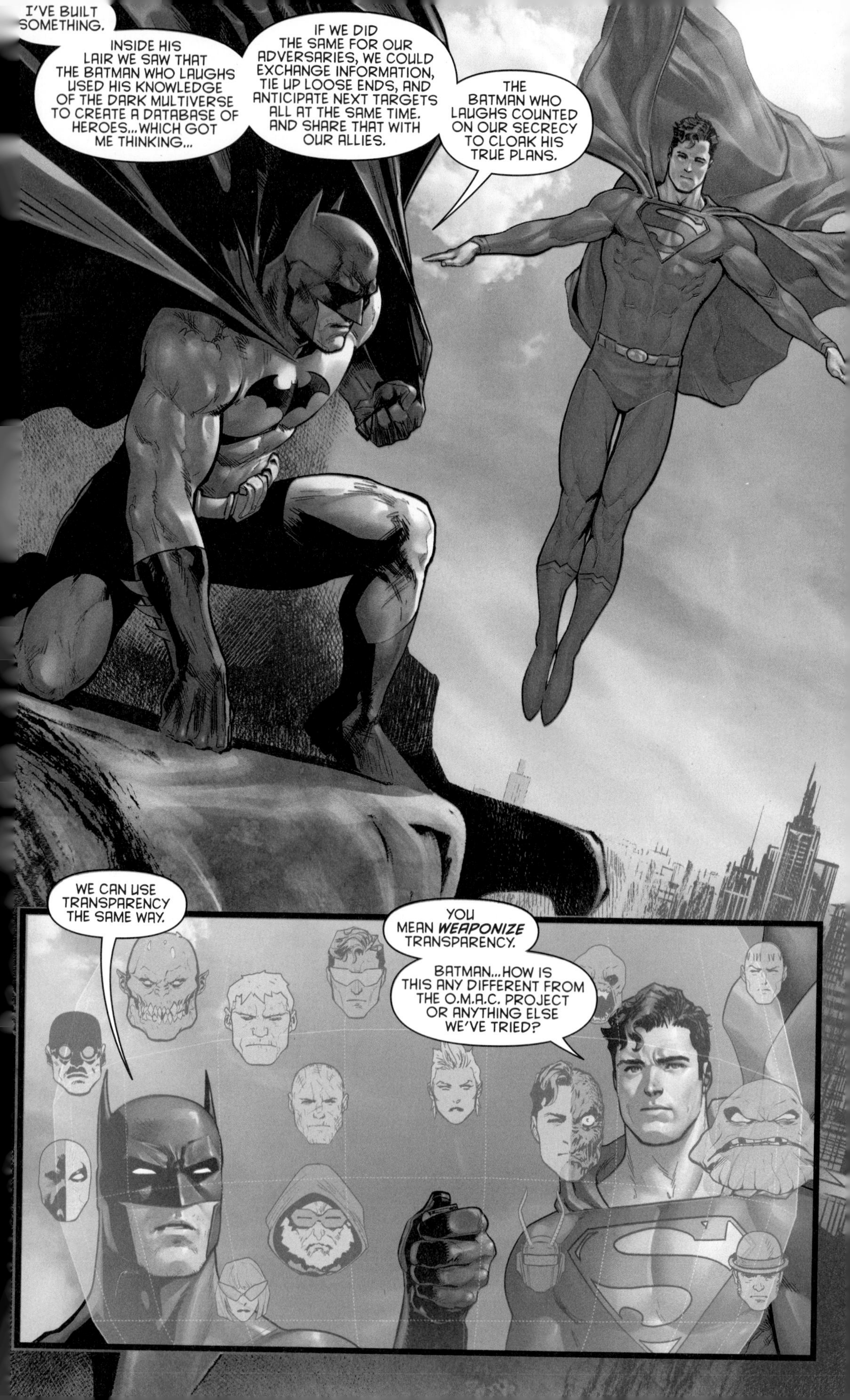
I'VE BUILT SOMETHING.
INSIDE HIS LAIR WE SAW THAT THE BATMAN WHO LAUGHS USED HIS KNOWLEDGE OF THE DARK MULTIVERSE TO CREATE A DATABASE OF HEROES...WHICH GOT ME THINKING...
IF WE DID THE SAME FOR OUR ADVERSARIES, WE COULD EXCHANGE INFORMATION, TIE UP LOOSE ENDS, AND ANTICIPATE NEXT TARGETS ALL AT THE SAME TIME. AND SHARE THAT WITH OUR ALLIES.
THE BATMAN WHO LAUGHS COUNTED ON OUR SECRECY TO CLOAK HIS TRUE PLANS.
WE CAN USE TRANSPARENCY THE SAME WAY.
YOU MEAN ***WEAPONIZE*** TRANSPARENCY.
BATMAN...HOW IS THIS ANY DIFFERENT FROM THE O.M.A.C. PROJECT OR ANYTHING ELSE WE'VE TRIED?

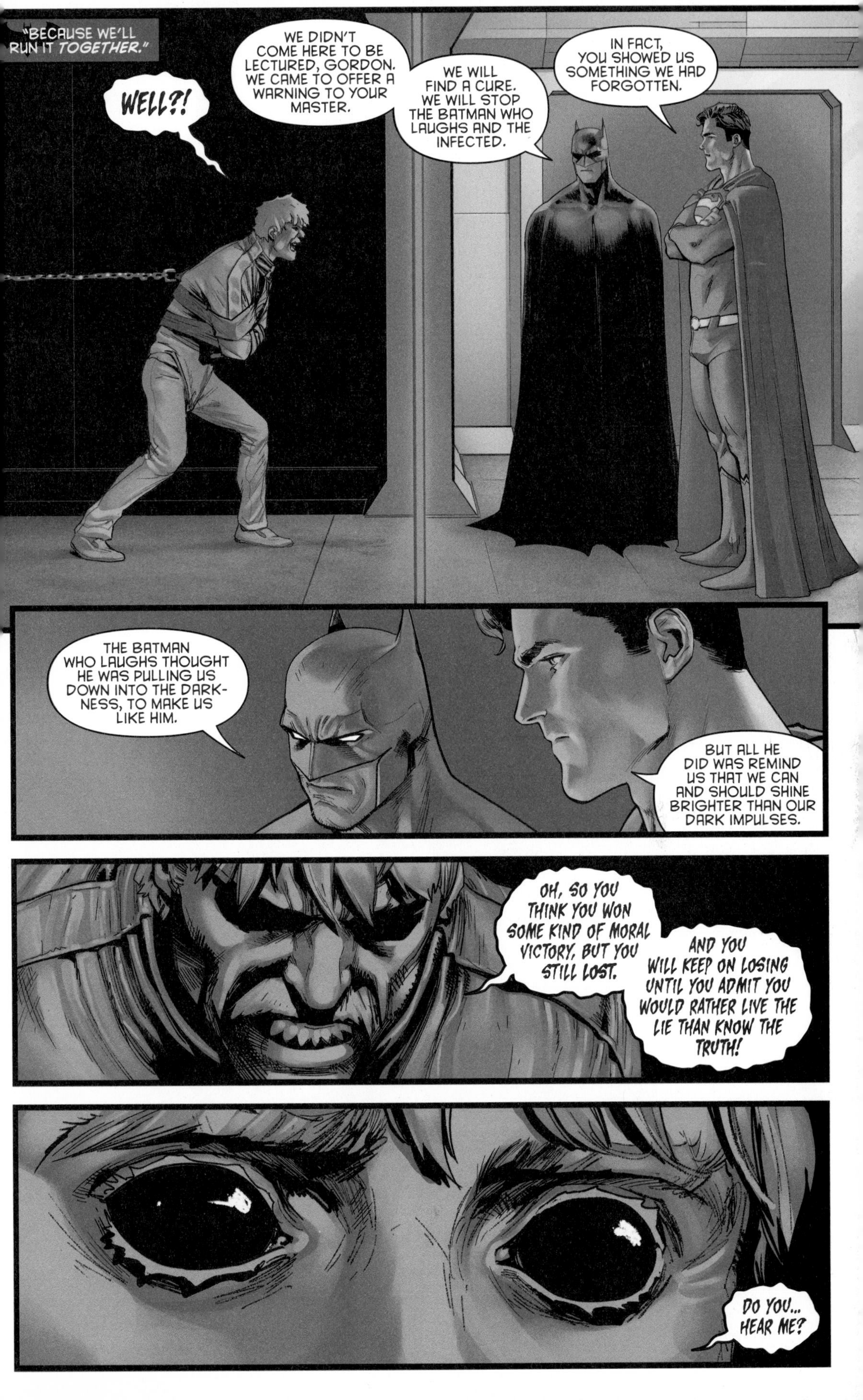
"BECAUSE WE'LL RUN IT *TOGETHER.*"
WELL?!
WE DIDN'T COME HERE TO BE LECTURED, GORDON. WE CAME TO OFFER A WARNING TO YOUR MASTER.
WE WILL FIND A CURE. WE WILL STOP THE BATMAN WHO LAUGHS AND THE INFECTED.
IN FACT, YOU SHOWED US SOMETHING WE HAD FORGOTTEN.
THE BATMAN WHO LAUGHS THOUGHT HE WAS PULLING US DOWN INTO THE DARK-NESS, TO MAKE US LIKE HIM.
BUT ALL HE DID WAS REMIND US THAT WE CAN AND SHOULD SHINE BRIGHTER THAN OUR DARK IMPULSES.
OH, SO YOU THINK YOU WON SOME KIND OF MORAL VICTORY, BUT YOU STILL LOST.
AND YOU WILL KEEP ON LOSING UNTIL YOU ADMIT YOU WOULD RATHER LIVE THE LIE THAN KNOW THE TRUTH!
DO YOU... HEAR ME?

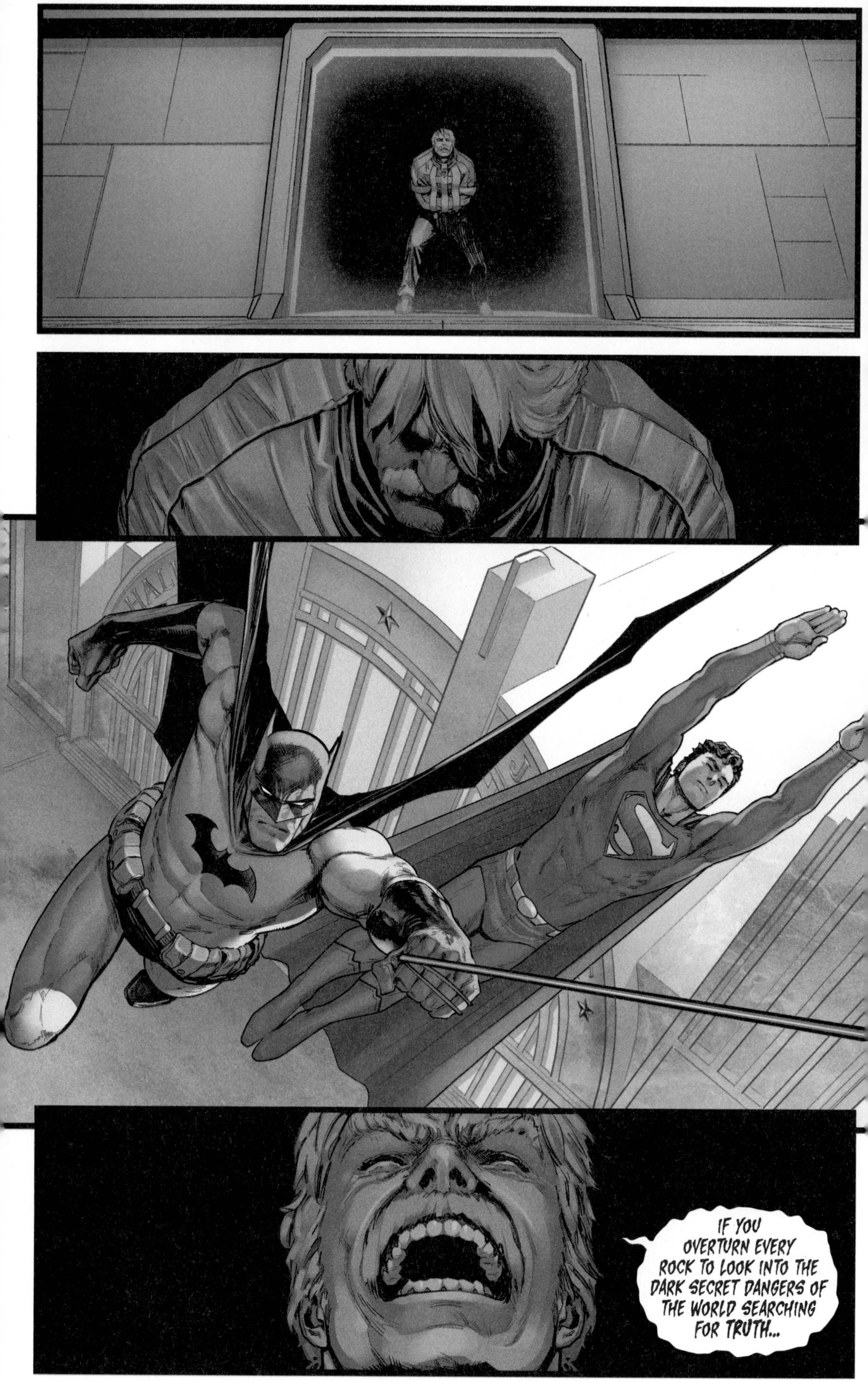
IF YOU OVERTURN EVERY ROCK TO LOOK INTO THE DARK SECRET DANGERS OF THE WORLD SEARCHING FOR TRUTH...

Batman/Superman #1 cover line art by **DAVID MARQUEZ**

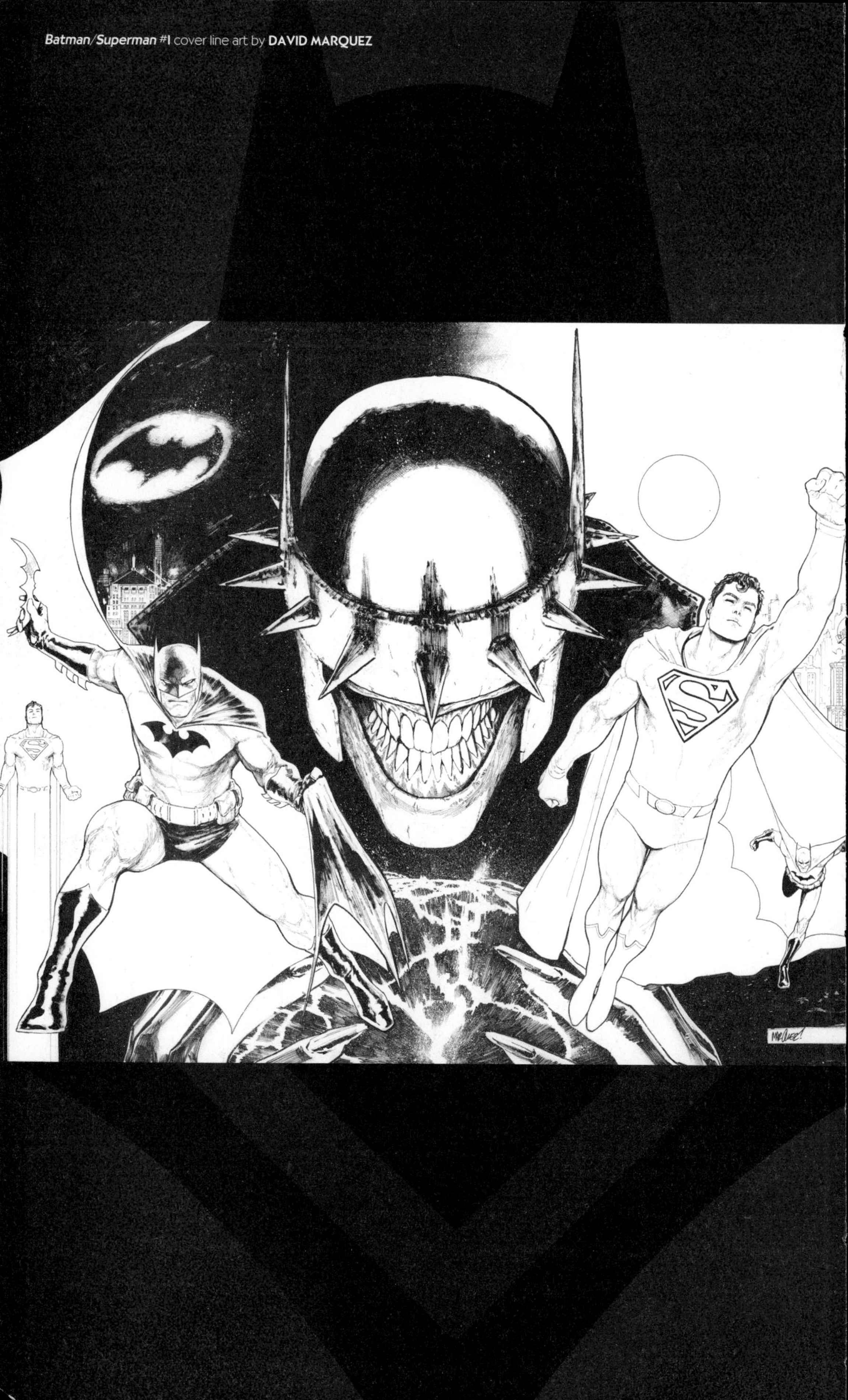

Batman/Superman #4 secondary cover image by
EMANUELA LUPACCHINO and REX LOKUS

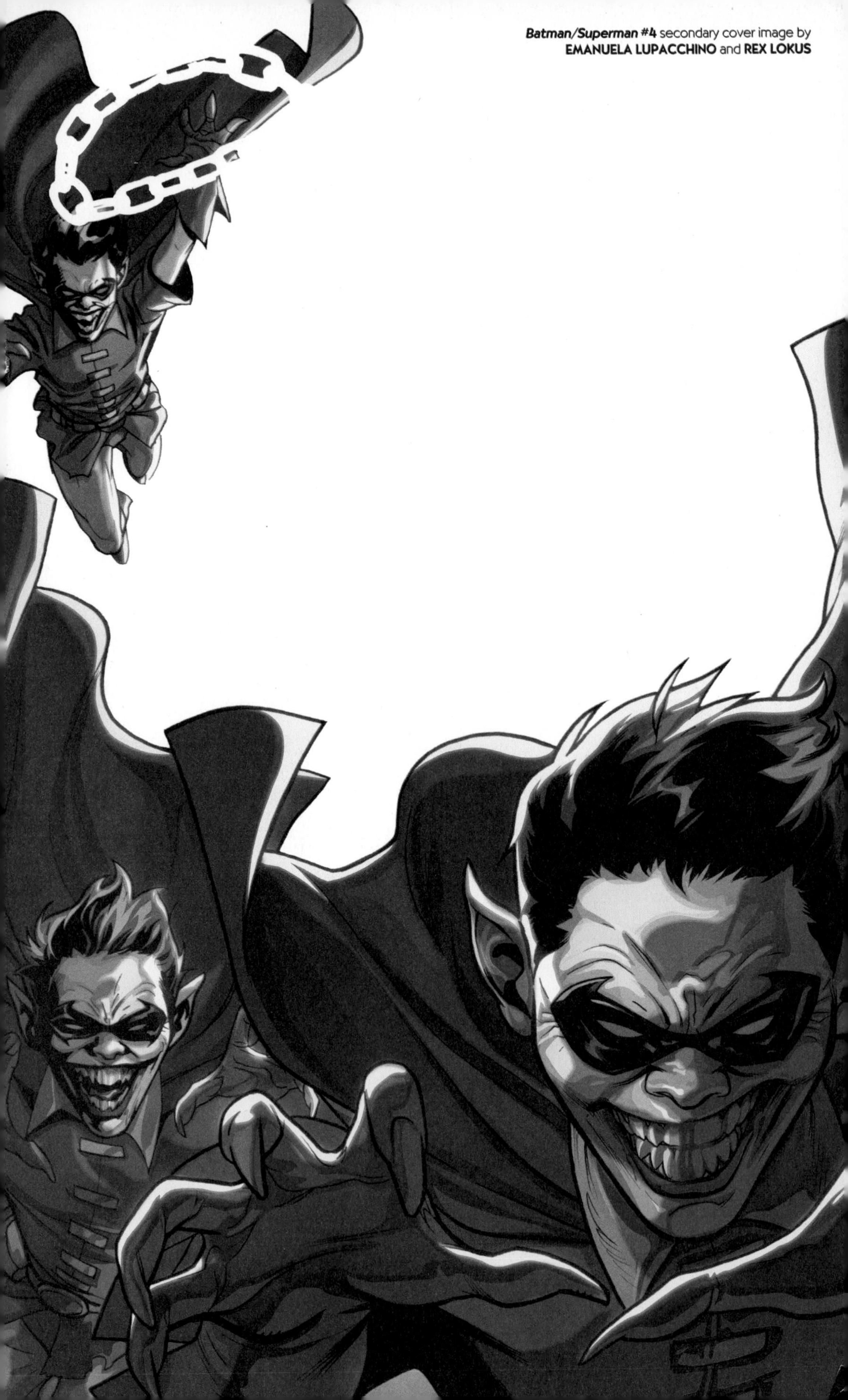

Batman/Superman #1 full wraparound cover by **DAVID MARQUEZ** and **ALEJANDRO SANCHEZ**

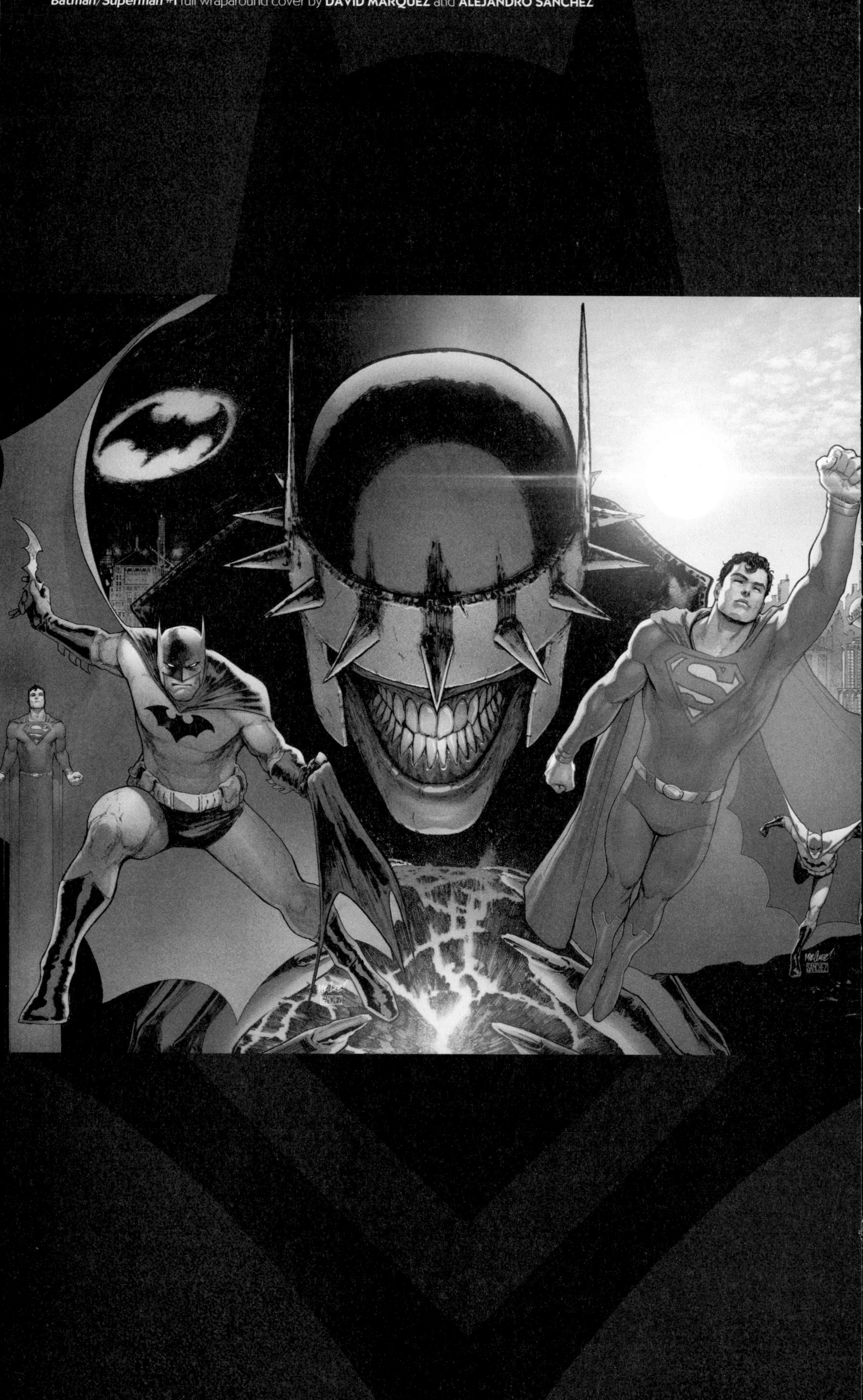

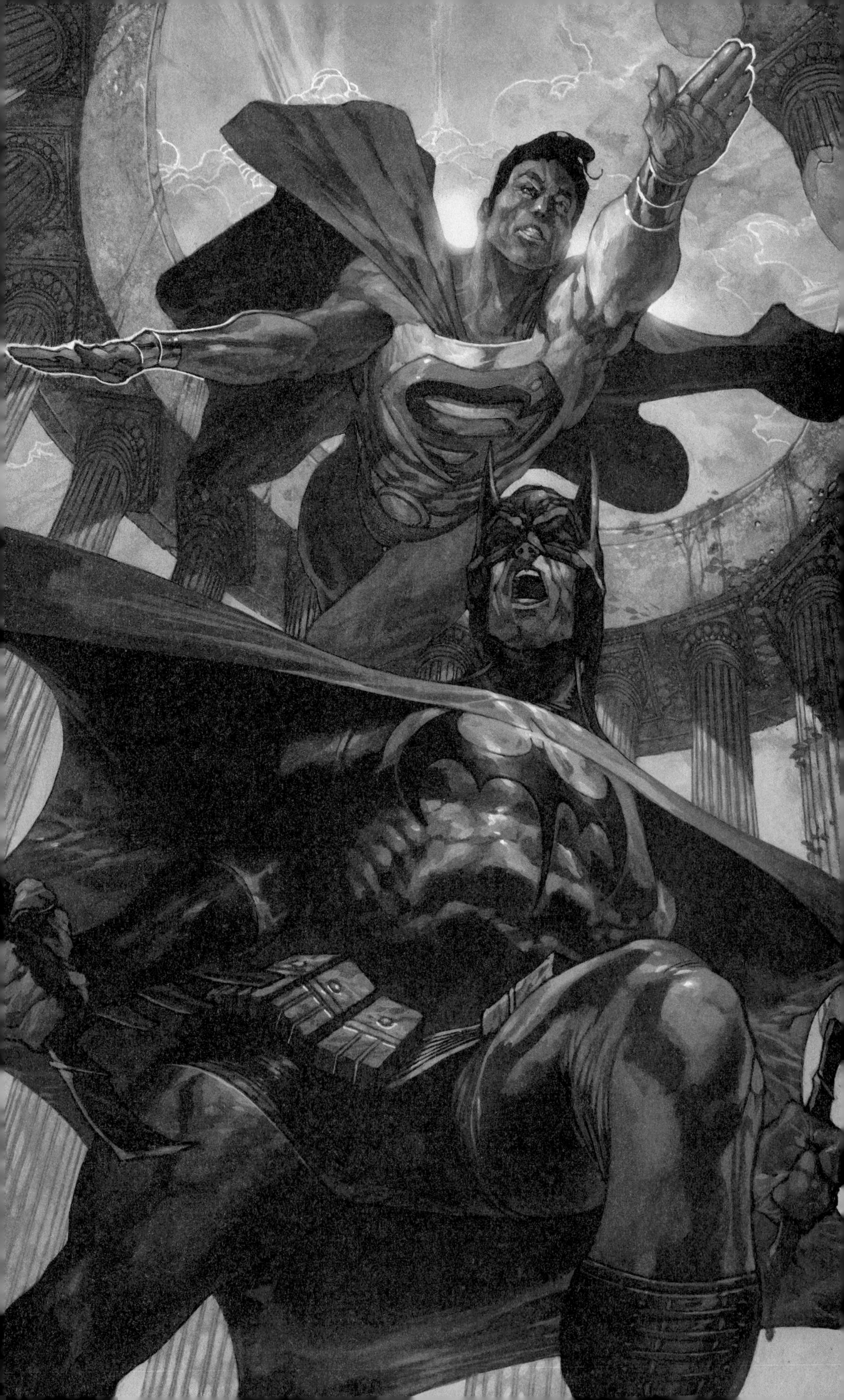

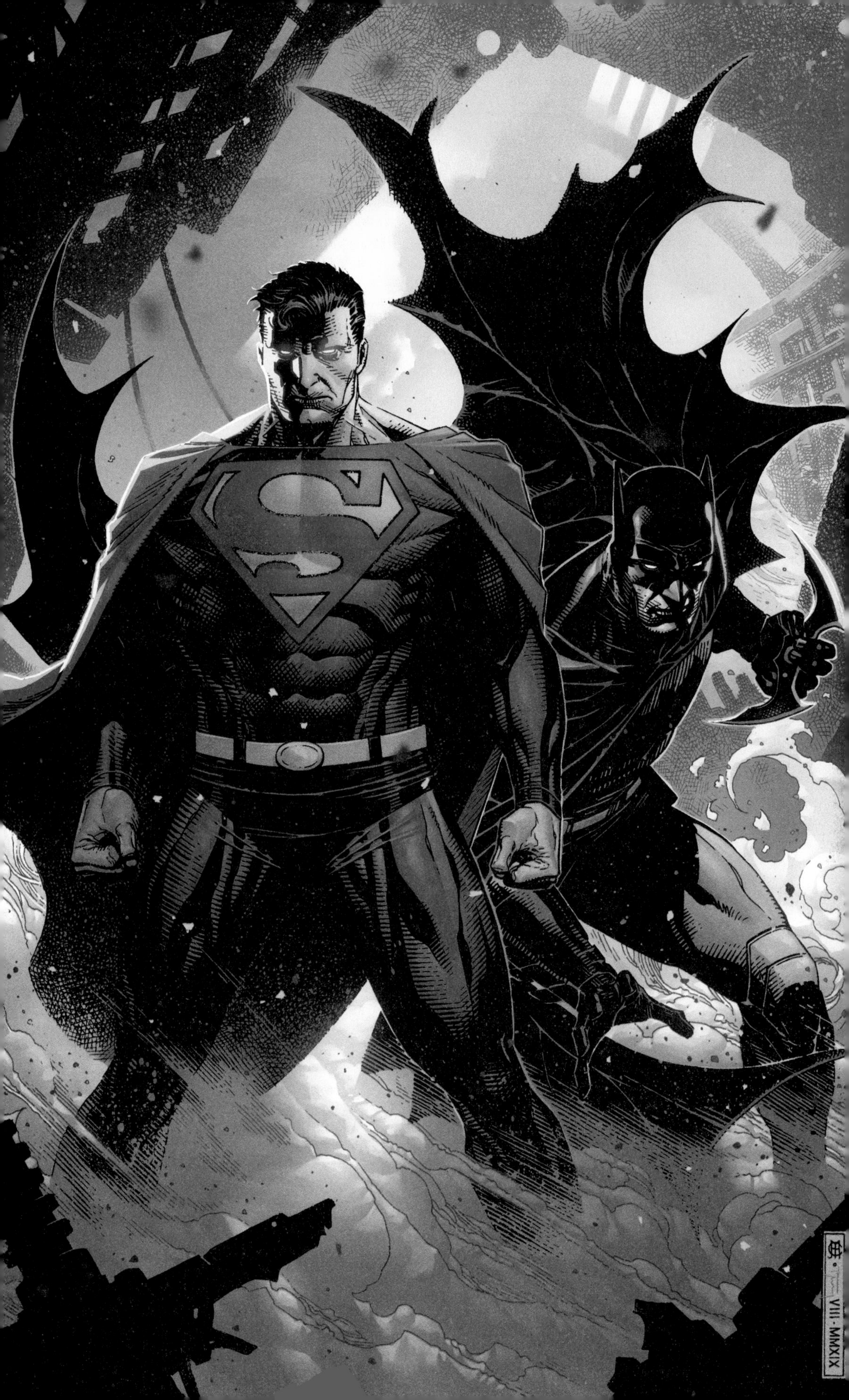
VIII·MMXIX

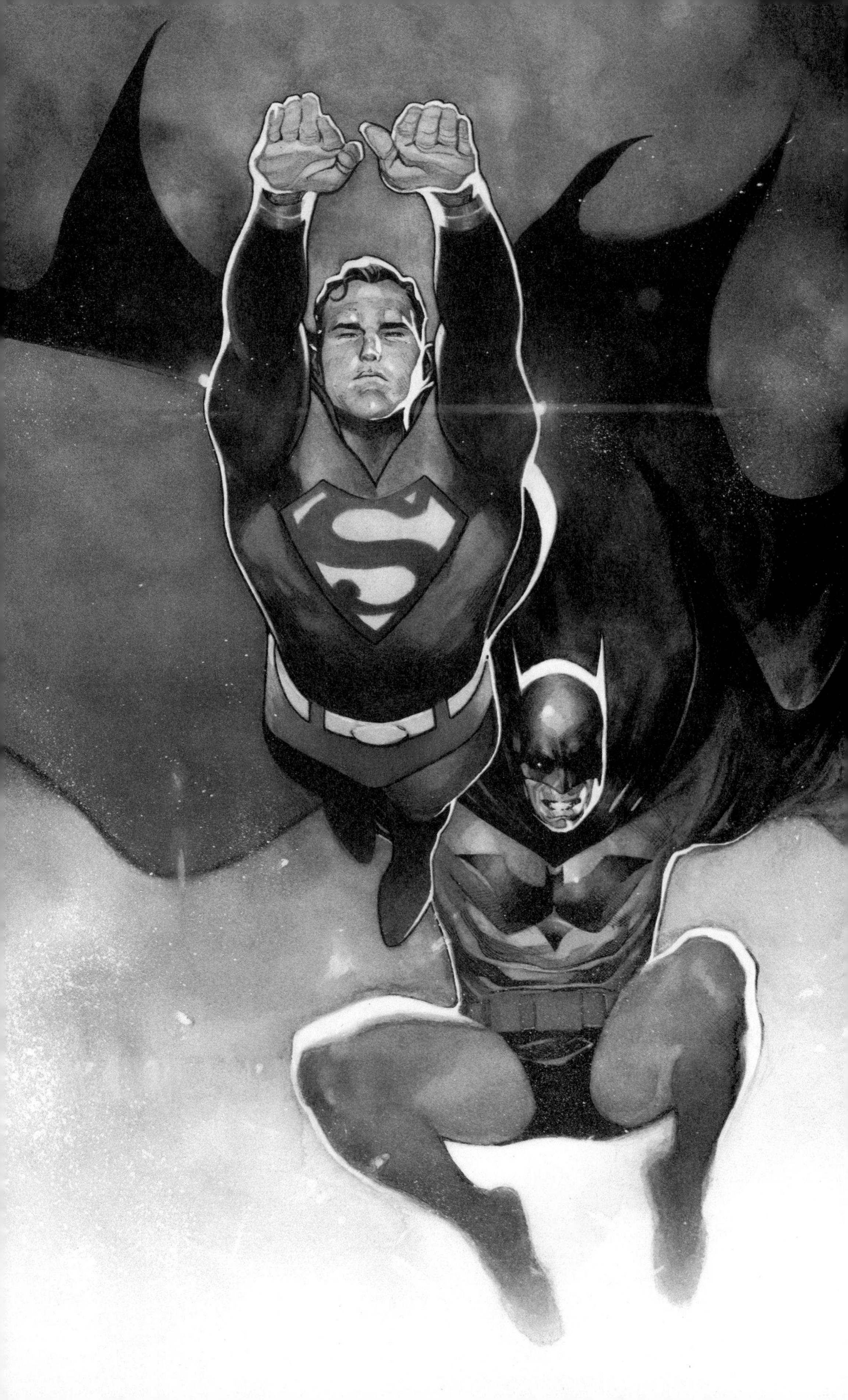

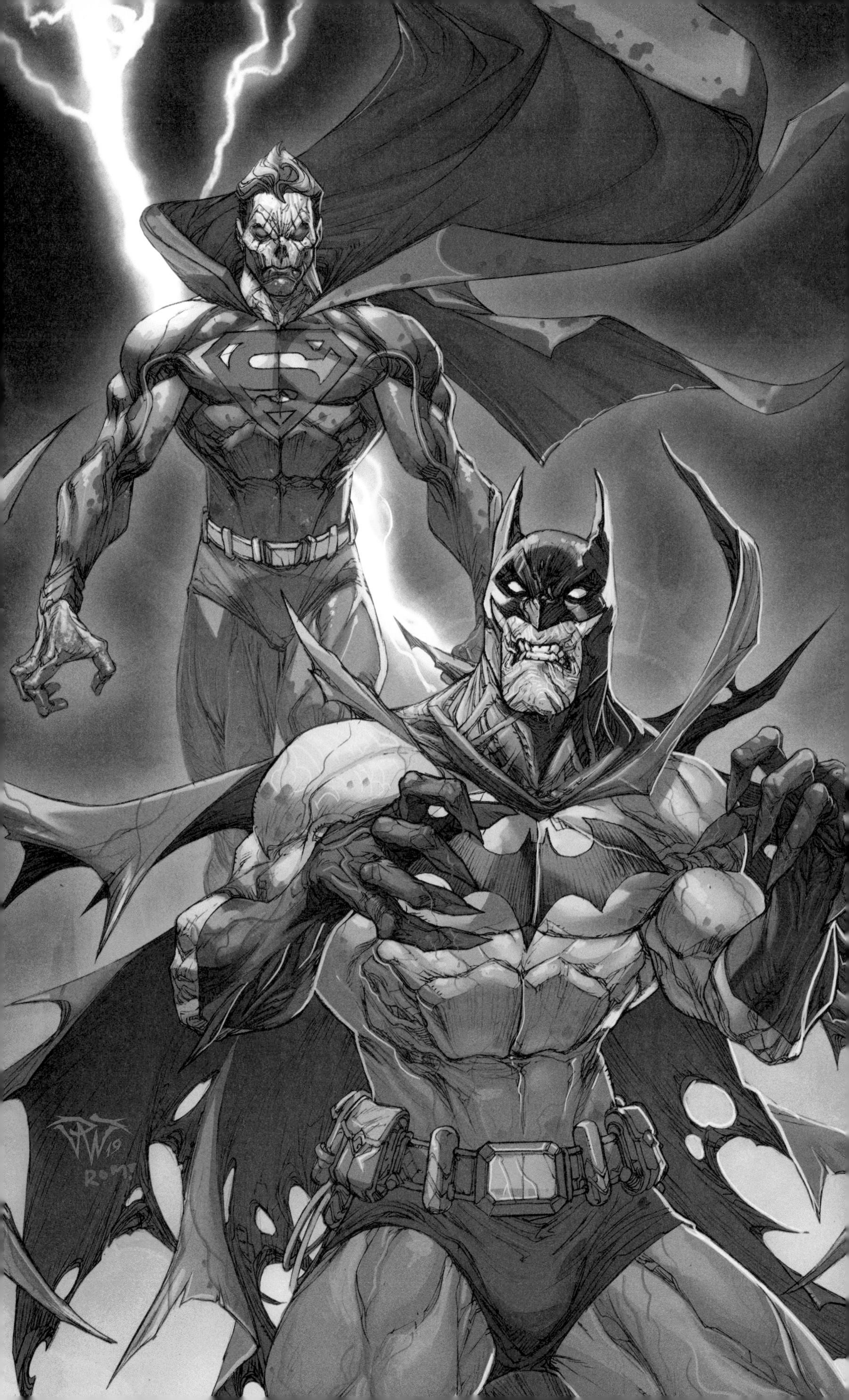

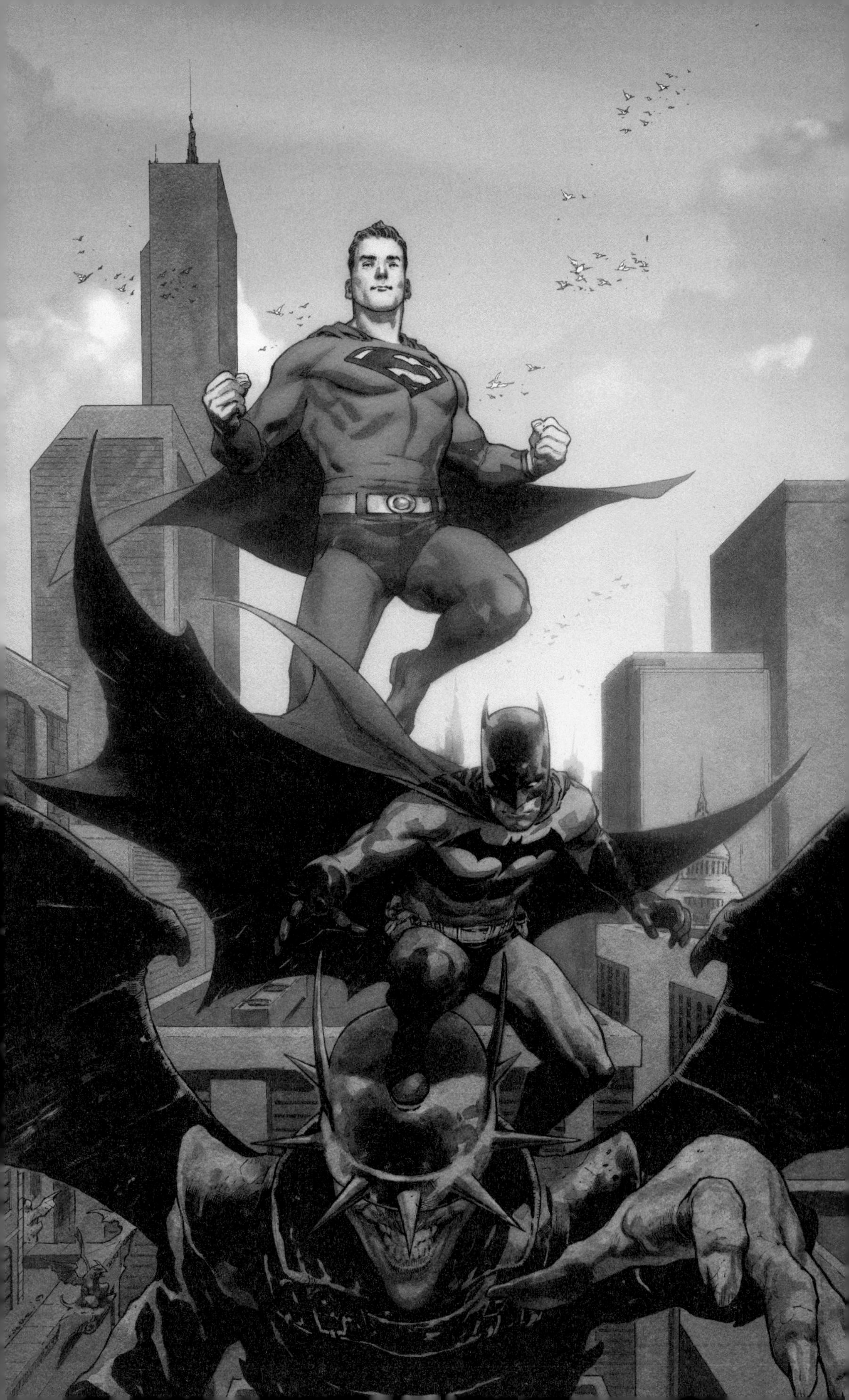

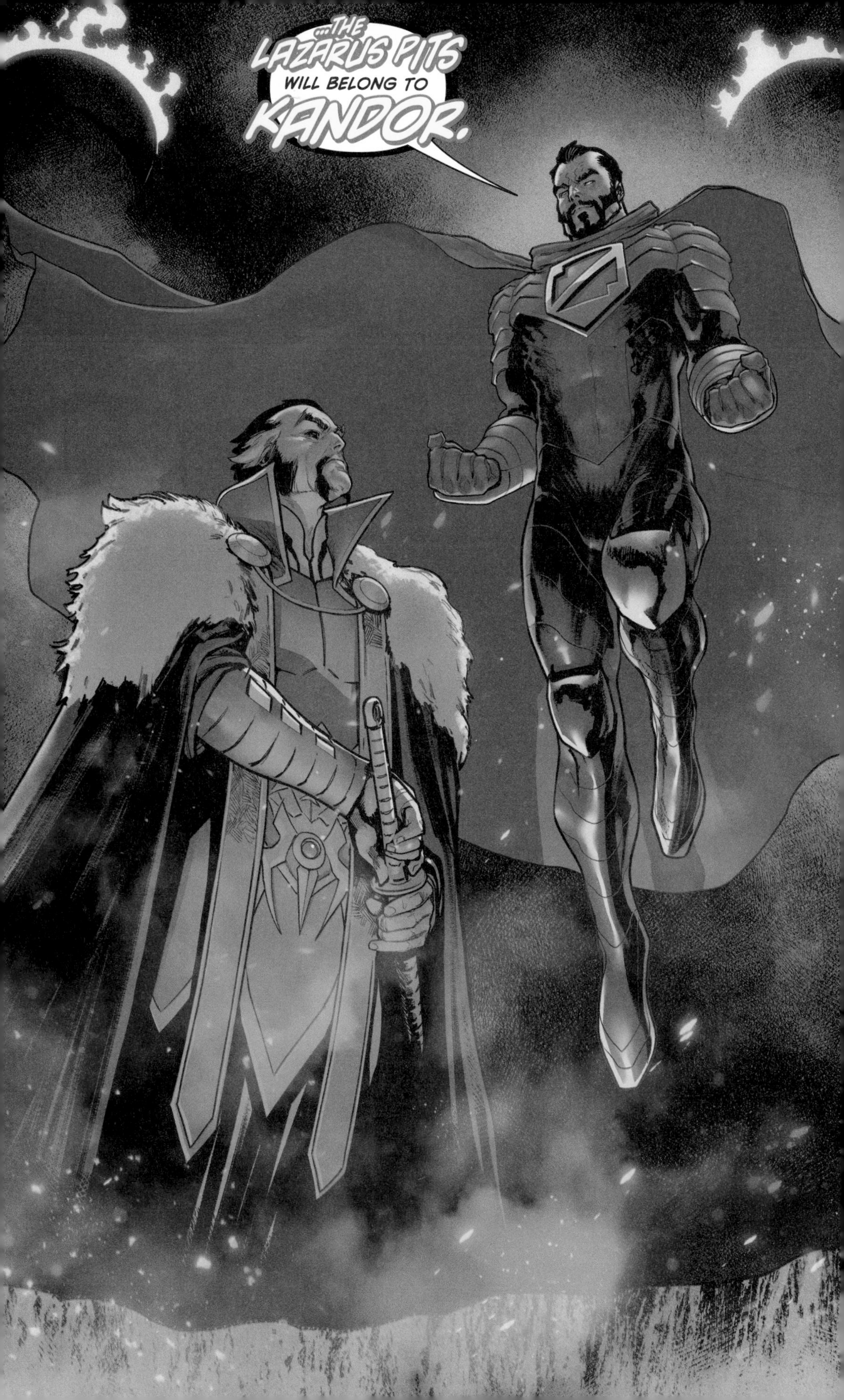
...THE LAZARUS PITS WILL BELONG TO KANDOR.

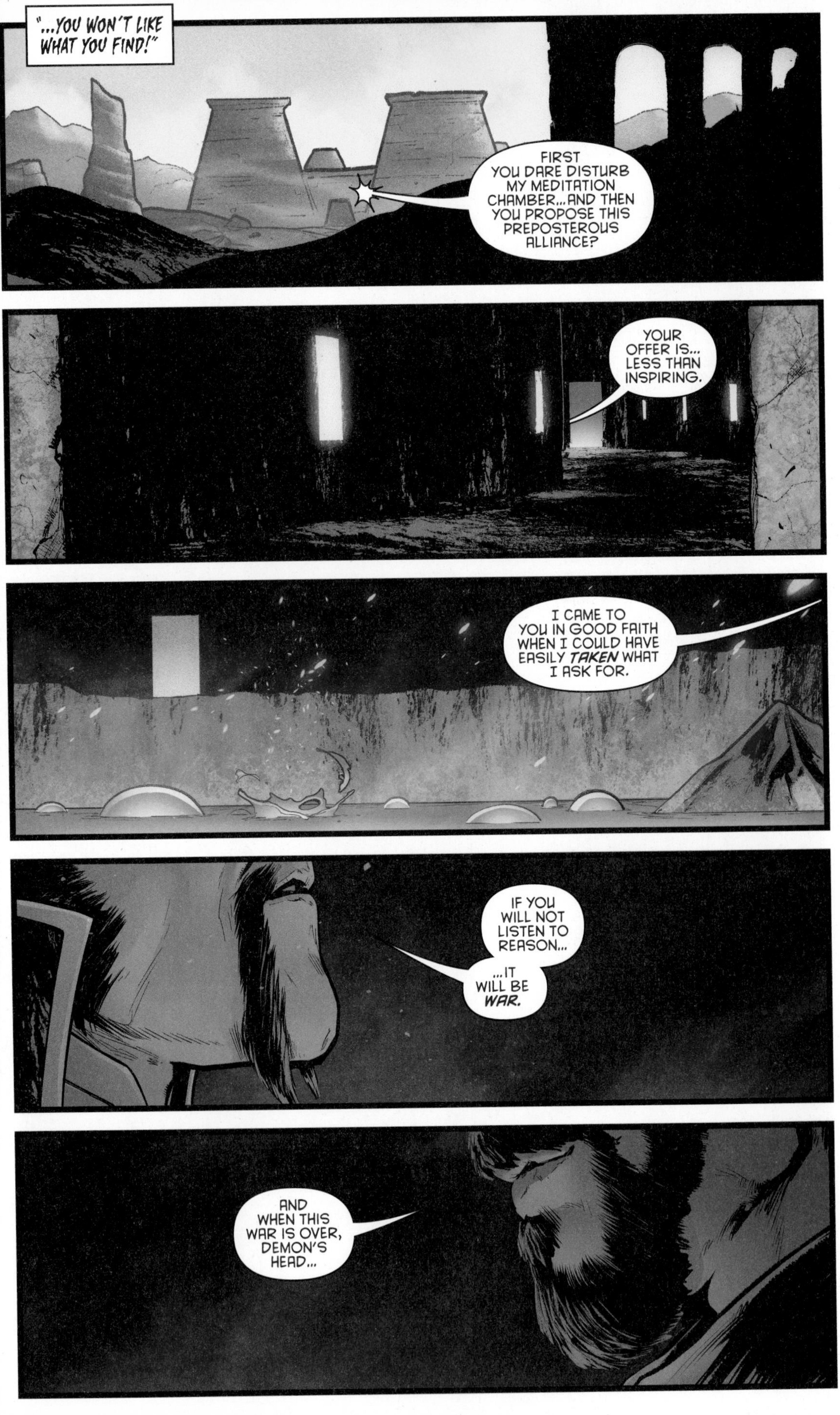
"...YOU WON'T LIKE WHAT YOU FIND!"
FIRST YOU DARE DISTURB MY MEDITATION CHAMBER...AND THEN YOU PROPOSE THIS PREPOSTEROUS ALLIANCE?
YOUR OFFER IS... LESS THAN INSPIRING.
I CAME TO YOU IN GOOD FAITH WHEN I COULD HAVE EASILY *TAKEN* WHAT I ASK FOR.
IF YOU WILL NOT LISTEN TO REASON...
...IT WILL BE ***WAR.***
AND WHEN THIS WAR IS OVER, DEMON'S HEAD...

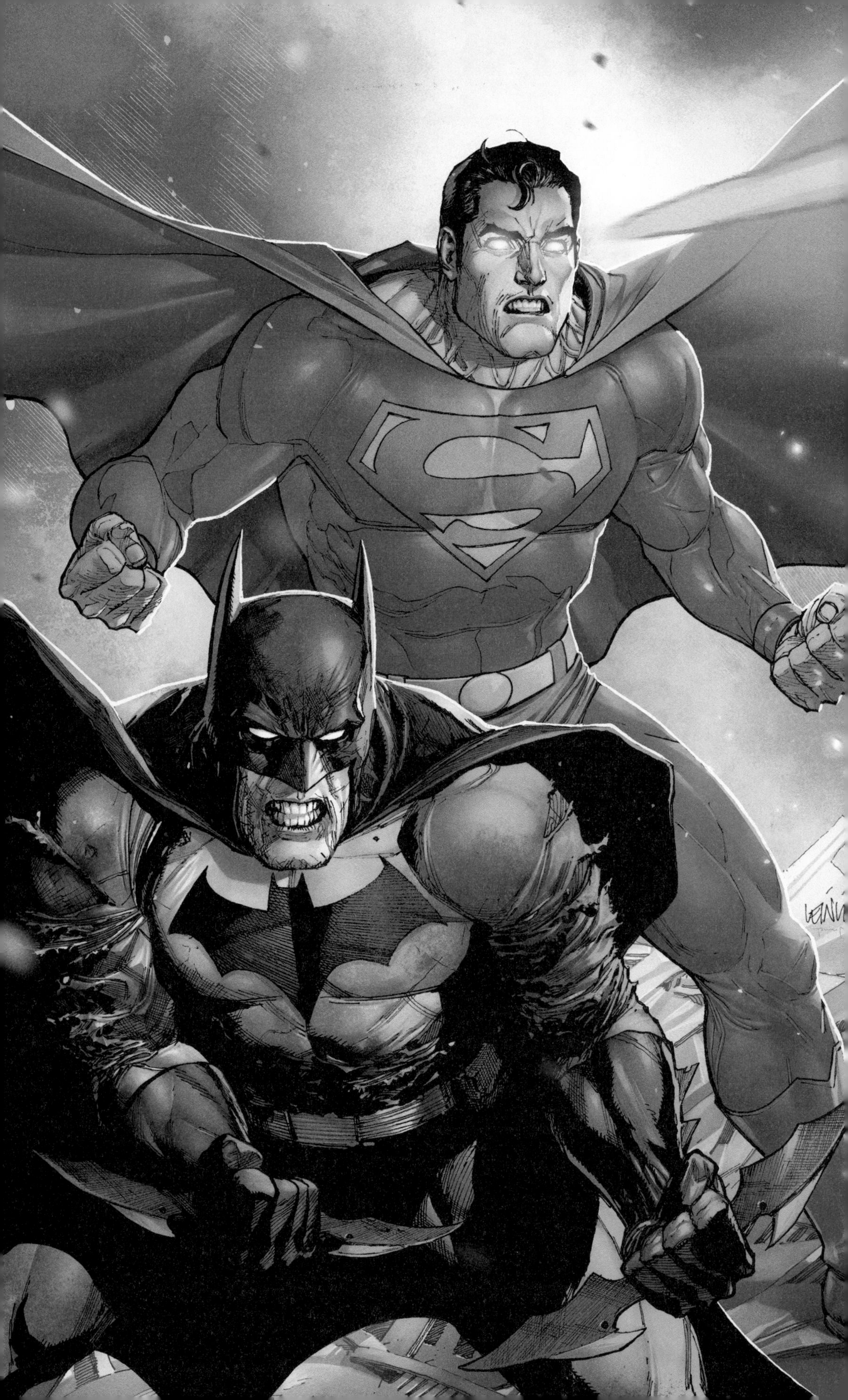

VARIANT COVER GALLERY

Batman/Superman #1
variant cover by
LEINIL YU and **TOMEU MOREY**

Batman/Superman #2
variant cover by
JEROME OPEÑA and **MORRY HOLLOWELL**

Batman/Superman #3
variant cover by
PAOLO PANTALENA and **ROMULO FAJARDO JR.**

Batman/Superman #4
variant cover by
OLIVIER COIPEL

Batman/Superman #5
variant cover by
JIM CHEUNG and **TOMEU MOREY**

Batman/Superman #6
variant cover by
SIMONE BIANCHI